# The
# San Francisco
# Chronicle
## Cookbook

# The San Francisco Chronicle
## Cookbook

edited by Michael Bauer and Fran Irwin

CHRONICLE BOOKS
SAN FRANCISCO

Page 411 is a continuation of the copyright page.

Library of Congress Cataloging-in-Publication Data:
The San Francisco Chronicle cookbook/edited by Michael Bauer and Fran Irwin.
      p. cm.
Includes index.
ISBN 0-8118-1445-9 (pbk.)
1. Cookery—California—San Francisco. 2. Cookery, American—California style.
I. Bauer, Michael. II. Irwin, Fran. III. San Francisco Chronicle.
TX715.S1825 1997
641.59794'61—dc20                     96-26460
                                      CIP

Printed in the United States of America
Book and cover design by Pamela Geismar
Composition by Candace Creasy, Blue Friday Type & Graphics
Engravings from the 19th century

Distributed in Canada by Raincoast Books
8680 Cambie Street
Vancouver, B.C. V6P 6M9

10 9 8 7 6 5 4 3 2 1

Chronicle Books
85 Second Street
San Francisco, CA 94105

Web Site: www.chronbooks.com

# Contents

# Acknowledgments

Putting together a compilation of recipes is a labor of love. Without the dedication and enthusiasm of our columnists and contributors we simply would have no materials. We believe we work with the best collection of columnists in the country, including Flo Braker, Georgeanne Brennan, Marion Cunningham, Laxmi Hiremath, Jacqueline McMahan and Marlena Spieler.

There are also a lot of people behind the scenes: Rosalie Wright, formerly assistant managing editor/features at *The Chronicle* (now editor-in-chief at *Sunset* magazine), and Matt Wilson, executive editor, who were enthusiastic and encouraging about the project. There are the Food Department editors who make everyone look good: Mary Ann Mariner, assistant food editor, and copy editors Christine Feldhorn and Karen Seriguchi. Then there is our food stylist Dan Bowe, who is also a fabulous cook. And we can't forget our writers Maria Cianci, Janet Fletcher and Karola Saekel.

We've received lots of help in recipe testing and followup from Shanna Masters and Carolyn Zezima.

We owe a particular debt to Richard Geiger, *The Chronicle*'s library director, who was able to download a decade's worth of recipes. Without him we'd still be leafing through stacks of yellowed newspapers. And without Mike Keiser, editorial systems director, our manuscript would forever be lost in cyberspace.

# Introduction

**SAN FRANCISCO IS THE METROPOLIS OF DIVERSITY.**
Although our ethnic neighborhoods are often distinct, they also inter-mingle: The very Italian North Beach and everyone's postcard-perfect Chinatown happily share their boundary streets.

Other neighborhoods, such as the Richmond, which stretches along the northern side of Golden Gate Park offer a true amalgamation of cultures and tastes. On Clement Street, for example, one of the city's finest French restaurants, Alain Rondelli, is a mere block from Murasaki, a haven for sushi fanatics. And in countless grocery stores a few steps away, the Mexican staple jicama sits next to bins of Chinese lotus root. There's also a Russian bakery near a Mid-Eastern deli, and an Italian trattoria next to a Chiu Chow Chinese restaurant.

The melting-pot nature of San Francisco also shows up in the foods we eat at home; it's become second nature for local cooks to mix and match ethnic flavors. Here, a rosemary-accented roast chicken might be served with a Thai cucumber salad (see page 46); the Thanksgiving turkey may get a tandoori treatment (see page 239) with a pomegranate-juice marinade.

The weekly Food Section of *The San Francisco Chronicle* has become a valued repository of these dishes. Created by scores of local columnists, contributors and chefs, each with a different background and approach to food, the recipes reflect our region's openness and abundance.

In the last 10 years, we've published about 13,000 recipes, and we've scrutinized each one to come up with the 350 found here, all tested and retested for home use.

Even though San Franciscans love to explore the exotic, we learned early on that Bay Area residents face the same constraints of time as everyone else. Speed is of the essence, and if a dish takes time to make, the results had better be worth it. That's why our bottom line has always been the time/value ratio of a given dish.

At first glance, some ingredients may seem a little esoteric for a busy-day meal, but these varied flavors quickly expand a cook's repertoire, with very little additional effort.

Asparagus is a good example of the ways that a single vegetable can be transformed. In one recipe, it's highlighted with a classic French orange-butter sauce (page 147); in another, it's paired with a Japanese wasabi-and-miso dip (page 148); and in still another, it gets aromatic flavors from a collection of Indian spices and pistachios (page 149).

A trip to an ethnic market might be required for some dishes, but after that the possibilities are limitless. We've also included mail-order resources for possibly hard-to-find ingredients (see pages 407–08), and when appropriate, we've offered reliable substitutions.

Still, the backbone of the book is honest, simple food, often with a gently creative twist: creamy beet and potato gratin (page 153); pan-seared chicken with lemon, mint and almonds (page 213); our 10-minute pasta with green beans, goat cheese and olives (page 84).

The creators of these recipes are a who's who of great cooks including Marion Cunningham, best known as the modern Fannie Farmer, and Flo Braker, an internationally respected baker and creator of *The Simple Art of Perfect Baking*. Georgeanne Brennan, who introduced arugula to Americans when she owned a seed company, also wrote the classic *Potager* and other cookbooks. Joyce Jue, who was raised in San Francisco's Chinatown, has written several cookbooks, including *Wok and Stir-Fry Cooking,* and Jacqueline Higuera McMahan, who grew up on one of the last California ranchos, has several books to her credit, including one devoted to aromatic chipotle chiles. (See pages 409–10 for a complete list of contributors.)

Through the years, we've also tapped the talents of well-known local chefs, including Alice Waters, Jeremiah Tower, Joyce Goldstein, Carlo Middione, Bradley Ogden and Madeleine Kamman, to name but a very few.

What we offer is truly the best of the best.

Chapter 1

# Soups and Salads

San Francisco is a soup and salad culture. Because the fog comes in during the summer, soup is a year-round staple. And just across the bay, where the sun shines bright, a cooling salad always seems right.

The ethnic diversity found in the city is highlighted in this chapter. Take corn, for example. We've included four recipes: one for a roasted corn soup with a California cachet; another flavored with chipotle chile for a Mexican flavor; a traditional Chinese velvet soup accented with crabmeat; and a creative Asian version with cream of ginger and chile bean paste.

Myriad other cultures are also represented: fresh tomato tarragon soup from France; turkey congee from China; fava bean soup from Italy; spicy summer squash soup from the Middle East; chicken soup with lemongrass and lime from Thailand; and a Tlalpeno-style soup from Mexico.

Salads are just as diverse, from a homey mustard-celery salad from Marion Cunningham to Japanese eggplant salad from David Vardy of O Chame in Berkeley. In between there are a Thai cucumber salad; dandelion salad with anchovy dressing; Egyptian feta salad with dill and mint; and an Indian papaya chaat with pine nuts.

# Pureed Artichoke Bisque

*Nearly all the artichokes produced in the United States come from Northern California. Marlena Spieler's simple bisque showcases these nutty-tasting giant thistles. Potato, garlic, basil and a vegetable or chicken stock are all that's really needed to make this show-stopping soup.*

8 artichoke hearts, cleaned, trimmed of sharp leaves and chokes, cut into halves or quarters (or 1 package frozen artichoke hearts, defrosted)

1 baking potato, peeled and diced

3 to 5 garlic cloves, chopped

2 tablespoons butter or olive oil

4 to 6 cups chicken stock or vegetable broth

Salt and pepper to taste

1 tablespoon thinly sliced fresh basil

◗◗ Sauté the artichokes, potato and garlic in butter or olive oil for 5 minutes, or long enough to partially cook both artichokes and potato. Add the stock or broth and bring to boil. Reduce heat and simmer until the vegetables are tender, about 10 minutes. Puree the soup, then season with salt and pepper.

Ladle into bowls and garnish with basil.

SERVES 2 TO 4

# Roasted Sweet Corn Soup

*Roasting brings out the sweetness of corn in this recipe from chef Mary Evely of Simi Winery in Healdsburg. A few teaspoons of cornmeal add flavor and give the soup texture.*

10 to 12 ears fresh corn, unshucked

4 tablespoons unsalted butter

4 large garlic cloves, unpeeled

4 cups low-sodium chicken stock

2 cups water

1 large baking potato, peeled and cut into eighths

4 teaspoons cornmeal

## Basic Chicken Stock

Put about 2 pounds bony chicken parts (backs, wings, necks) in a stockpot. Add about 10 cups cold water; 1 onion, halved; 2 carrots, cut in half; 3 celery stalks (with leaves), cut in half; a few parsley sprigs, 1 or 2 bay leaves, 10 peppercorns and a little salt. Bring to a boil, reduce heat and simmer for at least 1 hour. Strain. Season to taste with salt. Yields about 8 cups, depending on length of time the stock is cooked.

## Basic Vegetable Stock

In a large soup pot, combine 12 cups water; 2 carrots, cut into chunks; 3 or 4 celery ribs, including leaves, chopped; 1 large onion, quartered; several parsley sprigs; 12 to 15 whole peppercorns and 1 large bay leaf. Slowly bring to a boil, partially cover and simmer about 1½ hours. Add salt or lemon juice to taste. Strain. Refrigerate until ready to use, or freeze. Yields about 10 cups.

1 cup heavy cream
Salt and pepper to taste
Basil oil and basil sprigs (optional)

☙ Preheat the oven to 450 degrees.

Pull back husk partway on each corn ear. Using all the butter, put a small piece inside each husk, replace the husk and place ears in a single layer on a baking sheet (or two). Scatter the garlic around the ears. Bake for 20 minutes. Let cool, then peel the garlic and shuck the corn. Scrape the kernels from the cobs; set aside 2 cups of the kernels. Reserve 6 of the cobs.

Combine the stock, water and the 6 reserved corn cobs in a large pot. (Cut cobs in half if necessary.) Add the peeled garlic and potato. Simmer until potato is soft. Discard corn cobs. Transfer the mixture to a food processor. Add the corn kernels (except the reserved 2 cups) and the cornmeal; puree. Return the puree to the pot and stir in the cream. Thin, if desired, with a little stock. Heat just to a boil. Stir in the reserved corn kernels. Season with salt and pepper.

Serve immediately, garnishing, if desired, with a swirl of basil oil and a basil sprig.

SERVES 8

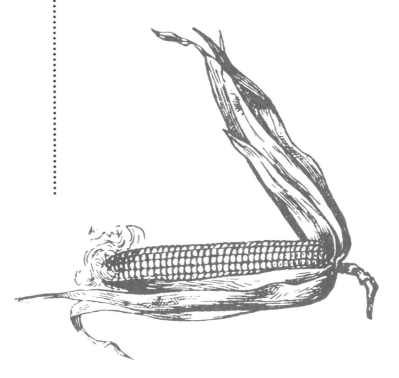

# Chilled Cucumber Soup

*Jane Benet, late food editor of* The Chronicle, *created this refreshing, uncooked soup that gets a jolt of flavor from garlic and a cool and soothing texture from cucumbers and yogurt.*

4 cucumbers

4 garlic cloves, peeled

1 quart plain yogurt

¼ cup snipped fresh dill

Salt and pepper to taste

Dill sprigs

❧ Peel the cucumbers, cut in half and scoop out the seeds; cut the cucumbers into chunks.

With the steel blade in place and the motor running, drop the garlic down the feed tube of a food processor and process until finely chopped. Add the cucumbers and process with on/off pulses until finely chopped but not pureed.

Combine the cucumber mixture with the yogurt and dill; season with salt and pepper. Chill.

Serve in cups or small mugs, garnished with sprigs of fresh dill.

SERVES 8 TO 12

## Chopping Garlic

One of the best ways to keep garlic from clinging to the knife as you chop it is to sprinkle a little salt on the cloves. In addition, the salt absorbs the flavor that otherwise would be lost to the cutting board.

# Chicken Lime Soup

*Chicken and lime is a classic Latin duo, as showcased in this recipe from Jacqueline McMahan. The soup contains no added fat. Instead, it gets a flavor boost from garlic, red bell peppers, tomatoes, cilantro and salsa.*

Olive oil cooking spray

3 half chicken breasts, boned and skinned

4 limes

1½ quarts chicken broth, preferably homemade

1 cup diced red bell pepper

2 garlic cloves, minced

½ cup diced celery

1 cup diced carrot

1¼ cups diced zucchini

1 cup diced skinned and seeded tomato

¼ cup minced fresh cilantro

½ cup very picante homemade salsa (optional)

Spray olive oil over the chicken breasts, then squeeze the juice of 1 lime over them. Grill (or broil) the chicken over medium heat for 5 minutes per side. Cool for a few minutes, then dice. Set aside.

Bring the chicken broth to a simmer. Add the bell pepper, garlic, celery and carrot. Cook over low heat for 15 minutes. Stir in the zucchini and cook for 5 minutes. Add the reserved chicken, the juice of the remaining limes and the tomato. Simmer for a couple of minutes. Remove from heat. Stir in the minced cilantro and the optional salsa.

SERVES 6

# Chicken-Lemongrass Soup with Long-Grain Rice, Lime Juice, Basil and Cilantro

*Versions of this soup are made throughout Cambodia. This recipe is from Sovan Boun Thuy, proprietor of Chez Sovan in San Jose. The combination of lemongrass, lime, basil and cilantro is exotic and hauntingly fragrant. The soup is excellent served before a platter of stir-fried vegetables, broiled fish or with a grilled vegetable salad. It could also precede meat, but if so, you might want to omit the diced chicken.*

5 cups chicken broth

¾ pound boneless, skinless chicken (dark meat), cut into 1½-inch dice

3 stalks fresh lemongrass, bulbous part only, smashed with the side of a cleaver

1 teaspoon sugar

2 cups cooked long-grain rice (¾ cup raw)

3 to 4 tablespoons fresh lime juice

Salt to taste

½ cup packed cilantro leaves, coarsely chopped

½ cup lightly packed basil leaves, coarsely chopped

Combine the chicken broth, chicken, lemongrass and sugar in a large saucepan. Bring to a boil, reduce heat and simmer for 4 minutes, skimming occasionally. Add the cooked rice. Simmer for 1 minute. Add enough of the lime juice for a pleasantly tart flavor. Season with salt, if necessary. Stir in the cilantro and basil.

YIELDS ABOUT 8 CUPS

## Jazzing Up Canned Chicken Broth

For a quick, almost homemade chicken broth, Jacqueline McMahan suggests the following:

Pour a 49½-ounce can defatted chicken broth into a large saucepan. Add 3 cups water; ¼ cup dry white wine; ½ white onion; 1 tomato, halved; 2 smashed garlic cloves and 1 skinned whole chicken breast. Simmer for 30 minutes. Remove the chicken (reserve it for another use) and strain the broth.

## Basic Brown Vegetable Stock

This good basic vegetable stock with intense flavor is from Joyce Goldstein.

Combine in a heavy baking pan 2 yellow onions, cut in quarters; 1 red onion, cut in quarters; 5 carrots, cut in chunks; 3 leeks, cut in chunks; 3 stalks celery, cut in chunks; and 1 head garlic, cut in half. Roast in a 450-degree oven for about 1 hour, stirring occasionally.

Transfer the vegetables to a stockpot. Add 1 bay leaf and 1 gallon water. Bring to a boil, reduce heat and simmer, covered, for 1 hour. Strain. Chill. This may be made ahead and frozen. Yields 1 gallon.

# Creamy Corn Soup with Chipotles

*There's something magical about the smoky-hot flavor of chipotle when it combines with cream. However, if you prefer a reduced-fat version of this Jacqueline McMahan recipe, omit the cream; low-fat milk and pureed sweet corn lend a wonderful creaminess of their own.*

2 tablespoons butter
1 cup coarsely chopped onion
2 garlic cloves
8 cups frozen petite sweet corn, thawed
4 cups low-fat milk
1 teaspoon salt
2 dried chipotle chiles, slivered
¼ cup heavy cream (optional)
4 corn tortillas, cut into strips
Olive oil cooking spray
Pure ground chile
3 tablespoons coarsely chopped fresh cilantro

◉ Preheat the oven to 350 degrees. Heat the butter in a soup pot. Add the onion and sauté until softened, adding the garlic the last couple of minutes.

Puree 2 cups of the corn with 1 cup of the milk. Place a wire strainer over a large bowl and push the puree through the strainer. Puree the remaining corn with the remaining milk and the onion-garlic mixture. Strain, pressing to get all of the juices. (Remember to scrape off the good stuff on the bottom of the strainer.) Transfer the mixture to soup pot; add the salt and chipotles. Heat well but do not boil or the soup will curdle.

Just before serving, stir in the cream.

Place the tortilla strips on a baking sheet; mist with olive oil spray and sprinkle with salt. Bake for 8 minutes. Turn and bake for 5 minutes, or until crisp.

Ladle the soup into bowls. Garnish with a tiny sprinkle of chile powder, cilantro and a few tortilla strips.

YIELDS ABOUT 7½ CUPS; SERVES 6

# Velvet Corn Soup and Crabmeat

*Here's a Chinese version of corn soup by Joyce Jue, this one with crabmeat and a hint of ginger and sesame oil. Use fresh sweet corn if possible. In a pinch, cream-style corn or frozen corn niblets may be substituted.*

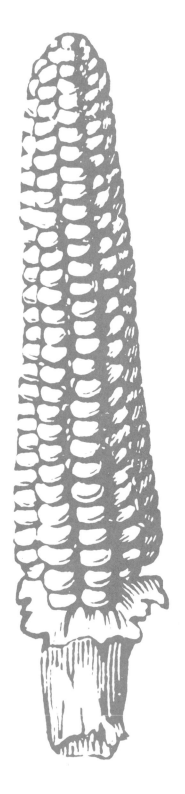

4 ears of corn (or 2 cups frozen corn kernels, or a 17-ounce can cream-style corn)

1 tablespoon vegetable oil

1 teaspoon minced peeled ginger

2 shallots or scallions, minced

2 tablespoons rice wine or dry sherry

4 cups chicken stock

1 tablespoon light soy sauce

Dash white pepper

6 ounces fresh crabmeat, flaked

1 teaspoon Asian sesame oil

1 to 1½ tablespoons cornstarch mixed with 3 tablespoons water

2 large egg whites

Pinch salt

1 tablespoon minced scallions

1 tablespoon chopped fresh cilantro

1 tablespoon minced Smithfield ham or prosciutto

⊚⊚ Cut the corn kernels off the cobs, scraping cobs with the back of the knife to extract the corn "milk," and place in a food processor. Process into a coarse puree; set aside.

Heat the oil in a medium-sized soup pot. Add the ginger and shallots or scallions; lightly sauté until aromatic. Increase heat to high. Add the corn and wine; stir for 30 seconds. Add the chicken stock, soy sauce and pepper. Stir until the soup reaches a boil, then add the crab and sesame oil. Reduce heat to medium-high. Pour the cornstarch mixture into the soup, stirring until the soup thickens, about 15 seconds. Turn off the heat.

Lightly beat the egg whites with the salt until almost frothy. Pour the egg whites into the soup in a slow, steady stream and in a circular motion. Gently stir, allowing the lacy ribbons to surface.

Ladle the soup into serving bowls. Garnish with the minced scallions, cilantro and ham.

SERVES 6

# Cream of Ginger and Corn Soup with Chile Bean Paste

*In this recipe, Chinese chef Ken Hom takes one of his favorite creamed corn soups and heightens its flavor with the addition of lemongrass, ginger and chile bean paste.*

2 tablespoons butter

1 tablespoon finely chopped fresh ginger

2 tablespoons very finely chopped fresh lemongrass

2 tablespoons finely chopped shallots

½ cup finely chopped yellow onions

2 cups fresh corn kernels

4 cups homemade chicken stock

Salt and freshly ground white pepper to taste

2 teaspoons sugar

½ cup half-and-half

2 teaspoons chile bean paste, or to taste, for garnish

Fresh cilantro leaves for garnish

◎◎ Heat the butter in a medium-sized pot. Add the ginger, lemongrass, shallots and onions. Cook over low heat for 2 minutes. Add the corn and cook 1 minute or so longer. Add the chicken stock and bring the mixture to a simmer. Continue cooking over low heat for about 5 minutes. Add salt and pepper, then the sugar and half-and-half. Take the pot off the heat and let cool to room temperature.

Puree the soup in a blender (do this in several batches). Puree each batch for at least 2 or 3 minutes. Return the soup to the pot and bring to a simmer.

To serve the soup in a large tureen, add the chile bean paste in the center and stir to make a swirling pattern. To serve in individual bowls, add ¼ teaspoon chile bean paste or less to each bowl and swirl or mix in. Garnish with cilantro leaves.

SERVES 4 TO 6

# Mixed Greens Soup with Fennel-Scented Croutons

*This jade green soup by Laxmi Hiremath gets a pleasantly spicy flavor from mustard greens and fresh chile pepper. To turn it into a silky-textured main-dish soup, cook 1 or 2 peeled and diced potatoes with the greens (potatoes will thicken the mixture and prevent it from separating as it sits). For a special presentation, spoon plain yogurt into a squeeze bottle and pipe a design on top of each serving. Crunchy fennel- and cumin-topped croutons add a fragrant counterpoint.*

2 cups lightly packed chopped spinach

1 cup lightly packed chopped Swiss chard

½ cup lightly packed chopped mustard greens

½ cup packed chopped kale

1 fresh hot green chile, stemmed and chopped

4 cups water

3 tablespoons unsalted butter

2 tablespoons rice flour or whole-wheat flour

½ teaspoon salt, or more to taste

½ teaspoon freshly ground white pepper

Fennel Croutons (recipe follows)

∞ Combine the greens, chile and water in a large heavy pot. Bring to a boil. Reduce heat and simmer until the greens are tender, about 20 minutes. Remove from heat and puree in a food processor, blender or food mill. Set aside.

Melt the butter in a heavy saucepan over medium heat. Add the flour, stir and cook until lightly browned, 6 to 8 minutes. Return the pureed mixture to the pan and cook until heated through. Season with salt and pepper. If not using immediately, cool, cover and refrigerate up to 5 days.

When ready to serve, reheat over medium heat, stirring constantly. Taste and add more salt and pepper if needed.

To serve, ladle into shallow soup bowls and pass croutons at the table.

SERVES 4

## Fennel Croutons

1 tablespoon light olive oil or peanut oil
1½ tablespoons unsalted butter, melted
8 slices French baguette (½ inch thick)
½ teaspoon ground cumin
¼ teaspoon cayenne pepper
¼ teaspoon ground fennel seed

◉ Preheat the oven to 350 degrees.

Combine the oil and butter. Lightly brush one side of each crouton with the mixture. Combine the spices in a small container and sprinkle over the croutons. Place the croutons on a baking sheet and bake on the middle rack of the oven until golden and crisp, about 5 to 7 minutes.

YIELDS 8 CROUTONS

# Hot and Sour Soup

*You've had many versions of hot and sour soup in Chinese restaurants, but we think Bruce Cost's is the best you'll ever taste. While tiger lily buds and tree ear mushrooms may seem exotic, they're readily available in Asian markets.*

3 dried black Chinese mushrooms

1 heaping tablespoon tree ear mushrooms (black tree fungus)

20 dried tiger lily buds (golden needles)

2 blocks (about 14 ounces) firm bean curd (tofu)

¼ pound lean pork, cut into matchstick-sized shreds

2 teaspoons dark soy sauce

1 tablespoon light soy sauce

5 tablespoons white vinegar

2 teaspoons salt, or to taste

1 tablespoon peanut oil

¼ cup bamboo shoots, cut into matchstick-sized shreds

5 cups chicken stock (if using canned, cut back on the salt)

3 tablespoons cornstarch mixed with ¼ cup water

2 eggs, lightly beaten

1 teaspoon freshly ground white pepper

1 tablespoon Asian sesame oil

2 tablespoons chopped scallions, green part included

2 tablespoons chopped fresh cilantro leaves

⊛ Put the mushrooms, tree ears and lily buds into separate bowls and cover with boiling water. Let stand 30 minutes.

Meanwhile, slice the bean curd into strips (thick matchsticks), and set aside.

Combine the pork shreds with the dark soy sauce in a small bowl. In a different container, combine the light soy sauce, vinegar and salt.

Drain the black mushrooms, cut off the woody stems and discard, then slice the mushrooms thinly and put into a bowl. Drain and rinse the tree ears and add them to the mushrooms. Drain the lily buds, cut off the woody tips, cut each in half, then pull each half into shreds by hand; add to the mushrooms.

Heat the oil in a large pot. Add the pork and stir-fry until it changes color. Add the tree ears, mushrooms, lily buds and bamboo shoots; cook, stirring, for 1 minute. Add the stock and bring to a boil. Stir in the vinegar mixture. Reduce heat to medium and cook for 1 minute, then add the bean curd and cook for another minute.

Recombine the cornstarch and water and stir into the soup. Cook until the soup thickens and clears slightly. Turn off the heat and slowly swirl in the beaten eggs. Sprinkle with the pepper, drizzle in the sesame oil, garnish with the scallions and cilantro and serve.

SERVES 4 TO 6

# Kale and Black Bean Soup with Ham Hocks

*Kale, slow-cooked in chicken broth, and tiny black beans simmered with a ham hock come together with olive oil and fresh herbs. Served with buttered squares of corn bread and a plateful of raw vegetables, this soup is a good choice for a hungry crowd after Christmas caroling, says Georgeanne Brennan. It may be made in advance and reheated—the flavors just get better and better.*

1 cup dried black beans

1 ham hock

8 to 10 cups water

2 bunches kale, stemmed

6 cups chicken broth

2 tablespoons olive oil

¼ cup chopped onion

4 garlic cloves, chopped

2 potatoes, scrubbed and diced

2 tablespoons chopped fresh parsley

2 tablespoons chopped fresh thyme

1 teaspoon salt (optional)

∞ Soak the beans overnight in water to cover.

Drain the beans, then place in a large saucepan. Add the ham hock and water. Bring to a boil, reduce heat, partially cover and simmer 2 to 3 hours. When the beans are soft, mash some with the back of a wooden spoon to thicken the liquid. Bone the ham hock and cut the meat into bite-sized pieces; set aside.

Simmer the kale in the chicken broth until tender, about 30 minutes. Using a slotted spoon, remove the kale from the broth; reserve broth. Squeeze as much liquid as possible from the kale, then chop it.

Heat the olive oil in a deep, heavy-bottomed soup pot over medium heat. Add the onion and garlic and sauté lightly for a few minutes. Add the reserved chicken broth and chopped kale; simmer for 30 minutes.

Add the cooked beans with their broth, the ham, potatoes, parsley and thyme. Simmer for 30 minutes, or until the potatoes are tender. Taste and add salt, if necessary.

SERVES 6 TO 8

# Kale, Chorizo and Potato Soup

*Full of robust flavors, this is another winter soup from Georgeanne Brennan. Potatoes are cooked and pureed, then added to simmering kale and broth, thickening the soup and giving it a satisfying "heft."*

1 pound kale, stemmed

1 pound chorizo, hot Italian or other spicy sausage

½ teaspoon salt

6 large red potatoes, cut into ½-inch slices

10 cups chicken broth

8 slices French bread, grilled or toasted

1 tablespoon freshly ground black pepper

◉◉  Mince the kale. (A food processor does this job well.)

Prick the sausages with a fork and simmer for 15 minutes. Drain and cut into thin slices.

Fill a saucepan with water, add the salt, bring to a boil, then add the potatoes. Cook for 10 to 15 minutes, or until tender. Puree the potatoes, adding enough of their cooking water to make a thick paste.

## Easy Garnishes for Soup

◉◉ Salsa. Add your favorite to a variety of soups: tomato-rice, meatballs and spinach, pepper and tomato, seafood, chicken or vegetable. A wedge of lemon or lime is a nice counterpoint.

◉◉ Pesto. Good with pureed zucchini and chicken broth, or diced asparagus and potatoes simmered in stock.

◉◉ Pureed vegetables and herbs. Try pureeing roasted red peppers with garlic and a little olive oil; pureed spinach mixed with yogurt, garlic and mint; curry-scented tomatoes; or cilantro, mint, chile and onion. All add spice and body to soup.

◉◉ Diced spicy sausage. Brown lightly and blot well on paper towels. Adds rich texture and flavor.

◉◉ Pureed roasted garlic. Mix with a little chopped parsley and stir in well.

◉◉ Chopped raw garlic. Warm it in a little olive oil, then combine with chopped parsley.

Wine. Add a splash of dry sherry or red wine to each bowl at serving time.

Mild red chile paste. Mix 2 chopped garlic cloves with 1 teaspoon ground cumin, 2 tablespoons chopped cilantro, 2 tablespoons pasilla chile powder, 2 tablespoons orange juice and 1 tablespoon or so olive oil. Season with salt and cinnamon to taste.

Onion-chipotle. Mix minced onion with a tiny bit of chipotle chile sauce or a chipotle salsa.

Tomatoes and fresh herbs. Chop together, then add to soup.

Low-fat tortilla chips. Add to a spicy vegetable soup, along with a little chopped cilantro and raw onion.

Sautéed scallions. Gently heat 2 or 3 thinly sliced green onions with a tablespoon of vegetable oil until the onions are wilted. Remove from heat and cool. Use a small amount as a condiment for vegetables or soup.
—*Marlena Spieler*

Bring the chicken broth to a boil in a soup pot; reduce heat and add the kale. Simmer for 5 minutes, then stir in the potato paste, little by little, thickening the broth. Add the sausages and taste for seasoning.

Put a slice of grilled or toasted bread into each soup bowl. Ladle the soup over the bread and sprinkle with pepper.

SERVES 4

# Mu-Shu Soup

*While many of us are familiar with mu-shu pork in one form or another, there also is a mu-shu soup. It's generally prepared in the home and is rarely, if ever, found in restaurants. This version, by Bruce Cost, is especially delicious.*

2 tablespoons small dried tree ear mushrooms (sometimes labeled "black tree fungus")

20 dried lily buds (golden needles)

¼ pound boneless pork loin

2 teaspoons dark soy sauce

12 to 15 fresh spinach leaves

⅓ cup bamboo shoots, cut into matchstick shreds

6 cups rich chicken broth (see Note)

3 tablespoons peanut oil

2 teaspoons salt

2 tablespoons light soy sauce

5 tablespoons cornstarch dissolved in ½ cup water

3 eggs, lightly beaten with 1 teaspoon Asian sesame oil

½ teaspoon freshly ground white pepper

Place the mushrooms and lily buds in separate bowls and cover with boiling water. Let stand 20 minutes or so.

Meanwhile, thinly slice the pork, stack the slices and cut into matchstick shreds. Mix well with the dark soy sauce. Set aside.

Drop the spinach leaves into a saucepan of boiling water. When they wilt (almost immediately), drain and run under cold water to stop the cooking. Set aside.

Drain the mushrooms and lily buds. Cut the tough little knobs off the end of each lily bud, cut in half and pull each half into 2 or 3 shreds. Combine the mushrooms, lily buds and bamboo shoots. Set aside.

Bring the stock to a boil.

Heat a wok or skillet and add the peanut oil. When hot, add the pork shreds and stir briefly to separate. Add the mushrooms, lily buds and bamboo shoots; stir over high heat for about 1 minute, then remove from heat.

When the stock boils, season with the salt and light soy sauce. Add the pork-mushroom mixture and, when it comes to a boil again, give the cornstarch mixture a stir to combine and add it to the soup. When it thickens slightly and boils, remove from heat. Add the spinach leaves and, while stirring in one direction, slowly add the egg. Sprinkle with the white pepper and serve.

SERVES 6

**NOTE:** Make rich chicken broth by first cutting up a whole chicken. Put it in water to cover and bring to a boil. Skim any foam that comes to the top, reduce the heat to low, cover and simmer for 3 to 4 hours. Let sit for an hour to cool. Strain.

# Roasted-Onion Soup with Chiles, Coconut Milk and Salsa

*Guajillo chile, coconut milk and achiote lend tropical notes to this deliciously unusual soup by Marlena Spieler. It makes refreshing fare for a sweltering afternoon or evening, and is especially suited to kick off a Latin-inspired barbecue.*

2 guajillo or other mild, fruity, smooth red chiles

1 onion, unpeeled, cut in half

5 garlic cloves, unpeeled

2 teaspoons achiote seeds ground to a powder or 1 tablespoon achiote paste,
   made by simmering and pureeing the seeds

1½ cups diced tomatoes

1 tablespoon oil

3 cups chicken broth

1 zucchini, cut into bite-sized pieces

¾ cup cooked and drained corn kernels

1 cup unsweetened coconut milk

1 skinless, boneless chicken breast half (about 4 ounces), diced (optional)

Large pinch dried oregano, crumbled

Pinch ground cumin

Salt and pepper to taste

½ ripe but firm banana

1 lime

1 tablespoon chopped fresh cilantro

Hot pepper sauce (optional)

◉◉  Place the chiles in a bowl and pour hot water over them. Let soak until softened, about 30 minutes. Remove the stems and seeds, then cut the chiles into small pieces. Puree in a blender using just enough of the soaking liquid to make a puree.

Toast the onion and garlic in an ungreased frying pan until lightly charred. When cool enough to handle, peel the onion and garlic, then dice and combine with achiote and half of the tomatoes. Puree. Blend in the chile puree.

Heat the oil in a saucepan. Add the puree and cook until concentrated, pastelike and darkened in color. Do not let burn. Add the chicken broth and zucchini. Bring to a boil, reduce heat and cook until the zucchini is cooked through.

Add the corn, coconut milk, diced chicken, oregano and cumin; heat through (the chicken will take just a moment or two to cook, and the coconut milk will slightly thicken the soup). Season with salt and pepper.

Just before serving, dice the banana and toss with the juice of half of the lime.

Serve each bowlful of hot soup with a sprinkling of banana, the remaining tomato, the coriander and the rest of the lime, cut into wedges. Offer hot pepper sauce if desired.

SERVES 4

# California Garden Minestrone

*The last of summer's ripe tomatoes and squash combine with fall's tender shell beans and sweet early cabbage in Georgeanne Brennan's minestrone.*

4 tablespoons olive oil

2 tablespoons butter

1 onion, chopped

2 garlic cloves, chopped

4 potatoes (if possible, Yukon Gold or another buttery type), peeled and chopped (about 5 cups)

1 baby fennel bulb, plus 3 inches of stalk, chopped

2 cups mixed snap beans, such as Romano, Blue Lake, yellow wax

2 medium-small zucchini, chopped

2 cups coarsely chopped cabbage

2 cups ripe tomatoes, peeled and coarsely chopped

6 cups chicken, beef or vegetable broth

¾ to 1 pound fresh cranberry or other shell beans, shelled

2 tablespoons chopped fresh marjoram or oregano leaves

Rind from a wedge of Parmesan or Romano cheese (optional)

Freshly grated Parmesan cheese (optional)

## Keep the Rinds

When you buy a wedge of Parmesan, save the rind. It's great added to a pot of minestrone or other bean soup, and to meat-based and vegetable soups. Store the rind in a heavy-duty plastic bag in the freezer until soup-making day.

⊚⊚ Combine the olive oil and butter in large soup pot. Place over medium heat. When the butter foams, add the onion and garlic; cook 2 or 3 minutes, stirring constantly. Add the potatoes; cook for 2 or 3 minutes, stirring constantly.

Continue this process, adding the vegetables one variety at a time, in the order given (except for the shell beans), and cooking each addition for 2 or 3 minutes, stirring. When the tomatoes have been added, pour in the broth. Bring to a boil, reduce heat to low, cover, and cook for 2 hours, stirring occasionally. The soup should be rather thick.

Add the shell beans, marjoram and optional cheese rind. Cook until the shell beans are tender, about 30 or 40 minutes, stirring often.

Garnish with grated Parmesan if desired.

SERVES 6 TO 8 AS A MAIN DISH

# Pancotto (Bread Crumb and Egg Soup)

*Carol Field, who is one of the country's foremost experts on Italian food, gave us this recipe for a rustic soup that uses dried bread. Because the ingredients are so simple, genuine Parmigiano-Reggiano cheese is a must.*

3 to 4 tablespoons olive oil

3 garlic cloves

4½ cups chicken broth, preferably homemade

Bread crumbs from 6 to 8 slices stale country-style bread, crusts removed

¼ cup shredded or torn fresh basil

½ cup chopped fresh Italian parsley

¼ cup freshly grated Parmigiano-Reggiano cheese

3 to 4 eggs, lightly beaten

Salt and pepper to taste

⊚⊚ Heat the olive oil over medium-low heat in a 2-quart saucepan. Add the garlic and sauté until it is soft, but be careful it doesn't burn. Pour in the broth and bring to a boil. Reduce heat and simmer about 5 minutes.

Combine the bread crumbs, basil, parsley and grated cheese. Whisk the mixture into the broth and cook, whisking constantly, until the soup is hot but not boiling. At the last minute, whisk the eggs into the hot broth; simmer for about 1 minute, until the eggs are cooked and have shredded. Do not let the broth boil. Season with salt and pepper and serve immediately.

SERVES 4 TO 6

# Fresh Pea Soup with Blossoms

*This soup, by Georgeanne Brennan, takes only minutes to prepare. It's also delicious made with fresh asparagus or fava beans.*

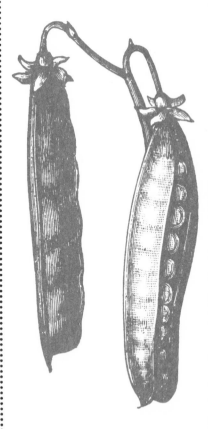

2 pounds unshelled English peas (about 2 cups shelled)

3 cups chicken or vegetable broth

½ cup water

½ teaspoon salt

½ teaspoon freshly ground black pepper

2 tablespoons crème fraîche, yogurt or sour cream thinned with milk

2 tablespoons minced chive blossoms or fresh chives

Shell the peas and set aside. Reserve the pods.

Bring the broth to a boil in a medium-sized saucepan. Add the pea pods and the water, cover, reduce heat to medium-low and simmer for 15 to 20 minutes. Strain, discarding the pods.

Return the broth to the saucepan and add the peas. Bring to a boil, cover, reduce heat to medium low, and simmer until the peas are tender. This will take anywhere from 15 to 40 minutes, depending upon the size and maturity of the peas. When tender, put the peas and broth in a food processor or blender and puree. Return to the saucepan, add the salt and pepper and heat to just below boiling.

Ladle into soup bowls and garnish with a little crème fraîche and a sprinkling of chive blossoms or chives.

SERVES 3 OR 4

# Pork-Rib Tea Soup (Bak Ku Teh)

*Chris Yeo serves this Chinese Hokkien-style soup at his Straits Cafe in San Francisco. It's a simple two-part meal in a bowl. First, the pork ribs are lifted out, dipped into a chile–soy sauce mixture and eaten with a rice garnish. Then the soup is eaten, along with pieces of Chinese cruller, which help sop up every drop of the aromatic broth.*

1 pound pork back ribs, chopped into 2-inch lengths

1 large garlic clove, crushed

6 cups water

1 cinnamon stick

3 whole star anise

1 teaspoon white peppercorns

1½ teaspoons sugar

2 teaspoons salt

3 tablespoons dark soy sauce, or to taste

**Garnishes**

1 serrano chile, thinly sliced

2 tablespoons soy sauce

2 tablespoons crisp-fried shallot flakes (see Notes)

6 cups steamed white rice

2 Chinese crullers, sliced (see Notes)

∞ Combine the pork, garlic and water in a large saucepan; bring to a boil and boil for 5 minutes. Skim the scum that rises to the top. Add the cinnamon, star anise, peppercorns, sugar, salt and soy sauce. Simmer over low heat for 45 minutes, or until the pork is tender. Skim off the fat.

Mix together the chile and soy sauce.

Divide the soup among serving bowls, allowing 3 to 4 ribs per serving. Scatter about 1 teaspoon of the shallot flakes over each bowl. Dip the ribs into the soy-chile dipping sauce and eat with rice. Dunk the cruller slices into the broth.

SERVES 6

**NOTES:** Commercially prepared crisp-fried shallot flakes are sold in Southeast Asian grocery stores.

Chinese crullers (also called "deep-fried devils") resemble long doughnuts, and may be purchased in some Chinese bakeries and delis. If you cannot find them, substitute French or country-style bread.

# Spicy Pumpkin Soup with the Works

*Here's the perfect way to use those Halloween pumpkins. Jacqueline McMahan says the toppings are fun to add when you have guests. If you prefer to dine simply, just top the soup with chopped fresh chives.*

1 tablespoon butter

1 onion, chopped

1½ teaspoons minced fresh thyme

3 cups steamed and pureed pumpkin or acorn squash, or canned pumpkin puree

2 cups chicken broth, preferably homemade

1 dried chipotle chile, or 2 dried New Mexico chiles

Salt to taste

¼ cup finely ground toasted almonds

½ cup milk

½ cup heavy cream

**Toppings**

¼ cup snipped fresh chives

6 strips bacon, cooked crisp and crumbled

1 tablespoon ground red chile

1 cup sour cream thinned with 2 tablespoons milk

Heat the butter in a soup pot; add the onions and thyme and sauté, stirring, until the onions are translucent, about 10 minutes.

Transfer to a food processor; add the pumpkin or squash puree and process to a smooth mixture. Return to the soup pot. Add the broth and the chile (do not break up). Simmer for 20 minutes. The chipotle will add a hint of smoky spiciness to the soup. Season with salt. Add the ground almonds, then whisk in the milk and cream. Gently simmer for 2 minutes just to heat

## About Pumpkins

A fresh pumpkin can keep up to 6 months in a cool, dry place (below 50 degrees). The best eating pumpkins are 10 to 12 inches in diameter; they have more flesh and a smaller seed cavity and they're less stringy. Those cultivated for cooking are labeled "pie" or "sugar" pumpkins.

Fresh pumpkin may be baked or boiled; leftovers may be frozen up to two months.

To bake, preheat the oven to 350 degrees. Cut the pumpkin in half and cut off the stem. Remove the seeds and stringy portions. Tent with foil to prevent drying. Bake skin side up on a baking sheet for 30 to 40 minutes, or until tender. Peel off the skin with a sharp knife. Puree the flesh in a food processor or with a potato masher.

To boil, cut the pumpkin in half, discarding stringy portions and seeds. Peel and cut into 3- to 4-inch pieces and place in a large pot. Cover with boiling water and simmer for 15 to 20 minutes. Drain, then force through a food mill, puree in a food processor, or mash with a potato masher or large fork until smooth.

and blend flavors. Do not boil. If the soup becomes too thick, add a little more broth or milk.

The soup may be made earlier in the day and reheated just before serving (it will thicken when refrigerated). Remove chile before serving.

Let diners add toppings of their choice at the table.

SERVES 6

**TIP:** Put the sour cream–milk mixture in a plastic squeeze bottle and drizzle lines across the surface of soup, then draw a butter knife through the lines to create a decorative pattern.

# Shellfish Soup with Couscous

*Created by Joanne Weir, this Mediterranean soup features four kinds of shellfish: mussels, clams, shrimp and scallops. It's a good choice for a casual dinner where people stand around the kitchen watching the cook and inhaling the wonderful aromas of things to come.*

3 cups fish stock, or half bottled clam juice, half water

2 pounds assorted shellfish (mussels, clams, shrimp, scallops), washed

2 tablespoons extra-virgin olive oil

1 small onion, minced

3 garlic cloves, minced

Pinch red pepper flakes

1 cup dry red wine

2 bay leaves

1¼ cups chopped, peeled and seeded tomatoes

2 teaspoons red wine vinegar

Freshly ground pepper to taste

1 cup water

1 cup couscous

½ teaspoon salt, plus salt to taste

3 tablespoons chopped fresh parsley

Large pinch saffron threads

∞ Bring stock to a simmer in a soup pot. Add the mussels, cover and cook until they open, 2 to 5 minutes. As the mussels open, remove them with a slotted spoon, place in a large bowl and cover with foil.

Add the clams to the pot, cover and cook 2 to 5 minutes. As soon as they open, remove with a slotted spoon; add to the mussels. Strain the cooking broth and reserve.

Peel the shrimp and add to cooked shellfish.

Remove the muscle from the side of each scallop. Add the scallops to the cooked shellfish.

Heat the olive oil in a soup pot. Add the onion and sauté until soft, about 7 minutes. Add the garlic and red pepper flakes; sauté 1 minute. Increase heat to high and immediately add the wine. Cook until the liquid has reduced by half, about 2 minutes. Add the bay leaves, tomatoes, vinegar, reserved shellfish broth and pepper. Cover and simmer slowly about 15 minutes.

Meanwhile, bring the water to a boil and remove from heat. Add the couscous and ½ teaspoon salt, stir, cover and let sit 10 minutes. Uncover and fluff with a fork.

Add the parsley, saffron and shellfish to the soup and simmer slowly, about 2 minutes. Season with salt and pepper.

Divide the couscous among serving bowls. Ladle the soup over the couscous.

SERVES 6

# Hot and Spicy Thai Shrimp Soup

*This seductive Thai soup by Maria Cianci has a complexity of flavors and illustrates one of the basic tenets of Thai cuisine: a balance of hot, sour, sweet and salty. A big bowl of the soup with a crunchy lettuce or brown rice salad makes a meal. As an appetizer, it could precede roasts, chops or grilled fish.*

¾ pound shrimp (31 to 35 count), about 24

1 large stalk lemongrass

1 teaspoon vegetable oil

10 cilantro stems, chopped

4 small dried red peppers, split in half and seeded

4 slices fresh ginger, each smashed with the side of a knife

1 garlic clove, smashed

5 cups chicken stock

2 teaspoons sugar

3 tablespoons plus 2 teaspoons fresh lime juice

2 tablespoons plus 2 teaspoons Asian fish sauce

1 can (5½ ounces) straw mushrooms, drained

⅓ cup packed fresh cilantro leaves

## About Straw Mushrooms

Canned straw mushrooms come peeled and unpeeled. Choose the peeled ones; they're more tender, and more decorative, too— they look like miniature umbrellas that are halfway open.

👓 Shell and devein the shrimp; reserve shrimp and shells separately.

Cut bulbous portion of lemongrass on the diagonal into ¼-inch-thick slices. Separate slices into rings; set aside. Coarsely chop the long slender stalk and reserve separately.

Heat the oil in a heavy medium-sized saucepan over high heat. Add the shrimp shells and sauté until pink, about 1 minute. Add the chopped lemongrass stalk, the cilantro stems, 1 of the peppers, the ginger and garlic; sauté for 1 minute. Add the stock and sugar; bring to a boil. Reduce heat to low, cover and simmer for 25 minutes. Strain and discard the solids.

Return the stock to the saucepan. Add the lime juice, fish sauce, lemongrass rings and the remaining 3 peppers. Boil for 3 minutes. Check the seasoning. The soup should be highly seasoned, with a balance of hot, sour, sweet and salty. Add more lime, fish sauce or sugar, if necessary. (The pepper will intensify as the soup stands.)

Add the mushrooms and shrimp; simmer until the shrimp turn opaque and are just cooked through, 1½ to 2 minutes. Do not overcook. Stir in the cilantro leaves.

YIELDS 6 CUPS

# Mexican Pasta Soup

*Jacqueline McMahan's Mexican pasta soup is lightly kissed with fresh and dried chiles. Good chicken stock is important in the dish, as is the quality of the cheese that's grated over the top at serving time.*

12 ounces Mexican fideos, or vermicelli

1 cup chopped onion

2 cups peeled and seeded tomatoes or canned plum tomatoes

2 quarts chicken stock

1 teaspoon minced garlic

1 fresh Anaheim chile, seeded and chopped

1 teaspoon mild ground red chile, such as New Mexico Dixon chile

Salt to taste

¼ cup grated Asiago or Parmesan cheese

Salsa for garnish (optional)

◎ Break up the coils of fideos on a jelly-roll pan and toast in a preheated 350-degree oven for 8 to 10 minutes. They should be a golden brown.

Chop the onion and tomatoes in a food processor just until coarse; there should be no large pieces.

Pour the chicken stock into a soup pot. Add the onion-tomato mixture, the garlic, chopped Anaheim and ground red chile. Simmer for 15 minutes to blend flavors. Season with salt. Stir in the toasted fideos and simmer for 4 minutes.

Ladle the soup into wide bowls and sprinkle with grated cheese. Pass salsa at the table.

SERVES 6 TO 8

# Sorrel and Potato Soup

*Spring is the best time to use sorrel. The long, sword-shaped leaves are bright green and as mildly sour as they will ever be. Alternatively, this soup, by Georgeanne Brennan, may be made with young spinach or dandelion greens.*

2 tablespoons olive oil

1 tablespoon butter

8 potatoes (yellow-fleshed, if possible), cut into ½-inch cubes

2 large leeks (including tender green portions), well cleaned and chopped

2 quarts chicken or vegetable broth

15 large or 30 small sorrel leaves, cut into julienne

½ teaspoon freshly ground black pepper

⊚ Combine the olive oil and butter in a large pot; place over medium heat. When the butter melts, add the potatoes and leeks and gently sauté until the leeks are translucent and the potatoes have begun to glisten, about 5 to 10 minutes.

Add the broth, reduce heat to low and simmer until the potatoes are tender, 15 to 20 minutes. About 5 minutes before the potatoes are done, add half of the sorrel and the pepper. Taste the soup for salt and adjust according to taste.

Ladle the soup into bowls; stir 2 or 3 tablespoons of the remaining sorrel into each serving.

SERVES 4

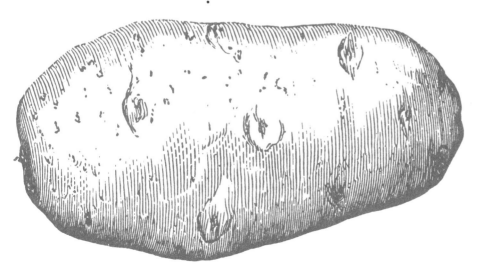

# Spicy Summer Squash and Yellow Split Pea Soup

*The spice in this Ayla Algar recipe doesn't come from chiles, but a mix of turmeric, cumin, ginger, mustard and black pepper. The split peas and squash, pureed together, create a very enticing combination. It's particularly good with coconut milk stirred in at the very last, but cream works, too.*

¾ cup yellow split peas, soaked overnight in water to cover

1 teaspoon ground turmeric

3 slices (each about ⅛ inch thick) fresh ginger

2 quarts water

1 large onion, chopped

2 garlic cloves, chopped

2 tablespoons clarified butter or vegetable oil

1 teaspoon whole cumin seed, ground

2 teaspoons whole coriander seed, ground

¾ teaspoon black mustard seed, ground

⅓ teaspoon pepper

⅛ teaspoon fenugreek seed, ground (optional)

2 large tomatoes, chopped

1 pound summer squash and crookneck squash, cubed

1 cup chopped fresh cilantro leaves

4 cups light chicken stock or water

¾ cup coconut milk or cream

Salt to taste

⊗ Drain the split peas. Place in a large saucepan; add ½ teaspoon of the turmeric, the ginger and water to the saucepan. Simmer until the peas are soft.

Cook the onion and garlic in the butter or oil for 5 minutes. Stir in the spices, including the remaining turmeric, and cook 30 seconds. Add the tomatoes, squash and ½ cup of the cilantro; cook 15 minutes. Stir in the cooked split peas and the chicken stock or water. Simmer, covered, 30 minutes. Cool slightly and puree the soup in a blender. Return to the pan and stir in the coconut milk or cream and salt; heat through.

## How to Make Clarified Butter (Desi Ghee)

Melt 1 pound unsalted butter in a large heavy pan over low heat. Cook uncovered until the butter stops sizzling and sputtering and turns golden in color, about 15 minutes. Remove from the heat and let stand for a couple of minutes. Skim the foam off the top and pour the clear golden liquid into a storage container. Discard the solids in the bottom of the pan. Clarified butter will keep up to 3 months in the refrigerator. Yields 1⅔ cups.

If the soup is too thick, thin it with water. Serve hot, garnished with the remaining cilantro leaves.

SERVES 6

# Four-Squash Soup with Tomatoes, Orzo, Salsa and Lime

*This intriguing combination by Marlena Spieler offers a cross-cultural kick. Orzo, a ricelike pasta, along with oregano, adds an Italian touch. The salsa and lime give a Mexican twist. Together they are dynamite.*

½ cup (4 ounces) orzo pasta

1 cup tiny cherry tomatoes, or 1½ cups regular cherry tomatoes, cut into halves

2 tablespoons olive oil

3 or 4 garlic cloves, chopped

1 yellow pattypan squash, diced

1 green pattypan squash, diced

1 green zucchini, diced

1 golden zucchini, diced

6 cups chicken stock or vegetable broth

½ teaspoon dried oregano

Salt to taste

2 to 3 tablespoons red salsa

1 lime, cut into wedges

◉ Cook the pasta in boiling salted water until al dente. Drain and set aside.

Quickly sauté the tomatoes in olive oil until lightly browned in places (if using halved cherry tomatoes, cook until slightly saucy); add the garlic and cook a few moments, then stir in the squash. Continue to cook another minute or two. Add the stock or broth and cook 10 minutes, or until the squash is just tender. Season with oregano and salt.

Place a few spoonfuls of pasta into each serving bowl, then ladle in the soup. Garnish each with a dab of salsa and a wedge of lime.

SERVES 2 TO 4

# Yellow Squash Soup with Cumin and Salsa

*Marlena Spieler's pale yellow puree, flecked with bits of red tomato, is one of the most refreshing soups around—and it's low in calories, about 65 per serving.*

4 yellow crookneck squash or golden zucchini, diced

3 cups chicken stock or vegetable broth

2 cups diced tomatoes, including juices

¼ teaspoon ground cumin

3 garlic cloves, chopped

Salt to taste

1 tablespoon red salsa

∞ Combine the squash with the stock or broth, tomatoes, cumin and garlic in a saucepan. Bring to boil and cook until the squash is tender, about 10 minutes.

Puree the soup, then season with salt, more cumin if desired, and salsa.

SERVES 2 TO 4

# Simple Tlalpeño-Style Soup

*This classic Mexican soup comes from the town of Tlalpán, which is in the state of Michoacán. It is one of the quickest from-scratch soups to be found— if you have homemade chicken broth on hand, says Jacqueline McMahan. The chipotle lends a rich earthiness, while avocado and minced green onions offer a refreshing counterpoint.*

1 whole chicken breast, skinned and halved

8 cups homemade chicken broth

1 dried chipotle chile

4 green onions, minced

2 tablespoons minced fresh cilantro

¼ cup diced tomato

1 avocado, pitted, peeled and cut into neat cubes

## Nonslip Cutting Board

To keep a cutting board from bouncing and moving during chopping, place a damp towel underneath it.

Place chicken breast in a large saucepan. Add the broth, bring to a boil, reduce heat and simmer for 20 minutes. Let chicken cool in the broth, then remove and cut into strips.

Bring the broth to a simmer. Add the chicken strips and chipotle. Cover and simmer for 5 minutes. Add the green onions, cilantro, tomato and avocado. Ladle into shallow bowls.

SERVES 6

# Fresh Tomato-Tarragon Soup with Fennel Crouton Crust

*Tarragon subtly flavors Georgeanne Brennan's late-season tomato soup, giving it a surprise finish that combines ideally with the toasted crunch of fennel seeds.*

1 tablespoon butter

2 shallots, finely sliced

13 or 14 medium tomatoes (4 to 5 pounds), peeled, seeded and chopped (save the juices)

4 tablespoons chopped fresh tarragon

½ cup dry white wine

4 cups water

½ teaspoon salt

**Croutons**

½ loaf day-old unsliced bread

2 tablespoons olive oil

1 tablespoon fennel seeds

5 or 6 whole black peppercorns

¼ teaspoon salt

Melt the butter in a large saucepan over medium heat. Add the shallots and sauté 3 or 4 minutes, or until translucent. Add ¾ cup of the chopped tomatoes and their juices, and half of the tarragon. Cook over medium heat, stirring occasionally, for 10 minutes. Add the wine and bring to a boil. Reduce heat to low and simmer about 20 minutes. (You should have about

½ cup liquid.) Add the remaining tomatoes, the water and salt. Increase heat to medium-low and cook 20 to 30 minutes, or until the soup has reduced to about 6 cups.

The croutons: Preheat oven to 350 degrees. Cut the bread into ½-inch-thick slices. Cut each slice in half lengthwise to make biscotti-shaped pieces. Place the slices on a baking sheet and brush with olive oil. Bruise the fennel seeds, grind or crush the peppercorns and mix them with the salt. Sprinkle the mixture over the bread slices, gently pressing it into the bread. Bake for 15 minutes, or until the croutons are slightly golden. Remove and set aside.

Just before serving, add the remaining tarragon to the soup and simmer 2 to 3 minutes. Ladle the soup into bowls and top with the croutons.

SERVES 4

## Adding Orange to Soup

To add a pleasant, fresh taste to a leftover tomato-based soup (including minestrone), try adding an orange half and simmering it in the soup for 15 to 30 minutes.

# Turkey Congee

*Congee is a rice porridge that's a staple in many San Francisco Chinese restaurants. In China, congee may be made with water, duck or chicken stock. Here, Joyce Jue uses turkey stock. It's a perfect way to recycle that all-American after-Thanksgiving carcass. There are many accompaniments served with congee, including Chinese crullers, thin slices of Chinese barbecued pork, chopped chives, green onions or cilantro, preserved eggs, pickled vegetables, and fresh sliced meat, fish and poultry. Pick two or three of your favorites, or serve it unadorned. Traditionally, congee is eaten for breakfast or as a late-night snack, but it also makes a satisfying lunch or supper.*

1 turkey carcass

1-inch lump fresh ginger

2 green onions

3½ quarts water

⅔ cup rice, washed until the water runs clear

Salt to taste

**Condiments**

White pepper

Soy sauce

Asian sesame oil

Chopped green onions

Cilantro sprigs

Chinese crullers, sliced (see page 22)

  Chop the turkey carcass into large pieces. Place in a large stockpot with the ginger, green onions and the water. Bring to a boil, cover and simmer for 2 hours. Strain the stock and remove any fat. Measure out 8 cups of stock.

  Put the rice in a deep saucepan. Add the 8 cups turkey stock and bring to a boil. Stir well. Reduce heat to low, cover, and simmer until the rice thickens to a porridge consistency, about 1½ hours, stirring occasionally. The congee is ready when there is no separation of the rice and liquid. Season with salt.

  Serve with accompaniments of choice.

SERVES 4 TO 6

# Zuppa di Fave (Fava Bean Soup)

*This creamy, pale green soup, from chef Giuseppe Naccarelli of Il Fornaio in San Francisco, is worth the time it takes to shell and peel 5 pounds of fava beans. However, if time is short, or favas are hard to find, a delicious version may be made using packaged frozen lima beans.*

> 5 pounds fava beans, or 2 packages (10 ounces each) frozen lima beans
>
> 3 tablespoons olive oil, plus more for garnish
>
> 1 small yellow onion, chopped
>
> 2 russet potatoes, peeled and diced
>
> 8 cups vegetable broth
>
> ½ cup heavy cream
>
> Salt and freshly ground black pepper to taste
>
> ¼ cup freshly grated Parmesan cheese, plus more for garnish
>
> 6 slices baguette, toasted and rubbed with garlic

Shell the fava beans. To skin them, blanch in a large quantity of boiling water for 2 minutes, then transfer to ice water. When cool, drain and pinch open the thick skin of each bean. The peeled bean will slip out easily. (You should have about 1 pound of peeled beans.)

Heat 3 tablespoons olive oil in a large pot over medium heat. Add the onion and sauté until softened, about 5 minutes. Add the potatoes and beans. Sauté for 2 to 3 minutes. Add the broth, bring to a simmer and cook until the potatoes and beans are very soft, about 20 minutes. Add the cream; season with salt and pepper, and simmer 5 minutes longer. Stir in ¼ cup cheese, then puree soup in a blender or food processor.

Serve in warm bowls, topping each portion with a drizzle of olive oil, a sprinkle of Parmesan cheese and a slice of garlic toast.

SERVES 6

## How to Prepare Fava Beans

First, shell the beans. Slit the skin on the kidney-shaped beans with your thumbnail or the tip of a knife. Then peel back and discard. Or squeeze at the bottom of the bean and it should pop out.

The beans also can be skinned by plunging them into boiling water for a few seconds to pop the skin. Rinse beans in cold water to stop cooking and peel back the skins.

# Tamarind Vegetable Soup

*This light soup is fragrant with Indian spices and tamarind, a sweet-sour fruit used much like lemon. But unlike lemon, tamarind's tartness does not dissipate with cooking. Originating in southern India, this soup is based on a recipe from Savera Restaurant in San Jose, adapted for home use by Maria Cianci.*

2 teaspoons vegetable oil

1 small onion, finely chopped

1 small carrot, finely chopped

2 tablespoons coriander seed, crushed

2½ teaspoons sugar

1¼ teaspoons cumin seed

1 small dried red pepper, split

2 tablespoons tomato puree

4 cups chicken stock

1 cup water

1 walnut-sized lump tamarind pulp (see Note)

½ pound green beans, cut into ½-inch lengths

2 teaspoons butter

1 medium tomato, peeled, seeded and cut into medium dice

1 large carrot, cut into small dice

1 large celery stalk, pared and cut into small dice

½ cup cilantro leaves

⊚⊚ Heat the oil in a large saucepan over medium heat. Add the onion and carrot and sauté until the onion is golden, 10 to 12 minutes.

Add the coriander seed, sugar, cumin seed and red pepper; sauté until the spices are fragrant, about 45 seconds. Stir in the tomato puree, then add the chicken stock, water and tamarind. Bring to a boil, reduce heat, cover and simmer 25 minutes. Strain the liquid, pressing on the solids and scraping some of the tamarind pulp from the bottom of the strainer into the soup. Discard the remaining solids. There should be about 3¾ cups liquid.

Blanch the beans in boiling water until just tender; drain, rinse under cold water. Set aside.

## Quick Soup Ideas

⊚⊚ Simmer red potatoes and cubed squash (acorn or hubbard) in canned chicken broth; add kale or spinach, leeks or fennel. Just before the potatoes are tender, add macaroni shells and adjust the seasoning.

⊚⊚ Poach escarole in butter and cream. Puree and add milk and seasonings. Reheat.

⊚⊚ Cook kale or other winter greens in chicken stock along with cubes of potatoes and onions. Near the end of the cooking time, stir in a few capers and salt-cured olives.

⊚⊚ Sauté onions, garlic and carrots for a few minutes. Add dry lentils and stir until they darken slightly. Add water to generously cover and cook with a ham hock, some bacon and fresh herbs.

*—Georgeanne Brennan*

Melt the butter in a medium saucepan over medium heat. Add the tomato and sauté, stirring, for 2 minutes. Add the carrot and celery; sauté for 3 minutes. Add the soup and simmer for 5 minutes. Stir in the beans and heat through.

Ladle the soup into serving bowls. Garnish with cilantro leaves.

SERVES 4

**NOTE:** Blocks of tamarind pulp are available in Asian and Indian grocery stores.

# Shell Bean and Haricot Vert Salad

*Fresh flageolets, black-eyed peas, baby lima, cranberry, pinto and black turtle beans all have a unique flavor, texture and appearance. Georgeanne Brennan showcases these qualities by combining several types with a few tiny fresh green beans and green or yellow Romano beans. Toss all with a simple herb vinaigrette and you've got a memorable late-summer salad. The same vinaigrette can work with a variety of dried beans, too.*

2 pounds mixed fresh shell beans in the pod (flageolet, cranberry, pinto, españa, dragon, black-eyed pea, baby lima)

½ pound haricots verts or baby Blue Lake beans

½ pound young green and/or yellow Romano beans

2 quarts water

1½ tablespoons salt

**Vinaigrette**

⅓ cup red wine vinegar

½ cup olive oil

½ teaspoon salt

1 teaspoon freshly ground black pepper

2 shallots, peeled and minced

2 tablespoons minced fresh summer savory, tarragon or parsley for garnish

∞ Shell the beans, keeping the different varieties separate. Trim the haricots verts or Blue Lakes and Romano beans, removing stems and tips. Leave the haricots whole; cut the Romanos on the diagonal into ½-inch lengths. Set aside.

Taste the raw shell beans. Those that are still so small and "green" that you can bite through them easily will need to cook only about 10 minutes. The beans that are less green (they have already begun to dry, and will offer resistance to your bite) will need to cook longer, up to 30 minutes, especially if they are large as well as dry.

To preserve their individual flavors, the shell beans will need to be cooked separately. They may be cooked in one pan, one variety at a time, changing the water each time, or at the same time, in separate pans. Bring the water and salt to a boil and cook the shell beans until just tender.

Steam the haricots or Blue Lakes for 3 to 4 minutes, until just tender but still bright green. Plunge them into cold water for 30 seconds, drain and set aside.

Steam the Romano beans about 5 minutes, or until tender but still brightly colored. Remove from steamer and set aside to cool.

To make the vinaigrette: Combine all the ingredients, mix well and let stand 30 minutes before assembling the salad.

To assemble: Reserve 12 to 15 haricots verts or Blue Lakes, an equal number of Romanos and about 24 of the shell beans. Combine the remaining beans with the vinaigrette. Divide equally among 6 plates. Garnish with the reserved beans and the herbs.

SERVES 6

# Cannellini all'Insalata

*This refreshing salad is perfect as an antipasto for a summer lunch or picnic, created by chef Luca Loffredo of Prego in San Francisco.*

1 pound dried cannellini beans

4 garlic cloves (1 whole, 3 sliced)

1 sprig fresh sage

3 celery stalks (1 whole, 2 chopped)

½ red onion, julienned

5 tablespoons extra virgin olive oil

2 lemons

Salt and pepper to taste

Leaves from 1 bunch parsley

⊚⊚ Combine the beans, the whole garlic clove and the sage in a large bowl. Cover with cold water and let soak overnight.

The next day, discard the garlic and sage, drain and rinse the beans.

Place the beans in a large pot, cover with fresh water and add the whole celery stalk. Bring to a boil, reduce heat and simmer until the beans are al dente, from 30 to 40 minutes. (Don't let them turn mushy.) Drain the beans, reserving about 1 cup of the cooking liquid. Discard the celery. Let the beans cool to room temperature.

Combine the sliced garlic, the onion and olive oil in a medium-sized bowl. Squeeze the juice from 1½ of the lemons over the top and season with salt and pepper. Whisk lightly until emulsified. Add the beans, chopped celery, parsley and reserved cooking liquid. Cover and set aside for at least 1 hour to allow flavors to blend. (If holding for more than 1 hour, refrigerate.)

' Serve at room temperature, garnished with lemon wedges from the remaining lemon half.

SERVES 4

# Salad of String Beans, Shell Beans and Tomatoes

*There is a vast difference between fresh and dried shell beans, as shown in this recipe from Chez Panisse. Fresh beans are distinctly sweeter and are not at all starchy. Choose shell beans with pods that are tight and vividly colored: This is the best way of telling if they have been recently picked. Although it is much easier to remove the beans from dried pods, they will be much less sweet. Serve this salad as an appetizer with slices of prosciutto and/or dry-cured Italian sausages.*

**Vinaigrette**

1 small red onion, finely diced

3 tablespoons red wine vinegar

¼ teaspoon salt

⅛ teaspoon freshly ground black pepper

1 small garlic clove

4 salt-packed anchovy fillets, soaked and squeezed dry

⅓ cup extra-virgin olive oil

3 cups shelled fresh shell beans (1 cup flageolets, 1 cup black-eyed peas or purple-hulled crowders, 1 cup cranberry beans, or any combination available)

6 quarts water

6 teaspoons salt, plus salt to taste

4 ounces mixed string beans (yellow wax, haricots verts, Romanos)

2 small red tomatoes, peeled, diced

1 large yellow tomato, peeled, diced

3 tablespoons chopped fresh Italian parsley

8 salt-packed anchovy fillets, soaked, squeezed dry, cut in half lengthwise and tossed in 2 teaspoons olive oil

◎ To make the vinaigrette: Mix the onion with the vinegar in a bowl. Add the salt and dissolve it in the vinegar. Add the pepper. Pound the garlic and anchovies to a paste in a mortar and add them to the bowl. Stir in the olive oil.

## Basic Vinaigrette

Marion Cunningham suggests this basic oil and vinegar salad dressing for any type of greens or as a marinade:

Combine 2 teaspoons lemon juice, 2 teaspoons vinegar and ¼ teaspoon salt in a jar with a tight-fitting lid. Let sit for a minute, then put the lid on the jar and shake well. Add 4 tablespoons olive oil and 2 tablespoons water; put the lid on the jar and shake until thoroughly mixed. Yields about ½ cup.

Cook each type of shell bean in a separate pan in 1 quart water with 1 teaspoon salt. Depending upon the variety, each will take from 20 to 25 minutes. Sample the beans. When they are tender, take them off the heat.

Combine all the shell beans in one container and remove all but enough of their cooking liquid to just cover them. Let beans cool in the cooking liquid in the refrigerator.

Parboil each type of string bean in a separate pan in 1 quart water with 1 teaspoon salt. When they have softened but are still slightly crunchy, remove the beans from the water with a sieve or slotted spoon. Spread out on a plate to cool. (Cooked string beans absorb water quickly, so do not soak them in cold water to cool them.) Combine the string beans in 1 container and put in the refrigerator.

To assemble: When the dried and fresh beans are cool, drain off the water in the bowls and combine all of the beans.

Season the tomatoes with 2 tablespoons of the vinaigrette and 1 tablespoon of the parsley. Taste the tomatoes and correct the seasonings with salt, pepper and vinegar, if desired. Pour the rest of the vinaigrette over the beans and shell beans, add the remaining parsley and mix well.

Place the beans on a large plate, then arrange the tomatoes over the top. Add all vinaigrette and juices to the plate and garnish the top with the anchovy strips.

SERVES 6 AS AN APPETIZER

# Belgian Endive and Watercress Salad with Smoked Trout

*Peppery watercress and slightly bitter crunchy endive make a wonderful contrast to bite-sized pieces of smoked trout in this Georgeanne Brennan recipe. A warm shallot/tarragon dressing is drizzled over just before serving.*

## The Secret to Great Cooking

Taste every ingredient before you add it to a dish. Some chiles are mild, some are hot; sometimes cabbage is sweet, other times it's strong. By tasting first, you have a head start in creating a pleasing balance.

5 bunches watercress, washed and patted dry

5 heads Belgian endive

8 to 10 smoked trout fillets (about 2½ pounds)

2 tablespoons butter

3 shallots, minced

¼ teaspoon salt

1 cup dry white wine

4 tablespoons fresh lemon juice

¼ cup chopped fresh tarragon leaves

¼ cup olive oil

Choose 10 small clusters of watercress leaves; set aside for garnish. Remove the leaves from the remaining watercress; set aside. Discard stems.

Cut the cores from the Belgian endive by cutting an inverted "v" at the base of each head. Discard cores. Separate each head into individual leaves, setting aside the small leaves for garnish. Chop the remaining leaves into bite-sized pieces.

Cut or break the smoked trout into bite-sized pieces, discarding any skin. Set aside.

Melt the butter in a small skillet over medium heat. When the butter foams, add the shallots and sauté until translucent, 2 or 3 minutes. Add the salt, wine, lemon juice and 3 tablespoons of the tarragon. Cook over medium heat until the liquid is reduced by one third. Remove from heat, add the remaining tarragon, more salt if desired, and the olive oil.

To serve: Divide the chopped endive, watercress leaves and trout among individual salad plates. Drizzle a little dressing over each salad and garnish with the reserved watercress clusters and small endive leaves.

SERVES 10

# Caesar Salad

*It seems that every restaurant in San Francisco does Caesar salad, but the benchmark is Zuni Cafe's version, which has a perfect balance of acid, anchovies and Parmesan cheese. Be sure the romaine leaves are well chilled and dry so the dressing doesn't become watery.*

2 salt-packed anchovies, filleted, rinsed, dried and chopped

½ generous tablespoon minced garlic

½ scant tablespoon red wine vinegar

Sea salt to taste

Freshly ground pepper to taste

⅓ cup plus 1 tablespoon olive oil

¼ pound chewy rustic French or Italian bread, cut into ¾-inch cubes

Juice of 1 lemon (about 2 tablespoons), or to taste

½ cup freshly grated Parmigiano-Reggiano cheese

2 eggs, well beaten

2 hearts of romaine lettuce, cored, leaves left whole and chilled

∞ Combine half of the anchovies and garlic in a bowl. Add the vinegar, a pinch of salt, pepper and ⅓ cup olive oil. Let stand for 20 minutes.

Preheat the oven to 300 degrees. Toss the bread cubes with the remaining 1 tablespoon olive oil and a pinch of salt. Spread out on a baking sheet and bake until golden, about 10 minutes.

At serving time, add the remaining anchovies and garlic, the lemon juice and 1 tablespoon of the cheese to the dressing base. Whisk in the eggs to form an emulsion.

Thoroughly toss the lettuce leaves with the dressing, being careful not to bruise them. Taste for salt and add more, if necessary.

Divide the salad among chilled serving plates. Add the croutons, dust with more freshly ground pepper and sprinkle with the remaining cheese.

SERVES 4

# Mustard-Celery Salad

*Three common ingredients—mustard, celery and parsley—combine in this surprisingly simple but satisfying salad by Marion Cunningham. It's great for a luncheon side dish, or as a contrast to roast chicken or grilled steak. As a variation, garnish with a handful of toasted walnuts or pine nuts.*

3 cups finely diced celery
1 cup (loosely packed) finely chopped fresh parsley
½ cup mayonnaise
1 tablespoon "ballpark" mustard
Pepper to taste
Butter lettuce leaves (optional)

Combine the celery and parsley in a bowl; toss to combine.

Blend together the mayonnaise and mustard; taste and add more of either to balance the flavor. Stir and toss into the celery mixture and season with pepper. Chill until needed; serve on butter lettuce, if desired.

SERVES 4

# Fennel Coleslaw

*Fred Halpert, chef/owner of Brava Terrace in St. Helena in the Napa Valley, invented this creative twist on traditional coleslaw. Fennel, golden raisins, red and purple cabbage pair well with the dressing, which is accented with curry and horseradish. Serve with hamburgers, grilled sausages or roast chicken.*

2 medium fennel bulbs

1 small head green cabbage

1 small head red cabbage

2 medium carrots, peeled and cut in matchsticks

1 tablespoon fennel seeds

¾ cup mayonnaise

3 tablespoons white wine vinegar

1 large bunch Italian parsley, minced (about 1½ cups)

3 tablespoons prepared horseradish

½ teaspoon curry powder

½ teaspoon freshly ground black pepper

½ cup golden raisins

Salt to taste

Shred the fennel and cabbages by hand or in a food processor. Combine with the carrots.

Toast the fennel seeds in a dry skillet over medium-low heat until fragrant. Let cool.

Combine the mayonnaise and vinegar in a large bowl; whisk until smooth. Stir in the fennel seeds, parsley, horseradish, curry powder and pepper. Add the cabbage mixture and raisins. Toss until well mixed. Season with salt.

SERVES 8

## Easy Fennel Salad

The licorice taste and crunchy texture of fennel make a wonderful salad. Slice the bulb as thinly as possible. Toss with a vinaigrette made with lemon, olive oil, salt and pepper (and a dab of Dijon mustard, if desired). Add either mint or parsley and top with shavings of Parmesan cheese. Thinly sliced mushrooms may also be added to the salad.

# Salad of Grilled Corn, Red Pepper and Wilted Greens

*The smoky flavors of the still warm, slightly browned corn and roast peppers are great without further adornment. But Georgeanne Brennan found that when she added wilted greens, the combination took on a new dimension.*

1 bunch spinach, dandelion or chard

2 teaspoons salt

6 ears fresh corn, silk and husks intact

2 red bell peppers

1 tablespoon butter

1 teaspoon freshly ground black pepper

½ tablespoon finely chopped fresh oregano

Wash the greens, trim and discard the stems. Put the greens in a steamer, sprinkle with 1 teaspoon of the salt and steam until wilted but still bright green, less than a minute for spinach; 4 to 5 minutes for chard. Remove the greens, gather them into a ball and squeeze them dry. Slice through the dry ball of greens, making thin shreds. Set aside.

Pull back the husks from the ears of corn to expose the silk. Pull out the silk and discard. Wrap the husks back around the ears. Grill the ears about 10 minutes, turning once or twice. Fold back the husks, and put the corn directly on the grill; cook 3 or 4 minutes longer, turning often. You want the kernels slightly browned, not burnt.

The red peppers may be grilled at the same time. Grill them over the hottest spot until they are charred on all sides, about 5 or 6 minutes. Place the roasted peppers in a plastic bag and let sweat for 4 or 5 minutes. Peel, seed and stem the peppers, then chop them; set aside.

When the corn is done, remove from the grill and cut the kernels off cobs with a sharp knife. Put the kernels into a bowl and toss with the butter. Add the peppers, the remaining 1 teaspoon salt, the pepper and oregano; toss to combine. Stir in the greens and serve warm.

SERVES 4 TO 6

# Thai Cucumber Salad

*Bruce Cost's salad is cool and refreshing, with the bright, complex flavor characteristic of Thai food. The spicy chiles, the salty dried shrimp and the acidic lime juice are balanced by a hefty dose of sugar and the crunch of peanuts. It's perfect for a picnic and is great with any grilled meat or fish.*

  2 cucumbers

  3 tablespoons thin round fresh red chile slices (with seeds)

  3 tablespoons chopped red onion

  2 heaping tablespoons dried shrimp, ground to a coarse powder in a mortar
      or food processor

  3 tablespoons fresh lime juice

  1½ tablespoons fish sauce

  2 tablespoons sugar

  1 tablespoon peanut oil

  ¼ cup crushed roasted or fried peanuts

⊚⊚  Peel the cucumbers and trim off the ends. Cut the cucumbers in half lengthwise and scrape out the seeds using the tip of a spoon. Slice the cucumbers into thin half-moons. Place the cucumbers in a bowl with the chile and onion. Add the ground shrimp, lime juice, fish sauce, sugar and peanut oil; toss well.

Serve immediately, or let sit at room temperature for up to 1 hour. Just before serving, garnish with the peanuts.

SERVES 4

# Dandelion Salad with Anchovy Dressing

*For serious lovers of robust flavors, this salad by Georgeanne Brennan is a must. Serve with thick slices of chewy bread.*

  2 bunches dandelion greens

  6 anchovy fillets

  3 garlic cloves

¼ cup olive oil

3 tablespoons balsamic vinegar

Freshly ground pepper to taste

☙ Wash the dandelion greens thoroughly and remove any bits of dirt, root or damaged leaves. Dry. Trim any large leaves into 2-inch-long slivers; leave smaller ones whole. Mash the anchovies with the garlic; blend in the olive oil and balsamic vinegar.

Toss the greens with the dressing, then divide among serving plates and grate pepper over the top.

SERVES 4 TO 6

# Japanese Eggplant Salad

*David Vardy cooks with a Japanese sensibility at his O Chame restaurant in Berkeley. Fingers of eggplant are fried before being tossed with grated daikon, scallions and a tangy-sweet dressing.*

8 large Japanese eggplants

1 quart canola or peanut oil

4 tablespoons soy sauce (preferably Japanese)

2 tablespoons mirin

2 tablespoons rice vinegar

6 tablespoons finely grated daikon (giant white radish)

3 green onions, finely minced

☙ Cut the calyx off each eggplant. Quarter the eggplants lengthwise, then cut each quarter in half, widthwise.

Pour the oil into a deep, heavy pan; heat to 375 degrees. Add the eggplant, a few pieces at a time (do not crowd the pan), and fry until lightly golden. Remove with a slotted spoon to paper towels to drain and cool.

Mix together the soy sauce, mirin and vinegar; stir in the daikon and green onions, then lightly toss with the eggplant.

Serve at room temperature.

SERVES 4

## Quick Salads

Here are some quick fall salad ideas from Georgeanne Brennan:

☙ Combine chopped pears, apples and grapes with walnuts and any creamy dressing (or mayonnaise).

☙ Combine crisp leafy winter greens with cubes of hot fried potatoes and chunks of Swiss cheese.

☙ Combine slices of fresh quince with spinach leaves and feta cheese; toss with a vinaigrette dressing.

☙ Combine persimmons, Chinese cabbage and toasted pecans in a lemony vinaigrette.

# Ensalada Pico de Gallo

*The term* pico de gallo *commonly refers to the uncooked, very hot table salsa found in taquerias. In central Mexico, however, pico de gallo is a salad composed of oranges, onions and romaine lettuce—a perfect, cooling accompaniment for chili, according to Jacqueline McMahan.*

**Dressing**

¼ cup fresh orange juice

1 tablespoon fresh lime juice

1½ tablespoons honey

½ teaspoon ground cumin

½ teaspoon ground red chile

½ teaspoon salt

1½ tablespoons canola oil

2 tablespoons minced fresh cilantro

1 cup thinly sliced red onion

1 cup julienne-cut peeled jicama

5 cups loosely packed torn romaine leaves

2 cups sliced, peeled navel oranges

¼ cup toasted pecans or peanuts, coarsely chopped

◖◗ Whisk together all the dressing ingredients.

Drizzle half of the dressing over the onion and jicama; refrigerate for at least 1 hour.

Just before serving, remove the onion and jicama from the marinade and toss with the romaine. Arrange oranges on top and drizzle the remaining dressing over the salad. Garnish with the nuts.

SERVES 8

## Toasting Seeds

Place the seeds in an ungreased small, heavy skillet and toast over medium heat, stirring constantly, until the seeds darken slightly and are aromatic. Remove from heat and pour into a small bowl.

# Fennel, Orange and Red Onion Salad

*This simple salad, by Georgeanne Brennan, combines the classic refreshing flavors of fennel, orange and red onion. It can be served with rich meats, such as sausage, pork or pot roast, but it also goes well with poached fish and chicken.*

2 medium fennel bulbs

2 oranges

½ red onion

¼ cup olive oil

2 tablespoons balsamic vinegar

3 tablespoons finely chopped fresh chervil, arugula or parsley leaves

Trim the fennel bulbs, removing the stalks and any discolored pieces. Cut into ¼-inch slices; set aside.

Peel the oranges, divide them into sections and remove the white pith. Set aside 6 sections and cut the remainder in half; set aside.

Cut the onion into thin slices; set aside.

Combine the juice of the 6 orange sections, the olive oil, vinegar and herbs to make a dressing.

Toss the salad ingredients with the dressing and let stand at room temperature for about 30 minutes. Stir occasionally.

Serve as is or on a bed of butter lettuce.

SERVES 4 TO 6

# Egyptian Feta Salad with Dill and Mint

*The clean tang of feta and the coolness of cucumbers allow fresh herbs—parsley, mint and dill—to shine in this recipe from Joanne Weir.*

8 ounces feta cheese

3 tablespoons extra-virgin olive oil

2 tablespoons fresh lemon juice

Salt and freshly ground pepper to taste

1 large cucumber, peeled, seeded and cut into ½-inch dice

1 small red onion, cut into ¼-inch dice

1½ tablespoons chopped fresh mint

1½ tablespoons chopped fresh parsley

1½ tablespoons chopped fresh dill

3 lemon wedges

Dill and mint sprigs for garnish

◉◉ Crumble the feta into a bowl and mash with the olive oil and lemon juice. Season with salt and pepper. Add the cucumber, onion and chopped herbs. Toss to combine. Place on a serving plate and garnish with lemon wedges and herb sprigs.

Accompany with warm pita bread. (The salad also is terrific in a pita sandwich paired with slices of roast lamb.)

SERVES 6

**NOTE:** May be prepared 1 day ahead of time and refrigerated. Bring to room temperature before serving.

# Arugula with Figs, Roquefort and Toasted Walnuts

*Marlena Spieler first tasted this salad in a tiny bistro in France. When she returned to California, she brought the recipe back with her. If sweet ripe figs are not in season, substitute fresh pears.*

1 quart arugula leaves or spring salad mix

1 or 2 tablespoons walnut oil

1 or 2 tablespoons bland vegetable oil

1 or 2 tablespoons raspberry vinegar

1 fennel bulb, trimmed and thinly sliced

6 to 8 ripe figs, cut into halves

6 ounces Roquefort or similar blue cheese, broken into bite-sized bits

½ to ⅔ cup walnut bits or halves, toasted

1 to 2 tablespoons chopped fresh chervil

◐ Place the greens in a salad bowl. Toss with the oils and vinegar. Arrange the fennel and figs on top and scatter the cheese and toasted walnuts over all. Portion onto serving plates and garnish with chervil.

SERVES 4

# The Iceberg Salad

*Cold iceberg lettuce, moist and crisp, is perfectly refreshing in summer's heat and a great vehicle any time of the year for bold dressings. Blue cheese lovers will revel in this one by Steve Simmons of Bubba's Diner in San Anselmo.*

4 plum tomatoes, halved lengthwise

½ cup plus 1 tablespoon olive oil

1 tablespoon plus 1 teaspoon chopped fresh basil

¼ cup red wine vinegar

Salt and freshly ground pepper to taste

3 tablespoons minced onion

1 garlic clove, minced

4 ounces domestic blue cheese

2 teaspoons fresh lemon juice

2 heads iceberg lettuce, trimmed of all outer loose leaves

◐ Preheat the oven to 400 degrees. Toss the tomatoes with 1 tablespoon olive oil, 1 teaspoon basil, 1 teaspoon of the vinegar and the salt and pepper.

Place the tomatoes cut side up on a baking sheet. Roast for 20 minutes. Let cool.

Combine the minced onion, garlic and the remaining 1 tablespoon basil in a medium bowl. Whisk in the remaining ½ cup olive oil. Crumble in half of the cheese; whisk in the remaining vinegar and the lemon juice. Season with pepper. Let stand at room temperature for 30 to 45 minutes. Taste for tartness (the dressing should be pungent). Add more vinegar or lemon juice, pepper and a pinch of salt, if necessary.

Holding 1 head of lettuce at the top, rap the base firmly on the counter to dislodge the triangular core. Remove and discard it. Using your fingers and thumbs, pull the head into 2 large sections. Pull each section into 3 smaller sections. Repeat with the second head of lettuce. You will have 12 slightly triangular-shaped sections. Wrap airtight and chill thoroughly.

Arrange the lettuce sections on a chilled platter so they lean against one another in a tepee shape. Sprinkle lightly with salt and pepper.

Whisk the dressing and drizzle over the lettuce. Crumble the remaining cheese over the lettuce. Garnish the platter with the tomatoes.

SERVES 4

# Lotus Root Salad

*Lotus root, which is found in Asian markets, looks like the Swiss cheese of root vegetables as the round root is riddled with holes. It has a crunchy, nutty flavor that only needs a little salt, fresh ginger and sesame oil to bring it to life. Created by Bruce Cost, this salad is great for a picnic, or used as a side dish with just about any meat or sandwich. It's also an interesting addition to a cocktail party buffet.*

1 pound lotus root

3 tablespoons white vinegar

3 tablespoons sugar

1 teaspoon salt

1 teaspoon chopped fresh ginger

1 tablespoon Asian sesame oil

## Storing Oils

Because salad and cooking oils turn rancid at room temperature, store them in the refrigerator. Some oils, including olive oil, will congeal when chilled, so either keep a small cruet in the kitchen—just enough for a week's use—or remove the oil from the fridge an hour or two before you plan to use it.

∞∞ Wash the lotus root under cold water. Pare away the skin, and trim and discard both ends of the root. Cut the root into ⅛-inch-thick slices, dropping them as you go into cold water mixed with a little vinegar.

Combine the vinegar, sugar and salt in a small stainless steel or enameled saucepan and heat just until the sugar and salt dissolve. Turn off the heat and stir in the ginger.

Bring a quart of water to a boil in another pot.

Drain the lotus root slices and add them to the boiling water. Turn off the heat and let sit for 4 minutes.

Drain the lotus slices and pat dry. Then toss them with the vinegar/sugar mixture and the sesame oil. Let marinate for at least 30 minutes.

Serve the slices overlapping on a round, flat platter.

SERVES 3 OR 4

# Papaya Chaat Salad with Pine Nuts

*This potpourri of fruit, onions and fresh chiles bombards the palate with contrasting flavors and textures. Pass cayenne, lime wedges and additional chaat masala at the table to complete this Laxmi Hiremath creation.*

½ honeydew melon or large cantaloupe

1 cup diced ripe papaya

¼ cup chopped white onion

2 tablespoons fresh lime juice

1½ to 2 fresh red chiles, stemmed and slivered

¼ cup chopped fresh cilantro leaves

2 tablespoons toasted pine nuts

1 teaspoon chaat masala (see Note)

∞∞ Using a melon baller, scoop out balls of melon flesh to make 1 cup. Or, cut the melons into wedges, peel, then cut the flesh into even dice. Combine the melon, papaya, onion, lime juice, chiles and cilantro in a bowl; mix well. Cover and let stand for 15 minutes. Or, cover and chill up to 2 hours. Just before serving, fold in the pine nuts and sprinkle with chaat masala. Spoon into a clear glass serving bowl.

SERVES 4

**NOTE:** Chaat masala is a seasoning blend used specifically for Indian chaats (similar to our salads). It is available in Indian markets. If you cannot find it, simply omit it.

# Insalata di Patate con le Capperi e Olive Neri (Potato Salad with Capers and Black Olives)

*Carlo Middione, who creates superior Southern Italian food at his two Vivande restaurants, devised this excellent salad. Assertive seasonings—garlic, capers, olives, anchovies—turn mundane potatoes into exciting fare.*

2 pounds unpeeled white potatoes

½ cup boiling water from the potatoes

3 garlic cloves, finely chopped

¼ cup white wine vinegar or lemon juice

Scant ⅓ cup virgin olive oil

½ cup finely chopped Italian parsley

Salt and freshly ground black pepper to taste

1½ ounces capers, drained

4 ounces or so Gaeta or kalamata olives

4 anchovy fillets (or more), finely chopped

◎◎ Boil the potatoes in plenty of water until tender.

Heat a crockery salad bowl and keep it handy in a warm place.

When the potatoes are done, carefully remove them from the water and leave it boiling. Handling the potatoes carefully, peel them and cut them into large pieces. Place them in the warm salad bowl and pour the ½ cup boiling

## The Joys of Vinegar

A splash of vinegar in the cooking water of green beans helps them retain their crunch. In a pot of potatoes it prevents the potatoes from crumbling, which is great when using them for potato salad.

potato water over them. (Discard the remaining water or save it to add to soups or to make potato bread, etc.)

Quickly add the remaining ingredients to the potatoes and gently toss with large spoons. Cover the bowl with a plate and let the salad mellow for about 30 minutes before serving.

Serve tepid.

SERVES 6

# Sichuan Sweet and Sour Shrimp Salad with Cucumbers and Tree Ears

*This Chinese recipe by Bruce Cost has an intriguing sweet, sour and spicy dressing that unites the main ingredients: sweet shrimp, cool cucumbers and slightly crunchy tree ear mushrooms (available in Asian markets).*

¾ pound extra-large shrimp (about 20)

2 teaspoons salt

¼ cup small dried tree ear mushrooms

2 cucumbers

12 small dried red peppers

2 tablespoons Sichuan peppercorns

¼ cup Asian sesame oil

1 tablespoon peanut oil

½ cup red wine vinegar

¾ cup sugar

⊚ Bring a pot of water to a boil.

Meanwhile, toss the shrimp with 1 teaspoon salt; set aside.

When the water boils, add the shrimp. When the water returns to a boil, after about 1½ minutes, drain the shrimp and rinse under cold water to stop the cooking.

Pour hot water over the tree ears and set aside to soften. Trim off the ends of the cucumbers. Cut in half lengthwise, scoop out the seeds, then slice the cucumbers into thin half-moon slices; set aside.

## Salad-Making Tips

Count on 2 cups of lettuce leaves for each serving. Wash the lettuce under cold running water; gently dry with paper towels. Put the lettuce into a large salad bowl, cover the bowl with a damp paper towel and refrigerate until just before serving.

Combine the red peppers, peppercorns and both oils in a saucepan; heat until the peppers smoke and blacken. Remove from heat and strain the oil, discarding the spices.

Wipe out the saucepan, add the seasoned oil and place over medium heat.

Blend the vinegar, sugar and remaining 1 teaspoon salt and add to the saucepan. Cook, stirring, for about 3 minutes, until the sugar dissolves. Remove from heat and let cool.

Arrange the cucumber in 1 layer on a serving platter. Drain the tree ears, dry and arrange in a layer over the cucumbers. Peel the shrimp, cut in half lengthwise, and arrange over the tree ears.

When ready to serve, pour the sauce over the salad.

SERVES 4

# Tabbouleh

*This is Jeff Cox's interpretation of the classic Middle Eastern salad made with bulgur wheat. Spearmint, rather than peppermint, gives it a more subtle flavor.*

1 quart boiling water
1½ cups bulgur wheat
2 cups minced fresh parsley
¼ cup minced fresh spearmint
¾ cup finely diced scallions
2 tomatoes, chopped
½ cup fresh lemon juice
4 tablespoons olive oil
1 to 2 teaspoons salt, or to taste
Freshly ground pepper to taste

Pour the boiling water over the bulgur and let stand until cool, about 2 hours.

Drain the bulgur, then shake it or lightly press out the remaining excess water. Combine with the remaining ingredients. Toss lightly and chill at least 1 hour before serving.

SERVES 6

# Tongue of Fire Beans with Parmesan and Anchovy Vinaigrette

*The name Tongue of Fire comes from the beautiful flamelike markings on these beans. We tasted this salad at Oliveto Restaurant in Oakland and had to have the recipe.*

3 cups dried Tongue of Fire or Borlotti beans

1 small carrot, peeled

1 celery stalk

1 small yellow onion, peeled, studded with 2 whole cloves

Bouquet garni: fresh thyme sprig, bay leaf and 6 black peppercorns tied in
     a cheesecloth bag

12 cups water

Salt to taste

**Vinaigrette**

1 tablespoon minced anchovies

1 teaspoon minced garlic

2 tablespoons fresh lemon juice

Salt and freshly ground black pepper to taste

6 tablespoons extra virgin olive oil

**Garnish**

Parmesan cheese shavings

Chopped fresh parsley

## Salting a Salad

When preparing a salad, salt each component separately. The salad tastes better and each component retains its individual flavor.

Rinse the beans and place in a large bowl. Cover with 12 cups cold water and soak, refrigerated, for about 12 hours. Drain.

Put the beans in a large pot; add the carrot, celery, onion, bouquet garni and water. Bring to a simmer over high heat, reduce heat to maintain a bare simmer and cook until the beans are just tender, about 45 minutes to 1 hour. Remove from heat, season with salt and let cool in the liquid.

To make the vinaigrette: Combine the anchovies, garlic, lemon juice, and salt and pepper in a bowl. Gradually whisk in the oil. Taste and adjust seasoning. To serve, drain the beans and place in a large skillet. Add the anchovy vinaigrette and reheat over low heat. When warm (not hot), transfer to a serving platter and top with shavings of Parmesan and chopped parsley.

SERVES 8 TO 10

# Watercress and Fresh Water Chestnut Salad

*If you've never tried fresh water chestnuts, you're in for a big surprise. They taste nothing like the canned; instead, they have a sweet, juicy, almost applelike flavor. If you cannot find them fresh for this salad by Bruce Cost, substitute jicama. Reserve canned water chestnuts for use in cooked dishes where they will play only a minor role.*

4 or 5 bunches watercress

10 fresh water chestnuts, peeled and finely chopped

1 teaspoon light soy sauce

1 tablespoon Asian sesame oil

½ teaspoon salt

½ teaspoon sugar

Start bringing a large pot of water to a boil.

Meanwhile, trim and discard any large stems from the watercress.

When the water boils, drop in the cress, stir briefly, then immediately drain and run under cold water to stop the cooking. Squeeze the watercress with your hands to get rid of most of its liquid, then chop it finely and put in a mixing bowl with the chopped water chestnuts.

Combine the remaining ingredients and add to the bowl. Toss and serve.

SERVES 4

# Sweet and Spicy Zucchini Salad

*Brad Levy serves "home cooking from around the world" at his Firefly
Restaurant in San Francisco's Noe Valley. Here, he gives one of the most
common vegetables, zucchini, a special Chinese home-style treatment. Serve
with grilled meats or fish.*

4 medium zucchini, preferably 2 green and 2 golden

½ cup distilled white vinegar

4 tablespoons sugar

1½ teaspoons salt

1 teaspoon Chinese chile paste with garlic

1 tablespoon coarsely chopped fresh cilantro

1 small carrot

½ small red onion, thinly sliced

◎◎ Trim the zucchini, cut in half lengthwise, then cut into ¹⁄₁₆-inch-thick
slices on a 45-degree angle. Combine the zucchini, ¼ cup of the vinegar,
2 tablespoons of the sugar and 1 teaspoon of the salt in a bowl. Toss well
and let stand at least 1 hour.

Drain the zucchini well. Add the remaining ¼ cup vinegar, 2 tablespoons
sugar and ½ teaspoon salt, the chile paste and cilantro; mix well.

Peel the carrot, cut in half lengthwise, then slice as thinly as possible on a
45-degree angle. Blanch the carrot slices in boiling water for 10 seconds, then
transfer to ice water to stop the cooking. Drain, pat dry and add to the
zucchini. Add the onion and let stand 30 minutes before serving.

SERVES 6 TO 8

# Warm Spring Vegetable Salad

*Chef Deborah Madison, who opened Greens, San Francisco's pioneering vegetarian restaurant, created this simple but absolutely stunning warm vegetable salad that highlights the season's first fava beans and asparagus.*

1½ pounds fava beans, shelled

1 small red onion, thinly sliced

3 tablespoons extra-virgin olive oil

3 tablespoons chopped fresh chervil

8 ounces asparagus, thinly sliced on the diagonal

4 ounces (or 4 small) carrots, peeled, thinly sliced or julienned

1 pound green peas, shelled

½ small fennel bulb, cored, thinly sliced crosswise

½ teaspoon salt, plus salt to taste

Pepper to taste

Tarragon vinegar to taste

◉◉ Bring 3 quarts of water to a boil, put in the shelled fava beans and cook 1 minute. Take them out with a slotted spoon (save the water), rinse briefly to cool, then remove their outer skins. Put the peeled beans in a bowl along with the sliced onion, olive oil and chervil.

Return the water to a boil.

Prepare the rest of the vegetables and add to the boiling water, along with ½ teaspoon salt. Check after a minute to see if the vegetables are done; cook longer if necessary. Drain the vegetables in a colander and shake off as much water as possible. Add them to the onions and beans and gently mix everything together using a rubber spatula. Taste and season with salt, if desired, and a grinding of pepper. Gradually add vinegar until it is as tart as you like. Serve right away.

SERVES 4

# Chapter 2

# Pasta and Grains

*San Franciscans are in love with pasta, but then again so is the rest of the country.*

*As we've learned, it's a quick-fix meal on those always harried weeknights. So throughout this chapter you'll get some fresh ideas for pastas and grains that can be prepared in a hurry: ditali (short hollow tubes) with asparagus; fusilli (corkscrew-shape) with strong greens and mushrooms; spaghetti with parsley; and a 10-minute pasta with green beans, goat cheese and olives.*

*Some well-known chefs also weigh in on this chapter: Joyce Goldstein, Carlo Middione and Gerald Hirigoyen. We're also lucky to have a pasta expert on staff, Janet Fletcher, who's even written a book on the subject.*

*The list of grain recipes is equally as impressive. There's a soft polenta from Gary Danko at the Ritz-Carlton; roasted polenta with balsamic sauce from Michael Chiarello, chef at Tra Vigne in the Napa Valley; paella from Marimar Torres, owner of Torres Winery; and wild rice pilaf with fennel and pine nuts from Annie Somerville of Greens.*

# Orzo with Smoked Salmon and Capers

*Capers provide a sharp, crisp note, balancing well with the smoked salmon and creamy orzo (rice-shaped pasta) in this quick-to-the-table dish. A small salad of watercress and endive plus buttered toasts will round out Marion Cunningham's creation.*

1½ quarts water

1 teaspoon salt, plus salt to taste

1 cup orzo

3 tablespoons olive oil

Pepper to taste

3 ounces smoked salmon, cut into strips

¼ cup capers, drained

∞ Put the water and 1 teaspoon salt into a saucepan and bring to a boil. Slowly pour in the orzo and stir once or twice. Cook about 8 minutes, or until the pasta is tender. Drain. Add the olive oil and season with salt and pepper. Stir to mix well. Stir in the smoked salmon and capers.

Serve with thin slices of buttered toast.

SERVES 2

# Ditali with Asparagus

*Janet Fletcher created this quick one-pot dish, in which the pasta and asparagus cook together and are sauced in the serving bowl. Datali are short hollow pasta tubes, related to elbow macaroni but shorter.*

2½ to 3 pounds thick asparagus spears

1 pound dried ditali ("thimbles") or canneroni ("large reeds")

4 tablespoons unsalted butter, cut in pieces

1 cup freshly grated Parmesan cheese

Salt and freshly ground black pepper to taste

## Identifying Pasta Shapes

**Bucatini:** A spaghetti-shaped pasta with a hole in the middle. Great for meat sauces.

**Capellini ("fine hairs"):** This pasta is often used in soups or with the simplest of sauces. A slightly thicker version is known as angel hair pasta.

**Conchigliette ("tiny shells"):** About the size of lima beans, this pasta is excellent in soups.

**Ditali ("thimbles"):** Similar to elbow macaroni, but cut into shorter lengths.

**Farfalle ("butterflies" or "bows"):** Bow tie–shaped pasta that comes in a variety of sizes.

**Fettuccine ("small ribbons"):** These ¼-inch-wide noodles are one of the most versatile pastas.

**Fusilli ("twists" or "small corkscrews"):** This pasta is great with hearty sauces.

**Gemelli ("twins"):** These resemble two short pieces of spaghetti twisted together.

**Linguine ("little tongues"):** These thin, flat noodles are used like spaghetti.

**Mostaccioli ("little mustaches"):** These pasta tubes are about 2 inches long; the ends are cut on the diagonal. Use with hearty meat sauces or for baked dishes.

**Orecchiette ("little ears"):** These are disc-shaped, with a thumbprint impression in the middle. Great with many sauces, especially vegetable sauces.

**Orzo ("barley"):** This tiny pasta resembles rice and, in general, is used in soups or as a side dish.

**Pappardelle:** Long, wide ruffle-edged noodles from Tuscany, these are great with game sauces and other rich preparations.

**Penne ("pens"):** These pasta tubes are versatile and may be used with almost any sauce; the generous hole traps the sauce.

**Rigatoni ("large grooved"):** These large pasta tubes have ridges.

**Rotelle ("small wheels"):** A variation of fusilli.

**Tagliatelle:** These narrow-cut noodles are a bit wider than fettuccine, but may be used interchangeably.

**Tortellini ("small twists"):** A type of stuffed pasta, these are shaped into rings.

**Ziti ("bridegrooms"):** Large tubular macaroni similar to penne.

◎◎ Holding an asparagus spear in both hands, bend it gently; it will break naturally at the point where the spear becomes tough. Repeat with the remaining spears. Discard the tough ends. You should have about 1½ pounds of tender spears. Cut the spears crosswise into ⅓-inch slices (about the same length as the ditali).

Bring a large pot of salted water to a boil. Add the asparagus and partially cover the pot. When the water returns to a boil, add the pasta. Cook until al dente. Drain. Transfer the pasta and asparagus to a large warm bowl. Add the butter, cheese and salt and pepper. Toss to coat. Serve immediately on warm dishes.

SERVES 4

# Fusilli alla Carlo

*Carlo Middione, author of the excellent* The Food of Southern Italy, *and owner of the two Vivande restaurants, created this cream-based pasta dish featuring mushrooms and pancetta, an unsmoked Italian-style bacon. A mild-cured bacon will work in a pinch.*

¾ cup (1½ sticks) unsalted butter

4 ounces pancetta, sliced ⅛ inch thick, then cut into ¼-inch-long pieces

6 ounces chopped domestic mushrooms (about 2 cups)

⅓ cup pine nuts

1 cup finely chopped cored and peeled tomatoes

2¼ cups heavy cream

Salt and pepper to taste

1½ pounds imported Italian fusilli ("twists")

¾ cup grated Parmesan cheese

⅓ cup grated pecorino romano cheese

◎◎ Melt the butter in a large frying pan. Add the pancetta and mushrooms and sauté until they are golden. Add the pine nuts and sauté until they are golden. Add the tomatoes and toss everything together. Add the cream and simmer over medium heat until the cream is thick and coats the back of a spoon, about 5 minutes. Season with salt and pepper.

Cook the pasta in a large pot of salted boiling water. When the pasta is al dente, drain it but do not shake out all the water—it should be moist, not wet. (See Note.)

Toss the pasta and the Parmesan in a warm large bowl. Add the sauce and mix again. Serve in pasta plates or basin-shaped plates. Sprinkle on the pecorino cheese and add a bit more black pepper to garnish. Pass more cheese at the table if you like.

SERVES 6

**NOTE:** Reserve about 1 cup of the pasta water to add to the dish should it become too dry; you will not need it all. Add a tablespoon or two at a time, as needed.

# Fusilli with Mushrooms and Strong Greens

*Sharon Cadwallader wrote a natural foods column for* The Chronicle *long before "natural" went mainstream. Here she simply sauces a corkscrew-shaped pasta with olive oil and balsamic vinegar.*

1 pound collard, kale or mustard greens

¾ pound fusilli (rotini or penne also are good)

⅓ cup extra-virgin olive oil

1 large onion, thinly sliced

1 tablespoon minced garlic

½ pound mushrooms, sliced

¼ teaspoon red pepper flakes

1½ tablespoons balsamic vinegar

Salt to taste

Freshly grated Parmesan cheese

ᴓ Wash the greens, then trim and discard the tough stems. Coarsely chop the greens. Cook in boiling salted water until tender. Drain.

Cook the pasta in boiling salted water until al dente; drain.

## Cooking Pasta

Pasta should cook in a lot of water—at least 4 quarts and preferably 5. Put a lid on the pot to bring it to a fast boil. Add 1 tablespoon salt to the water after it comes to a boil.

Boiling salted water bubbles up vigorously when the pasta first goes in. To prevent it from boiling over, add a single piece of pasta and let the water bubble up, then add the rest.

After adding pasta to the water, stir immediately to prevent sticking. Stir occasionally during the cooking, too.

Pasta should cook at a brisk boil so it's continually moving. If necessary, partially cover the pot to keep the water boiling.

While the pasta is cooking, heat 3 tablespoons of the olive oil in a large skillet. Add the onion and garlic and sauté until the onion is softened. Add the mushrooms and red pepper flakes and sauté until the mushrooms soften slightly. Add the greens, the pasta, vinegar and remaining olive oil (if desired); cook, stirring, until heated through. Season with salt.

Serve in warm shallow pasta bowls. Top with a generous amount of Parmesan.

SERVES 4

# Fusilli with Green and Golden Zucchini

*You can use all green or all golden zucchini, but half and half makes the prettiest presentation in Janet Fletcher's tomato-based dish. The sauce gets extra flavor from red pepper flakes and capers.*

¾ pound small zucchini (half green, half golden), trimmed

8 ounces plum tomatoes, cut in small dice

3 tablespoons olive oil

2 garlic cloves, minced

⅛ teaspoon red pepper flakes

Salt to taste

12 to 20 leaves basil, torn into small pieces

1½ tablespoons capers, coarsely chopped

8 ounces dried fusilli

½ cup freshly grated pecorino romano cheese

Cut the zucchini into lengthwise slices about ¼ inch thick. Stack the slices and cut crosswise into thin, short sticks.

Combine the zucchini, tomatoes, 2 tablespoons of the olive oil, the garlic, pepper flakes and salt in a 12-inch skillet. Cook over medium-high heat, stirring often, until the zucchini is tender but not soft and the tomatoes have collapsed and formed a thick sauce, 6 to 8 minutes. Toward the end, the mixture will be rather dry and will need to be stirred almost constantly to prevent sticking. Add a few drops of water if necessary. Remove from heat and stir in basil and capers. Taste and adjust seasoning.

Cook the pasta in a large pot of boiling salted water until al dente. Drain and transfer to a warm serving bowl, reserving a little of the cooking water. Toss the pasta with the remaining tablespoon oil. Add the sauce and cheese and toss again, adding a tablespoon or two of the cooking water if necessary to thin the sauce. Transfer to warm plates.

SERVES 2 TO 4

# Macaroni and Wild Mushroom Gratin

*This sophisticated but comforting gratin is from Gerald Hirigoyen of Fringale and Pastis restaurants in San Francisco.*

½ pound small elbow macaroni

½ pound oyster mushrooms, chopped into ½-inch or smaller pieces

½ pound shiitake mushrooms, chopped into ½-inch or smaller pieces

½ pound chanterelle mushrooms, chopped into ½-inch or smaller pieces

4 garlic cloves, finely chopped

3 shallots, finely chopped

4 tablespoons olive oil

1 tablespoon chopped fresh chives

1 tablespoon chopped fresh parsley

¼ pound coarsely grated cheese (Swiss or Parmesan type)

◉◉  Preheat the oven to 350 degrees.

Cook the macaroni in 2 quarts salted rapidly boiling water until al dente. Drain and rinse with cold water; set aside.

While the macaroni is cooking, sauté the mushrooms, garlic and shallots in the olive oil until golden brown, 3 or 4 minutes, then add the chives and parsley.

Toss the drained macaroni with the mushrooms and arrange in an oven-safe dish. Bake for 10 minutes, stirring occasionally, until the mixture is

## Mushroom Tip

To store mushrooms, place in a brown paper bag, fold over the top of the bag and refrigerate. The mushrooms will stay fresh for about 5 days.

heated through. Remove from the oven, sprinkle with the cheese and broil for
1 or 2 minutes, just until the cheese is melted and has browned.

SERVES 4

# Gemelli with Artichokes, Olives, Feta and Capers

*Fresh baby artichokes are the star of Janet Fletcher's olive oil–based sauce,
which gets a boost from capers and salty niçoise olives. If you can't find
gemelli, which looks like short pieces of spaghetti twisted together, substitute
penne or fusilli.*

Juice of ½ lemon

20 baby artichokes (1½ to 2 ounces each)

5 tablespoons olive oil

2 garlic cloves, minced

Salt to taste

Red pepper flakes to taste

1 pound dried gemelli ("twins"), penne rigati (ridged tubes) or fusilli ("twists")

½ cup freshly grated Asiago cheese

¼ cup capers, rinsed

48 niçoise olives, pitted

4 ounces Greek or Bulgarian feta cheese, crumbled

◎ Fill a bowl with cold water; add the lemon juice. Peel back the tough outer leaves on each artichoke until they break off at the base. Keep removing leaves until you reach the pale green heart. Cut about ⅓ inch off at the top of the heart to remove the pointed leaf tips; cut away any stem. Trim the base to remove any dark green parts. Immediately drop the trimmed hearts into the acidulated water to prevent browning. Drain the artichokes, halve them lengthwise, then cut each half into neat dice by slicing 2 or 3 times in each direction.

Heat 4 tablespoons of the oil in a 12-inch skillet over medium heat. Add the garlic and sauté 1 minute. Add the artichokes, salt and pepper flakes. Toss to coat with oil. Cover and reduce the heat to medium low. Cook the artichokes, stirring occasionally, until tender and appetizingly browned in spots, about 15 minutes. You should not need additional liquid, but you may add 1 or 2 tablespoons water if the artichokes begin to stick.

Cook the pasta in a large pot of boiling salted water until al dente. Drain. Transfer to a large warm bowl. Add the remaining 1 tablespoon olive oil and ¼ cup of the Asiago cheese; toss. Add the artichokes, capers, olives and feta. Toss to mix well.

Serve on warm plates, topping each serving with a little of the remaining Asiago.

SERVES 4

## A Quick Pasta with Vegetables

Cut a selection of fresh vegetables into bite-sized pieces, then toss them into the hot pasta water when the noodles are about half cooked. This works with a single vegetable or several, and nearly any shape of pasta. Once the pasta and vegetables are drained, sauce the whole thing simply: garlic and olive oil; tomato; pesto; reduced broth; butter; a few shakes of hot sauce; or Asian sesame oil and soy sauce.

# Spicy, Mustardy, Tangy Macaroni and Cheese

*This version of macaroni and cheese is as comforting as a favorite book—and anything but bland, thanks to Marlena Spieler's addition of a roasted mild green chile, a few dashes of Tabasco and whole-grain mustard.*

12 ounces short elbow-type macaroni

3 tablespoons butter

1 tablespoon flour

1 cup milk

½ to 1 mild green chile (Anaheim or poblano), roasted, stemmed, seeded
    and cut into strips, or chopped raw green chile to taste

Several dashes Tabasco

2 tablespoons sour cream

1 to 2 teaspoons whole-seed mustard

2 to 3 garlic cloves, chopped

2 teaspoons paprika

3 cups (12 ounces) shredded sharp cheddar cheese

Preheat the oven to 375 degrees.

Cook the pasta in a large pot of boiling salted water until al dente; drain and set aside.

Heat the butter until foamy, then sprinkle in the flour and cook a few minutes. Remove from heat and whisk in the milk. Cook, whisking, until the sauce thickens (ignore any lumps unless they are large and obvious).

Combine the pasta and sauce with the chile, Tabasco, sour cream, mustard, garlic, paprika and two thirds of the cheese. Pour into a baking dish and top with the remaining cheese.

Bake until the cheese topping is melty and lightly browned, and the macaroni is sizzling hot, about 20 minutes.

SERVES 4

# Pasta all'Amatriciana

*This simple tomato sauce from Narsai David gets its flavor from bacon and just a haunting note of spice from red pepper flakes.*

6 to 8 strips of bacon, cut crosswise into ¼-inch slices
1 tablespoon olive oil
1 medium onion, chopped
¼ to ½ teaspoon red pepper flakes
4 cups tomatoes, peeled and chopped, or two 15-ounce cans diced tomatoes
1 pound dried pasta, such as penne
½ cup (2 ounces) grated Parmesan

◎ Cook the bacon until most of the fat is rendered and the bacon is cooked but not crisp. Drain the bacon and discard the fat. Add the olive oil and onion to the pan and sauté until the onion is translucent. Add the red pepper and tomatoes and simmer until the sauce is nicely thickened, about 10 minutes.

Cook the pasta in a large pot of boiling salted water until it is al dente. Drain and rinse with hot water. Toss with the sauce and reserved bacon. Top with the cheese.

SERVES 4

**NOTE**: Although garlic is not used traditionally, 3 or 4 cloves, chopped and sautéed with the onion, are a fine addition.

## Basic Uncooked Tomato Sauce

Peel and seed vine-ripened tomatoes, then cut into cubes. Place in a large pottery bowl. Add extra-virgin olive oil to taste, some finely minced garlic if desired, salt and a grinding of pepper. Tear fresh basil leaves into pieces and add them to the bowl. Place in an oven, on low heat, while the pasta is cooking. When the pasta is done, quickly drain and toss in the bowl with the tomato mixture.

# Orecchiette with Fava Beans and Prosciutto

*Fava beans are so sweet and delicate in the spring that Janet Fletcher takes great care not to cover them up with bold flavors. A little mild green onion and a bit of minced Italian ham are perfect complements.*

4 pounds fava beans

2 tablespoons unsalted butter

2 tablespoons olive oil

2 bunches green onions (white and pale green parts only), minced

Salt and freshly ground black pepper to taste

½ cup water

1 pound dried orecchiette ("little ears") or gnocchi

3 ounces prosciutto di Parma, minced

1 cup freshly grated pecorino romano cheese

⚭ Shell the favas. To peel individual beans, bring a large pot of water—at least 5 quarts—to a boil. Add the favas and cook until just tender, 2 to 4 minutes depending on size; lift one out and pinch it open to test. Transfer with a skimmer to a bowl of ice water. Pinch open the end of the bean opposite the end that connected it to the pod. The peeled bean will slip out easily. Reserve the cooking water.

Heat the butter and oil in a 12-inch skillet over medium-low heat. Add the onions and cook until softened and fragrant, about 3 minutes. Add the fava beans and toss to coat with the onions and fat. Season well with salt and pepper. Add the water, bring to a simmer and keep warm.

Add salt to the reserved cooking water and bring to a boil. Add the pasta and cook until al dente, stirring often to keep the orecchiette from sticking together. Just before the pasta is ready, add the prosciutto to the fava beans.

Drain the pasta, reserving about ½ cup of the cooking water. Transfer the pasta to a large warm bowl. Add the contents of skillet and toss to coat. Add the cheese and toss again, adding some of the reserved cooking water if needed to moisten the dish. Serve immediately on warm dishes.

SERVES 4

## Basic Cooked Fresh Tomato Sauce

Wash and quarter vine-ripened tomatoes. Place in a large saucepan, cover and gently cook over low heat for 10 minutes. Puree in a blender or food processor; strain and return to the saucepan. For each pound of tomatoes, add ½ cup (1 stick) butter, half a peeled onion, ¾ teaspoon salt and a pinch of sugar. Gently simmer about 45 minutes. Discard onion; taste for seasoning.

# Ken Hom's Fresh Pasta with Cilantro, Ginger and Basil Pesto

*In this dish, the assertive flavors of fresh ginger, cilantro, basil and garlic "titillate the palate," says Ken Hom, who credits fellow cookbook author Bruce Cost for inspiring this Asian twist on traditional pasta with pesto. Regular basil may be used—better yet, try to find the Asian tropical variety, which has a distinctive basil-anise flavor.*

**Pasta**

1¼ cups all-purpose flour

3 large eggs

2 tablespoons peanut oil

1 teaspoon salt

**Sauce**

1 tablespoon finely chopped fresh ginger

1 tablespoon finely chopped fresh cilantro

3 tablespoons finely chopped fresh basil

2 tablespoons finely chopped garlic

1 tablespoon peanut oil

2 teaspoons Asian sesame oil

2 teaspoons salt

1 teaspoon freshly ground black pepper

⊚⊚ Combine the flour, eggs, oil and salt in a bowl or a food processor. Knead or process the dough until smooth and satiny. Run the pasta through a pasta machine twice on each setting, stopping at the thinnest setting. Cut the pasta into thin noodles. Flour lightly and set aside.

Combine all the sauce ingredients in a blender; mix thoroughly.

Bring a large saucepan of water to a boil. Add the pasta and cook for 1 minute. Drain and toss with the sauce.

SERVES 6

## A Chef's Favorite Combinations

Julian Serrano, chef of the famed Masa's in San Francisco, is intrigued by flavors. Here are some of his favorite combinations:
⊚⊚ ginger and lime;
⊚⊚ orange and rosemary, particularly in a sorbet or granita;
⊚⊚ white asparagus and mint;
⊚⊚ red cabbage and cloves;
⊚⊚ eggplant and cumin.

# Penne with Tomato and Olive Sauce

*Here's a rustic, peppery sauce with the rough texture of chopped olives and capers. Janet Fletcher suggests using the French picholine olives, if possible, which are easy to pit.*

2 tablespoons olive oil

1 large garlic clove, minced

⅛ teaspoon red pepper flakes

12 ounces plum tomatoes, diced

3 anchovy fillets, minced to a paste

⅔ cup coarsely chopped pitted green olives (preferably French picholine)

1 scant tablespoon capers, rinsed and coarsely chopped

1½ tablespoons minced fresh parsley

Salt to taste

8 ounces dried penne ("pens" or "feathers")

◍ Heat the olive oil in a 10-inch skillet over medium-low heat. Add garlic and sauté for 1 minute. Add the pepper flakes and tomatoes. Raise heat to medium high. Cook, stirring often, until the tomatoes have collapsed and formed a thick sauce, 8 to 10 minutes. Stir in the anchovies, olives, capers and 1 tablespoon of the parsley. Season with salt. Remove from heat. Reheat sauce gently just before the pasta is ready.

Cook the pasta in a large pot of boiling salted water until al dente. Drain, reserving about ¼ cup of the pasta cooking water. Place the pasta in a warm bowl and toss with the sauce, adding a little of the reserved water if necessary to thin the sauce.

Serve the pasta on warm plates. Top each serving with a little of the remaining parsley.

SERVES 2 TO 4

## Basic Garlic and Oil Sauce

Pour a generous amount of olive oil into a skillet. Peel and thinly slice a handful of garlic cloves and add to the skillet; sauté over low heat until the garlic turns golden. Discard the garlic. Toss the garlic-scented oil with freshly cooked and drained pasta. Season with salt and freshly ground pepper. Optional additions: crisp-fried slivers of pancetta or bacon; chopped pitted Mediterranean-style olives. The sauce is also great tossed with steamed vegetables.

# Pasta with Red Peppers, Greens, White Beans, Garlic and Lemon Zest

*In this hearty dish by Joyce Goldstein, the flavor and texture of fleshy bell peppers play off the mellow richness of white beans. Tart greens and lemon provide flavor accents.*

½ cup dried white beans, soaked in water overnight

2 cups water

1 bay leaf

4 garlic cloves

6 ounces dried pasta (shells, farfalle, orecchiette)

⅓ cup vegetable stock

2 red bell peppers, seeded, deribbed and cut in ½-inch strips

4 cups Swiss chard or escarole, cut in ½-inch strips and well washed

1 tablespoon grated lemon zest

Salt and freshly ground pepper to taste

2 tablespoons fresh lemon juice

◎◎ Drain and rinse the beans. Put them in a saucepan with the water, bay leaf and 2 of the garlic cloves. Bring to a boil over high heat, then reduce heat and simmer until tender, 45 to 60 minutes. Set aside.

While the beans are cooking, bring a large pot of salted water to a boil; add the pasta, cover, and cook until just done.

Finely chop the remaining 2 garlic cloves. Set aside.

Pour the stock into a sauté pan; bring to a simmer over medium heat. Add the pepper strips and simmer for 5 to 8 minutes. Add the greens and lemon zest, stirring until greens are wilted, about 3 or 4 minutes.

Using a slotted spoon, remove beans from their cooking liquid and add them to the peppers and greens. Warm through. Season with salt and pepper, then stir in the lemon juice.

Drain the pasta, place it in a heated serving bowl and toss with the bean mixture. Add the chopped garlic and toss to mix. Serve immediately.

SERVES 2

## Arrabbiata Sauce

*This feisty Italian sauce gets its assertive character from garlic and red pepper flakes. Use it on any pasta. The recipe may be doubled, tripled, etc.*

6 tablespoons olive oil

1½ teaspoons (or more) red pepper flakes, or about 1 teaspoon cayenne pepper

4 cups pureed tomatoes

Salt and pepper to taste

6 to 8 garlic cloves, chopped

◎◎ Heat the oil in a saucepan, then add the pepper flakes. Cook over medium heat but do not let burn. Be careful not to inhale the fumes of the chiles. Add the tomatoes, bring to a boil, reduce heat and simmer until reduced in volume by about one third. Season with salt and pepper and stir in the garlic.

YIELDS ABOUT 4 CUPS

**NOTE:** You could also make this with roasted peppers; in which case, steam the greens, fold in the beans and peppers, add lemon zest, season and toss with pasta.

# Rigatoni with Creamy Artichoke Sauce

*Cream is one of the best mediums to carry the nutty flavor of artichokes. However, if you want a less fatty sauce, Marlena Spieler also gives a creamless variation.*

    4 or 5 large artichokes
    1 tablespoon flour
    1 lemon, cut in half
    ½ onion, chopped
    1 garlic clove, chopped
    2 tablespoons butter
    ¾ cup broth (vegetable or chicken)
    1½ cups heavy cream
    Pepper to taste
    1 pound rigatoni or other medium-large tubular pasta
    Freshly grated Parmesan to taste

Prepare the artichokes by bending back the outer leaves until they snap off. The edible bit at the end should remain on the heart, which you will cook for the sauce. When all the tough leaves have been snapped off and only the tenderest ones remain, trim them with a knife: First strip the stem of its tough skin, trim the base, and cut off the sharp top of the tender inner leaves. You now have artichoke hearts. Cut each heart into quarters and trim the inner choke away.

Place the quarters in a saucepan with water to cover. Mix in the flour and add the lemon halves. Bring to a boil, reduce heat and cook a few minutes until the artichoke quarters are al dente. Drain. Discard the lemon and let the artichokes cool. (This may be done up to 3 days ahead.)

Dice the artichoke quarters. Lightly sauté the onion and garlic in the butter. When softened, add the diced artichokes and cook for a few minutes. Add the broth and bring to a boil. Reduce heat and simmer several minutes until the artichokes are quite tender. Add the cream and cook until sauce is thickened. Season with pepper. Salt is unlikely to be needed because both broth and Parmesan are salty.

Cook the pasta in a large pot of boiling salted water until al dente. Drain and toss with the sauce. Sprinkle with Parmesan and serve immediately.

SERVES 4 TO 6

**VARIATION:** For a lemony, olivey sauce rather than a creamy one, omit the cream and add 2 to 3 tablespoons chopped fresh parsley, 5 to 10 pitted and halved kalamata olives, and a teaspoon or 2 of capers to the broth along with the artichokes. Cook down until reduced by about half, then add a squeeze of lemon. Serve on a thin pasta such as spaghetti.

## Béchamel Sauce

*With this classic sauce on hand, lasagne, pasticcio or plain old macaroni and cheese aren't far behind. The recipe may be doubled, etc.*

2 tablespoons butter
2 tablespoons flour
2 cups milk, heated until hot but not boiling
Salt, pepper and nutmeg to taste

◉ Heat the butter in a saucepan. Add the flour and cook for a minute or two, stirring occasionally. Remove from heat and whisk in the milk, then return to the stove. Cook over medium heat, whisking constantly, until sauce is thickened and smooth. Season with salt, pepper and nutmeg.

YIELDS 2 CUPS

# Japanese Moon-Viewing Noodles

*This Bruce Cost recipe could be either a soup or a main course. Raw eggs are placed in nests of noodles and served in hot seasoned broth. The yolk takes on the appearance of the moon.*

4 dried shiitake mushrooms

1 pound dried udon noodles

8 ounces spinach, stemmed

4 cups chicken broth

2 tablespoons soy sauce

1 teaspoon salt

½ teaspoon sugar

4 eggs

3 scallions, chopped

Asian sesame oil

 Cover the mushrooms with boiling water and let soak for 30 minutes. When the mushrooms are pliable, remove them from the water. Cut off stems and discard; cut the caps into thin strips. Set aside.

Cook the noodles in a large quantity of boiling water until tender; drain and rinse under cold water to stop the cooking.

Pick the best leaves from the spinach, drop them into boiling water, then immediately drain and rinse under cold water to stop the cooking. Set aside.

Combine the broth, soy sauce, salt and sugar in a saucepan; heat to boiling.

Meanwhile, arrange the noodles into "nests" in 4 soup cups (you may not use all of the noodles), divide the mushroom slices among the nests and pour in the boiling broth. Slide an egg into the center of each noodle nest. Arrange the spinach in the bowls, sprinkle with the scallions, drizzle about ½ teaspoon sesame oil into each and serve.

SERVES 4

# Japanese New Year's Eve Soba

*A traditional Japanese New Year dish, this recipe is from Delphine and Diane J. Hirasuna.*

1 package (12.7 ounces) dried soba (buckwheat) noodles

**Broth**
5½ cups dashi (see Note), or pork, beef or chicken stock
¼ cup soy sauce
1 tablespoon sake
1 tablespoon mirin
1 teaspoon salt, or to taste

**Toppings** (optional)
4 slices red kamaboko (fish cakes; see Note)
4 hard-cooked eggs, peeled and sliced
8 shrimp, boiled, shelled and deveined
2 green onions, chopped

◉◉ Bring about 2 quarts of water to a boil in a large pot. Drop in the noodles and cook until tender but still firm. Drain in a colander and rinse well under cold water to stop the cooking.

To make the broth: Combine the dashi, soy sauce, sake, mirin and salt in a saucepan; bring to a quick boil.

To serve: Dip the cooked noodles into hot water to reheat. Drain off the water and divide the noodles among serving bowls. Pour the broth over the noodles. Eat plain or top with garnishes of choice.

SERVES 4

**NOTES:** Excellent instant dashi flavorings now come in granule, cube and small tea-baglike form. Any will work fine. If the package instructions are not in English, a good rule is that one granule packet, bag or cube makes 4 to 5 cups of stock. Just bring water to a boil and add the flavoring (you may have to adjust the salt, depending on the brand).

Kamaboko (fish cakes) may be found in the refrigerator section of Japanese markets.

# Perciatelli with Spicy Tomato Sauce

*The tomato sauce is irresistible and would taste good on almost any dried pasta shape, but Janet Fletcher likes it with perciatelli (also called bucatini), the hollow strands that look like thick spaghetti.*

1 tablespoon olive oil

2 ounces pancetta, minced

1 large garlic clove, minced

Scant ¼ teaspoon red pepper flakes

12 ounces plum tomatoes, diced

Salt to taste

8 ounces perciatelli or bucatini pasta

½ cup freshly grated ricotta salata or pecorino romano cheese

1 tablespoon minced fresh parsley

◉◉  Put the olive oil and pancetta in a 10-inch skillet. Cook over medium-low heat, stirring often, until the pancetta begins to crisp, 3 to 5 minutes. Add the garlic and sauté 1 minute. Add the red pepper flakes, tomatoes and a generous pinch of salt. Raise the heat to medium-high and simmer, stirring often, until the tomatoes collapse and form a thick sauce, 8 to 10 minutes. Add a little water if necessary to keep the mixture from sticking.

Cook the pasta in a large pot of boiling salted water until al dente. Transfer with tongs to a warm serving bowl. Add the sauce and toss to coat, adding a little of the pasta cooking water if needed to thin the sauce. Transfer to warm plates.

Top each serving with some of the grated cheese and minced parsley.

SERVES 2 TO 4

## Saucing Pasta

Chuck Williams, founder of Williams-Sonoma, swears by this method of saucing pasta: Drain the pasta in a strainer; allow some of the water to cling to the noodles. Immediately transfer the pasta back into the warm pot and toss with the sauce.

# Spaghetti alla Puttanesca

*Carlo Middione provides his version of a classic recipe with a colorful history. The dish, according to legend, was invented by prostitutes working the streets of Naples.*

2 to 3 tablespoons olive oil

2 garlic cloves, minced

½ cup (2 ounces) kalamata olives, pitted and coarsely chopped

1 teaspoon capers, coarsely chopped

1 large fresh tomato, peeled and coarsely chopped

4 or 5 anchovy fillets, coarsely chopped

1 pound spaghetti

¼ cup chopped fresh Italian parsley

Salt and pepper to taste

Red pepper flakes to taste

Heat the olive oil in a frying pan over medium heat. Add the garlic and sauté until golden, then add the olives, capers, tomato and anchovy; stir well and cook until heated through, about 6 minutes.

Cook the pasta in a large amount of boiling salted water until it is al dente. Drain. Transfer the pasta to a warm bowl. Add half of the sauce and toss. Add the remaining sauce and the parsley. Season with salt and pepper.

Sprinkle red pepper flakes over the top before serving.

SERVES 4 TO 6

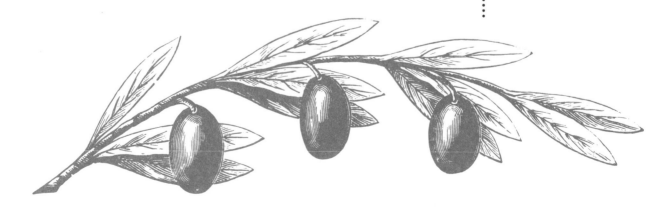

# Spaghetti with Salsa Cruda

*You need great-tasting tomatoes for this uncooked sauce, created by Janet Fletcher. Be sure to have plenty of bread on hand for sopping up the delicious juices that collect on the plates.*

12 ounces vine-ripened tomatoes (choose a mix of red and yellow varieties)

3½ tablespoons extra-virgin olive oil

4 anchovy fillets, finely minced

1 garlic clove, minced

3 tablespoons minced fresh parsley

1 teaspoon red or white wine vinegar

⅛ teaspoon red pepper flakes

Salt to taste

8 ounces spaghetti

◎◎ Bring a large pot of salted water—at least 4 quarts—to a boil. Cut an "x" in the end of each tomato; blanch for 30 seconds, then transfer to ice water. Peel the tomatoes, then core, halve and squeeze out the seeds. Cut the tomatoes into small, neat dice. Put in a bowl and add 2 tablespoons of the olive oil, the anchovies, garlic, parsley, vinegar, pepper flakes and salt. Stir and set aside.

Place a serving bowl in a low oven with the remaining 1½ tablespoons oil and a large pinch of salt.

Cook the pasta in a large pot of salted boiling water until al dente. Drain. Transfer to a serving bowl and toss to coat with oil. Serve the pasta on warm plates. Top with the tomatoes and their juices.

SERVES 2 TO 4

## Wild Pasta

When wild mushrooms are in season, enjoy them on pasta: Just sauté in butter with garlic, pour on a bit of brandy and broth, cook down and finish with a dash of heavy cream. Season with salt, pepper and a grating of nutmeg. Serve over fettuccine.

# Spaghetti Sauce with Vodka

*Michael Bauer adapted this recipe, a Christmas Eve tradition at his family home in Kansas, to bolder California tastes. The onions and garlic are sautéed, then reduced with vodka, which gives a complex peppery flavor to the ground meat and tomato sauce. Green olives and fresh mushrooms round out the sauce. Make a double batch and freeze half. When you defrost and reheat it, stir in chopped fresh parsley to give it a lift.*

2 white onions, peeled and chopped

6 garlic cloves, chopped

2 tablespoons olive oil, or as needed

Salt to taste

Lots of freshly ground black pepper

¾ cup vodka mixed with 1 tablespoon vinegar

2 pounds lean ground beef

2 large cans whole tomatoes

Basil (fresh or dried) to taste

1 pound mushrooms, cleaned and sliced

6- to 8-ounce jar pimiento-stuffed green olives (plus juices from jar), sliced

Chopped fresh Italian parsley

◎◎ Sauté the onions and garlic in olive oil until limp, about 10 minutes. While the onions are cooking, season them with salt and a generous amount of pepper, and add the vodka mixture in 3 additions, letting it reduce to a glaze after each addition. Add the beef to the onion mixture and sauté until browned.

Puree (or crush) the tomatoes and their juices and add to the beef mixture, along with basil, mushrooms, olives and their juices, and parsley. Simmer for 2 to 3 hours, stirring occasionally. Taste before serving. The sauce should be on the salty side.

YIELDS 12 TO 13 CUPS; SERVES 12

## Preparing Pasta Ahead

If cooking for guests use this method for precooking pasta: Cook until almost done. Drain and toss with a bit of olive oil to keep it from sticking. Refrigerate until ready to use. To serve, bring water to a boil, add the pasta and cook for about 2 minutes. In some cases chilled pasta can be reheated in the sauce.

# Whole-Wheat Spaghetti with Arugula

*This is one of those astonishingly simple sauces that you can make in the time it takes to cook the pasta, says Janet Fletcher.*

4 tablespoons extra virgin olive oil

12 garlic cloves, thinly sliced

¼ teaspoon red pepper flakes

¾ pound small young arugula leaves, washed and thoroughly dried

Salt to taste

1 pound whole-wheat spaghetti

¾ cup freshly grated pecorino romano cheese

☙ Preheat the oven to the lowest setting.

Heat 2 tablespoons of the olive oil in a 12-inch skillet over medium-low heat. Add the garlic and pepper flakes and cook until the garlic is soft and mild, about 10 minutes. Add the arugula (it will be bulky but will quickly cook down) and salt. Toss with tongs until the arugula has just barely wilted, about 2 minutes. Remove from heat.

Put the remaining 2 tablespoons oil in a large bowl and set the bowl in the oven.

Cook the pasta in a large pot of boiling salted water until al dente. Just before it is done, gently reheat the arugula. Using tongs, transfer the pasta to the warm bowl, leaving a little water clinging to the noodles. Toss well. Add the contents of skillet and ½ cup of the cheese; toss again. Portion among heated serving plates and top with the remaining cheese.

SERVES 4

## Classy Pasta

Pasta is a great way to showcase caviar for a special midnight supper or dinner party appetizer. Marion Cunningham suggests cooking ½ pound capellini, a thin pasta, for about 2 minutes. Drain, season and add ½ cup (1 stick) butter, cut into cubes. Divide the pasta between serving plates (2 for an entree, 4 for an appetizer). Spoon on a tablespoon of caviar. Place a wedge of lemon on the plate, and pass any remaining caviar.

# 10-Minute Pasta and Green Beans with Goat Cheese and Olives

*Trimming the beans is the most involved task in this quick pasta from Marlena Spieler. If available, use the thin green beans known as haricots verts. When yellow wax beans are in season, those are good, too. It's a recipe that begs for variations: You can omit the olive paste and toss in toasted walnuts, for example. If tomatoes are in season, dice one or two and toss them in the blend. Any pasta works well: flat fettuccine, tubular ziti, penne, even ordinary spaghetti.*

1 pound fresh pasta, or ¾ to 1 pound dried pasta

½ pound green beans, trimmed and cut into bite-sized pieces

3 garlic cloves, chopped

3 tablespoons olive oil, or as desired

⅓ to ½ cup coarsely chopped fresh basil, or 1 to 2 tablespoons fresh marjoram, thyme or oregano

1 log (5 to 6 ounces) fresh goat cheese, such as Montrachet, cut into small pieces

3 to 4 tablespoons olivada, or black olive paste

☙ Cook the fresh pasta and beans in a large pot of salted boiling water until the pasta is al dente, 2 to 3 minutes. Dried pasta will take longer; add beans the last 3 or 4 minutes of cooking time.

Meanwhile, lightly mix together the garlic, olive oil, basil (or other herbs), goat cheese and olive paste.

Drain the pasta and beans. Toss with the cheese mixture.

SERVES 4

## Quick Pasta Fixes

The slight bitterness of radicchio plays off the blandness of spaghetti in this extra-quick dish. Cut radicchio into strips and sauté in olive oil with a generous amount of garlic. When the spaghetti is done, toss with the contents of the pan and season with salt, pepper and a few squirts of lemon juice.

Toss just-cooked fettuccine with a handful of good-quality black cured olives, some chopped fresh rosemary, shreds of prosciutto (or crisp bacon), chopped garlic and just enough butter to add a glaze.

# Spaghetti with Collard Greens and Pancetta

*You could substitute other greens (mustard, kale or turnip greens) in this Janet Fletcher recipe, but collards have a particularly rich flavor.*

¾ pound collard greens

2 tablespoons olive oil

2 ounces pancetta, minced

2 garlic cloves, minced

⅛ teaspoon red pepper flakes

Salt

8 ounces spaghetti

¾ cup freshly grated pecorino romano cheese

 Cut away the tough rib and stem on each collard leaf. Stack the leaves together, a few at a time, and cut crosswise into ½-inch-wide ribbons. Set aside.

Put 1 tablespoon of the oil and the pancetta in a 10-inch skillet. Cook over medium-low heat, stirring often, until the pancetta begins to crisp, 3 to 5 minutes. Add the garlic and sauté 1 minute. Add the pepper flakes and set aside.

Put the remaining 1 tablespoon olive oil and a large pinch of salt in a serving bowl and place in a low oven.

Cook the pasta in a large pot of boiling salted water until al dente. About 5 minutes before it is done, add the greens, stirring them down into the water until they wilt. Drain the spaghetti and greens well. Transfer to a warmed serving bowl. Add the contents of the skillet and toss to separate the greens and coat everything with oil. Add the cheese and toss again. Transfer to warm plates.

SERVES 2 TO 4

# Oven Polenta (Soft)

*Gary Danko, the impressive chef who made his name at the Ritz-Carlton in San Francisco, saved us loads of angst when he created this easy soft polenta that cooks slowly in the oven. Once done, it can easily be held for several hours in a water bath.*

4 tablespoons olive oil

½ cup minced onion

1 cup polenta

6 cups boiling water (measured after it comes to a boil)

2 teaspoons salt

◉◉ Preheat the oven to 350 degrees.

Heat the olive oil in a Dutch oven; add the onion and sauté over medium heat until translucent. Add the polenta, stirring to coat with the oil, and cook until heated through. Gradually whisk in the boiling water and return to a boil. Add the salt.

Bake for 35 to 45 minutes. The finished polenta should mound slightly. Remove from the oven and whisk until well blended.

May be made a few hours ahead of time and held in a water bath until needed.

SERVES 4 TO 6

**VARIATON:** For a firm polenta, brush a 12-inch cake pan with 1 tablespoon olive oil. Follow above recipe, using 4 cups boiling water. Bake 25 to 30 minutes, or until most of the water has been absorbed. Remove from the oven and whisk until well blended. Pour into the greased pan and smooth the top. Let cool. (May be made 1 to 2 days ahead of serving; cover with plastic wrap and refrigerate.)

To serve, turn the polenta out of the pan and cut into desired shapes. Brush with olive oil and grill or pan-fry until golden brown on the outside and warm on the inside.

## Basic Polenta

*This is great with any meat, as a bed for stew, or with cheese stirred in as a side dish.*

4 cups water

1 teaspoon salt, plus
    salt to taste

1 cup polenta

Pepper to taste

◉◉ Bring the water and 1 teaspoon salt to a boil in a large saucepan and slowly stir in the polenta. Cook, stirring constantly, over medium-low heat until thickened and tender, about 45 minutes. Season with pepper and additional salt, if needed.

SERVES 6

# Roasted Polenta with Balsamic Sauce

*Two of the most popular foods on the Bay Area restaurant scene come together in this combination by Michael Chiarello, the chef/owner of Tra Vigne in St. Helena in the Napa Valley. The polenta is baked and topped with a dark, rich balsamic sauce, making a quick do-ahead appetizer.*

### Polenta

3 cups chicken stock

3 cups heavy cream

Pinch ground nutmeg

1 teaspoon salt

¼ teaspoon ground white pepper

1 cup polenta

1 cup semolina

½ cup grated fontina cheese

1 cup grated Parmesan cheese

### Balsamic Sauce

2 cups balsamic vinegar

1 shallot, chopped

2 quarts stock (chicken or veal)

6 peppercorns

2 bay leaves

8 tablespoons unsalted butter

Salt and pepper to taste

To make the polenta: Combine stock, cream, nutmeg, salt and pepper in a heavy pot. Bring to a boil, then gradually add the polenta and semolina, stirring constantly. Cook over medium heat, stirring constantly, until the polenta pulls away from the sides of the pot, about 15 minutes. Remove from heat and stir in all the fontina and ¾ cup of the Parmesan. Spread the polenta evenly in an oiled tray or pan to a thickness of ¾ inch. Cool to room temperature, then cover and refrigerate.

To make the sauce: Combine the vinegar and shallots in a heavy saucepan; reduce over high heat to a syrup consistency. Add the stock, peppercorns and bay leaves and reduce to a sauce consistency. Strain.

To assemble: Preheat the oven to 500 degrees. Cut the polenta into squares or triangles. Place on a buttered sheet pan, sprinkle with the remaining Parmesan and bake until golden brown.

Bring the strained sauce to a simmer, then reduce heat to low. Whisk in the butter 1 tablespoon at a time. Season with salt and pepper. Divide the sauce among the serving plates. Top with polenta.

SERVES 6

# Basic Risotto

*Here's a basic risotto that is delicious as is. It can also be dressed up with sautéed asparagus, wild mushrooms, slivers of prosciutto, or any number of items. Just remember that a risotto waits for no one. It should be eaten the minute it is done.*

> 4 cups broth (chicken or beef)
> ½ cup (1 stick) butter
> 1 small onion, chopped
> 1 cup Arborio rice
> ½ cup dry white wine
> 2 tablespoons heavy cream
> ½ cup freshly grated Parmesan cheese
> Salt and freshly ground black pepper to taste

Bring the broth to a boil in a saucepan; reduce heat and keep at a low simmer on a back burner.

Melt half of the butter in a large skillet. Add the onion and cook over medium-low heat until translucent. Add the rice and stir rapidly until the grains are coated with butter. Add the wine and cook until it almost evaporates, stirring constantly. Add a ladle of broth (about ½ cup) and cook, stirring, until it has almost evaporated. (The rice should never get completely dry, but it shouldn't be awash in liquid, either.) Add another ladle of broth, cooking and stirring until it has almost evaporated. Continue the process.

When the rice is almost done (about 25 minutes) stir in the cream, then the cheese, then the remaining butter. Season with salt and pepper. Serve immediately.

SERVES 4 OR 5

# Marimar Torres' Paella with Shellfish, Chicken and Pork

*Here in America, we think of paella as the "national dish" of Spain, but there are as many recipes for paella as there are cooks in Valencia. This classic recipe comes from one of Marimar Torres' favorite restaurants in the region, Galbis, located in L'Alcudia de Carlet, a little town 20 miles south of Valencia.*

1 chicken (3 to 4 pounds), cut in small serving pieces

1 pound lean pork, diced

2½ teaspoons salt

1½ teaspoons freshly ground black pepper

2 tablespoons olive oil, or as needed

8 large prawns in the shell

1½ pounds squid, cleaned and cut in rings

1 large red bell pepper, seeded, deribbed and cut in thin strips lengthwise

4 large garlic cloves, minced

1 large onion, minced

3 pounds tomatoes, peeled, seeded and chopped

8 live clams, scrubbed

8 live mussels, scrubbed

3 cups short-grain rice

¾ pound green beans, trimmed and cut in 1-inch pieces

1 teaspoon (.4 gram) saffron threads, or ½ teaspoon powdered saffron

24 fresh snails in the shell (optional)

1 or 2 lemons, cut in wedges

Pat dry the chicken and pork. Season them with 1 teaspoon of the salt and ¼ teaspoon of the pepper.

Heat the oil in a large skillet or paella pan; add the chicken and sauté over medium-high heat until golden. Remove the chicken to a colander (pour the drippings back into the skillet). Add the pork to the skillet and sauté until just golden; set aside.

Pat dry the prawns and squid; season the squid with ¼ teaspoon each of the salt and pepper. Sauté the prawns until just colored; set aside.

Finally, add the squid to the skillet and sauté for 2 or 3 minutes, stirring; set aside.

Reduce the heat to medium, add more oil if necessary and sauté the pepper until lightly browned; set aside. Add the garlic and onion and sauté until soft. Add the tomatoes and cook quickly until dry.

Bring 1 cup water to a boil in a large pot. Add the clams and mussels, cover and steam until they open, 4 or 5 minutes for mussels, 5 to 10 or more for the clams. Discard any that do not open.

Strain the cooking liquid through a fine-meshed strainer. Measure the liquid and add enough water to make 6 cups.

About 45 minutes before serving, bring the 6 cups of liquid to a boil.

Meanwhile, add the rice to the tomato sauce; stir and add the pork, squid, green beans, saffron, snails and remaining 1¼ teaspoons salt and 1 teaspoon pepper. Sauté for 2 or 3 minutes, stirring. Add the chicken pieces; push them down and distribute them evenly. Add the boiling liquid and cook over medium-low heat for 20 minutes. (Cooking this dish evenly throughout the skillet is essential. The rice should simmer with small bubbles, but not boil; stir a bit on the sides and turn the skillet around to prevent overcooking in the center.)

Five minutes before cooking time is up, arrange the shellfish and peppers on top. Turn off the heat and place a cloth over the skillet. Let sit for 10 minutes. Serve garnished with lemon wedges.

SERVES 8

TIP: Never let more than 20 minutes pass before eating; as the Spanish saying goes, rice doesn't wait for you—you wait for it!

# Basmati and Wild Rice Pilaf with Fennel and Pine Nuts

*Wild rice combined with plump basmati rice makes a wonderful side dish or meatless main course. Annie Somerville, the chef at Greens, flavors the combination with fennel and white wine.*

## Making Basmati Fluffy

To make basmati rice fluffier, soak it in salted water overnight; drain just before cooking.

¼ cup pine nuts

½ cup wild rice

4 cups cold water

Salt to taste, plus 1 scant teaspoon salt

½ diced onion

1 small fennel bulb, diced

1 tablespoon butter

½ tablespoon olive oil

3 garlic cloves, minced

½ cup dry white wine

1½ cups basmati rice

¼ teaspoon freshly ground black pepper

2¼ cups boiling water

¼ cup chopped fresh Italian parsley

◎◎ Toast the pine nuts in a 350-degree oven until golden brown, about 5 minutes. Set aside.

Rinse the wild rice in cold water and drain. Bring 4 cups water mixed with a few pinches of salt to a boil. Add the wild rice and cook at a low boil for 35 to 45 minutes, or until it is tender. Keep warm.

Sauté the onion and fennel in the butter and olive oil over medium heat; season with ½ teaspoon of the salt. When the vegetables begin to soften, add the garlic and wine and cook about 5 minutes, until the wine reduces. Add the basmati rice and sauté for 5 minutes, stirring frequently. Add the remaining ½ teaspoon salt, the pepper and the boiling water. Cover tightly and cook over low heat until tender, about 20 minutes.

Toss the pilaf with the cooked wild rice, the pine nuts and parsley. Season with more salt and pepper if necessary.

SERVES 6 TO 8

# Green Rice

*This pretty green-flecked rice from Jacqueline McMahan usually is reserved for special family occasions. If you add the vegetables, it becomes a complete meal.*

2 poblano or Anaheim chiles

½ cup chopped fresh cilantro

2 garlic cloves

2 cups water or chicken broth

1 tablespoon olive oil

1 cup long-grain rice (preferably basmati)

½ cup chopped onion

1 jalapeno chile, seeded and minced

1 teaspoon salt

Kernels from 1 ear of corn (optional)

1 carrot, diced (optional)

1 zucchini, diced (optional)

⅓ cup sour cream

Cilantro leaves

◉◉ Char the chiles over a gas burner or under the broiler. Place in a plastic bag and let sit until cool enough to handle. Peel the chiles and remove the seeds. Place the chiles in a blender; add the chopped cilantro, garlic and water or broth. Puree.

Heat the olive oil in a deep 2-quart pot. Add the rice and sauté until lightly toasted, stirring constantly. Stir in the onion and jalapeno. Sauté for a couple of minutes; then add salt and the poblano-cilantro puree; stir well. Cook over medium heat for 3 or 4 minutes. Sprinkle the optional corn and diced vegetables over the rice. Cover and cook over low heat for 19 minutes. Remove the lid to check: If the rice appears tender and the liquid has been absorbed, it is done. Cover and let sit for a few minutes before serving. If rice is still soupy, cover and cook for 5 or 6 minutes longer.

Garnish with sour cream and a few cilantro leaves.

SERVES 4 TO 6

# Indonesian Fragrant Rice

*Serve this coconut-scented rice by Jackie Mallorca with grilled chicken or prawns that have been brushed with a little vegetable oil mixed with red pepper flakes.*

1 (14-ounce) can coconut milk plus ¼ cup water

½ teaspoon pepper

½ teaspoon minced lemon zest

¼ teaspoon ground nutmeg

⅛ teaspoon ground cloves

1¼ teaspoons salt

1 cup long-grain white rice

∞ Combine the coconut milk and water, pepper, lemon zest, nutmeg, cloves and salt in a large saucepan. Bring slowly to a boil, uncovered. Stir in the rice and return to a boil. Reduce heat to low, cover and let cook for 20 minutes. Uncover and, using a fork, gently stir the rice from the sides of the pan to the center, mixing in any coconut milk that has not been absorbed. Test for doneness. If the rice needs more cooking, add a little boiling water. Cover and cook for another 5 minutes.

SERVES 4

# Braised Green Lentils with Ginger and Lemon

*Wendy Brucker of Rivoli in Berkeley gives a fresh edge to green lentils by adding ginger at the beginning of cooking and lemon at the end. Serve with chicken, fish or as a main course with rice, yogurt and chutney.*

1 tablespoon peanut oil

1 small onion, diced

1 medium carrot, diced

2 bay leaves

2 large garlic cloves, chopped

2-inch piece fresh ginger, minced

1 cup green lentils

2½ cups chicken broth or vegetable stock

½ cup white wine

½ teaspoon salt, or to taste

Juice of ½ lemon

¼ cup loosely packed, chopped fresh cilantro

◎◎ Heat the oil in a heavy 3-quart pot over medium heat. Add the onion, carrot, bay leaves, garlic and ginger. Cook, stirring occasionally, for 5 minutes. Add the lentils, broth or stock, wine and salt. Reduce heat to low, cover, and simmer until the lentils are tender, 45 minutes to 1 hour. Remove the bay leaves. Stir in the lemon juice and cilantro.

SERVES 4 TO 6

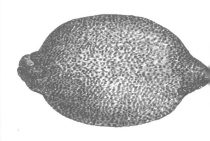

# Fragrant Creamy Lentils with Garlic (Dal)

*Mustard seed, cumin, chiles and garlic add a powerful punch to Laxmi Hiremath's recipe. Indian grocery stores carry toovar dal (dried yellow lentils), but if you cannot find them, yellow split peas may be substituted.*

1 cup plain toovar dal (dried yellow lentils) or yellow split peas

2 cups water

¼ teaspoon ground turmeric

1 tablespoon clarified butter (see page 28) or mild peanut oil

½ teaspoon black mustard seeds

¼ teaspoon cumin seeds

1 fresh hot green chile, stemmed and slit lengthwise

3 large garlic cloves, thinly sliced

¾ teaspoon salt, or to taste

1 tablespoon fresh lemon juice

Chopped fresh cilantro

Sort the lentils or peas and remove any debris. Wash in several changes of water. Transfer to a Dutch oven and add the water and turmeric. Bring to a boil, reduce heat, cover and cook until the lentils are tender, about 30 minutes. Set aside.

Heat the butter or oil in a heavy 2½-quart saucepan over medium heat. Add the mustard and cumin seeds. When the seeds begin to sputter (takes a few seconds), add the chile and garlic. Stir and cook 2 minutes, until the garlic is lightly browned.

Whisk the cooked lentils and add to the pan. Bring to a boil. Cover and simmer until thick, about 10 minutes. Season with salt. Stir in the lemon juice and sprinkle with cilantro.

SERVES 2 TO 4

Here are some tips from Janet Fletcher:

When buying beans, especially in bulk, choose plump-looking whole beans. Discard any that are broken, moldy, shriveled or spotted. Sort through, discarding any pebbles or bits of debris.

Store the sorted beans in an airtight container in a cool, dry place for up to a year.

Cooking time depends on the age of the legumes. Older beans can take twice as long to cook as new-crop beans. Small lentils and beans cook faster than larger beans; split beans cook fastest.

To test if legumes are cooked, remove one from the pan and press it between your thumb and finger. If it is soft, it is done. If there is a hard core, add water if required, cook longer, then test again.

# Braised Lentils with Bacon

*Gerald Hirigoyen, the Basque chef at San Francisco's much-acclaimed Fringale, created this recipe with only five ingredients—not counting salt, pepper and water. It shows how a few modest ingredients can make a truly memorable dish.*

¼ pound sliced bacon, cut crosswise into ½-inch pieces

¼ cup olive oil

½ large onion, coarsely chopped

¼ pound dried lentils

3 cups water

½ teaspoon salt

Freshly ground black pepper to taste

5 tablespoons butter

Put the bacon into a saucepan and add water to cover. Bring to a simmer, then remove from heat and drain in a sieve. Rinse the bacon and drain again.

Place the bacon in a large saucepan with the olive oil and onion. Sauté over medium-high heat until the onion has softened, about 3 minutes. Add the lentils, water, salt and pepper. Simmer until the lentils are tender and most but not all of the liquid has evaporated. (The lentils should be moist.)

Just before serving, add the butter and reheat, stirring, until it melts. Taste and adjust seasoning, if necessary.

SERVES 4

# Yellow Split Pea and Basmati Pilaf

*Traditionally, this pilaf is made from newly harvested rice and fed to the cattle in India. Laxmi Hiremath likes to use it as an out-of-the-ordinary stuffing for turkey.*

1 cup basmati rice, picked clean
½ cup yellow split peas, picked clean
2 tablespoons mild vegetable oil
1 teaspoon cumin seeds
½ teaspoon whole black peppercorns
½ cup finely chopped onion
½ teaspoon grated fresh ginger
2½ cups water or stock
½ teaspoon salt, or to taste
Toasted whole cashew nuts
Chopped cilantro leaves

◎◎ Combine the rice and split peas in a bowl. Wash in several changes of water and drain. Add enough water to cover by at least 1 inch and let soak for 10 minutes. Drain and set aside.

Heat the oil in a Dutch oven over medium-high heat. Add the cumin, peppercorns, onion and ginger. Stir and cook until the onion is lightly browned, about 4 minutes. Add the rice mixture, the water or stock and salt. Stir to mix. Bring to a boil. Reduce heat to low, cover, and simmer until the peas are fully cooked, 15 to 18 minutes. Remove from heat. Let rest, covered, for 5 minutes before serving.

To serve, gently fluff the pilaf with a fork and transfer to a heated platter. Garnish with cashews and cilantro.

SERVES 6

## Basic Steamed White Rice

2 cups water or chicken
  broth
1 cup long-grain white rice
Salt (optional)

◎◎ Bring the water or broth to a boil in a 2-quart saucepan. Slowly add the rice, stirring constantly. Season with salt, if desired. Cover, reduce the heat to a very low simmer, and cook for 19 minutes, or until the grains are tender but slightly firm and the liquid has been absorbed. Remove from heat and let sit, covered, for 15 minutes. Uncover and fluff with a fork.

YIELDS 4 CUPS

# Brown Rice and Lentils with Toasted Almonds

*A growing trend in the Bay Area is to combine dried legumes and grains as shown in this unusual side dish by Jackie Mallorca. It also may be served on its own like a risotto.*

5 cups water

1 teaspoon salt, plus salt to taste

1¼ cups long-grain brown rice

1¼ cups brown or green lentils

2 tablespoons vegetable oil

2 large onions, finely chopped

2 garlic cloves, finely chopped

½ teaspoon ground turmeric

⅛ teaspoon ground cloves

⅛ teaspoon ground cinnamon

Freshly ground black pepper to taste

4 tablespoons chopped fresh cilantro

¼ cup sliced almonds, lightly toasted

◌◌ Fill 2 saucepans with 2½ cups water each; bring both to a boil. Add 1 teaspoon salt and the rice to one, the lentils to the other. Stir the contents of each, cover, reduce heat and cook until tender and dry, about 40 minutes.

When the rice and lentils are almost ready, heat a large sauté pan over medium heat; add the oil and swirl in the pan. Add the onions and garlic and sauté until golden, stirring constantly, 7 to 8 minutes. Sprinkle with turmeric, cloves, cinnamon, and salt and pepper. Sauté for 1 minute. Stir in the rice, lentils and cilantro; mix well without crushing the grains. Taste and adjust seasoning if necessary. Transfer to a serving bowl and top with the toasted nuts.

SERVES 6

## Basic Brown Rice

2½ cups water or
   chicken broth
1 cup brown rice
Salt to taste
2 tablespoons butter
   (optional)

◌◌ Bring the water or broth to boil in a saucepan. Slowly add the rice, stirring constantly. Cover the pan, reduce the heat to a very low simmer and cook for 40 to 45 minutes, until the grains are tender but firm (check after 20 minutes by fishing a few grains out of the pan and tasting them).

When the rice is done, remove from the heat and stir in salt to taste and the optional butter.

YIELDS 3½ CUPS

# Chapter 3

# Meatless Main Courses

*Many home cooks in San Francisco prepare at least one meatless meal a week. And giving up the meat in restaurants is no effort either, because just about all of them feature at least one meatless item among the main courses.*

*At The Chronicle, our contributors and columnists have raised meatless cooking to a high art: vegetable cobblers, asparagus bread pudding, savory shortcakes topped with garden-fresh vegetables.*

*They've also created rich vegetarian cassoulets, spicy black bean stews and rustic spinach enchiladas spiked with tequila or vodka.*

*In addition to the recipes found in this chapter, you'll discover even more meatless dishes in the pasta and grains section and the vegetable chapter, which highlights a variety of satisfying gratins and casseroles.*

# Vegetable Mixed Grill

*Vegetables are never so satisfying as when they're cooked over coals. To further enhance the flavor, Marlena Spieler marinates a selection of vegetables—potatoes, bell peppers, zucchini, eggplant and tomatoes—in a garlic-laden vinaigrette before grilling. Almost any vegetable can be added to the lineup: red onions, mushrooms, radicchio. Experimentation is encouraged; if it grows it can be grilled.*

4 or 5 baking potatoes

1 cup olive oil

6 garlic cloves, chopped

¼ cup wine vinegar

1 to 2 tablespoons dried oregano leaves, crushed between your fingers

Salt and pepper to taste

4 to 6 heads garlic, broken into halves if large

2 red bell peppers, seeded, deribbed and cut into thick strips

2 yellow bell peppers, seeded, deribbed and cut into thick strips

2 green bell peppers, seeded, deribbed and cut into thick strips

4 zucchini, cut into thick slices lengthwise

1 eggplant, cut into medium slices (lengthwise or across)

4 to 8 large firm-ripe tomatoes, cut in halves

**Sauces/Relish** (optional, but nice)

Choose one or more of the following:

Olive-Pesto Aioli (recipe follows)

Sun-Dried Tomato Relish (recipe follows)

Tarragon-Mustard Creamy Dipping Sauce (recipe follows)

Garlic-Chive Butter (recipe follows)

∞ Parboil the potatoes. When half-cooked but tender enough to slice, drain and rinse under cold water; pat dry. Arrange in a glass baking dish and season with about 3 tablespoons of the olive oil, a generous sprinkling of the garlic, a drizzle of vinegar, a good pinch of oregano, and salt and pepper. Let marinate at least 30 minutes, preferably overnight.

Shortly before grilling, arrange each of the other vegetables in separate pans (combine the red, yellow and green peppers) and dress with the same mixture of olive oil, garlic, vinegar, oregano, salt and pepper.

## Quick Grilled Vegetables

To quicken the cooking of vegetables on the grill, partly cook them in the microwave beforehand. For extra flavor, make a marinade of soy sauce, rice wine vinegar, ginger, garlic, black pepper and a dash of oil. Microwave the vegetables for a minute or two. Let stand. When grilling, brush the marinade on the vegetables every few minutes.

Place the whole garlic on the grill first—place it to the side of the grill so it can cook more slowly to a sweet, soft consistency. Grill the vegetables quickly, letting the fire lick around them a bit to give them a smoky edge and slight patches of charring. Do not, however, overcook to a limp state. They should keep their fresh vitality. If your grill has widely spaced grids, use a length of foil for the smaller pieces.

Serve the vegetables on a platter, accompanied, if desired, with an assortment of sauces and relishes.

SERVES 6

## Olive-Pesto Aioli

2 tablespoons pesto (commercial or homemade)

3 tablespoons mayonnaise

1 tablespoon olive paste (tapenade or olivada)

2 tablespoons extra virgin olive oil

◎ Combine pesto, mayonnaise and olive paste. Slowly stir or whir in olive oil until it is absorbed into a smooth mixture.

YIELDS ABOUT ⅓ CUP

## Sun-Dried Tomato Relish

15 to 20 marinated sun-dried tomatoes, chopped or diced
2 garlic cloves, chopped
Large pinch fresh or dried thyme or oregano
3 tablespoons thinly sliced fresh basil leaves
Olive oil as needed

∞ Combine the tomatoes, garlic and herbs. Stir in enough olive oil to create a relishlike consistency.

YIELDS ABOUT ½ CUP

## Tarragon-Mustard Creamy Dipping Sauce

1 garlic clove, chopped
½ teaspoon minced fresh tarragon
½ cup mayonnaise
2 teaspoons mild Dijon mustard such as Maille
2 tablespoons unsalted butter, melted
Salt to taste
Fresh lemon juice to taste

∞ Combine the garlic, tarragon, mayonnaise and mustard. Slowly add the melted butter, whisking until smooth. Season with salt and lemon juice.

YIELDS ABOUT ⅔ CUP

## Garlic-Chive Butter

3 tablespoons unsalted butter
2 garlic cloves, chopped
Handful of chopped fresh chives
Salt and pepper to taste

∞ Soften butter; blend in garlic, chives and salt and pepper to taste. Smooth into a butter pot. For a particularly fanciful presentation, press the petals from lavender-hued chive blossoms onto the top of the butter.

YIELDS ABOUT 4 TABLESPOONS

# Meal-on-a-Wheel Pizza

*This ingenious all-in-one meal was devised by Marion Cunningham. Pizza dough is rolled into a circle, then a rope of dough is positioned down the center. Half of the pizza becomes a savory main course, the other half is layered with fresh fruit and sugar for an instant dessert.*

### Dough

1½ cups warm water

1 package active dry yeast

Pinch sugar

1 tablespoon olive oil

3½ cups all-purpose flour

1 teaspoon salt

### Peach Topping

6 ripe freestone peaches, peeled, pitted and sliced

⅔ cup sugar (more or less, depending on how sweet the peaches are)

### Tomato Topping

3 large garlic cloves, finely chopped

5 tablespoons olive oil

4 tomatoes, cut in half, gently squeezed to get rid of the juice and sliced
    about ¼ inch thick

Salt and pepper to taste

2 cups grated Monterey Jack or fontina cheese

⅓ cup grated Parmesan cheese (optional)

Fresh basil leaves

☙ To make the dough: Pour ¼ cup of the water into a large mixing bowl. Sprinkle the yeast and a pinch of sugar over it; stir and set aside for 5 minutes.

Stir in the remaining 1¼ cups water, the olive oil, 2½ cups of the flour and the salt. Stir thoroughly with a wooden spoon. If the dough feels very sticky, add another ½ cup flour and stir to mix. Knead the dough on a floured board for 7 to 8 minutes, adding additional flour if the dough seems too sticky to handle. Put the dough into a large bowl that has been coated with oil. Stretch a piece of plastic wrap over the top and put the bowl in a warm place until the dough has doubled in size, about 1 hour.

Preheat the oven to 450 degrees. Oil two 14-inch pizza pans.

Shaping the dough: Punch down the dough. Cut off about ½-cup chunk of dough and set aside. Divide the remaining dough in half. Roll out one half at a time on a floured board (or stretch and shape with your hands). The dough should be from ⅛ to ¼ inch thick. Transfer the dough to the pans and tuck it under all around the perimeter.

Divide the reserved chunk of dough in half and stretch each half into a 14-inch rope. Put a rope down the center of each pizza, pressing it firmly into the dough. (For a decorative touch, twist the dough rope into a spiral before securing to the pizza base.)

(Note: If you want to bake only one pizza, wrap half of the dough in plastic and refrigerate overnight, or freeze for later.)

The toppings: Place the peach slices overlapping on half of each pizza. Sprinkle the sugar evenly over the fruit. Combine the garlic and olive oil in a small bowl and stir. Season the tomato slices with a liberal amount of salt and pepper. Arrange the tomatoes in a single layer on the other half of the pizzas. Stir the garlic-oil mixture and drizzle over the tomatoes.

Bake for 15 minutes. Check at 12 minutes; the tomatoes and peaches should be bubbling a bit, and the sugar should have melted on the peaches. Sprinkle the cheeses evenly over the tomatoes and bake another minute or two, or until the cheeses have melted.

Sprinkle the basil leaves over the tomato topping. Cut the pizzas down the middle and cut each half into 4 wedges.

YIELDS TWO 14-INCH PIZZAS; SERVES 8

# Mélange of Artichokes, Fava Beans and Green Garlic

*Fava beans and green garlic both have a short season. Here they're paired with small artichokes. Georgeanne Brennan suggests serving the mélange with crusty country bread and red wine. If fava beans aren't available, substitute any other type of shelling beans, including limas.*

Juice of 1 lemon, or 1 tablespoon vinegar

16 very small artichokes (about 2 ounces each), or 6 medium artichokes

2 to 2½ pounds young fava beans (about 2 cups shelled)

½ cup olive oil

6 to 8 green garlic stalks, cut into 2-inch lengths

2 tablespoons chopped fresh winter savory

2 tablespoons chopped fresh thyme

½ teaspoon salt

½ teaspoon freshly ground black pepper

Fill a large bowl with water and add the lemon juice or vinegar.

Trim the stem end and cut off the top 1 to 1½ inches of each artichoke, depending upon the size. Peel away and discard the outer dark-green leaves until you reach the pale-yellow tender inner leaves. Cut the artichokes in half, from stem to top, and remove any bits of furry choke. Cut the halves in half again lengthwise; drop the pieces into the water.

Shell the fava beans. Because some people are allergic to the skins of the fava beans and because they are somewhat tough, you may want to peel the skins away, too. They are easily popped off by slitting the skin with the tip of a sharp knife or your thumbnail.

Heat the olive oil in a heavy saucepan over medium-high heat. Drain the artichoke pieces and dry them. Add them to the pan and sauté for 3 or 4 minutes. Add the fava beans and the garlic and cook for 10 minutes, stirring frequently. The artichokes will begin to change color to deep olive green; the favas, if peeled, will be bright green. Add the fresh herbs and the salt and pepper. Stir well, reduce heat to very low, cover and simmer until the artichokes are tender, 15 to 20 minutes.

SERVES 4 TO 6

# Vegetarian Cassoulet

*Concocted by Marlena Spieler, this casserole is hearty with beans and vegetables, and enlivened with the zing of pickled jalapeno. The bread crumb enrichment on top is flecked with parsley and lots of chopped garlic.*

1 pound dried white beans (haricots, Great Northerns, butter beans, cannellini or any combination of white beans—see Note)

3 to 4 tablespoons olive oil

2 to 3 heads of garlic, cloves separated and peeled but left whole

2 potatoes, peeled and diced

1 red bell pepper, seeded, deribbed and diced

1 carrot, diced

1 teaspoon herbes de Provence, crushed

¼ teaspoon dried thyme leaves, crushed

Salt and pepper to taste

1½ cups dry red wine (Zinfandel, Pinot Noir, etc.)

2 cups diced fresh or canned tomatoes

1½ to 2 cups vegetable broth (canned OK—Hain's makes a good vegetarian broth)

1 jalapeno en escabeche (pickled jalapeno), chopped

1 cup bread crumbs

3 to 4 tablespoons chopped fresh parsley

Onion-Jalapeno Relish (recipe follows)

◎ Pick over the beans for any bits of grit, rock or stone, then place in a heavy saucepan and pour in water to cover by at least 3 inches. Bring to a boil, boil for 1 or 2 minutes, cover and remove from heat. Let sit for 1 hour.

Drain the beans and add fresh water to cover by at least 3 inches. Bring to a boil, reduce heat and slowly simmer, partially covered, until the beans are tender, 1 to 2 hours depending upon age and variety of beans. Drain the beans and set aside.

Preheat the oven to 325 degrees.

Heat 2 to 3 tablespoons olive oil in a sauté pan. Add all but 4 to 6 of the garlic cloves, the potatoes, red pepper and carrot; lightly sauté for 5 minutes.

Layer the beans with the vegetables in an earthenware casserole or Dutch oven, sprinkling the layers with herbes de Provence, thyme, salt and pepper as you go. Top with the wine, tomatoes, broth and jalapeno en escabeche. Cover

## The Long and the Short of Soaking Dried Beans

The vote is split on which method of soaking beans is best. What it all boils down to is choosing the method that's best for you.

For the long method, soak the beans in an ample amount of cold water for 8 to 12 hours.

For the short method, boil the beans for a minute or two in a large quantity of water, then remove from the heat, cover and let soak for 1 hour.

with a tight-fitting lid and bake for about 1½ hours, checking every so often to be sure the mixture is not too dry. Add a little boiling broth or water if needed to keep the mixture slightly soupy.

Chop the reserved garlic and combine with the bread crumbs and parsley. Spread half of the bread crumb mixture over the cassoulet. Increase the oven temperature to 400 degrees and bake for 15 minutes; a golden-brown crust will form (if your oven gets terribly hot, set the thermostat at 375 degrees; you do not want the crumbs to burn).

Using a spoon, break the crust and stir into the bean mixture. Spread the remaining crumbs over the top and drizzle with remaining olive oil. Bake another 15 minutes.

Serve with the Onion-Jalapeno Relish. Pickled red bell peppers also are very good with this.

SERVES 4 TO 6

**NOTE:** Large kidney-shaped white beans make a particularly good cassoulet. They have lots of flavor and don't completely disintegrate into mush.

## Onion-Jalapeno Relish

*A spoonful or two of this sprightly relish enhances the flavor of cassoulet, much the same way a salsa enlivens a bowl of frijoles refritos.*

1 onion, chopped
2 garlic cloves, chopped
3 to 4 jalapenos en escabeche, chopped
Juice of 1 lemon, or more to taste
A spoonful or 2 of the brine from the jalapenos

☙ Combine all ingredients.
YIELDS ABOUT 1½ CUPS

## Hit of Garlic

Rather than chopping a lot of garlic before making a long-simmered dish, Marlena Spieler suggests waiting until the end. Then use a mortar and pestle to crush garlic and mash to a paste with good olive oil and salt. Stir into the dish just before serving for a wonderfully intense flavor.

# Black Bean Chili

*Cumin, chile powder and smoky chipotle chiles give Jacqueline McMahan's black bean chili distinction.*

2 cups dried black beans, picked over for stones and washed well

2 tablespoons olive oil

2 cups diced onions

1 tablespoon minced garlic

1 diced tomato

2 bay leaves

2 teaspoons crushed cumin seeds

1 teaspoon ground red chile, such as New Mexico

6 cups water

1 or 2 dried chipotle chiles, or 1 canned chipotle en adobo

3 tablespoons white vinegar

1 tablespoon brown sugar

2 teaspoons salt

☙ Place the beans in a large bowl; add water to cover. Let soak at least 6 hours or overnight.

Heat the oil in a frying pan; add the onions and sauté until translucent. Stir in the garlic and tomato. Sauté for 3 minutes, adding the bay leaves, cumin seed and ground chile.

Drain the beans and place in a heavy pot; add 6 cups fresh water. Add the onion-spice mixture and the chipotles (add 1 for a mildly spicy-smoky flavor; 2 if you want the beans really spicy). Stir in the vinegar and brown sugar. Simmer the beans over low heat for 1½ hours, or until tender to the bite but not mushy. Add the salt during the last 30 minutes of cooking.

SERVES 6 AS A SIDE DISH

## Hot and Smoky Flavors

Chiles add kick to salsas, sauces, stews and soups. The habanero, a beautiful 2-inch chile that ranges in color from orange sherbet to lime green, is considered the hottest domesticated chile in the world: Its Scoville units range from 100,000 to 300,000. At the moment, it's also one of the trendiest, which makes it not only hot, but haute. Chipotles are red jalapeno chiles that have been through a long, slow smoking process, which makes them seem hotter and more complex than fresh jalapenos. The chile's rather low Scoville rating— 2,500 to 5,000 units—can be deceiving, because the heat is felt on the lips and front of the mouth, increasing the burning sensation. They are available dried and canned in adobo sauce. See pages 314–15 for more about chiles.

# Black Bean Stew with Spinach

*When Laxmi Hiremath first tasted black beans in a Mexican restaurant, she went home and invented this recipe. The beans are a substitute for Indian black gram beans. If you like your beans hot, toss in 2 or 3 minced serrano chiles along with the garlic.*

1 cup dried black (turtle) beans

2¾ to 3 cups water

2 tablespoons mild oil

1 tablespoon minced garlic

1 tablespoon minced fresh ginger

1½ tablespoons ground coriander

1 tablespoon ground cumin

¼ teaspoon ground cinnamon

¼ teaspoon freshly ground pepper

5 whole cloves, ground

1 cup finely chopped tomatoes

4 cups packed finely chopped fresh spinach (leaves and tender stems
     from 1 large bunch)

½ cup unflavored nonfat or low-fat yogurt

Salt to taste

Cherry tomatoes (halved or whole) for garnish

@@ Sort through the beans and remove any debris. Wash the beans in cool water, then drain. Place the beans in a pot and add water to cover by at least 2 inches. Let soak at least 6 hours, or overnight.

Drain the beans and place in a large, heavy saucepan. Add 2½ cups water and bring to a boil. Reduce heat to medium, cover (partially at first, until the foam settles, then snugly), and cook until the beans are tender but still hold their shape, 30 to 40 minutes.

Heat the oil in a heavy skillet over medium heat. Add the garlic and ginger and cook for about 1 minute. Stir in the ground spices and cook until aromatic, about 30 seconds. Add the tomatoes and cook, stirring occasionally, until soft, 6 to 8 minutes. Stir in the spinach and cook until wilted, about 5 minutes.

Whisk together the yogurt and remaining ¼ to ½ cup water, then gradually add to the stew. Add the beans and season with salt. Bring to a boil, stirring constantly, reduce heat and simmer until the sauce has thickened, 10 to 12 minutes. Transfer to a serving dish and garnish with cherry tomatoes.

SERVES 4

# Black Bean–Stuffed Chiles with Chipotle Cream Sauce

*Anaheim chiles have only a mildly spicy kick; they're a perfect partner to black beans in Jacqueline McMahan's recipe. The sauce is made with chipotle, a smoked chile available dried or canned in Mexican groceries and some supermarkets.*

**Beans**

½ pound dried black beans

8 cups water

½ cup chopped onion

2 garlic cloves, chopped

1 chipotle chile

Black pepper to taste

1 teaspoon salt

**Sauce**

1 cup sour cream

1 tablespoon pureed chipotles en adobo

4 fresh green Anaheim or New Mexico chiles, charred, peeled and seeded

1 cup grated Monterey Jack cheese

Paprika or ground mild red chile

◉◉ To cook the beans: Pick over the beans for debris. Place in a sieve and rinse well. Place the beans in a large pot. Add the water, onion, garlic, chipotle and black pepper. Simmer for 2 to 3 hours, until tender. Add the salt during the last 30 minutes of cooking.

## To Salt or Not to Salt?

The When-to-Salt Bean Debate goes on.

Salt before?

Salt after?

Many cooks insist that salt toughens bean skins and should be added only after cooking. Others swear the beans will never taste right if they aren't salted from the start.

Grower Valerie Phipps of Phipps Ranch in Pescadero (San Mateo County) salts at the end, but says that the main reason beans are sometimes tough is that they're old.

To make the sauce: Combine the sour cream and pureed chipotle; stir to mix.

Preheat the oven to 350 degrees.

When the beans are tender, discard the chipotle and place a scant ¼ cup beans, drained of excess liquid, in the cavity of each chile. Arrange the chiles in a baking dish, pour the sauce over them and top with the grated cheese. Bake for 15 minutes. Dust with paprika or ground chile just before serving.

SERVES 4 TO 6

# Creamed Kidney Beans and Lentils

*In this rich Indian curry from Laxmi Hiremath, fiery fresh chiles play against soothing butter and cream. Served with steamed rice or a pilaf, this aromatic stew is a meal in a bowl. For an extra garnish, pass plain yogurt and chopped red or green onions at the table. The recipe may be doubled or tripled— leftovers keep well for up to 5 days in the refrigerator. And, like many stews, this gets better each time it's reheated. Pinto beans, Great Northerns or cannellinis may be substituted for the kidney beans.*

½ cup dried red kidney beans, picked over

½ cup dried brown lentils, picked over

2½ cups water

1 tablespoon unsalted butter

½ cup minced onion

1 teaspoon crushed garlic

½ tablespoon minced fresh ginger

2 fresh hot green chiles, minced

¼ cup tomato paste

½ teaspoon ground coriander seeds

½ teaspoon ground cumin seeds

¼ teaspoon pepper

½ teaspoon salt, or to taste

¼ cup milk

¼ cup heavy cream or half-and-half

1 tablespoon minced fresh cilantro

@@ Wash the kidney beans in several changes of water. Place in a pan and add water to cover by at least 2 inches. Let soak for 8 hours or overnight. Drain and rinse the beans.

Rinse the lentils and combine with the kidney beans. Place in a large, heavy saucepan; add the water and bring to a boil. Reduce the heat to medium, cover (partially at first, until the foam settles, then snugly), and cook until the beans and lentils are tender but still hold their shape, about 40 minutes. Remove the pan from the heat and let stand, covered, for 5 minutes.

Heat the butter in a large nonstick saucepan over medium-high heat. Add the onion, garlic, ginger and chiles and cook until the onion is lightly browned, about 4 minutes. Add the tomato paste, coriander, cumin and pepper; cook 2 minutes, stirring constantly. Add the cooked beans and lentils, the salt and milk. Bring to a boil, reduce the heat to low, cover, and cook until most of the liquid is absorbed, 6 to 8 minutes. Add the cream and heat through. Transfer to a warmed serving bowl and garnish with cilantro.

SERVES 3 OR 4

# Mixed Vegetables Jaipur-Style (Vegetable Curry)

*Laxmi Hiremath devised this delicious and colorful vegetarian curry. The ingredients are easy to find, but the combination of coriander, cloves, cardamom and cinnamon, smoothed with butter and tomato lend an exotic taste, especially with the raisins, which add a quick burst of sweetness.*

    1 teaspoon cumin seeds

    1 teaspoon coriander seeds

    1 tablespoon mild vegetable oil

    1 medium onion, sliced

    2 tablespoons tomato paste

    10 whole cashew nuts

    1 cup half-and-half

    1 tablespoon ghee, clarified butter (see page 28) or butter

    5 whole cloves

    5 cardamom pods

## Save the Stalk

When preparing broccoli, save the stalk, peel it with a vegetable peeler and cut it into coins for soups and stews.

1-inch piece cinnamon stick
1 tomato, peeled and chopped
½ cup cauliflower florets
½ cup broccoli florets
5 Brussels sprouts, cut in half
1 carrot, cut into 2-inch sticks
½ cup diagonally cut green beans
½ cup water
½ teaspoon cayenne pepper
½ teaspoon salt, or to taste
¼ cup raisins
Fresh mint sprigs for garnish

◉ Combine the cumin and coriander in a small skillet and dry-roast over medium heat for 6 to 8 minutes. Remove and set aside.

Heat the oil in the same pan, add the onion and stir-fry until brown. Combine the cumin-coriander, the fried onion, tomato paste, nuts and ½ cup of the half-and-half in a blender; blend into smooth paste and set aside.

Heat the ghee or butter in a heavy 2-quart saucepan over medium-high heat. Add the cloves, cardamom and cinnamon and stir until fragrant. Add the tomato and cook until soft. Add the remaining vegetables and stir-fry for 5 minutes. Stir in the reserved spice/onion paste, the remaining half-and-half, the water, cayenne, salt and raisins. Cover and cook over medium heat until the vegetables are tender. Serve with rice and garnish with mint sprigs.

SERVES 4 TO 6

# Ragout of Spring Vegetables

*The flavor and texture of new spring vegetables are so delicate that all they need is to cook quickly in butter, says Georgeanne Brennan. For meat eaters, feel free to add tender cubes of lamb or veal.*

½ pound asparagus, trimmed

4 or 5 young green shallots, or 8 green onions

4 tablespoons butter

8 small fingerling carrots

¾ pound small new potatoes, cut in halves

2 or 3 small young turnips, cut in halves

½ teaspoon salt

½ teaspoon freshly ground black pepper

½ teaspoon sugar

1 pound fava beans, shelled

¾ pound young peas, shelled

½ cup dry white wine

1 teaspoon finely chopped fresh thyme leaves

1 tablespoon chopped fresh parsley

1 teaspoon chopped fresh mint

∞ Cut the asparagus diagonally into 2-inch lengths. Cut the shallots or onion greens into 2-inch lengths, including all but the last inch or so of green tops.

Heat 3 tablespoons of the butter in a heavy saucepan. When it has melted, add the carrots and potatoes. Cover, reduce heat to low and cook 5 to 7 minutes. Add the turnips, salt, pepper and sugar; cover and cook for 3 or 4 minutes. Add the shallots, cover, and cook for 3 to 4 minutes. Add the fava beans and peas, adding more butter if needed. Cover, and cook for 8 to 10 minutes. By now, the vegetables should be almost tender.

Uncover the pan and increase the heat to medium. Add the wine, stirring and scraping up any bits clinging to the bottom. Stir in the herbs, the asparagus and any remaining butter. Cover, reduce heat and cook 5 to 7 minutes, or until the asparagus is just tender.

SERVES 4

**VARIATION:** For a meatlover's version, sauté ¾ pound cubed lamb or veal sirloin in 1 tablespoon butter for 10 minutes, covered, then add the carrots and potatoes and proceed with the recipe.

# Vegetable Tian

*Marlena Spieler's tian is a homey vegetable casserole, a specialty of Provence. Although this recipe calls for onions, bell peppers, eggplant, zucchini and tomato, the preparation lends itself to variations, depending on whatever is fresh or at hand.*

2 onions, peeled and sliced lengthwise

1 red bell pepper, seeded, deribbed and sliced

1 green bell pepper, seeded, deribbed and sliced

1 eggplant, thinly sliced, then cut into strips

6 tablespoons olive oil

5 to 8 garlic cloves, chopped

2 teaspoons or more chopped fresh herbs: marjoram, thyme, rosemary, savory

Salt and freshly ground pepper to taste

Pinch sugar

2 pounds young, tender zucchini, cut into thin slices

2 pounds vine-ripened tomatoes, sliced

½ cup grated Parmesan or other grating cheese (Asiago, locatelli romano, pecorino), or bread crumbs if the dish is to be eaten cool

◉◉ Preheat the oven to 375 degrees.

Lightly sauté the onions, peppers and eggplant in 4 tablespoons of the olive oil; when softened and lightly browned, add half of the garlic and cook a few minutes longer. Season with half of the herbs, as well as salt, pepper and sugar. Spoon the vegetables into a large baking dish. Arrange the sliced zucchini and tomatoes on top, in overlapping rows so you see stripes of white-green, red, white-green, then red again, etc. Sprinkle the top with salt, pepper and the remaining herbs, garlic and olive oil.

Bake for 30 minutes. Sprinkle with cheese (if serving hot) or bread crumbs (if serving at room temperature), then bake for 15 to 25 minutes longer.

SERVES 4

# Portobello Mushroom Fritters

*Wendy Brucker serves these delightful fritters at her restaurant, Rivoli, in Berkeley. They are presented on a bed of dressed peppery greens, accompanied with a classic aioli.*

### Aioli

2 garlic cloves, finely chopped

2 egg yolks

3 teaspoons fresh lemon juice

½ teaspoon salt

¾ cup pure olive oil

¼ cup extra virgin olive oil

### Vinaigrette

1 tablespoon minced shallots

3 tablespoons sherry vinegar

5 tablespoons extra-virgin olive oil

4 tablespoons pure olive oil

1 tablespoon salt

½ tablespoon freshly ground black pepper

### Fritters

1 pound portobello mushrooms, stemmed

4 cups all-purpose flour

Pinch salt, plus 1 tablespoon salt

4 eggs

¼ cup water

4 cups panko crumbs (see Note)

1 tablespoon chopped fresh thyme

6 cups peanut oil

4 cups loosely packed arugula

½ cup thinly shaved Parmesan

1 tablespoon rinsed and coarsely chopped capers

## Selecting Prime Portobellos

The mushrooms should be clean and firm. Look at the gills on the underside; they should be in good shape, not mashed or bent. Stored in a paper bag in the refrigerator, they will keep for several weeks.

◉ To make the aioli: Combine the garlic, egg yolks, lemon juice and salt in a bowl. Whisk to blend. Whisk in the oil very slowly, as for mayonnaise.

## Baking Portobellos

One of the easiest ways to prepare portobello mushrooms is to bake them. Preheat the oven to 350 degrees. Oil a sheet pan and arrange the stemmed mushrooms on it gill-side down. Drizzle olive oil (flavored ones work great) over the mushrooms, then add salt, pepper and any fresh herbs you desire. Bake for 15 minutes. Turn the mushrooms and bake 10 to 15 minutes longer. Serve on sourdough bread as a sandwich, or slice and arrange over dressed arugula or a mound of soft polenta.

To make the vinaigrette: Combine all ingredients in a bowl and whisk to blend.

To make the fritters: Slice the mushrooms ½ inch thick. Combine the flour and a pinch of salt in a large bowl. In another bowl, whisk the eggs and water until frothy. In a third bowl, combine the crumbs, thyme and 1 tablespoon salt. Dip the mushroom strips 1 at a time in the flour, then into the egg mixture, then into the crumbs. Transfer to a baking sheet until ready to fry. May be done 3 to 4 hours ahead of time.

Heat the peanut oil in a large saucepan to 350 degrees. Fry the mushrooms 6 at a time until golden-brown. Drain on paper towels.

Toss the arugula with 9 tablespoons of the vinaigrette. Divide among salad plates. Top with the hot mushrooms. Scatter shaved Parmesan over the salads. Mix the capers with the remaining vinaigrette and drizzle over the salads.

Serve the aioli separately for dipping.

SERVES 6

**NOTE:** Panko (Japanese bread crumbs) are available in Japanese markets and many other markets.

# Portobello Mushrooms with Soft Polenta

*Chef Reed Hearon reigns over the kitchen at Rose Pistola, one of the hottest restaurants in San Francisco. His recipe for portobello mushrooms is typical of the gutsy Mediterranean food served at his previous restaurant, LuLu. Portobellos are simply common brown button mushrooms, grown up a bit. Under proper conditions, they grow an inch a day, to more than 6 inches in diameter.*

4 whole portobello mushrooms, stemmed

¼ cup olive oil

1 tablespoon chopped fresh thyme

1 tablespoon chopped garlic

2 teaspoons chopped fresh rosemary

1 teaspoon freshly ground pepper, plus pepper to taste

1 teaspoon salt, plus salt to taste

3½ cups water

¾ cup polenta

¼ cup mascarpone at room temperature

1 tablespoon white truffle oil

◉ One day ahead: Rub both sides of the mushrooms with olive oil, thyme, garlic, rosemary, 1 teaspoon pepper and 1 teaspoon salt. Cover the mushrooms and refrigerate overnight.

Bring the water to a boil in a heavy pot. Whisk in the polenta, reduce heat to low and cook 2 hours, stirring occasionally. Season with salt and pepper. Keep warm until ready to serve.

Preheat the oven to 400 degrees.

Combine the mascarpone and truffle oil and set aside at room temperature.

Place the marinated mushrooms in a baking dish. Cover with foil and bake 20 minutes.

To serve, divide the polenta among serving plates. Top each serving with a mushroom and a tablespoon of the mascarpone mixture.

SERVES 4

To keep chopped parsley
from clumping when you
want to scatter it as a
garnish: Chop it, then put
it in cheesecloth or a paper
towel. Run it under cold
water and squeeze until the
water runs clear. The
parsley will become fluffy.

# Wild Mushroom Ragout Over Toast

*Georgeanne Brennan remembers having this dish at a friend's house in
Southern France. It was the end of mushroom season, and a whole group had
spent the day combing the pine- and oak-covered hills collecting mushrooms.
This recipe uses both wild and cultivated mushrooms, and the sautéed
mixture is spooned over wheat or multigrain bread.*

1 pound oyster mushrooms

1 pound mixed mushrooms (chanterelles, Italian field, shiitakes, cultivated buttons)

6 tablespoons butter

2 tablespoons chopped shallots

1½ tablespoons flour

½ teaspoon salt

½ teaspoon black pepper

½ cup dry white wine

8 thin slices wheat or mixed-grain bread

2 tablespoons finely chopped fresh parsley

Clean the mushrooms carefully. Cut the large ones into several pieces,
including the stems. Leave the small mushrooms whole, or halve them.

Heat 4 tablespoons of the butter in a heavy saucepan. When the butter
foams, add the shallots and sauté for 3 or 4 minutes, until translucent. Reduce
heat to low and add the mushrooms. The oyster mushrooms will begin to
release their juices almost immediately, creating the beginning of the broth.
Cook the mushrooms, turning them often, for 5 or 10 minutes.

Increase the heat to medium. Sprinkle the flour, salt and pepper over the
mushrooms. Turn several times to coat them with the flour. Add the wine and
stir for 3 or 4 minutes. The mushrooms will be reduced in volume by half or
more, depending upon your mixture, and you will have about 1 cup of broth.
Remove mushrooms and set aside.

Reduce the broth over high heat to ¾ cup. Return the mushrooms to the
pan and keep them warm over low heat while you toast and butter the bread
with the remaining 2 tablespoons butter.

Serve the ragout spooned over toast; garnish with parsley.

SERVES 3 OR 4

# Sambar

*Sambar, kind of a cross between a soup and stew, is an everyday dish in Southern India. If you are short on time, Laxmi Hiremath recommends using MTR brand sambar powder, available in Indian markets. This dish often is paired with Indian crepes (dosas) and rice cakes (idlis). For a truly authentic flavor, make this stew with toovar dal.*

1 cup toovar dal or dried yellow split peas

3½ cups water

1 cup chopped tomato

½ cup cauliflower, cut in ½-inch pieces

¼ cup sliced carrots

¼ cup green beans, cut into ½-inch lengths

½ teaspoon tamarind concentrate, dissolved in ½ cup water

1 tablespoon Sambar Powder (see following recipe, or use
    commercial sambar powder)

¼ teaspoon cayenne pepper

1 teaspoon kosher salt

¼ teaspoon sugar

2 tablespoons chopped fresh cilantro, plus more for garnish

1 tablespoon mild vegetable oil

½ teaspoon black mustard seeds

½ teaspoon cumin seeds

⅛ teaspoon ground turmeric

15 fresh kari leaves

2 small dried red peppers, stemmed and broken into pieces

◎ Combine the dal and water in a large saucepan. Bring to a boil, reduce the heat to medium and cook until the dal is soft, about 30 minutes. Add the tomato, cauliflower, carrots and beans. Simmer, covered, until the vegetables are tender, about 10 minutes. Add the tamarind liquid, sambar powder, cayenne, salt, sugar and cilantro. Cover and simmer for 10 minutes longer. Transfer to a large tureen, cover and set aside.

Heat the oil in a small frying pan over medium-high heat. Add the mustard and cumin seeds. When the seeds pop, immediately add the turmeric, kari leaves and peppers. Stir for half a minute, then pour over the sambar.

Ladle into bowls; garnish with a sprinkling of cilantro.

SERVES 6 TO 8

**NOTE:** Toovar dal and tamarind concentrate are available at Indian and some Middle Eastern markets.

## Sambar Powder

2 teaspoons dried yellow split peas, or chana dal

2 teaspoons urad dal

½ teaspoon white or black peppercorns (optional)

4 tablespoons coriander seeds

1 tablespoon cumin seeds

2 teaspoons fenugreek seeds

2-inch cinnamon stick, broken into pieces

30 fresh kari leaves

2 or 3 small dried red peppers, broken into pieces

Combine all ingredients in a 12-inch frying pan. Dry-roast over medium heat, stirring constantly, until the mixture is aromatic and the seeds are lightly browned, about 6 minutes. Cool slightly, then transfer to a spice grinder and grind to a fine powder.

Store in an airtight glass jar. This keeps well up to 3 months at a cool room temperature, or up to 6 months in the refrigerator. Freeze for longer storage.

YIELDS ⅔ CUP

# Zesty Tomato Shortcakes

*Who says shortcakes are only for strawberries? Shanna Masters created these innovative savory corn bread shortcakes, which are heaped with tomatoes, olives, herbs and vinegar and layered with sour cream.*

**Topping**

2 medium tomatoes, chopped

⅔ cup pitted and chopped black olives

3 or 4 green onions, sliced thinly

2 tablespoons chopped fresh basil

2 tablespoons chopped fresh Italian parsley

2 tablespoons minced bell pepper

2 tablespoons balsamic vinegar

Salt and black pepper to taste

**Corn Bread Shortcake**

1 cup all-purpose flour

1 cup yellow cornmeal

1 tablespoon baking powder

½ teaspoon salt

3 tablespoons sugar

2 green onions, chopped

2 garlic cloves, minced

1 egg, lightly beaten

3 tablespoons olive oil

1 cup milk

1 cup (8 ounces) sour cream, stirred

◉◉ Preheat the oven to 400 degrees. Grease an 8- or 9-inch square baking pan.

To make the topping: Combine the tomatoes, olives, onions, herbs, bell pepper and vinegar. Season with salt and pepper; stir to mix. Set aside, allowing flavors to blend while you make the shortcakes.

To make the shortcakes: Combine the flour, cornmeal, baking powder, salt and sugar in a mixing bowl; stir to blend. Add the onions and garlic, stirring to coat with the flour mixture. Make a well in the center; add the egg, oil and milk. Stir quickly, just to moisten the dry ingredients. Don't overmix. Spread the batter into the prepared pan.

Bake for 20 minutes. Cool and cut into 16 small or 8 large squares.

To assemble: Split each square in half horizontally. Place the bottom halves on individual plates. Top each with a dollop of sour cream, add a spoonful of the tomato mixture, then place the remaining shortcake halves on top. Add another dollop of sour cream and spoonful of tomato mixture.

SERVES 8 FOR LUNCH, 16 AS AN APPETIZER

**NOTE:** Try baking the shortcakes in muffin tins, for 12 to 14 minutes, and serving them upside-down, split and topped as above. The batter will fill 12 muffin cups.

# Muffaletta Shortcakes

*Black and pimiento-stuffed olives, celery and onions are the basis for a salad that is spooned over Parmesan shortcakes, all layered with cream cheese. Shanna Masters' shortcakes work both as a meatless main course or as a clever first course for a company dinner.*

½ cup chopped black olives

½ cup chopped pimiento-stuffed green olives

¼ cup brine from the green olives

¼ cup chopped onion

¼ cup chopped celery

3 garlic cloves, minced

1 tablespoon chopped fresh parsley

¼ cup olive oil

8 ounces cream cheese, softened

**Shortcakes**

1 cup all-purpose flour

1½ teaspoons baking powder

½ teaspoon baking soda

½ teaspoon salt

½ teaspoon garlic powder

5 teaspoons grated Parmesan cheese

2 tablespoons olive oil

1 tablespoon white wine vinegar

6 tablespoons milk

◎◎ Combine the olives, brine, onion, celery, garlic, parsley and olive oil in a mixing bowl; mix well. Set aside.

Beat the cream cheese until soft and creamy (if necessary, thin with a little of the olive brine); set aside.

To make the shortcakes: Preheat the oven to 400 degrees. Grease a baking sheet or line with bakers' parchment.

Combine the flour, baking powder, baking soda, salt, garlic powder and Parmesan in a mixing bowl; stir to blend. Make a well in the center and add the oil, vinegar and milk. Stir quickly just to moisten all ingredients, being careful not to overmix. Drop by heaping tablespoonfuls onto the baking sheet, making 6 equal mounds. Space them a few inches apart. Press the top of each with dampened fingers to make a shallow indentation.

Bake for 12 minutes, or until golden brown. Let cool.

To assemble: Split the shortcakes in half horizontally. Place the bottom halves on individual plates. Top with a good-sized dollop of the cream cheese, then with a spoonful of the olive salad. Place the tops on the shortcakes. Add a large dollop of cream cheese, then more olive salad.

SERVES 6

# Grapefruit and Avocado Shortcakes

*Grapefruit, avocado, walnuts and Gorgonzola cheese make an unusual and totally satisfying light supper dish. For a more formal meal, Shanna Masters recommends these as a tangy prelude to a perfectly grilled steak.*

2 medium grapefruit, peeled, sectioned, seeded, cut into ½-inch pieces (save the juice)

¼ cup chopped red onion

2 ripe avocados, pitted, peeled and cut into ½-inch chunks

¼ cup coarsely chopped walnuts

¼ teaspoon salt, or to taste

Black pepper to taste

4 ounces Gorgonzola, softened

4 ounces cream cheese, softened

**Shortcakes**

½ cup whole-wheat flour

½ cup all-purpose flour

1½ teaspoons baking powder

½ teaspoon baking soda

½ teaspoon salt

1 teaspoon dried rosemary, crushed, or ½ teaspoon chopped fresh rosemary

1 or 2 garlic cloves, minced

2 tablespoons olive oil

1 tablespoon wine vinegar

6 tablespoons milk

@@ Combine the grapefruit and its juice, the onion, avocados, and walnuts. Add the salt and pepper; toss well. Set aside. Before serving, stir thoroughly and check for salt, adding more if necessary.

Blend together the Gorgonzola and cream cheese, adding a little water, if necessary, to achieve a smooth consistency.

To make the shortcakes: Preheat the oven to 400 degrees. Grease a baking sheet or line with bakers' parchment.

Combine the flours, baking powder, baking soda, salt, rosemary and garlic in a mixing bowl; stir to blend. Combine the olive oil, vinegar and milk. Make a well in the center of the dry ingredients and pour in the oil mixture. Stir quickly just to moisten all ingredients, being careful not to overmix. Drop by heaping tablespoonfuls onto the baking sheet, making 6 equal mounds. Space them a few inches apart to keep them from baking together. Press the top of each mound with 2 dampened fingers to make a shallow indentation.

Bake for 12 minutes, or until golden brown. Let cool completely.

To assemble: Split each shortcake in half horizontally. Place the bottom halves on individual plates. Top each with a good-sized dollop of the cheese mixture (about a rounded tablespoonful—it's quite rich), then with a spoonful of the grapefruit mixture. Place the tops on the shortcakes, then top with another dollop of cheese and grapefruit mixture.

SERVES 6

# Red Onion Shortcakes

*These shortcakes make a beautiful presentation: The marinated onions turn the filling mixture a striking pink. The whole-wheat base is good with other toppings, too, and with other herbs substituted for the dill.*

1 large sweet red onion, thinly sliced

½ cup corn kernels, frozen or fresh

2 tablespoons thinly sliced celery

½ teaspoon dried dill weed

¾ to 1 teaspoon salt

Juice of 3 limes

1 teaspoon grated lime zest

2 teaspoons minced jalapeno chile (optional)

2 tablespoons pumpkin seeds, chopped (optional)

½ cup (4 ounces) sour cream

4 ounces goat cheese

**Herbed Wheat Shortcakes**

½ cup whole-wheat flour

½ cup all-purpose flour

1½ teaspoons baking powder

½ teaspoon salt

½ teaspoon baking soda

½ teaspoon garlic powder

½ teaspoon dried dill weed

½ teaspoon dried parsley

2 tablespoons olive oil

1 tablespoon wine vinegar

6 tablespoons milk

◎◎ Combine the onion, corn, celery, dill, ¾ teaspoon salt, the lime juice and zest, and the jalapeno and pumpkin seeds, if using; toss to mix. Let marinate at least 3 hours. Before using, stir thoroughly and taste for salt. Add the remaining ¼ teaspoon, if necessary.

Blend the sour cream and goat cheese until smooth; set aside.

To make the shortcakes: Preheat the oven to 400 degrees. Grease a baking sheet or line with bakers' parchment.

## A Vegetable Sandwich

Bitter greens work well in a supper sandwich. Sauté dandelion, arugula, escarole or other greens in a bit of oil and garlic, finishing with a squeeze of lemon. Spoon into a crusty roll and top with a few thin slices of mozzarella.

Combine the flours, baking powder, salt, baking soda, garlic powder, dill weed and parsley in a mixing bowl; stir to combine. Make a well in the center. Add the olive oil, vinegar and milk. Stir quickly just to moisten all ingredients, being careful not to overmix. Drop by heaping tablespoonfuls onto the prepared baking sheet, making 6 equal mounds. (Space them a few inches apart.) Press the mounds with 2 dampened fingers to make a shallow indentation in the top of each one.

Bake for 12 minutes, or until the shortcakes are golden brown. Remove to a rack to cool.

To assemble: Split each shortcake in half horizontally. Place the bottom halves on individual plates. Top each with a good-sized dollop of the goat cheese mixture (about a rounded tablespoonful), then with some of the onions. Replace top halves of the shortcakes and add another layer of cheese and onions.

SERVES 6

# Greek Salad Shortcakes

*Shanna Masters uses a lemon-herb shortcake to complement a salad of tomatoes, cucumbers, peppers and red onions. Feta cheese may be added for a quick variation, or to make the dish a bit more substantial.*

1 medium tomato, chopped

½ cup diced cucumber

½ cup diced green bell pepper

2 tablespoons diced red onion

2 teaspoons chopped fresh oregano

1 large peperoncini pepper, thinly sliced into rings

1 or 2 teaspoons fresh lemon juice

2 tablespoons olive oil

2 garlic cloves, minced

Salt and pepper to taste

4 ounces cream cheese, softened

½ cup (4 ounces) plain yogurt

**Lemon-Herb Shortcakes**

1 cup all-purpose flour

1 tablespoon cornmeal

¾ teaspoon salt

½ teaspoon baking soda

1½ teaspoons baking powder

1 teaspoon sugar

1 teaspoon dried oregano, or 2 teaspoons chopped fresh oregano

Grated zest of 1 lemon

2 tablespoons fresh lemon juice

2 tablespoons olive oil

⅓ cup milk

6 Greek olives for garnish (optional)

Combine the tomatoes, cucumber, bell pepper, onion, oregano, peperoncini, lemon juice, olive oil and garlic. Season with salt and pepper. Stir well. Set aside.

Blend the cream cheese and yogurt until smooth; set aside.

To make the shortcakes: Preheat the oven to 400 degrees. Grease a baking sheet or line with bakers' parchment.

Combine the dry ingredients in a mixing bowl; stir to blend. Make a well in the center. Add the lemon zest and juice, the olive oil and milk. Stir quickly to moisten the dry ingredients; do not overmix. Drop by spoon or an ice-cream scoop onto the prepared baking sheet, making 6 equal mounds. Slightly indent the tops of each with 2 dampened fingers.

Bake for 12 to 15 minutes, or until golden brown. Remove to a rack to cool.

To assemble: Split each shortcake in half horizontally. Place the bottom halves on serving plates. Layer with some of the yogurt mixture, then the salad mixture. Place tops on the shortcakes and repeat layering. Garnish with olives, if desired.

SERVES 6

# Savory Bread Pudding Layered with Asparagus, Cheese and Fresh Herbs

*Save your leftover bread for a week or so, especially the ends and slices from baguettes and any pieces of specialty breads such as focaccia. Let them dry and you'll have the main ingredient for Georgeanne Brennan's savory bread pudding. Heavy, chewy breads make a dense pudding; lighter breads result in a softer, more traditional texture.*

12 to 16 thick slices of dry bread

2½ to 3 cups milk

1 pound asparagus

5 eggs

1 teaspoon salt

1 teaspoon freshly ground black pepper

½ cup chopped mixed fresh herbs (such as chives, parsley and tarragon;
    or sage, thyme and marjoram)

¼ cup freshly grated romano cheese

4 ounces fontina cheese, slivered

4 ounces Swiss cheese, slivered

1 tablespoon butter, cut into small bits

Place the bread in a single layer in a shallow dish. Pour 2½ cups milk over the bread. Let soak until the bread has absorbed the milk and becomes soft, about 30 minutes. Press the bread slices to extract the milk. Measure the milk; you should have ½ cup. If not, add milk to make ½ cup. Set aside.

While the bread is soaking, trim the asparagus, removing the woody ends. Cut the stalks on the diagonal into thin slivers, about 2 inches long and ⅜ inch thick. Arrange on a steamer rack and place over gently boiling water. Cover and steam until barely tender, 2 or 3 minutes. Immediately place the asparagus under cold running water to stop the cooking. Drain and set aside.

Preheat the oven to 350 degrees. Butter a 3-quart mold (a soufflé dish works well).

Beat together the eggs, salt, pepper and the ½ cup milk until well blended.

Layer one third of the bread in the prepared dish. Set 6 to 8 asparagus slivers aside; top the bread layer with half of the remaining asparagus and half of the mixed herbs. Strew one third of each of the cheeses over the asparagus. Repeat the layers, using half of the remaining bread, all of the remaining asparagus and herbs, and half of the remaining cheese. Arrange the remaining bread on top, strew the remaining cheese over it, and garnish with the reserved asparagus slivers. Pour the milk-egg mixture over all, then dot with the butter.

Bake until the top is crusty brown and a knife inserted in the center comes out clean, about 45 minutes.

SERVES 6 TO 8

# Warm Tomato, Leek and Cheese Tart

*Paul Bertolli, who was the chef at Chez Panisse for 10 years before he moved to Oliveto in Oakland, created this dish. Use tomatoes of various colors for flavor and visual appeal. Serve with a bowl of Mediterranean olives and a salad of various lettuces dressed with a simple vinaigrette.*

**Pastry**

2½ tablespoons cold unsalted butter

1 cup unbleached all-purpose flour

Pinch salt

5 tablespoons ice water

**Filling**

1 tablespoon unsalted butter

3 leeks (½ pound), white part only, diced

⅓ cup water

½ teaspoon salt, plus salt to taste

Flour

Fresh basil leaves, torn in pieces

½ cup (2½ ounces) grated medium-sharp cheddar cheese

2 large ripe tomatoes, cored and cut in ⅛-inch rounds

Freshly ground pepper to taste

To make the pastry: Cut the butter into ¼-inch cubes. Combine the flour, butter and salt in a mixing bowl. Mix with your fingertips until the butter is coated with flour. Add half of the water. Using 2 knives, cut through the mixture to disperse the water and reduce the size of the butter cubes. Add the remaining water, pouring it over the dry portions of the dough and continue to cut until all the flour is damp. Gather the dough into a rough ball, then knead it very briefly. Form the dough into a ball and dust with flour. Wrap in plastic and refrigerate for at least 1½ hours before rolling.

Roll the dough on a well-floured board into a 12-inch-diameter circle. Place the dough on a baking sheet and refrigerate (or place in the freezer) until well chilled.

To make the filling: Melt the butter in a sauté pan; add the leeks and water. Bring to a boil, reduce heat, cover, and simmer for approximately 10 minutes, or until the leeks are tender and the water has completely evaporated. Season with ½ teaspoon salt and let cool to room temperature.

Preheat the oven to 400 degrees.

To assemble: Remove the pastry from the refrigerator (or freezer) and, leaving it on the pan, dust the surface with flour. Sprinkle the leeks over the pastry, leaving a 1½-inch border around the perimeter. Scatter some of the basil over the leeks. Sprinkle the cheese evenly over the leeks and follow with more basil. Arrange the tomato slices over the top, forming a concentric circular pattern. Lightly season with salt and pepper. Fold the perimeter of the pastry up over the edges of the tomatoes.

Bake about 50 minutes, or until the pastry is golden brown. Serve warm.

SERVES 6

# Spinach Enchiladas with Tequila Sauce

*A dash of tequila or vodka gives the sauce a special kick. While Jacqueline McMahan's recipe calls for fresh tomatillos (a small green tomatolike vegetable with a dry husk), canned tomatillos will do—just skip the toasting step.*

**Filling**

1 tablespoon olive oil

½ cup chopped onion

10 ounces spinach, stemmed

¼ pound mushrooms, cleaned and sliced

½ teaspoon salt

**Sauce**

½ onion

4 garlic cloves

1 jalapeno chile

1½ pounds fresh tomatillos in the husk

¾ cup water

2 tablespoons mild tequila or vodka

2 tablespoons heavy cream

1 teaspoon salt

3 teaspoons olive oil

6 corn tortillas

1½ cups grated manchego or Monterey Jack cheese

◉◉ Preheat the oven to 350 degrees.

To make the filling: Heat the olive oil in a 10-inch nonstick skillet. Add the onion and place the spinach on top. Sauté, moving the spinach around so it wilts and cooks evenly, for about 3 minutes. Add the mushrooms and salt and cook for 2 minutes. Set aside.

To make the sauce: Wrap the onion, garlic and chile in foil and bake for 45 minutes. Stem and seed the chile.

Heat a dry skillet over medium heat. Add the unhusked tomatillos and toast until softened, about 10 minutes. Cool, then rinse. Remove the husks. Place the tomatillos, roasted onion, garlic and chile in a food processor and puree. Add a little of the water to help in pureeing. Push the puree through a sieve. Place the puree in a skillet. Add the remaining water, the tequila or vodka, cream and salt. Simmer over low heat for 10 minutes, until the sauce has thickened.

To assemble: Preheat the broiler. Heat 1 teaspoon of the olive oil in a nonstick skillet. Add 2 tortillas and fry until softened. Repeat with the remaining oil and tortillas. Place a scant ½ cup of the filling toward the edge of each tortilla; roll up into an enchilada. Place 2 enchiladas per serving on heat-proof plates. Pour about ½ cup of the sauce over each serving, then scatter ½ cup grated cheese over each pair of enchiladas. Place the plates under the broiler 10 inches from the heat source, or as far from it as you can; broil about 3 minutes, or until the cheese is bubbly.

YIELDS 6 ENCHILADAS, SERVES 3

## Making a Chiffonnade

To make a chiffonnade with lettuce leaves or herbs, place the leaves on top of each other and roll tightly. Then cut cross-wise, making thin strips.

# Polenta with Sautéed Chard and Bell Pepper Topping

*The simplicity of preparation belies the interesting range of flavors of this cheery dish by Georgeanne Brennan. Chard, bell peppers, garlic and greens are quickly sautéed in olive oil, then heaped onto a mound of creamy polenta.*

12 cups water

2½ teaspoons salt, plus more to taste

2 cups polenta

4 bunches chard (about 12 ounces per bunch), or a mixture of chard, spinach and
    dandelion greens

2 red and 2 yellow bell peppers, seeded and deribbed

4 tablespoons olive oil

3 garlic cloves, peeled and minced

4 tablespoons butter

2 cups (8 ounces) grated white cheddar cheese

1½ teaspoons freshly ground pepper

◎◎ Combine the water and 2 teaspoons of the salt in a large saucepan; bring to a boil. Add the polenta very slowly in a steady stream, stirring constantly. When all the polenta has been added, reduce the heat to low and cook for 20 to 25 minutes, stirring constantly. The polenta will be done when it thickens and pulls away slightly from the edges of the pan.

Wash the greens carefully to remove any bits of sand or grit. Remove the white ribs from the chard. Remove the stems from dandelion greens and spinach, if using. Cut the chard crosswise and the dandelion and spinach lengthwise into ½-inch-wide strips. Dry the strips in a salad spinner or roll them in a clean towel to dry.

Cut the bell peppers lengthwise into 1½-inch strips.

Just before the polenta is ready, heat the olive oil in a large skillet over medium heat. When the oil begins to smoke, reduce the heat and add the garlic and bell peppers. Sauté briefly, 2 or 3 minutes, then add the greens. Sprinkle with ½ teaspoon salt. Reduce heat and cover the skillet for 3 or 4 minutes. The greens will steam and reduce considerably in volume. Remove

## Preventing Tummy Troubles

The part of the bell pepper that causes gastric distress is the skin. Remove it and you're home free.

the cover, increase the heat to medium-high. Continue cooking and stirring until the greens are limp but retain their bright green color, 2 or 3 minutes.

Heat a serving platter for the polenta. Stir the butter, cheese and black pepper into the polenta. Taste for salt, adding more if desired. Remove the polenta from the heat and spoon it onto the platter in a mound. Top it with the sautéed greens and peppers.

SERVES 8

# Casserole of Winter Roots with Whole Shallots

*The meaty consistency of root vegetables—turnips, parsnips, rutabagas and carrots, along with shallots and chard—create a grand meal. Georgeanne Brennan begins by sautéing the mixture, which caramelizes and intensifies flavors. Raisins are added before baking, adding a surprising burst of sweetness to the heady mixture.*

12 large shallots

4 parsnips

2 turnips

2 rutabagas

2 carrots

½ bunch chard

3 tablespoons butter

1 tablespoon olive oil

2 tablespoons flour

½ teaspoon salt

½ teaspoon pepper

1 teaspoon ground turmeric

⅓ cup dry white wine

2 cups vegetable stock

1 cup water

4 tablespoons raisins

¼ cup chopped fresh dill

¼ cup chopped fresh tarragon

¼ cup chopped fresh mint

¼ cup chopped fresh chives

1 cup plain yogurt

@@ Preheat the oven to 350 degrees.

Parboil the shallots (in their skins) in 2 cups water for 5 minutes. Let cool, then remove the papery skins. Trim off tips and trim root ends, but don't cut into flesh or shallots may not stay whole when cooked. Set aside.

## Tip for Cutting Fat Effortlessly

Use mashed vegetables—potatoes, carrots, parsnips or onions—to thicken soups and gravies. They add flavor and texture without the calories.

Scrub the vegetables, but don't peel them. Cut the thick upper parts of the parsnips into 1½-inch-long pieces; leave the thin root end (a piece about 2 inches long) intact. Quarter the turnips and rutabagas, then halve the quarters to make 8 pieces each. Cut carrots into 1½-inch-long pieces. Remove white ribs from the chard (reserve for another use). Cut the chard greens into chiffonnade strips by rolling the leaves lengthwise into a thin cigar shape, then cutting across into ⅛-inch-wide threads.

Heat 2 tablespoons of the butter and the olive oil in an 8-quart Dutch oven over medium heat. When the mixture foams, add the parsnips, turnips, rutabagas and carrots. Sauté for 5 to 6 minutes, turning the vegetables frequently.

Mix together the flour, salt, pepper and turmeric and sprinkle over the vegetables. Cook, turning the vegetables, for 3 or 4 minutes, until the flour mixture begins to brown. Add the wine, stir for a minute or two, then add the stock, water, half of the chard and the raisins. Cover and bake for 45 minutes, or until the vegetables are tender when pierced with a fork.

Heat the remaining 1 tablespoon butter in a frying pan over medium heat. Add the shallots and increase the heat to medium-high. Cook 3 to 4 minutes, stirring and turning constantly. The shallots will begin to brown and caramelize slightly. Remove the pan from the oven and stir in the shallots and the remaining chard.

Combine the herbs in a serving bowl. Top each serving of vegetables with several spoonfuls of yogurt and a generous spoonful of mixed herbs. Pass the remaining yogurt and herbs at the table.

SERVES 4 TO 6

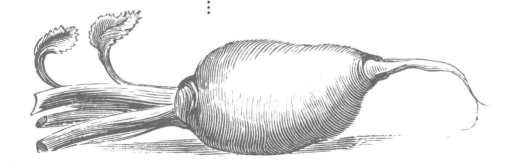

# Winter Vegetable Pot Pie

*Cornmeal makes a substantial crust for Flo Braker's savory vegetable pot pie.*

**Crust**

2 cups all-purpose flour

½ cup yellow cornmeal

¾ teaspoon salt

1 cup (2 sticks) unsalted butter

6 tablespoons ice-cold water

**Filling**

2 tablespoons butter

1 tablespoon olive oil

6 or 7 small leeks, washed well, halved lengthwise and sliced crosswise

1 garlic clove, minced

2 celery stalks, halved lengthwise and cut into ¼-inch pieces

1 large carrot, halved lengthwise and cut into ¼-inch pieces

1 small turnip, peeled and diced

1 small rutabaga, peeled and diced

4 or 5 small zucchini, cut in ⅛-inch-thick rounds

3 fresh Italian tomatoes, diced

½ teaspoon dried thyme

⅛ teaspoon cayenne pepper (optional)

Salt and freshly ground pepper to taste

3 tablespoons freshly grated Parmesan cheese

To make the crust: Stir together the flour, cornmeal and salt in a large bowl. Using a pastry blender, cut in the butter until the mixture is crumbly. Sprinkle the water over the dough, 1 tablespoon at a time, tossing with a fork just until a cohesive dough forms. Divide the dough in half. Shape each half into a disc about 1 inch thick. Wrap in plastic and refrigerate at least 1 hour.

To make the filling: Heat the butter and olive oil in a large frying pan. Add the leeks and garlic and sauté over medium heat, stirring occasionally, until soft and translucent. Add the celery, carrot, turnip, rutabaga and zucchini; cook, stirring occasionally, for 5 minutes. Add the tomatoes, thyme and cayenne and cook 5 minutes longer. Season with salt and pepper.

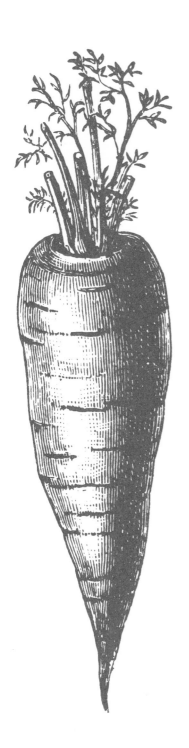

To assemble: Adjust the rack in the lower third of the oven; preheat the oven to 400 degrees.

Place one pastry disc on a lightly floured surface and roll out to a 14-inch circle, about ⅛ inch thick. Fit into a 9-inch pie pan. Trim the pastry, leaving a 1-inch overhang. Roll the remaining dough into a 14-inch circle. Spoon the filling into the pastry-lined pan. Sprinkle the Parmesan over the top. Cover with the top crust and trim the overhang even with the bottom crust. Press the edges together to seal, then fold under and flute the rim. Cut 5 or 6 slits in the top crust for steam to escape.

Bake 35 to 40 minutes, or until the pastry is golden. Cool on a wire rack about 10 minutes before serving.

SERVES 6

# Winter Vegetable Cobbler

*Marion Cunningham adapted a recipe for dessert cobbler to make a homey savory casserole filled with potatoes, celery root, turnips and carrots.*

**Dough**

1¾ cups all-purpose flour

1 tablespoon baking powder

½ teaspoon salt

6 tablespoons chilled butter, cut into pieces

¾ cup heavy cream

**Vegetables**

1 turnip, peeled and cut into bite-sized wedges

1 russet potato, peeled and diced

1 celery root, peeled and diced (about 1½ cups)

1 onion, coarsely chopped

3 carrots, peeled and sliced

½ cup chopped fresh parsley

1 cup broth (vegetable or chicken)

2 tablespoons cornstarch

1 teaspoon salt

Freshly ground pepper to taste

4 tablespoons butter

● Preheat the oven to 325 degrees.

To make the dough: Mix together the flour, baking powder and salt in a large mixing bowl; stir with a fork to blend. Scatter the butter pieces over the flour and quickly rub in with your fingertips until the mixture resembles coarse crumbs. Using a fork, slowly stir in the cream until roughly mixed. Gather the dough into a shaggy mass and knead 5 or 6 times. Cover and set aside.

To make the vegetables: Put the turnip, potato, celery root, onion, carrots and parsley in a 2-inch-deep 8-cup ovenproof baking dish. (You should have about 6 cups of vegetables.)

Blend together the broth and cornstarch; pour over the vegetables and mix well. Season with salt and pepper; mix to blend. Dot the vegetables with butter.

Roll out the dough on a lightly floured board until it is the size of the top of the baking dish. The dough should be about ¼ inch thick. Place the dough over the vegetables.

Bake for 55 to 65 minutes, or until the vegetables are cooked through and the crust is brown. Test the vegetables for doneness with the tip of a sharp knife or a skewer.

SERVES 6

Chapter 4

# Vegetables

*California is the most agricultural state in the country, and fresh produce is the backbone of most meals. In many homes fresh produce is the star.*

*For variety, San Franciscans love to experiment with some of the more unusual vegetables including cardoon, pea shoots, escarole, taro root, Chinese long beans and burdock root. Most of these can be found in specialty produce stores or ethnic markets. Many are easy to prepare and add interest to weekday meals.*

*Many recipes in this chapter are gratins: vegetables blanketed with cheese, cream, bread crumbs and the like. These are particularly recommended for the busy cook because they can often be assembled ahead and baked later. In addition, they go a long way in adding a special touch to the standard roast chicken or grilled steak. They also carry another bonus: The leftovers are great reheated the next day.*

# Baby Artichokes à la Castroville

*Maria Cianci took the classic preparation of fried artichokes as prepared in Castroville, where the majority of the U.S. artichoke crop is produced, and punched them up with powdered onion and garlic. Instead of the traditional mayonnaise dipping sauce, she prefers them plain with only a squeeze of lemon.*

16 baby artichokes (1 ounce each or less)

2 cups water mixed with 1 tablespoon lemon juice or vinegar

½ cup all-purpose flour

1¾ teaspoons powdered garlic

¾ teaspoon powdered onion

½ teaspoon salt, plus more to taste

½ teaspoon ground pepper, plus more to taste

Oil for deep-frying

2 eggs, beaten

Lemon wedges

To prepare baby artichokes for cooking, rinse them, trim the stem ends and snip off or pull off the outside, tougher leaves. When you come to the inner pale yellow-green cone, cut off the top quarter using a serrated knife. There is no choke to remove. Cut the artichokes in half lengthwise and drop into the acidulated water.

Thoroughly combine the flour, garlic powder, onion powder, salt and pepper.

Pour 3 inches of oil in a heavy medium saucepan and heat to 360 degrees.

Drain the artichokes and pat dry. Dip into egg, letting the excess drip off. Coat with the flour mixture, tapping off excess.

Fry the artichokes in batches until they are golden brown, turning once, 5 to 7 minutes. Drain on paper towels. Sprinkle with additional salt and pepper, if desired. Serve immediately with lemon wedges.

SERVES 4 AS AN APPETIZER

## Artichoke Fact

More than 90 percent of the artichokes in the nation are produced in Monterey County, south of San Francisco.

## Storing Artichokes

Sprinkle the artichokes with a little water, place in plastic bag and refrigerate. Although they'll keep for a week, they are best prepared as soon as possible.

When buying baby arti-
chokes, choose the
smallest, most compact
buds available. A pound
contains about 16 to 19.
They should have a true
"artichoke green" color
and appear moist, with no
sign of dry, woody exterior
bracts (leaves). Superficial
brown spotting can occur
in winter buds. Fall, winter
and spring buds are round
or globe-shaped; summer
buds flare slightly.

To prepare baby arti-
chokes for cooking, rinse
them, trim the stem end
and completely snip off or
pull off the outside tougher
leaves. When you come to
the inner pale yellow-green
cone, cut off the top
quarter using a serrated
knife. There is no choke to
remove. Leave buds whole
or cut them in half lengthwise, depending on the
recipe. Drop trimmed buds
into acidulated water
(2 cups water mixed with
1 tablespoon lemon juice
or vinegar) to retard dis-
coloration. Drain arti-
chokes just before cooking.

# Baby Artichoke Puttanesca

*Here, Maria Cianci pairs a classic spicy Italian tomato sauce with tiny fresh
artichokes. They may be served as a side dish, or tossed with cooked penne or
macaroni as a light main course.*

20 baby artichokes (1 ounce each or less)

2 cups water mixed with 1 tablespoon lemon juice or vinegar

2 tablespoons olive oil

1 medium onion, diced

2 large garlic cloves, minced

4 anchovy fillets, mashed

2 cups crushed tomatoes

10 kalamata olives, pitted and coarsely chopped

2 teaspoons capers

Salt and pepper to taste

Tabasco sauce to taste

Rinse the artichokes, trim the stem ends and remove the outside, tougher
leaves. When you come to the inner pale yellow-green cone, cut off the top
quarter using a serrated knife. Cut the artichokes in half lengthwise and drop
into the acidulated water.

Heat the olive oil in a saucepan over medium-high heat. Add the onion
and garlic and sauté, stirring frequently, until the onion begins to color, about
5 minutes. Add the anchovies and sauté 1 minute. Add the tomatoes, bring to
a boil, reduce heat and simmer until the sauce thickens slightly, 8 to 10
minutes. Stir in the olives, capers, salt, pepper and Tabasco sauce. Simmer for
3 minutes. Remove from heat and let stand, covered, for 15 minutes.

Drain the artichokes. Boil in salted water until they are just tender, about
5 minutes. Drain. Add to the sauce and toss thoroughly over medium heat
until well coated and heated through.

SERVES 6

# Artichoke and Potato Truffade

*Nancy Oakes, the creative chef/owner of Boulevard in San Francisco, is a master of side dishes, and this is one of her best. She fries a little bacon, cooks some potatoes and artichokes until tender and mashes it all together with seasonings and cheese. Then she briefly bakes the mixture until the top is deliciously brown and crusty. Oakes likes to serve this with game or roast chicken.*

4 ounces bacon, diced

2 tablespoons olive oil

2 pounds Yukon Gold potatoes, peeled, thinly sliced

Salt and pepper to taste

4 cups sliced cooked artichoke hearts

1 cup (¼ pound) coarsely grated Gruyère cheese

⊚⊚ Preheat the oven to 500 degrees.

Render the bacon in a large, heavy frying pan until lightly browned. Remove the bacon with a slotted spoon, leaving the fat in the pan. Add the oil to the pan, then the potatoes; season with salt and pepper. (Remember that bacon and cheese are salty.) Cover and cook over low heat for 10 minutes. Turn the potatoes. Add the bacon and artichokes; cover and cook 10 minutes. Turn the mixture again, crushing the potatoes. Cover and cook 20 minutes, or until the potatoes are tender. Turn the mixture, crushing potatoes again. Sprinkle cheese over the top and let melt.

Put the skillet into the oven until cheese browns, about 5 minutes. Turn out onto a platter and serve immediately.

SERVES 8

## How to Prepare Globe Artichokes

Cut off the top inch of the artichoke, then trim the stem. Using kitchen shears, cut off the spiked tip of each leaf. Rinse the artichoke well.

Artichokes may be steamed or boiled in salted lemon water (or try seasoning the water with a little vinegar, dried thyme, a few garlic cloves) until the leaves pull out easily, about 40 minutes, depending on the size of the artichoke. Serve hot, tepid or cold. Be sure to scrape out the fuzzy choke in the center (a spoon works well for this, and it can either be done before serving or each person can handle the chore at the table).

# John Carroll's Asparagus with Orange Butter Sauce

*John Carroll, a classic American cook who studied with James Beard, pairs asparagus with a hollandaiselike sauce in which orange juice and zest take the place of lemon.*

1½ pounds asparagus

3 egg yolks

¼ cup orange juice

⅔ cup unsalted butter, melted and hot

2 teaspoons grated orange zest

¼ teaspoon salt

Pinch freshly ground pepper

Trim the asparagus and, if the butt end is tough, peel the outer skin with a vegetable peeler.

Start bringing a large pot of salted water to a boil. Prepare the sauce before cooking the asparagus.

Combine the egg yolks and 2 tablespoons of the orange juice in a small, heavy pan; whisk until creamy. Set the pan over medium heat and cook, whisking constantly, for about 3 minutes, until the yolks are thickened and you see faint wisps of steam rising. You will also begin to see the bottom of the pan between strokes. Don't let the eggs get too hot or they will scramble. Immediately remove from heat and continue whisking for about 30 seconds. Add the hot butter slowly, in a thin stream, whisking constantly. Whisk in the remaining 2 tablespoons orange juice and the orange zest; salt and pepper. The sauce should be thick enough to coat the asparagus lightly. Set the pan in a larger pan of warm—not hot—water, or near a faint heat, such as a pilot light, while you cook the asparagus.

Drop the asparagus into the boiling water, bring it back to a boil over the highest heat and cook for 3 to 5 minutes, until the spears are just tender and droop slightly when lifted. Drain thoroughly and serve with the sauce.

SERVES 4 TO 6

# Asparagus with Wasabi-Miso Dressing

*The pairing of wasabi, a Japanese horseradish, and miso, a salty bean paste, brings out the best in asparagus. Created by Bruce Cost, the asparagus can be served alone as an appetizer or as a side dish with salmon or roast chicken.*

2 teaspoons wasabi powder

2 teaspoons water

1 pound thin asparagus or green beans

1 egg yolk (see Note)

2 teaspoons white miso

2 teaspoons Japanese soy sauce

1 tablespoon fresh lemon juice

1 tablespoon white rice vinegar

2 tablespoons minced scallions

◉ Combine the wasabi and water and mix to a thin paste; let sit for 15 minutes.

Cut the asparagus or beans on the bias into oblong pieces about 1 inch in length. Cook in boiling water until barely tender, 1½ minutes or so. Drain and set aside.

Briskly beat together the egg yolk and wasabi paste, then toss with the asparagus and the remaining ingredients.

SERVES 4

**NOTE:** Raw eggs have been known to carry salmonella.

## Asparagus Tip

To store asparagus, remove the rubber band (if there is one) around the stalks and place the spears upright in a container of water. Cover loosely with a plastic bag or plastic wrap and place on the top shelf of the refrigerator. The asparagus will stay fresh for at least a week.

If you don't own an
asparagus steamer you can
still cook asparagus to
perfection. Trim, then peel
the asparagus stalks. Bring
a large skillet of water to
a boil, add the asparagus,
cover and simmer until
crisp-tender. Peeling the
stalks allows stalks and
tips to cook in the same
time.

# Asparagus Chaat with Pistachios

*Crisp-tender pieces of asparagus are tossed with onions, walnut or olive oil, lemon juice and cilantro. Just before serving, pistachios and optional garbanzo beans are folded in. This is a particularly fine dish for a dinner party because it may be made ahead and served at room temperature. Laxmi Hiremath suggests pairing it with grilled or roasted meats and poultry. We particularly like it with grilled butterflied leg of lamb.*

1 pound asparagus

1 cup chopped white or red onion

3 tablespoons walnut or olive oil

2 tablespoons fresh lemon juice

¼ cup chopped fresh cilantro

1 teaspoon salt, or to taste

1 teaspoon chaat masala, see page 54 (optional)

½ cup cooked garbanzo beans, drained and rinsed (optional)

⅓ cup pistachios or pine nuts, toasted

Trim off and discard the tough ends of the asparagus. Cut the spears on the diagonal into 1-inch pieces. Fill a large skillet with 2 inches of water and bring to a boil over high heat. Add the asparagus, cover and cook until tender-crisp, about 3 minutes.

Using a slotted spoon, transfer the asparagus to a bowl of ice water. Drain, pat dry and place in a serving bowl. Add the onion, oil, lemon juice and cilantro. Mix lightly, cover, and let stand about 15 minutes. If made ahead, cover and chill up to 2 hours. Bring to room temperature before serving.

Just before serving, season with salt and optional chaat masala, then stir in the garbanzos, if using, and the nuts.

SERVES 8

**NOTE:** Refrigerated leftovers will keep for 4 or 5 days, but the asparagus will lose its bright green color.

# Green Beans with Vodka

*In this recipe by Michael Bauer, onions are stewed in vodka and vinegar, then green beans are added and covered with water. The mixture is allowed to cook down until the liquid forms a peppery glaze. Although the beans have that long-cooked army green color, the vodka acts as a pickling agent and keeps them slightly crunchy.*

 1 tablespoon olive oil
 1 medium white onion, chopped
 ½ tablespoon freshly ground pepper
 1 teaspoon salt
 ¾ cup vodka
 1 tablespoon white vinegar
 1 pound green beans, trimmed

∞ Heat the olive oil in a large saucepan over medium-high heat. Add the onion, ½ teaspoon or so of the pepper, and a little of the salt. Sauté about 3 minutes. Increase heat to high and add ¼ cup of the vodka and all of the vinegar; reduce to a glaze. Add another ¼ cup vodka, and a little more salt and pepper; reduce to a glaze. Repeat with the final ¼ cup vodka. When the liquid has evaporated, add the green beans and cover with water. Add more salt and pepper and let boil over high heat until all the cooking liquid has evaporated and forms a glaze on the beans. This should take about 35 to 40 minutes.

SERVES 4

## Beans in a Flash

Give green beans an Asian twist. Cook the beans in salted water until crisp-tender. Toss with a little Asian sesame oil, soy sauce, rice wine vinegar and chopped cilantro. The beans can also be chilled, then tossed with the seasonings and served as a salad.

# Sichuan Dry-Fried Long Beans

*Chinese long beans, also called asparagus beans or yard-long beans, resemble pencil-thin green beans, except they can grow up to three feet long. Here, Bruce Cost cuts them into manageable lengths and gives them a "twice-cooked" treatment: First, they're quickly deep-fried until they wrinkle, then they're stir-fried with ground pork, chiles, wine, fresh ginger and seasonings. Both processes take only a few minutes, and the results are memorable.*

2 pounds Chinese long beans

2 cups plus 2 tablespoons peanut oil, or as needed

½ pound ground pork

2 tablespoons chopped fresh hot red chiles, seeds and all

1 tablespoon chopped fresh ginger

1 tablespoon dark soy sauce

1 teaspoon sugar

1 teaspoon salt

1 tablespoon dry sherry or Shaoxing wine

Rinse and cut the long beans into 3-inch lengths; dry thoroughly.

Heat 2 cups oil in a wok or heavy skillet to nearly smoking.

While the oil is heating, chop the ground pork briefly to a finer consistency. Combine the chiles and ginger and set aside.

When the oil is hot, add the beans and cook 5 minutes or longer, until they wrinkle. Remove and drain.

Drain off the oil (it may be strained and used again) and reheat the pan. Add the remaining 2 tablespoons oil and the pork. Cook, stirring over high heat just until the granules are broken up and the meat changes color. Add the soy sauce and stir for about 30 seconds, then add the chiles and ginger; cook for another 30 seconds. Add the beans, sugar, salt and wine. Cook, stirring, until piping hot.

SERVES 4 TO 6 WITH RICE AND ANOTHER DISH OR TWO

# Drunken Beans for a Barbecue

*Beer is the secret ingredient in these hearty beans created by Jacqueline McMahan. Charred tomatoes, cumin and a combination of chiles add a rich depth of flavor to a basically simple dish. They're a must for any barbecue.*

1 pound dried beans: black, pinto or pink

10 cups water

12 ounces beer (not dark)

1 cup chopped onion

2 teaspoons minced garlic

2 teaspoons salt

2 tomatoes, roasted, peeled and chopped

2 serrano chiles, roasted, peeled and chopped

3 teaspoons ground cumin

1 tablespoon ground California (mild) or New Mexico (hot) red chile

1 tablespoon pureed chipotle chile en adobo

¼ cup bottled barbecue sauce

4 strips bacon, fried until crisp, crumbled (optional)

◉◉ Pick over the beans; discard debris. Rinse. Place in 10-quart pot and add the water and beer. Discard any beans that float. Add the onion, bring to a simmer, partially cover and cook 1 hour. (Monitor the water level; it should always cover the beans by 1 inch. If necessary, add a little boiling water to the pot.) Add the garlic and salt, then cover and cook until the beans are tender, 1 to 1½ hours.

Add the tomatoes, chiles, cumin, ground chile, chipotle, barbecue sauce and bacon. Simmer for 45 minutes to blend flavors.

SERVES 6 TO 8

# Creamy Beet and Potato Gratin

*The combination of Parmesan and Gruyère cheeses, baked with potatoes and earthy beets, makes this a warming autumn dish. Often served by Georgeanne Brennan at Thanksgiving, the gratin is hearty enough to stand on its own as a main course.*

3 pounds beets

1½ pounds potatoes

4 tablespoons butter

½ cup grated Parmesan cheese

¼ cup grated Gruyère or Swiss cheese

1 teaspoon salt

1 teaspoon freshly ground black pepper

1 tablespoon minced fresh rosemary

1 cup heavy cream

¾ cup milk

⅓ cup fresh bread crumbs

Preheat the oven to 350 degrees.

Place the beets and potatoes in separate pots; cover with water and bring to a boil. Reduce heat, partially cover and simmer for 20 to 30 minutes, or until both the beets and potatoes are tender when pierced with the tip of a knife. Drain and peel the vegetables.

Cut the beets and potatoes into ¼-inch slices, still keeping them separated.

Butter a shallow gratin dish with 1 tablespoon of the butter. Arrange a layer of beets in the dish, sprinkle with one third of the cheeses, salt, pepper and rosemary; dot with 1 tablespoon of the butter. Cover with a layer of potatoes (using all the potatoes). Sprinkle with another third of the cheeses, salt, pepper and rosemary. Dot with another tablespoon of butter. Add a final layer of beets, and top with the remaining cheeses, salt, pepper and rosemary. Pour the cream and milk over all, top with the bread crumbs and dot with the remaining 1 tablespoon butter.

Bake for 30 to 40 minutes, or until the sauce is bubbling and the topping is golden brown.

SERVES 8

# Kimpira (Stir-Fried Burdock Root with Carrots)

*Delphine and Diane J. Hirasuna gave us this recipe for a Japanese New Year dish. It's a wonderful combination of carrots and burdock, a fibrous root with a nutty flavor. The dish fits in with almost any Western-style menu, but the crunchy delicate flavors make it particularly good with chicken or fish.*

3 or 4 slim young burdock roots (gobo)

1 carrot, peeled

1½ tablespoons Asian sesame oil

2 tablespoons sugar

¼ teaspoon red pepper flakes or cayenne pepper (optional)

¼ cup soy sauce

Toasted sesame seeds

∞ Scrub the burdock with a vegetable brush until the brown layer of skin comes off (or scrape the roots with a dull knife).

Cut burdock and carrot into thick matchstick-sized pieces, about 2 inches long. (You should have about 4 cups burdock and ½ cup carrot.) Keep the cut burdock in water until you are ready to cook, then drain and dry thoroughly with a dish towel.

Heat the sesame oil in a wok or heavy skillet until it is hot. Add the burdock and carrot and stir-fry over medium-high heat until the pieces are limp, about 5 minutes.

Sprinkle in the sugar and red pepper flakes or cayenne; stir briefly to blend. Then add the soy sauce and stir-fry until the liquid is absorbed, a minute or two. Remove from heat.

Sprinkle with sesame seeds before serving.

SERVES 4

**NOTE:** Burdock root is available in Asian grocery stores and some specialty and produce markets.

# Gratin of Cardoons, Anchovy and Cheese

*Paula Wolfert, an expert on Mediterranean cuisines, is an East Coast transplant who recently moved to San Francisco. In this recipe, Wolfert features cardoons, a vegetable popular in Spain, Italy and France. The cardoon looks a little like a head of celery and tastes like a cross between an artichoke and an oyster.*

1 bunch fresh cardoons (about 4 pounds)

⅓ cup fresh lemon juice, strained

9 cups water

⅓ cup flour

3 tablespoons extra-virgin olive oil

Pinch salt

3 tablespoons chopped onion

3 anchovy fillets, rinsed and diced

Freshly ground black pepper to taste

3 tablespoons grated Gruyère or Parmesan cheese

2 tablespoons fresh bread crumbs

Separate the cardoon ribs from the core and wash them. Cut away the prickly leaves and any damaged ribs. Rub the cut ends with a little of the lemon juice to prevent discoloring. Pare the stalks with a vegetable peeler. Cut into pieces about 3 inches long, then scrape away the inner white membrane. (Use the tip of the peeler to loosen it first.) Drop the slices into a bowl of acidulated water (1 tablespoon vinegar or lemon juice to 3 cups water) to prevent darkening. Pare and quarter the core and add to the bowl.

Put 2 cups of the water in saucepan. Whisk in the flour. Bring to a boil over medium heat, whisking. Add 6 cups of the water, 2½ tablespoons of the lemon juice, 1 tablespoon of the olive oil and a large pinch of salt; return to a boil.

Drain the cardoons and add to the saucepan. Cover and cook until tender, about 15 minutes. Remove from heat but do not drain until ready to use.

Preheat the oven to 350 degrees. Lightly oil a shallow 9-inch baking dish.

Heat the remaining 2 tablespoons olive oil in a medium skillet. Add the onions and sauté until soft. Add the anchovies, crushing them to a puree with a wooden spoon. Add the remaining 1 cup water and the pepper; bring to a boil. Simmer 5 minutes. Drain the cardoons and dry well.

Spread a thin layer of anchovy sauce in the prepared baking dish. Cover with an even layer of cardoons. Sprinkle with the remaining lemon juice. Top with the remaining sauce, the cheese and bread crumbs. Bake about 30 minutes, until golden and crusty.

SERVES 3 OR 4

# Parsleyed Carrots

*The secret to this dish from Marion Cunningham is to use perfectly fresh young carrots. Older, larger carrots can have a woody core and lack the sweetness of the younger vegetables.*

2½ pounds young carrots, peeled and cut on the diagonal into ½-inch chunks
4 tablespoons unsalted butter
Salt to taste
¼ cup finely chopped fresh parsley

Bring a large saucepan of salted water to a boil. Add the carrots and cook over medium heat until just tender, about 10 minutes. Drain well.

Add the butter to the saucepan and toss to coat the carrots. Season with salt, add the parsley and mix well. Transfer to a bowl and serve hot.

SERVES 8

# Cauliflower with Olives and Rosemary

*Chef John Caputo created this Mediterranean-flavored dish at Socca, his San Francisco restaurant. He usually pairs it with stuffed veal shoulder, but it's equally good with lamb, beef, pork or chicken.*

1 head cauliflower

2 tablespoons pure olive oil

20 Mediterranean-style black olives

2 teaspoons coarsely chopped fresh rosemary

Salt and pepper to taste

1 tablespoon extra-virgin olive oil

๑๑ Cut the cauliflower into florets about the size of a silver dollar.

Bring a large pot of salted water to a boil. Add the florets and blanch until almost cooked but still a little crunchy, about 2 minutes. Transfer to a bowl of ice water to stop the cooking. Drain and let dry.

Heat the pure olive oil in a sauté pan over medium heat. Add the cauliflower and sauté for 2 minutes. Add the olives and sauté until the cauliflower colors lightly, another minute or two. Add the rosemary and cook 30 seconds. Season with salt and pepper. Drain off the oil.

Transfer the cauliflower and olives to a serving platter. Drizzle with the extra-virgin olive oil.

SERVES 4

# Green Tomato and Fresh Corn Pie

*The sharp tang of green tomatoes and olives complements this spicy mixture of chorizo, peppers and corn, all tucked beneath a layer of herbed corn bread, which is just thick enough to soak up the wonderful juices. It's a specialty of Georgeanne Brennan.*

⅓ pound good-quality chorizo sausage, casings removed

½ medium onion, minced

1 red bell pepper, seeded, deribbed and minced

1 hot chile (jalapeno, Hungarian wax or serrano), seeded and minced

2 ears fresh sweet corn

¼ cup flour

2 tablespoons cornmeal

½ teaspoon salt

½ teaspoon freshly ground black pepper

4 to 5 large green tomatoes, chopped, about 2½ to 3 cups

1½ tablespoons butter

2 tablespoons vegetable oil

12 tart olives such as kalamata, pitted and coarsely chopped

**Topping**

2 tablespoons flour

1 teaspoon baking powder

½ teaspoon salt

½ teaspoon freshly ground black pepper

¾ cup cornmeal

2 tablespoons fresh thyme leaves

2 eggs, beaten

½ cup milk

1 tablespoon vegetable oil

⊚⊚ Preheat the oven to 425 degrees.

Cook the chorizo in a skillet over medium heat, stirring often, until it cooks through and becomes somewhat crumbly, about 5 minutes. Remove from skillet and set aside to drain on several layers of paper towels.

## Making Corn Sweet

If you're plagued with starchy corn, garden writer Jeff Cox suggests this trick: Cut the kernels from the cob and steam until just tender. Stir in some butter and a teaspoon of sugar.

Pour off any excess fat in the skillet, leaving a scant ½ teaspoon in the pan. Return the skillet to the heat. Add the onions and peppers and sauté over medium heat for 3 or 4 minutes, stirring often. Remove from the skillet and set aside.

Husk the corn. Holding it upright, place an ear of corn in a bowl. Using a knife, cut off the kernels as close to the cob as possible. Repeat with the other ear of corn. Discard the cobs and set the bowl of corn kernels aside.

Mix together the flour, cornmeal, salt and pepper in a bowl. Add the chopped green tomatoes and toss to coat them with the flour mixture.

Heat 1 tablespoon of the butter and the vegetable oil in a skillet. When the butter is foaming, remove the tomatoes from the bowl with a slotted spoon and place in skillet. Do not add the accumulated juice in the bottom of the bowl. Cook over medium-high heat for 3 or 4 minutes, or until the tomatoes have browned slightly. Turn and cook another 2 or 3 minutes. Remove the tomatoes, add the olives and set aside.

Make the topping by combining all the dry ingredients, including the thyme, in a bowl. Stir in the eggs, milk and oil; mix just until thoroughly moistened.

Use the remaining ½ tablespoon butter to grease a 1½-quart baking dish.

Combine the corn and its accumulated juices with the chorizo mixture and make a layer of it in the baking dish. Top with a layer of green tomatoes and olives. Pour the batter over the tomatoes and spread it evenly across the top.

Bake for 15 to 20 minutes, or until the topping is slightly puffed and cooked through. Let stand 10 to 15 minutes, loosely covered, before serving.

SERVES 4 TO 6 AS A MAIN COURSE

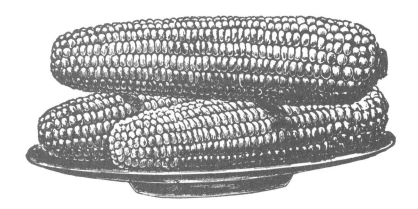

# Double-Corn Spoon Bread with Green Chiles

*The contrasting tastes and textures of cornmeal and fresh corn kernels enrich this simple custardy dish by Georgeanne Brennan. Anaheim chiles add a mild edge of heat to the cheesy mixture.*

2 tablespoons butter

6 large fresh green chiles (such as Anaheim), roasted, peeled and seeded

½ cup grated Monterey Jack cheese

¼ cup grated cheddar cheese

3 eggs, separated

Kernels from 2 ears fresh corn (yellow or white)

2 tablespoons yellow cornmeal

2 tablespoons flour

⅓ cup milk

2 tablespoons sour cream

½ teaspoon salt

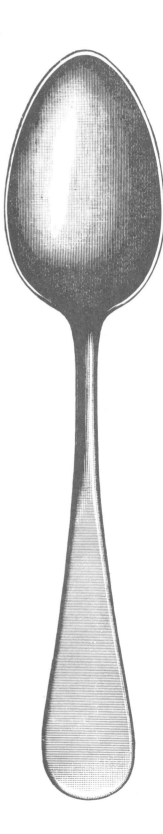

Preheat the oven to 350 degrees. Butter an 8-inch square baking pan with 1 tablespoon of the butter.

Place the chiles in a layer on the bottom of the pan; sprinkle with all but 2 tablespoons of the cheese.

Beat the egg whites until soft peaks form.

In another bowl, mix together the egg yolks, corn kernels, cornmeal, flour, milk, sour cream and salt.

Fold the whites gently into the yolk-flour mixture. Spoon over the cheese and peppers. Cut the remaining butter into small pieces and scatter over the top. Sprinkle the remaining cheese over all.

Bake for 25 to 30 minutes, or until all but the very center is set.

SERVES 8

# Eggplant Parmesan, Garden Style

*The best time to make this dish is near the end of summer, when eggplants and tomatoes are plentiful and at the peak of perfection. Eggplants that ripen just before the frosts have firm, dense flesh and the seeds have barely developed. And late-summer tomatoes are so sweet and full of flavor that any seasonings beyond salt and pepper are not really necessary, says Georgeanne Brennan.*

**Sauce**

3 pounds ripe tomatoes

2 tablespoons olive oil

2 garlic cloves, chopped

4 to 5 small globe eggplants, or 2 medium-large eggplants

¼ cup olive oil

1 teaspoon salt

2 or 3 tablespoons fresh thyme leaves

2 cups (8 ounces) grated mozzarella

1 tablespoon chopped fresh marjoram or oregano leaves

¼ cup freshly grated Parmesan cheese

1½ tablespoons butter

◎◎ To make the sauce: Peel and coarsely chop the tomatoes. Heat the olive oil in a large saucepan over medium heat. Add the garlic and sauté briefly without browning. Add the tomatoes, bring to a boil, reduce the heat to low and simmer over medium-low heat for 30 to 40 minutes, or until the tomatoes have cooked down into a sauce. Taste and add salt, if desired.

Preheat the oven to 450 degrees.

Cut the eggplants into ½-inch-thick slices and place them in a single layer on a large baking sheet. Sprinkle with half of the olive oil and half of the salt. Turn the slices and sprinkle with the remaining olive oil and salt. Top with the thyme. Bake for 10 minutes. Turn the eggplant and bake 2 to 3 minutes, then place under the broiler for 2 or 3 minutes, until a slightly golden crust forms. Remove and set aside.

Reduce oven temperature to 400 degrees.

Arrange a layer of eggplant in a 2-inch-deep baking dish. Top with one third of the sauce, half of the mozzarella, half of the marjoram or oregano, and one third of the Parmesan. Make a second layer of eggplant and proceed with the layering, ending with a layer of eggplant. Pour the remaining sauce over the eggplant and top with the remaining Parmesan. Dot with the butter.

Bake for 25 to 30 minutes, or until the top is lightly browned and bubbling. Let stand 10 minutes, loosely covered, before serving.

SERVES 4 TO 6

# Hand-Shredded Eggplant with Ginger-Garlic Dressing

*This simple dish by Bruce Cost is well worth the time it takes to hand-shred the eggplant. A pungent dressing of vinegar, sugar, garlic, ginger and sesame oil permeates the shreds, and toasted sesame seeds add the crowning touch.*

2 pounds globe eggplant(s)

2 tablespoons light soy sauce

3 tablespoons mild vinegar

1½ tablespoons sugar

4 tablespoons peanut oil

1 tablespoon chopped garlic

1 tablespoon chopped fresh ginger

2 tablespoons Asian sesame oil

1 tablespoon toasted sesame seeds

Put the eggplant(s) into a hot steamer and steam, covered, for 20 minutes (less if very fresh). When tender, take out and let cool.

Mix together the soy sauce, vinegar and sugar; set aside.

When eggplant is cool, cut crosswise into 2-inch rounds. Pull apart the flesh into thin 2-inch long strips. Discard any seeds.

Heat the peanut oil in a small saucepan. Add the garlic and ginger, stir briefly, then add the soy sauce–vinegar mixture. When it just reaches a boil, remove from heat and stir in the sesame oil; transfer to a bowl and let cool.

To serve, drain the eggplant and toss with the seasonings, sprinkle with the sesame seeds and serve.

SERVES 4 TO 6

**NOTE:** The eggplant should not sit long in the seasonings before serving.

## Garlic Tips

Buy garlic that is sold loose, by the pound, rather than in boxes. Select heads that are plump and firm; avoid those that are withered or soft.

Store garlic in a cool, dry dark place, not in the refrigerator.

Garlic may be frozen almost indefinitely, unpeeled and enclosed in an airtight container.

To peel garlic, place the cloves on a cutting surface and hit them with the flat side of a cleaver or heavy knife. The skins will separate instantly.

Add a small amount of salt to garlic while mincing or chopping. This prevents it from sticking to the knife and your hands.

# Gai Lan Dressed with Rice Wine and Oyster Sauce

*Bottled oyster sauce, found in Asian groceries, is mixed with chicken stock, rice wine, sugar and sesame oil to form the dressing for blanched Chinese broccoli. The simple dressing, created by Joyce Jue, works well with baby bok choy and regular broccoli, too.*

2 tablespoons oyster sauce

2 tablespoons chicken stock

1 tablespoon Shaoxing wine or dry sherry

½ teaspoon sugar

½ teaspoon Asian sesame oil

1 to 1½ pounds gai lan (Chinese broccoli)

1 teaspoon salt

1 tablespoon peanut oil

◉◉ Combine the oyster sauce, chicken stock, wine, sugar and sesame oil in a small saucepan. Bring to a boil and cook until the sauce thickens. Set aside.

Wash the gai lan in cold water. Trim off and discard the tough bottoms. Peel the stalks if they are thick and tough. Leave the gai lan whole or cut into thirds.

Bring 3 to 4 quarts of water to a boil in a wok or stockpot; add the salt and oil. Add the greens and bring back to a boil. Turn off the heat and let greens stay in the water for a minute or two. When the green stalks brighten, test one for doneness. It should be tender and crisp. Drain immediately and shake off the excess water.

Transfer to a platter and drizzle with the dressing.

SERVES 4 TO 6

# Braised Bitter Greens

*Traditional Pugliese cooking, says Joyce Goldstein, is both simple and delicious—and this recipe is a perfect example. Bitter greens, olive oil, garlic and chile quickly combine to produce an extremely comforting dish.*

2 to 2½ pounds assorted bitter greens (escarole, chicory, beet greens, mustard greens, collards, mizuna, broccoli rabe, endive, etc.)

Olive oil as needed

3 to 4 garlic cloves, finely minced

1 fresh very hot chile, finely minced, or 1 tablespoon red pepper flakes

2 to 3 tablespoons minced anchovies (optional)

Salt and pepper to taste

◎◎ Wash the greens well and trim off any tough stems or unsightly leaves. Cut or chop very large leaves into large bite-sized pieces.

Bring a large pot of salted water to a boil. Add the greens and cook, uncovered, for about 10 minutes, until quite soft. Drain well.

Heat a little olive oil in large sauté pan. Add the garlic, hot chile and anchovies, if using. Warm over medium heat for a few minutes. Add the drained greens, tossing them in the hot oil. Simmer gently for 5 minutes. Season with salt and pepper.

Serve at room temperature.

SERVES 4 TO 6

# Pork and Greens

*Smoky bacon, pungent horseradish and piquant red wine vinegar give spinach a lift in this Michael Bauer creation.*

2 strips bacon

¼ cup chopped white onion

1 medium garlic clove, minced

2 tablespoons red wine vinegar

½ to 1 teaspoon prepared horseradish

1 to 1½ pounds spinach, stemmed

Salt and freshly ground pepper to taste

## Low-Fat Vegetables

To cut the fat when preparing broccoli and other vegetables, flavor with gremolada instead of butter and oil.

Combine 2 tablespoons chopped fresh parsley, 4 teaspoons finely grated lemon zest and 2 minced cloves garlic. Toss with hot cooked vegetables.

&#8734; Fry the bacon in a large skillet over medium-high heat until crisp. Remove the bacon to paper towels to drain and cool, then crumble.

Add the onion and garlic to the bacon grease in the skillet and sauté about 3 minutes. Add the vinegar and horseradish and let reduce. (This may be done ahead, if desired.)

Add the spinach and toss well. Season with salt and pepper. Stir-fry until the spinach is limp and glistening. Just before serving, add more salt and pepper, if desired. Stir in the crumbled bacon.

SERVES 4

# Pugliese Peperonata

*Joyce Goldstein discovered this dish one summer during a visit to the Apulia region of Southern Italy. It's a simple but zesty mix of red and yellow bell peppers, tomatoes and onions. Serve it at room temperature as part of an antipasto; or serve it hot as a side dish with roast meats, or as a sauce for pasta.*

3 red bell peppers

3 yellow bell peppers

Olive oil, as needed

3 onions, peeled, halved and cut into ¼-inch slices

2 garlic cloves, minced

3 large tomatoes, peeled, seeded and chopped

¼ cup chopped fresh parsley

1 small fresh hot chile, minced

Salt and pepper to taste

&#8734; Wash the peppers, cut in half, remove the thick ribs and seeds and slice into ½-inch-wide strips.

Heat a little olive oil in a large sauté pan. Add onions and cook over medium heat until softened, about 5 minutes. Add peppers and sauté, stirring often, for about 10 minutes. Add garlic, tomatoes, parsley and chile and simmer for 25 minutes over very low heat. Season with salt and pepper.

SERVES 6 AS VEGETABLE OR PASTA SAUCE

**NOTE:** For a sweet and sour version, omit the chile and add a little sugar and a splash of white wine vinegar to the peppers as they are simmering.

## Onion Tip

To peel onions easily and with a minimum of tears, soak them in plenty of cold water for 20 to 30 minutes. This toughens the skin so it will pull off more easily. Also the cold inhibits the gasses that burn your eyes.

# Roast-Garlic Mashed Potatoes

*Jon Goldmark, a chef at Oliveto in Oakland, says that at first glance the garlic in this recipe may seem overpowering. However, it loses its bite when roasted and takes on a nutty, mellow taste. Any leftover puree may be added to sauces or spread on grilled or toasted bread.*

4 heads garlic, separated into unpeeled cloves

2 tablespoons olive oil

2 pounds russet potatoes, peeled

1 cup milk or heavy cream

4 tablespoons butter

Salt and pepper to taste

☙ Preheat the oven to 350 degrees.

Put the garlic cloves in a baking dish, drizzle with the olive oil and cover with foil. Bake for 20 minutes, or until the garlic is soft. Puree the garlic in a food mill; set aside.

Boil the potatoes in liberally salted water until tender, then drain. Mash with the milk or cream and butter. Stir in garlic puree to taste. Season with salt and pepper.

SERVES 4

## Roasted Garlic

You can roast a whole head of garlic, or just the cloves. In either case, do not peel the garlic. Place in a pan, brush with a little olive oil and roast in a preheated 325-degree oven for about 45 minutes, or until the flesh is soft. The papery skin will brown, but should not burn.

Some cooks wrap garlic in foil before roasting, in which case, cut off the top of the head of garlic to expose the cloves before wrapping, and add another 15 minutes to the roasting time.

# Anchovies and Potatoes in Rosemary Cream

*Georgeanne Brennan combines anchovies and rosemary to perfume a dish of humble potatoes. As the casserole bakes, the potatoes are bathed in the rich and pungent sauce.*

1 tablespoon butter

6 medium potatoes, peeled and cut into ½-inch-thick "fingers" (as for French fries)

6 anchovies packed in olive oil, cut into ½-inch pieces

1 tablespoon chopped fresh rosemary

2 large onions, peeled and thinly sliced

1½ cups heavy cream

Oil from the anchovy tin

1 teaspoon freshly ground pepper

Preheat the oven to 350 degrees. Butter a deep-dish casserole.

Arrange a layer of potatoes in the casserole, scatter a few anchovy pieces over, then sprinkle on a little rosemary. Add a layer of onions, then repeat the layering, ending with potatoes.

Mix half of the cream with all the oil from the anchovies; pour it over the potatoes.

Cover and bake for 35 minutes. Pour the remaining cream over the potatoes, sprinkle with the pepper, cover and bake 15 minutes longer, or until the potatoes are tender.

SERVES 4

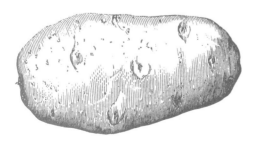

# Chard and Red Potato Gratin

*Alternating layers of chard and thinly sliced potatoes, interspersed with cheese and seasonings, resemble lasagne in construction if not in taste. Georgeanne Brennan's recipe makes a great side dish, but it can also be a glorious meatless main course. This reheats well in the microwave, so any leftovers can be enjoyed the next day.*

6 medium-sized red potatoes, about 2½ pounds

1 garlic clove, bruised

6½ tablespoons butter

1½ teaspoons salt

½ teaspoon freshly ground black pepper

18 baby chard leaves, or 9 large chard leaves with thick mid-ribs removed

½ to ⅔ cup (2 to 3 ounces) grated Swiss or Monterey Jack cheese

4 tablespoons heavy cream

◉◉ Preheat the oven to 350 degrees.

Slice the potatoes as thinly as you can; set aside.

Rub a 3-quart loaf pan with the garlic and ½ tablespoon of the butter. Put a layer of potatoes in the pan, sprinkle with one third of the salt and pepper, 1½ tablespoons of the butter and top with one-third of the chard leaves. Although the chard may seem incredibly bulky, it will wilt down during cooking. Sprinkle one third of the cheese over the chard. Repeat, making 2 more layers, ending with cheese.

Dot with the remaining 1½ tablespoons butter, pour the cream over the top, cover and bake about 1 hour and 15 minutes, or until the potatoes are thoroughly tender.

SERVES 4 TO 6

## About Green Garlic

Green garlic is harvested before the bulb has matured and before skins have formed around the cloves. It can be used like baby leeks. The flavor is mild but distinctly garlicky.

# Red-Chile Mashed Potatoes for the Blues

*Jacqueline McMahan turns to these potatoes when she "needs the fires to burn more brightly and the sun to shine at midnight." Roasted garlic and good-quality pure chile powder are the key to success, but you can play around with the amounts.*

1 head garlic

2 teaspoons olive oil

1 tablespoon dry white wine

4 russet or Yukon Gold potatoes

1 tablespoon butter

¾ cup milk (low-fat or whole)

¼ cup sour cream

2 tablespoons ground red chile (preferably New Mexico)

1 to 2 teaspoons salt

Freshly ground pepper to taste

◉◉ Preheat the oven to 350 degrees.

Place the garlic on a square of foil, drizzle with the olive oil and wine and wrap up tightly. Roast for 45 minutes, or until soft. Using the tip of a sharp paring knife, lift out each clove; set aside.

Peel the potatoes and place in a pot of boiling salted water. Cook for 30 minutes, or until very tender but not falling apart. Drain well.

Put the potatoes in a mixer fitted with the whisk attachment; break up potatoes with fork. With the mixer going, slowly add the butter, milk, sour cream, ground chile and roasted garlic to taste (from 1 tablespoon to the whole head—reserve the garlic you don't use for another dish). Add the salt and pepper and continue beating for a couple of minutes. Eat immediately.

If you are serving a friend, sprinkle the mound of rosy potatoes with ½ teaspoon ground chile and garnish with cilantro leaves.

SERVES 6

# Oven-Fried Potatoes

*These are unbelievably easy, and utterly delicious. As a variation, Georgeanne Brennan likes to roast a variety of root vegetables alongside, including sweet potatoes, rutabagas, turnips, parsnips, carrots, beets and even onions.*

  3 russet potatoes (about 1 pound)
  2 tablespoons olive oil
  ½ teaspoon salt
  ½ teaspoon freshly ground pepper

◎◎  Preheat the oven to 400 degrees.

  Peel the potatoes and cut them lengthwise into ½-inch-thick slices. Put them in a bowl and toss with the olive oil, salt and pepper. Arrange on a lightly oiled baking sheet in a single layer.

  Roast for approximately 45 minutes, turning once, until the potatoes are golden on the outside and tender inside.

  SERVES 2 OR 3

# Roasted Potatoes with Red Garlic and Fresh Herbs

*Annie Somerville, the chef at Greens, created these roasted potatoes. Unlike the recipe above, the potatoes are roasted whole and covered, which gives them a more tender, steamed texture. If red garlic isn't available, regular garlic works just fine.*

  1½ pounds small Rosefir, Yellow Finn or new potatoes
  8 to 10 unpeeled whole red garlic cloves
  2 teaspoons extra-virgin olive oil
  ¼ teaspoon salt, plus salt to taste
  Pepper to taste
  Sprigs and leaves of fresh herbs (rosemary, thyme, sage, oregano)

◎◎  Preheat the oven to 400 degrees.

## Crisp Vegetable Chips

Johnathan Robinette, formerly an instructor at the California Culinary Academy, suggests baking vegetable chips to add crunch to a plate: Spread the thinly sliced vegetables in a hot pan, sprayed with a bare mist of oil, and place in a preheated 375-degree oven. Bake just until the vegetables begin to curl and crisp.

Rinse the potatoes under cool water; pat dry. Toss them in a small baking dish with the garlic, olive oil, ¼ teaspoon salt and a few pinches of pepper. This should be just enough olive oil to coat the potatoes, and a little more. Add herbs; cover and roast for 35 to 40 minutes, until tender. Season with salt and pepper.

SERVES 4

# Parsnip and Potato Puree

*Parsnips are a vastly underrated vegetable. They have a nutty sweetness that complements a number of other vegetables. Here, Nancy Oakes, chef/owner of Boulevard, has combined them with Yukon Gold potatoes in a delectable puree. If you want a leaner dish, simply leave out the bacon and use low-fat or nonfat sour cream.*

6 parsnips, peeled and cut into 1-inch cubes

6 medium Yukon Gold potatoes, peeled and quartered

4 garlic cloves, peeled

3 heaping tablespoons sour cream

4 strips bacon, julienned, fried until crisp and drained

2 tablespoons chopped fresh parsley

Salt and pepper to taste

Blanch the parsnips in boiling salted water until fork-tender, about 10 minutes. Drain well; set aside.

Boil the potatoes and garlic in salted water until soft, about 20 minutes. Drain, leaving a tablespoon or two of cooking water in the pot. Mash potatoes or put them through a potato ricer or a food mill. Add the sour cream and blend well. Gently fold in the bacon, parsnips and parsley. Add salt and pepper (little salt will be needed).

SERVES 8

Often overlooked at the produce counter, these carrot-shaped roots have a wonderful nutty flavor. Georgeanne Brennan offers these ideas:

For oven-roasted chips, slice parsnips into thin rounds and season with salt, pepper and a little olive oil. Bake at 350 degrees until tender when pierced with a fork, about 20 minutes.

For pureed parsnips, cut into chunks, then boil until soft, about 20 minutes. Add a splash of milk or cream, along with salt and pepper. Garnish with a sprinkling of chopped mint.

# Oven-Fried Sweet Potatoes

*Thin slices of sweet potato become crispy and slightly caramelized in a hot oven, bringing out their natural sweetness. This easy preparation by Georgeanne Brennan is a great substitute for the ubiquitous casserole of candied yams that shows up regularly on the Thanksgiving table.*

12 to 15 sweet potatoes (about 5 pounds)

½ cup plus 3 or 4 tablespoons olive oil

2 tablespoons chopped fresh marjoram or thyme

1½ teaspoons salt

1½ teaspoons freshly ground black pepper

⊚⊚  Preheat the oven to 475 degrees.

Peel the sweet potatoes and cut them in half across the middle, then cut the halves lengthwise into ¼-inch-thick slices. Put the slices into a bowl and add ½ cup oil, the marjoram or thyme, salt and pepper. Toss several times to coat the slices with oil and seasonings.

Spread the slices evenly in a single layer on baking sheets. Bake for 8 to 10 minutes, then turn the slices and bake until slightly crisped and tender, 5 to 7 minutes longer.

Scoop the hot slices back into the bowl. Add the remaining 3 or 4 table-spoons oil and turn the slices until they glisten.

SERVES 10

## Making the Most of Sweet Potatoes

Here are some ideas from Georgeanne Brennan for roasting sweet potatoes: Slit open sweet potatoes and add butter, ground ginger and cayenne. Wrap in foil and bake in a preheated 400-degree oven until tender, about 1 hour.

To mash sweet potatoes: First peel and cut into chunks. Boil until soft, about 35 minutes. Drain. Add butter, salt and pepper and mash with a fork. Top with dollops of plain yogurt and a bit of chopped cilantro, if desired.

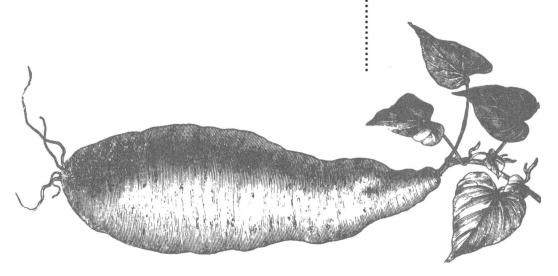

# Creamed Spinach with Bacon and Onions

*Bradley Ogden, who owns Lark Creek Inn in Larkspur and One Market in San Francisco, created this simple but delicious creamed spinach. It goes well with grilled steak, roast pork and lamb chops.*

½ cup diced bacon

½ cup minced onion

3 pounds spinach, washed, dried and stemmed

Salt and pepper to taste

1½ cups heavy cream

Freshly ground nutmeg to taste

⍟ Render the bacon in a Dutch oven over medium-low heat until crisp. Add the onion and sauté until softened. Add the spinach and cook, turning and stirring, until just wilted. Season with salt and pepper. Drain the excess liquid into a skillet. Add the cream to the juices in the skillet, bring to a boil and reduce by half. Season with nutmeg. Pour over spinach and stir to blend.

SERVES 6

# Crusty Buttered Taro

*Although taro isn't used much in Western cooking, it's a popular starch throughout Asia. Taro (a tuber) has the texture of a new potato and a nutty taste, especially when sautéed as in this recipe by Niloufer Ichaporia.*

1½ pounds small, slender taro roots

1 tablespoon butter

1 tablespoon vegetable oil

Coarse salt and freshly ground black pepper or chile powder

Lime wedges (optional)

Place the taro in a saucepan and cover with salted water. Bring to a boil, partially cover, reduce heat and simmer until the roots can be pierced easily with a knife, 12 to 15 minutes. Drain and peel while warm. When cool, cut into 1-inch chunks.

Heat the butter and oil in a nonstick or cast-iron skillet over medium-high heat. Add the taro and sauté until lightly browned and crusty. Season with salt and black pepper or chile powder.

Serve hot, with lime wedges, if desired.

SERVES 6

# Baked Cherry Tomatoes with Ricotta and Basil

*Cherry tomatoes, lightly covered with a custardy ricotta mixture, come out of the oven piping hot and plump. Created by Georgeanne Brennan.*

3 tablespoons olive oil

2 pounds cherry tomatoes (a mixture of red and yellow), stemmed

¼ cup fresh bread crumbs

1 garlic clove, peeled and minced

½ cup chopped fresh basil

¾ teaspoon salt

1 teaspoon or more freshly ground pepper

1 cup low-fat ricotta cheese

2 eggs

2 tablespoons flour

4 tablespoons heavy cream

∞ Preheat the oven to 425 degrees. Choose a shallow baking dish just large enough to hold the tomatoes snugly packed in a single layer.

Oil the bottom and sides of the dish with 2 tablespoons of the olive oil. Add the tomatoes, rolling them around to coat them with oil.

Combine the bread crumbs, garlic, 5 tablespoons of the basil, ¼ teaspoon of the salt and the pepper. Sprinkle half of the mixture over the tomatoes.

Combine the ricotta, the remaining basil and ½ teaspoon salt, the eggs, flour and cream. Pour over the tomatoes. Sprinkle with the remaining bread crumb mixture and drizzle with the remaining 1 tablespoon olive oil.

Bake for 15 minutes.

Serve hot or at room temperature.

SERVES 6 TO 8

# Scalloped Turnips, Potatoes and Celery Root

*This Georgeanne Brennan creation is lighter in taste and texture than traditional scalloped potatoes. The sharp tang of prosciutto is a good match for the delicately textured but distinctively flavored vegetables. Any leftovers reheat beautifully in the microwave.*

4 turnips (about 1½ pounds)

2 potatoes, preferably Yellow Finn (about ¾ pound)

1 large celery root (about 1 pound)

5 tablespoons butter

½ teaspoon salt

1 teaspoon freshly ground black pepper

2 tablespoons chopped fresh rosemary

4 ounces prosciutto, cut into 1-inch-wide strips

12 capers (optional)

3 cups milk

☙☙ Preheat the oven to 400 degrees.

Peel the vegetables and cut into thin slices. Butter a shallow ovenproof casserole with 1 tablespoon of the butter. Arrange a layer of turnips in the bottom of the casserole; top with a layer of potatoes. Dot with 1 tablespoon butter, season with a third of the salt, pepper and rosemary; sprinkle on half of the prosciutto and optional capers.

Add a layer of celery root, then another layer of potatoes. Dot with 1 tablespoon butter, season with half of the remaining salt, pepper and rosemary, then sprinkle on the remaining prosciutto and capers.

Top with a layer of turnips, dot with the remaining 2 tablespoons butter and season with the remaining salt, pepper and rosemary.

Slowly pour the milk over the vegetables. Put the casserole on a baking sheet (to catch any drips or boil-overs) and bake 10 minutes. Reduce oven temperature to 325 degrees and bake 50 minutes longer, or until a puffy brown crust has formed, the vegetables are tender, and about ½ inch of juices remain in the bottom of the dish.

SERVES 4 TO 6

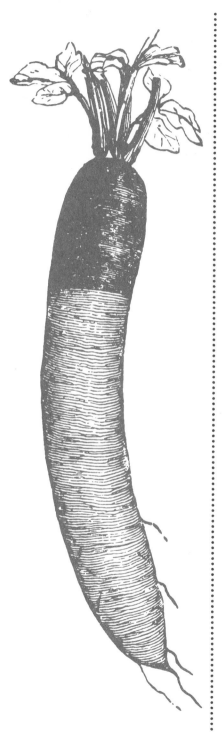

# White Lightning

*This recipe by Michael Bauer combines the contrasting flavors of three white root vegetables: The turnip adds an earthy nuance, the jicama a refreshing sweet note and the daikon (a large white radish) lends the peppery overtones. The flavors are brought together with cilantro, chiles and lime juice. The combination is particularly refreshing with grilled meats.*

2 medium turnips
½ pound daikon
½ pound jicama
2 tablespoons olive oil
Juice of 2 limes
1 red jalapeno chile, seeded and finely chopped
½ cup water, or as needed
Salt and pepper to taste
2 tablespoons finely chopped fresh cilantro

Cut the vegetables in julienne strips of equal size. Heat the olive oil in a large skillet or wok over high heat. Add the vegetables and stir to keep them moving in the pan. Squeeze in the juice of about half a lime and add the jalapeno. When the liquid evaporates, add several tablespoons water and more lime juice. Repeat the process so the vegetables are always kept slightly glistening and moist. Cook until the vegetables are just tender.

Season with salt and pepper, then add the cilantro and remaining lime juice. Mix well and serve.

SERVES 6

# Zucchini with Mint

*Quickly fried slices of young zucchini are layered with garlic, fresh mint leaves and a splash of wine vinegar in this Southern Italian recipe from Joyce Goldstein. The dish should be made at least 1 hour before serving for the flavors to develop and blend.*

1 pound young zucchini, cut into ¼-inch slices

Olive oil as needed

2 garlic cloves, cut into paper-thin slivers

12 whole fresh mint leaves

Mild white wine vinegar

∞ Place the zucchini between layers of towels and let dry for 2 hours.

Working in batches, quickly fry the zucchini in olive oil. Place the first batch in a serving dish, sprinkle with some garlic, mint and a dash of vinegar. Top with another layer of fried zucchini, then more garlic, mint and vinegar. Repeat until all ingredients have been used. Let sit at room temperature for about 1 hour, stirring from time to time, before serving.

SERVES 4

# Chapter 5

# Meats

*"This dish is even better the next day," is a phrase repeated throughout this chapter. It's a phrase that makes a harried cook jump for joy, because it also means leftovers.*

*We've gathered a flavor-packed collection of recipes that are great to cook on the weekends and then to reheat throughout the week: peppery beef daube; meatballs in chipotle sauce; lamb curry; and pork and potatoes with whole-grain mustard gravy, for example.*

*We've also collected recipes that are great for a crowd, including tamale pie and butterflied leg of lamb, which makes great sandwiches throughout the week. There's even an indulgent recipe for two: a pan-seared steak with a quick red wine sauce.*

# Theater Steak

*This is an ideal one-dish meal in which the meat, onions and mushrooms are sautéed and placed atop fried bread. The quality of the bread is very important, says Marion Cunningham. It needs to be sturdy enough to hold up to the steak juices and mushrooms.*

5 tablespoons butter

2 large onions, cut into thin rings

½ pound mushrooms, sliced

2 fillets of beef steak (8 ounces each, about 1 to 1¼ inch thick),
    cut in half horizontally

Salt and pepper to taste

4 thick slices white bread

2 bunches watercress, stemmed

∞ Melt the butter in a large skillet. When hot, add the onions and mushrooms. Cook for about 2 minutes, stirring constantly, just until soft. Remove the vegetables to a warm plate.

Increase the heat to medium-high and fry the steak quickly. Season both sides with salt and pepper and fry until the desired doneness is achieved. Remove the steak from the skillet and keep warm with the vegetables.

Quickly put the bread into the skillet and fry, turning it once, so it sops up all the pan juices.

To assemble, place a slice of fried bread on each plate. Put a quarter of the onions and mushrooms on each slice, pile some watercress on top, then top with the steak. Gently press down on the steak with a spatula so some of the warm juices drip down.

SERVES 4

## Eye Test for Doneness

For beef and lamb, the easiest way to tell doneness is to cut discreetly into a steak or chop and take a look.

A visual cue to the medium-rare stage is when droplets of blood appear on the upper surface.

Pork is both leaner and less prone to trichinosis today than in the old days, so it need not be cooked as long. A pork chop cooked just to the medium stage, with a bare hint of pinkness, will be juicier than one cooked well done.

## Touch Test for Doneness

Once you have a steak or chop cooked to your liking, press down on the top with your fingertip and get to know that feel (soft and yielding when very rare, slightly springy for medium rare, firm for medium); next time you can use it as a test while the meat is cooking.

# Bistro-Style Steak with Sauce Marchand

*You can't beat the classics, as shown in this Georgeanne Brennan recipe. Ready in minutes, the seasoned steaks are fried, then the pan juices are enhanced with red wine and reduced for a quick sauce. Great served with oven-fried potatoes.*

2 rib steaks, ½ to ¾ inch thick

½ teaspoon salt

1 teaspoon freshly ground black pepper

2 teaspoons finely chopped fresh thyme

2 tablespoons butter

4 tablespoons minced shallots

⅓ to ½ cup dry red wine

⊚ Trim the steaks of external fat. Pat them dry and sprinkle with the salt, pepper and thyme, pressing the seasonings into both sides.

Heat a heavy nonstick skillet over medium-high heat. Add 1 teaspoon of the butter. When it has melted and is near sizzling, put the steaks in the pan, searing them for 3 to 4 minutes on each side, depending upon thickness of the steaks and how you like them cooked. Keep the heat high, but don't let the butter burn. Test for doneness by cutting into a steak. When done, remove to a warm platter and cover loosely with foil while you prepare the sauce.

Pour off all but 1 tablespoon of the pan juices. Return the skillet to the heat and add the shallots; sauté until they are translucent. Add the wine and deglaze the pan, scraping up any bits clinging to it. Reduce the wine by half (it will thicken), then stir in the remaining butter. Pour the hot sauce over the steaks.

SERVES 2

# Sumatran Red Short Ribs of Beef

*This Southeast Asian stew from Copeland Marks is a brilliant blend of contrasting flavors: fiery chiles, tart lemon, rich beef and aromatic spices. Serve with rice pilaf, studded with tiny currants and tinged with ground turmeric.*

4 shallots, sliced

3 garlic cloves, sliced

1-inch piece fresh ginger, sliced

4 or 5 fresh hot red chiles, seeded and sliced

2 teaspoons ground coriander

⅛ teaspoon ground turmeric

1 teaspoon salt, or to taste

2 cups water

2 pounds lean short ribs of beef, cut into 3-inch pieces (see Note)

2 tablespoons corn oil

2 kari leaves

2 slices galangal

1 stalk lemongrass, tender bulb end only

1 or 2 lemon slices

⚱ Process the shallots, garlic, ginger, chiles, coriander, turmeric, salt and ½ cup of the water to a smooth sauce. Pour over the meat and let marinate for ½ hour. Heat the oil in a wok or Dutch oven. Add the beef and its marinade, the kari leaves, galangal, lemongrass and lemon slices. Stir-fry over medium heat for 5 minutes. Add the remaining 1½ cups water, cover, reduce heat and simmer until the meat is tender, 1 to 2 hours, depending on the cut of meat used. If the sauce evaporates too quickly, add another ½ cup water. Remove the galangal, lemongrass and lemon slices before serving.

SERVES 4

**NOTE:** Beef chuck, fresh brisket or rump roast also work well.

# Sunday Roast and Winter Roots

*A 2-inch-thick bone-in chuck roast (sometimes called a seven-bone roast) is the best cut to use in Georgeanne Brennan's recipe. This cut has a marvelous beefy flavor, plus it fits nicely into a shallow roasting pan with room for all the vegetables.*

1 beef chuck roast with bone, about 4½ to 5 pounds

1 teaspoon salt

1 tablespoon freshly ground black pepper

2 garlic cloves, bruised

1 tablespoon chopped fresh rosemary

1 tablespoon chopped fresh thyme

4 large onions

4 large carrots

3 turnips

2 rutabagas

4 large potatoes (any kind)

Rosemary and thyme sprigs for garnish

⊚ Preheat the oven to 325 degrees.

Rub the roast with half of the salt and pepper, the garlic, and half of the rosemary and thyme. Place in a roasting pan large enough to hold the meat and all the vegetables. Roast, uncovered, for 1½ hours.

While the meat is roasting, peel the onions but do not cut them through the root ends. Peel the carrots and cut them into 3-inch lengths. Peel the turnips, rutabagas and potatoes and cut them lengthwise into quarters.

When the meat has cooked for 1½ hours, tuck the vegetables around the roast, turning them in the pan juices. Sprinkle them with the remaining salt, pepper and herbs and return to the oven. Roast for another 1½ hours, turning the vegetables from time to time. The meat is done when it separates easily with a fork. The vegetables are done when they are easily pierced with the tines of a fork.

Cut the roast into ⅓- to ½-inch-thick slices and arrange on a warmed platter. Surround with the vegetables and drizzle with some of the pan juices. Garnish with sprigs of thyme and rosemary.

SERVES 6 TO 8

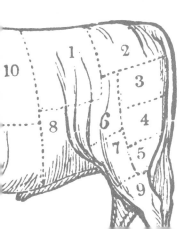

# California Fajitas

*Grilling gives soy, lime and tequila-marinated flank steak a smoky quality, and adds an extra dimension to these fajitas by Jacqueline McMahan.*

2 tablespoons soy sauce

¼ cup fresh lime juice

¼ cup tequila or beer

2 tablespoons olive oil

2 garlic cloves, pressed

½ teaspoon powdered garlic

½ teaspoon pepper

½ teaspoon salt

2 pounds flank steak

4 Anaheim chiles

12 flour tortillas, heated

Salsa of choice

◉◉ Combine the soy sauce, lime juice, tequila or beer, olive oil, garlic and spices. Cut 4 shallow slashes across the grain on each side of the flank steak. Place the steak in a glass dish and pour the marinade over it, rubbing the garlic into the slashes. Marinate at least 2 hours. If you refrigerate the meat, return to room temperature at least 1 hour before you barbecue it.

Light the coals at least 45 minutes before you plan to barbecue. When the coals are covered with white ash, they're ready to use.

Place the steak on the hot grill. Barbecue about 6 minutes per side for rare; 8 minutes for medium; 10 to 12 minutes for well-done. Exact timing will depend upon the thickness of the steak.

While the steak is cooking, place the chiles along the perimeter of the grill. Keep turning until they are charred. Remove and let cool.

When steak is done, place it on a cutting board and cut across the grain into thin slices.

Remove most of the charred skin, stems and seeds from the chiles. Slice into strips and toss with the meat.

Serve with hot flour tortillas and salsa.

SERVES 6

## Making Herb Butters

Herb butters make quick and easy sauces for steaks and chops. They can be made ahead, and store well in the refrigerator, or for a longer time in the freezer.

Basic Herb Butter: Work ¼ cup chopped fresh herbs (Italian parsley, chives, tarragon, basil or chervil, or a compatible combination) into ½ cup (1 stick) softened butter. Scrape onto a piece of waxed paper and form into a log. Wrap well, then refrigerate or freeze.

To use, simply slice off rounds and place on piping hot steaks or chops; the butter will slowly melt, blending in with the meat juices. (These butters are also delicious tossed with plain steamed vegetables, or slathered with abandon on freshly cooked ears of corn.)

# Peppery Beef Daube with Shiitake Mushrooms

*Loads of pepper, balanced by orange peel, is the secret to this rich beef stew created by Georgeanne Brennan. It's great for company because it's best done ahead. If possible, marinate the meat in wine and herbs the first day, simmer it the next day, and serve on the third day. Accompany with freshly cooked pasta, such as small shells or orecchiette, which will capture the rich sauce. The daube is also good spooned over soft polenta.*

4 pounds boneless beef chuck roast, or a combination of boneless chuck
    and beef shank

2 onions

3 carrots, cut in chunks

8 thyme sprigs

2 bay leaves

1 rosemary sprig

2 teaspoons salt

1 to 2 tablespoons freshly ground pepper

4 garlic cloves

A 4 x ½-inch strip orange peel

1 bottle (750 ml) dry red wine, such as Zinfandel or Cabernet Sauvignon

⅓ cup minced salt pork

Vegetable oil as needed

2 tablespoons flour

1 cup water

2 ounces dried shiitake mushrooms, some broken into 2 or 3 pieces,
    other left whole, rinsed

Cut the chuck into 2- to 2½-inch cubes. Trim off any large pieces of fat. If using shanks, cut the meat from the bone in pieces as large as possible. Place the meat in a large bowl.

Quarter 1 of the onions and add to the meat along with the carrots, thyme, bay leaves, rosemary, half of the salt and half of the pepper, 2 garlic cloves and the orange peel. Pour the wine over all and turn to mix and immerse the ingredients. Cover and let marinate in the refrigerator overnight, or at least 4 hours.

To cook, put the salt pork in a heavy-bottomed casserole large enough to hold all ingredients. Cook over medium-low heat until the pork releases its fat, about 5 minutes. Discard the crisped bits of pork.

Dice the remaining onion and mince the remaining garlic cloves. Add to the pot and sauté until translucent. (If there is not enough fat from the salt pork, add a little vegetable oil.) Remove the onion and garlic with a slotted spoon and set aside.

Drain the meat (reserve the marinade) and pat it as dry as possible. Add a few pieces of meat to the casserole (do not crowd) and sauté about 5 minutes, turning once or twice. The meat will darken, but will not truly brown. Remove the meat with a slotted spoon and set aside. Continue until all the meat has been sautéed.

Add the flour to the casserole and cook it until it browns, stirring often. Increase the heat to high and slowly pour in the reserved marinade. Deglaze the pan, scraping up any bits clinging to the bottom. Return the onions, garlic, meat and its juices to the pan. Add the remaining salt and pepper, the water and the mushrooms and bring to a near-boil. Reduce heat to very low, cover with a tight-fitting lid and simmer for 2½ to 3 hours, or until the meat can be cut with a spoon and the liquid has thickened. Remove from the heat. Discard the carrots, herb branches and the onion quarters. Skim off the fat.

Serve the daube directly from its casserole.

SERVES 6 TO 8

# Meatballs in Chipotle Sauce

*This is Jacqueline McMahan's easy, lower-fat variation on meatballs. Instead of frying the meatballs in oil, she bakes them until browned. Serve with mounds of steaming rice or mashed potatoes to help sop up the sauce, which gets a kick from smoked jalapenos (called chipotles). This dish is even better reheated.*

**Sauce**

½ onion, chopped

1 tablespoon olive oil

A Basic Red Meat Sauce

Here's a quick sauce from Hubert Keller, chef at Fleur de Lys:

Sauté the meat in a heavy pan with a little oil. Do not use a nonstick pan because you want the crusty bits that will form on the bottom. When the meat is done to your liking, remove it and keep warm. Pour out the fat in the skillet. Add thinly sliced onions and shallots and sauté over medium heat until brown. Pour in 2 tablespoons red wine or a shot of Cognac, brandy or other spirit. Let bubble for 30 seconds; add a tablespoon or two of broth or water, a dash of mustard, basil, chives or chopped tomatoes. Spoon over the meat.

1 garlic clove, minced

1 (28-ounce) can crushed tomatoes with added puree

1½ cups light chicken broth

2 canned chipotle chiles en adobo, seeded and minced (see Note)

**Meatballs**

1 slice bread, crust removed

½ cup low-fat milk

1 pound ground round

1 pound ground turkey or pork

4 green onions, minced

¼ cup minced white onion

¼ cup minced fresh parsley

1 egg

1 teaspoon salt

1 teaspoon dried oregano

½ teaspoon pepper

¼ teaspoon ground nutmeg

¼ teaspoon ground cinnamon

To make the sauce: Sauté the onion in the oil until softened, then add the garlic, tomatoes, broth and chiles. Simmer for 20 minutes. Set aside.

Preheat the oven to 400 degrees.

To make the meatballs: Soak the bread in milk for a minute, then squeeze dry. Crumble the bread over the ground meats. Add the remaining ingredients, sprinkling the spices over all. Blend with a large spoon, or use your hands. Form into golf ball–sized rounds.

Place the meatballs in a roasting pan and bake for 25 minutes, or until lightly browned. Transfer the meatballs to the sauce and simmer at least 15 minutes.

Serve immediately, or let cool, then refrigerate. They reheat beautifully.

SERVES 6

**NOTE:** Chipotles en adobo, or en vinagre, are pickled in vinegar, tomato juice, onion and spices. They may be found in the ethnic or Latino section of some large supermarkets or in small Mexican grocery stores. Once the can has been opened, store unused chiles in a glass jar in the refrigerator. They'll keep for 2 to 3 months.

# Mogul Beef Kheema Curry (Makkai Kheema)

*This hearty one-pot meal originated in the royal kitchens of India. Laxmi Hiremath has given the dish a decidedly Western touch by adding fresh corn kernels to the traditional mix of ground meat, onions, garlic, tomatoes, spices and yogurt.*

*Don't be alarmed by the long list of ingredients; all you do is combine and cook. The whole spices are not meant to be eaten and may be removed before serving. This keeps well in the refrigerator for 5 or 6 days, getting better each time it is reheated.*

2 tablespoons mild vegetable oil

½ teaspoon cumin seeds

½-inch cinnamon stick

4 whole cloves

3 green cardamom pods

1 cup chopped onion

2 garlic cloves, peeled and crushed

½-inch piece fresh ginger, crushed

¼ teaspoon ground turmeric

1 pound lean ground beef

1 cup chopped peeled tomato

½ teaspoon ground cumin

½ teaspoon ground coriander

½ teaspoon cayenne pepper

1 teaspoon paprika

½ teaspoon salt, or to taste

1 cup water

1 cup unflavored yogurt

8 almonds, blanched and ground to a paste with 2 tablespoons water

1 teaspoon garam masala, optional (see Note)

½ cup fresh corn kernels, blanched 1 minute in boiling water

3 tablespoons chopped fresh cilantro

## Easy Vegetable Sauces

Pureed cooked vegetables, such as fava beans or peas, thinned with lemon or lime juice and seasoned with fresh herbs, make a wonderful quick topping for grilled fish or meats.

Use your juicer to make juice, which can be heated, seasoned with herbs and poured over the meats. Cabbage and celery are great with shrimp; carrot and tarragon give a lift to pork; and beet juice can perk up grilled steak.

⊚⊚ Heat the oil in a heavy skillet over medium-high heat. Add the cumin, cinnamon, cloves and cardamom; stir until fragrant, about 1 minute. Add the onion, garlic, ginger and turmeric and cook, stirring, until the onion is lightly browned, about 4 minutes.

Add the beef and cook, breaking up the meat with a fork, until it is no longer pink, about 4 minutes.

Add the tomato, cumin, coriander, cayenne, paprika and salt; cook, stirring, for 2 minutes. Add the water, yogurt and almond paste; bring to a boil, stirring occasionally. Reduce heat, cover, and simmer until the mixture thickens and the flavors mellow, about 45 minutes. Skim off the fat.

Stir in the optional garam masala, corn and cilantro.

SERVES 4

**NOTE:** A spice blend available at Indian grocery stores and some specialty food stores.

# Tamale Pie

*Marion Cunningham, the modern-day Fannie Farmer, makes this impressive one-dish casserole when she entertains. The seasoned sausage and beef, flavored with onions, corn, celery, cumin, tomatoes and canned green chiles, cook and bubble in a thick cornmeal crust.*

6 cups water

1½ cups yellow cornmeal

3 teaspoons salt

¼ to ½ cup butter or lard

½ pound bulk sausage

2 tablespoons chili powder

¾ teaspoon ground cumin

1 garlic clove, minced

1 to 1½ cups finely chopped onions

1 small green bell pepper, seeded, deribbed and chopped

1 cup finely chopped celery

1½ pounds ground beef

3 cups canned Italian tomatoes (or 4 cups peeled and seeded fresh tomatoes)

2 cups fresh, frozen or canned corn kernels

4 ounces canned diced mild green chiles

1 teaspoon minced jalapeno chile (optional)

1 cup pitted ripe olives

2 cups grated medium or sharp cheddar cheese

◎◎ Bring 4 cups of the water to a boil in a 3-quart kettle. Stir the cornmeal into the remaining 2 cups (cold) water (this helps prevent lumping), then stir this into the boiling water. Continue to stir while the water returns to a boil. Reduce the heat to low, add 1½ teaspoons of the salt and the butter or lard, cover and simmer for 30 to 40 minutes, stirring often.

Mash the sausage in a large frying pan, and cook over medium heat until it begins to turn color. Add the chili powder and cumin, and cook about 5 minutes, stirring. Add the garlic, onions, green pepper, celery and the remaining 1½ teaspoons salt. Stir and cook until the vegetables are limp.

Crumble the beef into the pan and mash and cook until it loses its raw color. Add the tomatoes, corn and chiles. Simmer for 15 to 20 minutes.

Preheat the oven to 350 degrees.

Grease a 10 x 14 x 2–inch baking pan. Spread two thirds of the cornmeal mixture on the bottom and up the sides of the pan. Spoon in the filling and distribute the olives evenly over it. Top with the remaining cornmeal, then sprinkle with the cheese. Bake about 1 hour.

SERVES 6

# Hispanic American Meat Loaf

*Salsa, ground chile and cumin lend south-of-the border interest to a homey American dish by Jacqueline McMahan. Serve with mashed or baked potatoes and a green vegetable or salad. Leftovers make great sandwiches too.*

½ cup minced celery (including some minced leaves)

¾ cup minced yellow onion

¾ cup minced green onion

½ cup minced carrot

¼ cup minced green bell pepper

½ cup minced red bell pepper

2 teaspoons minced garlic

¾ cup minced fresh parsley

2 tablespoons olive or canola oil

1 teaspoon salt

½ teaspoon pepper

2 teaspoons ground New Mexico chile

1½ teaspoons ground cumin

½ teaspoon ground nutmeg

¾ cup fresh salsa, or good quality store-bought salsa

2 eggs

1 pound leanest ground beef

1 pound ground turkey

¾ cup dried bread crumbs

◎ Preheat the oven to 350 degrees. Line a small roasting pan with foil and lightly grease the foil.

Sprinkle a layer of salt on a wood cutting board to clean it and draw out moisture. Let sit for at least 15 minutes before wiping off.

Sauté the celery, onions, carrot, peppers, garlic and parsley in the oil until softened but not browned. Spoon into a large bowl and sprinkle with the spices. Add the salsa and eggs and blend well. Add the ground meats and crumbs. Mix well. Form into a rounded loaf, making it more flat than high. Place in the roasting pan.

Bake for 50 to 55 minutes. Let stand 10 minutes before slicing.

SERVES 6

# Home-Cured Corned Beef

*Merle Ellis, a columnist for* The Chronicle *for more than 25 years, created this mild-flavored corned beef. For this, you'll need a large earthenware, enamel or stainless-steel crock.*

3 cups salt

7 quarts water

1 brisket of beef (6 to 9 pounds)

3 garlic cloves, peeled

20 peppercorns

20 whole cloves

1 bay leaf

6 sprigs fresh thyme, or 1 teaspoon dried thyme

◍ Dissolve the salt in the water in a large earthenware, enamel or stainless-steel crock. The concentration should be about 10 percent salt (this will float a raw egg in the shell). Add the brisket to the salt brine. Add the garlic, peppercorns, cloves, bay leaf and thyme. Place a clean, heavy weight on the meat to keep it submerged. Cover the crock with the lid or with foil and refrigerate for 12 days, turning the meat every other day.

Remove the meat from the brine and rinse it in fresh water. The corned beef is now ready for cooking.

To cook: Place the meat in a large kettle. Cover with cold water and bring to a boil, reduce heat and simmer for 2 to 2½ hours. Transfer to a cutting board and slice thinly. Arrange the slices on a heated platter or serving plates. Serve with accompaniments of choice.

SERVES 8 TO 12

## Choosing the Cooking Wine

Choosing the right wine for the right sauce or poaching liquid shouldn't be intimidating. Think "weight" and match the wine to the amount of flavor in the main ingredient. Here are some ideas:

**Chenin Blanc or Sauvignon Blanc:** Light white fish, including sole and snapper.

**Chardonnay:** Meatier fish, such as shark or halibut. Try not to use one that has too much oak.

**Pinot Noir:** Braises, such as coq au vin, pork stews, pork tenderloin. Salmon and tuna also take well to this peppery red wine.

**Cabernet Sauvignon:** It's a perfect choice for lamb, beef and heavier meats, simply prepared.

**Zinfandel:** Though the style varies, the ripe berry flavor is wonderful with venison, squab and lamb.

**Champagne and sparkling wines:** Chicken, veal and lighter fish.

# Roast Leg of Lamb with Mustard Skin

*There are many versions of mustard-crusted lamb. Georgeanne Brennan tried several before coming up with this easy rendition, which is better than the more complex ones.*

1 leg of lamb (5 to 5½ pounds)
6 garlic cloves, peeled and cut into slivers
1 teaspoon salt
1 tablespoon freshly ground black pepper
¾ cup Dijon mustard
2 tablespoons dry red wine
2 tablespoons finely chopped fresh mint
½ cup dry white or red wine

◎◎  Preheat the oven to 350 degrees.

Using the tip of a sharp knife, make slits all over the leg of lamb. Insert garlic slivers into the slits. Rub the lamb with the salt and half of the pepper. Combine the remaining pepper, the mustard, red wine and mint to make a paste; spread all over the lamb.

Place the lamb on a rack in a roasting pan and roast, uncovered, about 1½ hours, or until a meat thermometer stuck in thickest part of the leg (do not let it touch bone) registers 145 degrees (medium rare).

Let the meat stand, on its rack and lightly covered with aluminum foil, for 10 to 15 minutes before carving.

Meanwhile, heat the juices in the roasting pan to boiling. Add the white wine and cook over high heat until reduced by half, stirring constantly.

Slice the lamb and serve with spoonfuls of the sauce.

SERVES 6

# Butterflied Leg of Lamb on the Grill

*Jane Benet, who was our food editor for more than 30 years, created this simple recipe. The lamb marinates for 5 days in a garlic, lemon and vermouth mixture before being grilled.*

1 leg of lamb, about 5 pounds

1 cup dry vermouth

3 garlic cloves, peeled

1 medium onion, peeled

½ lemon, with peel, seeds removed

1 sprig fresh rosemary

Salt and pepper to taste

Bone and butterfly the lamb (or have the butcher do it for you) and place it in a shallow pan. Pour the vermouth over the meat.

With the metal blade in place in a food processor and the motor running, drop in the garlic and process until finely chopped. Add the onion, lemon and leaves of rosemary and process with on/off pulses to a coarse puree; add to the lamb. Transfer to a large self-sealing plastic bag and refrigerate up to 5 days, turning every day.

Remove the lamb from the marinade. Season with salt and pepper.

Grill over hot coals (best in covered grill) about 20 minutes per side, or until done as you like it.

SERVES 6 TO 8

**OVEN-ROASTING METHOD:** Place the lamb in a roasting pan and roast in a 450-degree oven for 45 minutes, or until done as you like it.

# Narsai David's Assyrian Rack of Lamb

*Narsai David, a longtime* Chronicle *columnist, chef and television and radio personality created this juicy rack of lamb, marinated in pomegranate juice and red wine.*

1 large onion

2 or 3 garlic cloves

1 teaspoon dried basil

½ cup pomegranate juice

¼ cup dry red wine

½ teaspoon salt

½ teaspoon pepper

2 racks of lamb, each with 8 or 9 ribs

Puree everything but the lamb in a blender. Rub some of the mixture into the lamb; place the meat in a shallow glass pan and pour the remaining mixture over it. Cover and refrigerate overnight.

Bring the meat to room temperature. Preheat the oven to 450 degrees.

Wipe off the excess marinade. Place the racks in a roasting pan and roast for 15 to 20 minutes for medium rare.

SERVES 6

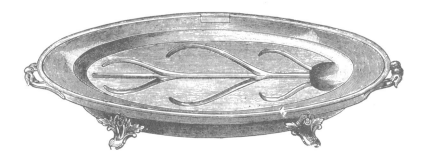

# Kashmir Lamb Curry
# (Kashmiri Gosht)

*Kashmir's cuisine combines the area's plentiful fruits and nuts with the rich ingredients and sophisticated cooking style of the Moguls. This adaptation by Laxmi Hiremath makes a marvelous main dish. Serve with rice or crusty breads.*

2 pounds boneless lamb, trimmed of all fat

¼ cup cashew nuts

3 tablespoons mild vegetable oil

2-inch cinnamon stick, broken

4 whole cloves

4 cardamom pods

1 teaspoon cumin seeds

1 large onion, chopped

1 tablespoon minced fresh ginger

3 garlic cloves, peeled and crushed

½ teaspoon ground coriander

¼ teaspoon ground turmeric

1 teaspoon paprika

½ teaspoon cayenne pepper

1 teaspoon salt, or to taste

2 medium tomatoes, peeled, seeded and chopped

3 medium boiling potatoes, peeled and diced

1 cup water

2 cups unflavored yogurt

¼ cup heavy cream

½ cup fresh peas, or frozen, thawed

Snipped fresh chives or green onion tops

⊚⊚ Cut the meat into 1-inch cubes; set aside.

Grind the cashews with a little water to make a paste. Set aside.

Heat the oil in a large, heavy skillet over medium-high heat. Add the cinnamon, cloves, cardamom and cumin seeds. Cook, stirring, until fragrant, about 1 minute. Add the onion, ginger and garlic. Stir and cook until the onion is soft, about 3 minutes. Add the coriander, turmeric, paprika, cayenne and salt. Stir for a minute. Add the lamb and stir-fry until it is no longer red. Add the tomatoes and potatoes. Cook, stirring constantly, for 5 minutes. Add ½ cup of the water.

Blend together the yogurt, cashew paste and remaining ½ cup water and add to the skillet. Reduce the heat, cover, and simmer 30 to 45 minutes, or until the meat is tender. Skim off the fat.

(May be prepared 1 day ahead to this point. Cool, cover and refrigerate. Warm over medium heat before continuing.)

Add the cream and peas and heat through. The sauce should be thick, but if it is too thick, add a few tablespoons water. If too thin, boil to reduce.

Serve in deep plates or soup bowls, garnished with chives or green onions.
SERVES 4

# Wine-Braised Lamb Shanks

*San Francisco has a passion for lamb shanks. They seem to be on every restaurant menu, and variations are continually showing up in* The Chronicle's *Food Section. This one, by Dan Bowe, is one of our favorites. Serve the shanks on a bed of soft polenta.*

6 large lamb shanks, about 1 pound each

8 small garlic cloves, peeled and each cut into 3 long slivers

**Marinade**

3 lemons, juiced (reserve the rind of 2 of the lemons)

4 cups dry vermouth or dry white wine

½ cup diced onion

2 teaspoons dried marjoram

**Braising Liquid**

1 cup Madeira

2 cups dry white wine

4 cups rich chicken stock

2 tablespoons balsamic vinegar

3 garlic cloves

2 bay leaves

2 teaspoons crushed fresh thyme

1 teaspoon minced fresh marjoram, or ½ teaspoon dried marjoram

4 to 5 tablespoons olive oil

1 cup diced onion

½ cup diced peeled carrots

1 tablespoon salt

2 teaspoons ground pepper

4 ounces fresh mushrooms (any variety), cleaned, sliced if large, left whole if small

**Gremolada**

2 tablespoons minced garlic

2 tablespoons minced lemon zest

1 tablespoon minced tangerine or orange zest

2 tablespoons finely chopped fresh parsley

## The Art of Braising

Braising is a combination of sautéing and poaching, used primarily for the less expensive, tougher cuts of meat.

First dust the meat (lamb shank, chuck roast, pork shoulder) lightly with flour and brown in a heavy Dutch oven or deep skillet.

Add liquid (water, wine, juice or stock) about halfway up the pot. Cover and simmer on top of the stove, or in a preheated 350-degree oven, which takes about 20 percent longer but cooks more evenly. Turn several times during the process, adding more liquid if necessary. Cooking times will vary, but braising is very forgiving ; longer cooking generally makes tougher cuts more and more tender, although when cooked too long, the flavor will diminish and leach into the liquid.

❦ Hold each shank by the bone end and, using a sharp thin knife, pierce the meat in 4 places almost parallel to the bone, down toward the wide meaty part. Insert the garlic slivers into the holes. Combine the marinade ingredients in a nonaluminum container that will accommodate the shanks in one layer. Add the shanks, being sure the marinade covers them. Cover and refrigerate overnight, or up to 1 day, turning once.

Combine the braising ingredients. Cover and refrigerate overnight.

Preheat the oven to 300 degrees.

Remove the shanks from the marinade and let dry for 5 to 10 minutes. Heat a large skillet over medium-high heat; add the olive oil. Toss in the onion and carrot and briefly sauté; remove and set aside.

Reheat the pan. Season the shanks with the salt and pepper. Add more oil to the pan, if needed. Just before the oil smokes, add the shanks—only as many as will fit comfortably in the pan. Brown quickly but well on each side, about 4 to 5 minutes. Transfer the shanks and the sautéed vegetables to a baking pan that will hold them in 1 layer. Add the braising liquid to almost cover. Cover the shanks with a piece of foil, pressing it around the shanks so there is little extra air space in the pan.

Roast the shanks for 45 minutes. Reduce the oven temperature to 200 degrees and roast 30 minutes longer. Turn the oven off and let shanks stay in the oven for 20 to 30 minutes.

Remove 4 cups of the braising liquid; skim off the fat. Put the liquid in a saucepan and bring to a high simmer. Add the mushrooms and simmer for 5 minutes.

Combine the gremolada ingredients.

To serve, arrange the shanks on serving plates and spoon the sauce over them. Top each shank with a spoonful of gremolada.

SERVES 6

# Zuni Stew with Kale, Hominy and Lamb

*Marlena Spieler was inspired by Native American cuisine when she created this rich, spicy stew, which combines the rustic flavors of kale, hominy and lamb. Serve with warm corn tortillas, or country-style bread. Like most stews, this is best made a day or two ahead.*

1 onion, chopped

4 or 5 garlic cloves, coarsely chopped

1 to 2 tablespoons vegetable oil

1 teaspoon dried oregano

1 to 1½ teaspoons ground cumin or cumin seed

1 pound lamb shoulder, or other lamb stew meat, cut into cubes

Flour for dredging

2 green bell peppers or Anaheim chiles, roasted, peeled, seeded and cut into strips

1 or 2 green jalapeno chiles, seeded and cut into strips

4 cups broth (beef, chicken or vegetable)

1 head kale, trimmed of tough stems

2½ cups drained canned hominy (preferably white)

2 tablespoons ground chile (or to taste), or ½ cup red chile or enchilada sauce
    (canned OK)

¼ cup chopped fresh cilantro

Salt and black or cayenne pepper to taste

Lightly sauté the onion and garlic in the oil until the onion is softened, about 10 minutes. Add the oregano and cumin.

Dust the meat with flour, then add it to the onion and sauté a few minutes until the meat is lightly browned. Add the pepper and chile strips and broth. Bring to a boil, cover, reduce heat and simmer for 1½ to 2 hours, or until the meat is very tender.

Meanwhile, blanch the kale in a large pot of boiling water; rinse and squeeze dry. Cut into bite-sized pieces. Add to the stew, along with the hominy and ground chile powder or chile/enchilada sauce. Simmer 30 minutes or so.

Stir in the cilantro, season with salt and pepper and extra chile powder or sauce if needed.

SERVES 4

# Mixed Greens with Lamb and Rice

*Paula Wolfert, inspired by a trip to her neighborhood produce market and by her love of Mediterranean foods, devised this satisfying one-pot meal.*

1 pound mixed spring greens (young mustard greens, spinach, miner's lettuce, arugula), stemmed

Salt

½ cup water

1 tablespoon olive oil

½ cup chopped onion

⅓ pound lean ground lamb

½ tablespoon tomato paste

¼ teaspoon pepper

¼ teaspoon ground allspice

2 tablespoons medium- or long-grain rice

Wash the greens well, then place in a pot with ½ cup lightly salted water. Cover and cook over medium-high heat until the greens are wilted, about 5 minutes. Drain, reserving 1 cup of the cooking water (if necessary, add water to make 1 cup). When the greens are cool enough to handle, squeeze dry and roughly chop.

Heat the oil in a large, heavy skillet over medium heat. Add the onion and sauté until soft, about 2 minutes. Add the lamb and cook, breaking up the meat with a fork, until lightly browned, about 3 minutes. Add the tomato paste, pepper, the allspice and salt to taste. Cook 2 to 3 minutes.

Stir in the chopped greens, reserved cooking water and the rice. Reduce heat to low, cover, and simmer until the liquid is absorbed and the rice is cooked, about 17 minutes. Taste and adjust seasoning. Serve warm.

SERVES 2 OR 3

# Florentine-Style Pork Loin with Rosemary and Garlic

*Joyce Goldstein, owner of the now closed Square One restaurant and an expert on Italian cuisine, prepares pork loin flavored with a generous amount of garlic, rosemary and black pepper. She then makes a light sauce from the bones and pan drippings.*

3½- to 4-pound pork loin roast, with bone

4 to 6 garlic cloves, peeled and cut into slivers

4 tablespoons fresh rosemary leaves

Salt and freshly ground black pepper to taste

2 to 3 cups chicken stock

4 tablespoons fresh lemon juice

½ teaspoon ground cloves

◉◉ Preheat the oven to 450 degrees.

Using a small, sharp knife, poke slits between the rib bones in the roast. Insert garlic slivers and some of the rosemary leaves into the slits; sprinkle a few rosemary leaves on top of the roast as well. Put the pork in a roasting pan, sprinkle with salt and pepper and roast for 45 to 50 minutes, or until the meat reaches an internal temperature of 140 degrees. Let the roast rest for 15 minutes, or until you can handle it comfortably, then cut the meat in one piece from the bones. Keep the roast covered and warm. Chop up the bones.

Skim the fat from the juices in the roasting pan. Add the bones and chicken stock to the pan and simmer over low heat for 20 minutes. Strain and add the lemon juice, cloves and remaining rosemary, chopped fine. Simmer about 5 minutes longer to meld the flavors. If you like, add a bit more finely minced garlic to the sauce. Adjust seasoning.

Warm the pork roast in the oven for a few minutes, if necessary, then slice it and spoon the hot sauce over the meat. (Or, you may preslice the meat, heat the sauce in a large pan and warm the slices very gently in the sauce for about 1 minute. Do not boil or the meat will toughen.)

SERVES 6

## Room-Temperature Meat

Allow meat to come to room temperature before grilling or roasting. Cold meat cooks unevenly.

# Chile-Orange Pork Brochettes

*In this simple recipe by Georgeanne Brennan, chunks of pork are marinated overnight in an orange-flavored mixture seasoned with dried chiles and fresh herbs. Just before serving, the pork is threaded onto skewers, along with pieces of poblano chiles, and quickly grilled or broiled. Diners construct their own meals by wrapping the pork and chiles in warm tortillas and adding garnishes of choice. Or, omit the accompaniments and serve the brochettes over steaming mounds of arroz verde.*

## Great Combinations

Cindy Pawlcyn, chef and co-owner of Fog City Diner, Mustards Grill and Bistro Roti, among others, recommends these combinations:

Angostura bitters bring out the best in beets.

Ginger is a natural with carrots.

Ginger and red chiles make a great combination playing off the sweet/hot theme.

Grapes and almonds are a natural duo.

2 large dried red chiles (New Mexico or California), seeded

¼ cup vegetable oil

1 teaspoon salt

1 teaspoon freshly ground pepper

3 tablespoons chopped fresh thyme

2 tablespoons chopped fresh rosemary

4 tablespoons orange marmalade

4 tablespoons red wine vinegar

1½ pounds boneless pork, trimmed of fat and cut into 1-inch pieces

4 poblano chiles, seeded, deribbed and cut into 1-inch pieces

### Accompaniments

1 tablespoon butter

2 tablespoons vegetable oil

2 sweet potatoes, peeled and cut into ½-inch cubes

2 plantains

Juice of 1 lemon, about 2 tablespoons

Warm corn tortillas

1 cup finely chopped fresh cilantro

½ cup Mexican crema or sour cream

◎ Tear or crumble the dried chiles into a glass or ceramic bowl; stir in the oil, salt, pepper, thyme, rosemary, marmalade and vinegar. Add the pork cubes and turn to coat. Refrigerate for 24 hours, turning from time to time.

Thread the pork and chile pieces onto skewers (metal skewers, or wooden skewers that have been soaked in water for 30 minutes). Broil about 6 inches from the heat source, for 5 to 6 minutes on one side, 3 or 4 minutes on the other.

The accompaniments: Melt the butter with the oil in a skillet. Increase the heat to medium-high and add the sweet potato cubes. Cook, stirring often, about 10 minutes. The potatoes should be golden and crispy on the outside, soft on the inside.

Peel the plantains and cut into ½-inch chunks. Squeeze lemon juice over them.

To eat, fill a warm tortilla with bits of pork and chile, a few cubes of sweet potato and plantain, a sprinkling of cilantro and a spoonful of crema or sour cream.

SERVES 4 OR 5

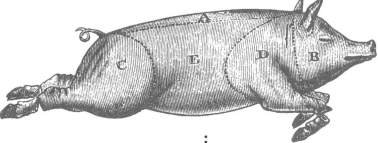

# Milanese Braised Pork

*Shirley Sarvis, an expert on wine and food matching, returned from a trip to Italy with a host of recipes. In this one, the meat is first roasted, then it is braised in milk, which makes it deliciously moist and fork-tender. The braising liquid is then reduced for a sauce.*

1 (3-pound) boneless pork butt (shoulder) roast
Salt and pepper to taste
Leaves from 4 (3-inch) sprigs fresh rosemary, or 1½ teaspoons dried rosemary
2½ cups milk
8 to 10 large garlic cloves, peeled and finely chopped
8 to 10 fresh sage leaves

◦◦ Preheat the oven to 350 degrees.

Trim the excess fat from the pork and tie the roast, if necessary. Wipe the meat dry. Season with salt and pepper and rub with the dried rosemary, if using. Place the roast in a large oiled Dutch oven, cover and bake for 2 hours.

Remove the meat and skim off the fat from the pan juices. Return the roast to the pan. Pour ½ cup of the milk into the pan. Add the garlic, sage and fresh rosemary (if not using dried). Cover and braise until the meat is very tender, about 1 hour, turning once or twice (see Note). Check occasionally, and add a little more milk, if necessary, to keep ¼ inch of liquid in the pan. Transfer the roast to a warm platter.

Add any remaining milk to the pan and cook over high heat, stirring, until the mixture turns light brown and thickens to the consistency of heavy cream (you should have about 1½ cups sauce). Season with salt and pepper.

Carve the roast and spoon some of the sauce over each serving.

SERVES 6

**NOTE:** You may braise the pork up to 2 hours, but you may need more milk—up to 1 quart. The pork will become almost spoon-slice tender.

# Pork Stew with Chestnuts and Ginger

*Meaty golden chestnuts cook with pork and white wine in this variation on an Old-World winter stew by Georgeanne Brennan. The addition of ginger lightens the taste and the spirit of this wonderful country dish. Fresh chestnuts are best, but canned are a better choice than poor-quality fresh nuts.*

1¾ pounds fresh chestnuts, or a 14-ounce can unsweetened whole chestnuts
    packed in water

2½ pounds boneless pork roast, or a 3½-pound pork shoulder roast, boned

1 teaspoon salt

1 teaspoon freshly ground black pepper

1 teaspoon minced fresh thyme

1 tablespoon olive oil

1 onion, peeled and chopped

1 garlic clove, peeled, and chopped

1 tablespoon minced fresh ginger

1 slice bacon, chopped

½ cup dry white wine

1¼ cups beef broth

◉◉ Preheat the oven to 350 degrees.

Score each chestnut with an "x" on its rounded side. Place the chestnuts on a baking sheet and bake about 20 minutes. Remove and let cool.

Meanwhile, start preparing the pork. Cut the meat into 2½-inch cubes, then season with salt, pepper and thyme. Set aside.

Heat the olive oil in a large, heavy saucepan or frying pan over medium heat. Add the onion, garlic, half of the ginger and the bacon. Reduce the heat and cook until the onion and bacon are translucent. Remove the bacon and vegetables with a slotted spoon.

Increase the heat to medium high. Add the pork and sauté until browned, turning often (this should take about 10 minutes). Remove the pork with a slotted spoon and set aside with the vegetables and bacon.

Pour the wine into the pan, scraping up the browned bits with a wooden spoon. Stir in the broth and the remaining ginger. Return the pork, bacon and vegetables to the pan. Cover, reduce heat to low and simmer for 1 hour, or until the pork is tender.

Peel the cooled chestnuts. Some will break, but don't worry. Add them to the pork and cook for 20 minutes, until the stew has thickened and the chestnuts and pork can be cut easily with a fork.

If you are using canned chestnuts, drain and rinse them. Cut extra-large ones into 2 pieces, leaving the smaller ones whole. Stir into the pork mixture 5 minutes before serving the stew. Mash a few of the chestnuts with the back of a wooden spoon to thicken the sauce.

SERVES 6

# Pork and Potato Stew in Whole-Seed Mustard Gravy

*This pork stew from Marlena Spieler has a wonderfully complex flavor; it's great on a winter evening. Whole-grain mustard is stirred in at the last minute, adding a refreshing jolt to the long-cooked dish. Although the recipe calls for only potatoes, feel free to add other root vegetables: parsnips, turnips and rutabagas. Corn would also be a good addition to the basic recipe.*

2 onions, coarsely chopped, or ¾ cup coarsely chopped shallots

2 tablespoons vegetable oil

2½ to 3 pounds boneless pork stew meat, cut in bite-sized pieces

## The Importance of Salt

Don't let anyone tell you to wait until the end of the cooking time to add salt. Salt blends and brightens flavors. In fact, in long-cooked tomato sauces and stews, salting lightly at the beginning, middle and end improves the flavor, and you end up using less.

1 to 2 tablespoons flour

2 cups dry red wine

2 cups beef or chicken broth

½ to 1 tablespoon chopped fresh sage leaves, or to taste

6 to 8 waxy potatoes, peeled and quartered

1 to 2 tablespoons whole-seed mustard, or to taste

Sauté the onions in the oil until softened. Add the pork and continue sautéing until the onions are browned and the pork is golden. Sprinkle in the flour, stir well, then add the wine, broth and sage. Bring to a boil, reduce heat and simmer over very low heat (or in a very slow oven, 300 to 325 degrees) until the pork is tender, about 2 hours.

Add the potatoes and continue to cook until they are just tender, about 30 minutes.

Just before serving, stir in the mustard, taking care not to break up the potatoes.

SERVES 6 TO 8

# Small Shanghai-Style Sweet and Sour Ribs

*These sweet-sour ribs, created by Bruce Cost, make a wonderful addition to picnics and casual buffets. Serve them warm or at room temperature—with plenty of paper napkins.*

3 pounds pork spareribs, cut across the bones into 1½-inch lengths

3 cups peanut oil

½ cup sugar

⅓ cup Chinese rice vinegar

1 teaspoon salt

1 tablespoon dark soy sauce

Rinse and dry the ribs; then cut them apart. Heat the oil in a wok. When it is very hot, add the ribs in small batches and fry until they are brown and crispy, about 5 minutes. Remove and drain on paper towels.

Combine the sugar, vinegar, salt and soy sauce in a small bowl.

Remove the oil from the wok, then place the wok over high heat. When it is hot, add the vinegar mixture. Cook, stirring over high heat until it is syrupy. Add the ribs and stir until they are well coated with the glaze.

SERVES 4

# Lemon, Caper and Green Peppercorn Veal Shanks

*Veal shanks often are cooked in tomato sauce, so Georgeanne Brennan's caper and lemon-sauced shanks are a dynamic change. The combination of puckery lemon, salty capers and the sweet fatty meat is unbeatable.*

1 tablespoon butter

4 slices veal shank, each 1 to 1½ inches thick (1½ to 2 pounds total)

2 tablespoons flour

½ teaspoon salt

1 teaspoon freshly ground black pepper

1 teaspoon minced fresh thyme

Juice of ½ lemon

½ lemon, cut into ½-inch pieces (including rind)

½ cup dry white wine

1½ to 2 cups chicken broth

1 tablespoon capers

1 teaspoon green peppercorns

◎◎  Melt the butter in a skillet over medium heat. When the butter foams, add the veal and sauté for 2 to 3 minutes, until it is just golden. Sprinkle the veal with the flour, salt, pepper and thyme. Sauté, turning the meat, for 1 minute. Add the lemon juice and pieces and cook for 1 minute, stirring. Add the wine and cook for 1 minute, stirring and scraping up any bits clinging to the pan.

Add the broth, reduce the heat to low, cover and simmer for 1½ to 2 hours, stirring often and basting meat with the juices, until the meat is tender and easily pierced with a fork. Add more broth if the meat gets too dry during cooking. There should be ¾ to 1 cup sauce at the end of the cooking time.

Just before serving, stir in the capers and peppercorns.

SERVES 4

# Homemade Chorizo

*Chorizo is a staple of the Mexican kitchen, and Jacqueline McMahan's make-at-home version is exceptional. The addition of ground turkey, mixed with the pork, makes this sausage lower in fat than the store-bought variety. Use as you would any spicy sausage: in a pot of beans, stews, chili, paella, omelets and scrambled eggs.*

2 to 4 tablespoons New Mexico chile caribe (crushed chile with seeds)

4 tablespoons ground New Mexico chile

½ cup apple cider vinegar, warmed

2 pounds unseasoned ground pork (not sausage)

1 pound ground turkey

1 tablespoon minced garlic

2 to 3 tablespoons dried oregano

1½ teaspoons ground pepper

1 tablespoon kosher salt

½ teaspoon canela (Mexican cinnamon)

4 tablespoons ground red chile, such as pasilla or ancho

◉◉  Marinate the chile caribe and 2 tablespoons of the ground New Mexico chile in the warm vinegar for 30 minutes to create a paste.

Place the ground meats in a bowl and mix in the remaining ingredients, including the chile paste. Cover and refrigerate overnight.

Divide the meat into portions, wrap airtight and freeze until needed. This keeps well in the freezer for up to 6 months.

YIELDS 3 POUNDS CHORIZO

# Spicy and Hot Tunisian Lamb Sausages (Merguez)

*Merle Ellis, "the Butcher," is a master sausagemaker, and we particularly like this unusual and spicy lamb version, which is flavored with pomegranate juice.*

3 pounds lean lamb stew meat and/or trimmings

1 tablespoon salt

1½ tablespoons cumin seeds

2 teaspoons coarsely ground pepper

4 tablespoons paprika

1½ teaspoons cayenne pepper

1 teaspoon ground cinnamon

½ cup pomegranate juice

1½ tablespoons minced garlic

1 teaspoon ground ginger

1 teaspoon dried thyme

Hog casings for stuffing

∞ Grind the lamb once through the medium (⅛-inch) plate of a meat grinder.

Mix together the remaining ingredients (except the casings) and add to the meat. Mix well with your hands. Grind through the ⅛-inch plate with a stuffing horn attached to fill casings. Twist or tie the sausages into 5-inch lengths.

Wrap and store in the refrigerator for up to 5 days, or freeze for up to 6 months.

To cook the sausages, prick them in several places, then fry over low heat, broil or barbecue.

YIELDS 3 POUNDS SAUSAGES

## Grilling Sausage

For even cooking, first poach sausages in water until about three quarters done and then finish cooking on the grill. The sausages will develop a pleasant smoky flavor and will be evenly cooked.

Chapter 6

# Poultry

*Chicken consumption in the United States just keeps growing. Unfortunately, today's supermarket chickens seem to be wanting in the flavor department. If you can find them, free-range chickens are nearly always better. If you can't find them, the secret for succulent birds, bursting with flavor, is to marinate them before cooking. That's why in many of our recipes we have included this extra step. If you plan ahead it only means a little more work and the results are well worth it.*

*In addition, we've also given several alternatives to the traditional roast turkey including a breast braised in wine, which is great for those who love white meat and are in a rush. We also have an intriguing recipe for preparing the whole bird tandoori style.*

*In between are many savory stews with Cuban, Thai, Italian, French and Chinese accents. Then there's an intriguing wok-smoked duck breast, and salt-seared duck legs with apricots.*

# Rosemary Roast Chicken with Onion-Garlic Gravy

*Chicken is roasted on a bed of onions and garlic in this recipe by Michael Bauer. When the bird is cooked through and golden, the vegetables are pureed with chicken stock to make a thick, rich gravy.*

1 chicken (about 3½ pounds)

1½ tablespoons olive oil

4 onions, cut in pieces

1 lemon, quartered

2 rosemary sprigs

8 garlic cloves

1½ cups chicken broth (unsalted canned is fine)

Salt and pepper to taste

Preheat the oven to 450 degrees.

Remove the giblets from the cavity, rinse the chicken, pat dry and remove excess fat from around the tail area. Rub the chicken inside and out with ½ tablespoon of the olive oil. Stuff the cavity with 1 of the onions, 2 wedges of lemon, a sprig of rosemary and 4 garlic cloves. Use a bit of the remaining olive oil to grease the bottom of a glass baking dish. Place the remaining onions and garlic in the dish. Drizzle the remaining oil over the onions. Use another quarter of the lemon to sprinkle on the chicken. Place the bird breast down on the onion mixture.

Roast for about 20 minutes per pound. Check the onion mixture; if it starts to blacken or stick, add a bit of the chicken broth. After about 30 minutes, turn the chicken breast up and add ¼ to ½ cup broth. Return to the oven and roast until the meat in the thickest part of the leg just loses its pinkness. Remove the chicken to a platter.

Scrape the onion mixture into the bowl of a food processor. Puree with the remaining broth. Season with salt and pepper. Chop the remaining rosemary and add it to taste to the pureed mixture. Squeeze in the juice of the remaining lemon quarter. Transfer to a pan and bring to a boil to meld flavors.

Cut the chicken in half and pour the gravy over each half.

Serve with rosemary roasted potatoes.

SERVES 2

## The Best Basic Roast Chicken

After trying many different methods, Chronicle food stylist Dan Bowe found that to keep the bird evenly moist, it should be roasted in a preheated 475-degree oven and turned during roasting. Here's how it's done.

Place a 3¾-pound chicken on its side in a roasting pan. Roast for 20 minutes. Turn the chicken on its other side for 20 minutes. Finally, turn the bird breast up and roast for 15 minutes longer, or until the internal temperature reaches 170 degrees. The turning technique distributes the juices and keeps the whole bird moist.

# Sicilian Chicken with Lemon, Mint and Almonds

*This chicken marinates in a lemon-garlic mixture overnight or for up to 2 days before being sautéed. A white wine sauce shows off the contrasting flavors of fresh mint and toasted nuts in Marlena Spieler's creation.*

1 chicken, cut into serving pieces

10 garlic cloves, coarsely chopped

1 cup fresh mint leaves

Juice of 3 lemons

3 tablespoons olive oil

Salt and pepper to taste

½ cup dry white wine

⅔ cup chicken broth

3 to 4 ounces slivered almonds, lightly toasted

Combine the chicken, garlic, ⅔ cup of the mint, the lemon juice, 1 tablespoon of the olive oil, and salt and pepper in a plastic container. Cover tightly. Refrigerate overnight, or up to 2 days.

Remove the chicken from the marinade and wipe dry. Reserve the marinade.

Heat the remaining 2 tablespoons olive oil in a sauté pan. Add the chicken legs, thighs and wings; sauté 20 to 25 minutes, turning several times. Add the breast pieces and sauté 10 to 15 minutes, turning occasionally. Remove the chicken and keep warm.

Discard the fat in the pan, then add the wine and cook over high heat until reduced by half. Add the chicken broth and reserved marinade and cook over high heat until reduced to ½ cup. Taste for seasoning, then pour the sauce over chicken. Garnish with almonds and the remaining mint.

SERVES 3 OR 4

# Lone Star Chicken

*This is one of those recipes that doesn't sound impressive from the list of ingredients, but is truly outstanding when cooked, says Marion Cunningham. It's a breeze to put together, may be served hot or cold, and yields extra sauce, which freezes well and is perfect over pasta.*

1 can (18¾ ounces) solid-pack tomatoes

1 large onion, chopped

4 garlic cloves, minced

2 bay leaves

2 teaspoons ground cumin

1½ teaspoons dried oregano, crumbled

2 tablespoons wine vinegar

Salt and pepper to taste

1 chicken (2½ to 3 pounds), cut into 8 pieces

∞ Put the tomatoes and their juices into a large, stove-top casserole and break the tomatoes into bits. Add the onion, garlic, bay leaves, cumin, oregano and vinegar; stir to blend. Season with salt and pepper. Simmer on top of the stove, stirring occasionally, for 30 minutes.

Preheat the oven to 350 degrees. Add the chicken parts, pushing them down into the sauce. Cover the casserole and bake for about 1 hour.

SERVES 4

# Poulet à la Niçoise

*This savory, tomatoey, Provencal-inspired chicken stew by Marlena Spieler pairs oranges with olives, potatoes and artichoke hearts. It's an interesting and satisfying combination for company, and is particularly good paired with a Pinot Noir.*

3 slices prosciutto or pancetta, diced

½ medium carrot, diced

½ to ¾ cup small pickling onions or shallots, peeled but left whole

2 tablespoons olive oil

1 chicken, cut into 8 serving pieces

---

## Poultry-Thawing Times

All frozen poultry should be thawed in the refrigerator, not at room temperature. To speed thawing, remove the giblets from the body as soon as the bird is pliable enough.

| Weight | Time |
| --- | --- |
| 3–12 lbs | Plan on 1–2 days |
| 12–20 lbs | Plan on 2–3 days |
| 20–24 lbs | Plan on 3–4 days |

1 head garlic, broken into cloves but left whole and unpeeled

¼ cup brandy

1 fresh tarragon sprig, 1 fresh thyme sprig, 3 fresh sage leaves,
    and 1 or 2 bay leaves tied together with string

1 cup diced tomatoes

1 cup dry white wine

1 tablespoon orange juice

Pinch grated orange zest

1 pound tiny new potatoes, parboiled

3 to 5 artichoke hearts, cut into quarters and blanched
    (or use frozen artichoke hearts)

½ cup mixed green and black Mediterranean olives

2 teaspoons capers

2 tablespoons chopped fresh parsley

## Doneness Test

Chicken and other poultry is done when the juices run clear when the meat is pricked with a fork or skewer. A springy feel to the meat is a good indicator, but it's best to use the juice test.

❦ Sauté the prosciutto or pancetta, carrots and onions or shallots in half of the olive oil for 5 to 8 minutes, or until the carrots are lightly browned. Remove from pan and set aside.

Add the remaining oil to the pan and sauté the chicken and garlic in it until lightly browned in spots. Remove from heat.

Pour the brandy into a long-handled ladle and carefully pour a little into the pan. It may ignite, so avert your face. Return the pan to the heat and cook until the brandy has evaporated. Add the remaining brandy, again being on the alert for any bursts of flame. Cook until the brandy has reduced to 1 or 2 tablespoons. Add the reserved prosciutto mixture, the herbs, tomatoes, wine, orange juice and zest. Simmer over very low heat or in a 325-degree oven for 2 hours.

Thirty minutes before serving, add the potatoes and artichokes.

Just before serving, add the olives and capers and heat through. Garnish with parsley.

SERVES 4

# Chicken in Spice-Laden Coconut Sauce

*In this Indian dish by Ayla Algar, creamy coconut milk makes a cooling counterpoint to fiery chiles and pungent spices.*

4 tablespoons peanut oil

1 large onion, finely chopped

8 garlic cloves, minced

1-inch piece fresh ginger, peeled and minced

8 to 10 small dried red peppers, seeded

1 tablespoon coriander seeds

2 teaspoons cumin seeds

Pinch salt

1 teaspoon ground turmeric

1 chicken (about 3 pounds), cut into small serving pieces

1 large tomato, peeled, seeded and chopped

2 cups fresh coconut milk, or a 14-ounce can coconut milk

½ cup water

∞ Heat the oil in a large skillet. Add the onion and cook about 20 minutes, until it turns almost reddish brown. Add the garlic and ginger and cook until the mixture looks reddish brown. While the onion is cooking, stir almost constantly to prevent it from burning. If the mixture begins to look too dry, add drops of water.

Grind the peppers, coriander and cumin seeds in a spice mill. Mix the ground spices with some salt and the turmeric and place near the pan with the onion. When the onion turns reddish brown, add the spices and let them cook a few seconds, stirring all the time, until they release their fragrance.

Add the chicken pieces and stir them well until they are coated with the spice mixture. Add the tomato; let cook until soft, and the fat separates from the sauce. Stir in the coconut milk and water and simmer, uncovered, about 40 minutes or longer, until the chicken is tender. If the sauce gets too thick, add a little water.

Serve with fluffy steamed rice.

SERVES 4

## It's an Un-Wrap

Never leave packaged supermarket chicken in its original package, advises chef and restaurant owner Jeremiah Tower. It's much safer to unwrap it when you get home from the market, wash it, dry it, and rub it with lemon juice (a natural disinfectant). Stuff the cavity with herbs and lemon, rub the surface with olive oil and refrigerate the bird, uncovered, until you are ready to cook it, even a couple of days later.

# Chicken Simmered with Tomatoes, Fresh Herbs and Red Wine

*Hunter's-style chicken is cooked in varying ways throughout Italy; this is Ayla Algar's delicious version.*

    3 tablespoons olive oil
    1 chicken (about 3 pounds), legs and thighs halved and breast quartered
    1 small onion, chopped
    1 garlic clove, minced
    ¾ cup dry red wine
    2 cups chopped tomatoes
    1 cup sliced mushrooms
    1 or 2 green bell peppers, seeded, deribbed and sliced
    1 teaspoon chopped fresh thyme
    1 teaspoon chopped fresh marjoram
    Salt and freshly ground pepper to taste

Heat the olive oil in a large skillet. Add the chicken, onion and garlic and sauté until the chicken is golden brown. Pour in the wine and let simmer, uncovered, about 10 minutes.

Stir in the tomatoes, mushrooms, green peppers, herbs, and salt and pepper to taste. Cover and simmer about 20 minutes, or until the chicken is tender.

SERVES 4

# Dynamite Chicken

*Nothing could be easier—and few dishes could taste better—than this simple baked chicken from Jacqueline McMahan. A blend of cilantro, garlic and chile powder is rubbed inside and outside a whole chicken, then the bird is baked in a savory blend of salsa and Mexican beer. The hardest part about this recipe is waiting for the chicken; the cooking aromas may drive you wild. Serve with plain steamed rice or a basic rice pilaf to collect the delicious juices. Leftovers are perfect for soft chicken tacos.*

1 chicken (about 3½ pounds)

½ cup cilantro leaves

4 garlic cloves

1 teaspoon salt

2 teaspoons ground chile, such as New Mexico Dixon

¾ cup salsa (chunky bottled salsa may be used)

½ cup Mexican beer

◎◎ Preheat the oven to 400 degrees. Coat a Dutch oven with oil.

Rinse the chicken, remove the innards and cut off any large pieces of fat or skin about the vent. Blot the chicken dry with paper towels.

Combine the cilantro, garlic, salt and ground chile in a food processor. Chop to a coarse puree. Rub 1 tablespoon of the mixture inside the chicken. Gently work your fingers under the skin of the breast to loosen it, then rub more of the mixture under the skin over the breast. Rub the remaining mixture over the outside of the bird. Place the chicken breast up in the Dutch oven. Pour ¼ cup of the salsa into the cavity of the chicken, then pour the remaining salsa over the bird. Add the beer to the pan, cover and bake for 1 hour. Uncover and roast 10 to 15 minutes longer, basting the chicken with the pan juices a couple of times.

SERVES 3 OR 4

## Chicken Cubes

Freeze homemade chicken stock in ice-cube trays, then transfer the cubes to plastic freezer bags and return to the freezer. When you need just a little stock, remove a cube or two— great for quick pan sauces, or to braise vegetables without butter or oil.

# Unfried Mexican Chicken

*Jacqueline McMahan often makes a double batch of this oven-fried chicken. It keeps beautifully for at least 3 days in the refrigerator, getting better each day.*

6 boneless, skinless chicken breast halves (about 4 ounces each)

16 ounces bottled thick, chunky salsa (see Note)

5 cups fresh bread crumbs (use day-old Italian or French bread)

2 garlic cloves

1 teaspoon dried oregano

½ teaspoon salt

1 teaspoon ground chile, such as New Mexico Dixon

Olive oil or canola oil spray

2 tablespoons melted butter

## Fryer's Helper

When preparing fried chicken for a next-day picnic, first marinate it for 30 minutes or so in lemon juice, then bread and fry as usual. The lemon helps prevent any "refrigerator flavor" and gives the chicken a lively, fresh taste.

◉◉ Place the chicken breasts in a single layer in a glass baking dish. Pour the salsa over the chicken, turning to coat well on both sides. Let marinate for 1 to 2 hours.

Preheat the oven to 375 degrees.

Combine the bread crumbs, garlic, oregano, salt and ground chile in a food processor; process to fine crumbs. Spread the crumb mixture on a long piece of waxed paper.

Remove the chicken from the salsa, keeping as many salsa chunks adhering to the chicken as possible. Place the breasts on top of the crumbs. Cover the breasts with more crumbs, pressing them on. Turn the chicken and press more crumbs on top.

Spray a nonstick baking sheet with oil. Arrange the breasts on the baking sheet; drizzle with melted butter and spray with oil.

Bake for 35 minutes. The chicken should be golden around the edges.

SERVES 6

**NOTE:** For this recipe, bottled salsa is better than fresh, which can become watery.

# Mexican-Cuban Chicken with Rice

*This recipe is a combination of Jacqueline McMahan's grandmother's arroz con pollo and a Cuban version of the classic dish. What makes it particularly good is the aromatic seasoning paste that is rubbed into the chicken pieces before they are browned.*

3 garlic cloves, minced

1 teaspoon salt (preferably kosher)

2 teaspoons ground chile, such as New Mexico Dixon

1 teaspoon cumin seeds

3 tablespoons olive oil, or as needed

1 chicken (about 3½ pounds), cut into serving pieces and skinned

1 cup chopped onion

1½ cups long-grain white rice

1 slice ham (4 ounces), cut into strips

½ pound sweet Italian sausages or good-quality chorizo, sautéed, cut into slices and drained on paper towels

4½ cups water or chicken broth (or a combination)

1 bay leaf

2 tablespoons dry sherry

2 tablespoons pimientos, cut into strips (optional)

Using a mortar and pestle or the blade of a large knife, mash together the garlic, salt, ground chile and cumin seeds. Add 1 tablespoon of the olive oil, blending the mixture into a paste.

Pat chicken pieces dry (saving the back for stock), then rub with the seasoning paste; set aside at room temperature for 30 minutes, or cover and refrigerate overnight.

Preheat the oven to 350 degrees.

Heat 1 tablespoon of the olive oil in a heavy pot with a lid. Add the chicken and sauté until golden brown. (Do not crowd the pan; work in batches, if necessary, adding more olive oil when needed.) Set aside.

Sauté the onion in the remaining 1 tablespoon olive oil until softened. Stir in the rice and sauté until it is very lightly browned. Add another tablespoon of olive oil if needed.

Return the chicken to the pot, then add the ham, sausage, water or broth, bay leaf and sherry. Bring to a simmer on top of the stove; cook for 10 minutes. Arrange the optional pimiento strips on top. Cover tightly and bake for 45 minutes. Remove from the oven and let rest, covered, for 10 minutes before serving.

SERVES 6 TO 8

# Grilled Chicken Breasts with Santa Fe Green Chile Sauce

*Santa Fe Green Chile Sauce, a perfect complement to grilled chicken breasts, is one of Jacqueline McMahan's most requested recipes.*

3 whole chicken breasts, halved, skinned and boned

2 tablespoons olive oil

Juice of 2 limes

2 garlic cloves, pressed

½ teaspoon salt

½ teaspoon or more freshly ground pepper

**Green Chile Sauce**

8 Anaheim or New Mexico chiles, or 1 large can roasted green chiles

1½ cups chicken broth

2 garlic cloves, minced

1 teaspoon dried oregano

½ to ¾ cup sour cream

Place each half chicken breast between 2 pieces of waxed paper and pound with a mallet until it has attained an even thickness. Place the chicken in a shallow dish.

Combine the olive oil, lime juice, garlic, salt and pepper; pour over the chicken. Make sure the chicken is well coated. Refrigerate for at least 1 hour. Bring to room temperature before grilling.

To make the sauce: Char the chiles over a gas burner or a charcoal fire, then place them in a paper bag, seal and let steam about 15 minutes. Remove the chiles; peel, seed and chop them. Combine the chiles, chicken broth, garlic and oregano in a saucepan and simmer for 20 minutes, or until the liquid is reduced by half. Set aside to cool. Just before serving, add the sour cream and stir until smooth. (This sauce also is good with fish or pasta.)

Grill the chicken breasts 5 to 6 minutes per side, depending on the heat of your fire and the thickness of the breasts. Serve with the green chile sauce.

SERVES 6

# White Chili

*This chili, created by Jacqueline McMahan, pairs white-meat chicken, white beans, white cheese and beer for a variation on the traditional tomato-based chili. But don't be fooled by its pale image; this dish packs a powerhouse of flavor. Although it may be served the day it's made, the chili is better reheated the second or third day. It also freezes well for up to 1 month.*

**Beans**

1 pound Great Northern or navy beans

8 cups water

½ cup chopped onion

2 garlic cloves, minced

Pepper

1 teaspoon salt

**Chili**

12 ounces Mexican beer (not dark)

2 cups diced onions

1½ tablespoons minced garlic

1 cup diced red bell pepper

2 jalapeno chiles, seeded and diced

4 Anaheim or New Mexico green chiles, roasted, peeled and seeded

1 tablespoon dried oregano

1 tablespoon crushed cumin seeds

1¼ pounds skinned, boned chicken breasts

1 can (14½ ounces) chicken broth

## Toasting Spices

One of the best ways to bring out the flavor in spices is to toast them first. Simply place them in a skillet over medium-high heat and continue to move and shake the pan until the aromas intensify and the spices start to darken slightly.

2 tablespoons ground New Mexico chile

1 pound tomatillos, husks removed by soaking

1 cup minced fresh cilantro

1 tablespoon rice vinegar

1 teaspoon salt

2 cups grated sharp white cheddar cheese

Cilantro leaves, for garnish

To make the beans: Pick over the beans for debris, then place in a sieve and rinse well. Place in large pot. Add the water, onion, garlic cloves and a grating of black pepper. Simmer for 2 to 3 hours, until the beans are tender. Add the salt during the last 30 minutes of cooking.

To make the chili: While the beans are cooking, place the beer in a 4-quart pot. Add the onions, garlic, bell pepper, jalapenos, green chiles, oregano and cumin. Simmer for 10 minutes.

Cut the chicken into strips, then dice. Add to the pot along with the chicken broth. Sprinkle in the ground chile and simmer for 15 minutes.

Place the tomatillos, minced cilantro, vinegar and salt in a food processor and process to a salsa consistency. Stir into the chili. Add the drained cooked beans and simmer for 20 minutes. Taste for seasoning; add salt, if desired.

Ladle into serving bowls. Sprinkle ⅓ cup of the cheese over each serving and broil until the cheese is golden (or skip this step and simply let the cheese melt into the hot chile). Garnish with cilantro.

SERVES 6

# Moroccan Chicken with Olives and Lemons

*Rod Smith, a wine writer and cook, found this recipe written in the back of a copy of Paula Wolfert's* Couscous and Other Good Food from Morocco. *Intrigued, he made the dish, and has been grateful to the anonymous writer ever since.*

⅓ cup olive oil

1 large onion, thinly sliced

1 garlic clove, minced

1½ tablespoons chopped fresh parsley

1 tablespoon chopped fresh cilantro

1 teaspoon salt

½ teaspoon pepper

⅛ teaspoon powdered saffron

1 broiler-fryer, cut in serving pieces

1½ lemons, cut in wedges

⅓ cup cracked green olives

⊚⊚ Heat the oil in a Dutch oven. Add the onion, garlic, parsley, cilantro, salt, pepper and saffron; stir to mix. Add the chicken pieces and turn to coat well. Arrange the lemon wedges on top. Cover and simmer about 2 hours, turning the chicken pieces from time to time.

Transfer the chicken to a warm serving platter and arrange the lemon wedges on top; keep warm.

Cook the liquid in the Dutch oven over high heat until it has reduced to a thick sauce. Add the olives, cook until heated through, then pour over the chicken.

SERVES 3 OR 4

# Chicken Quarters in Chermoula

*Permeated with the flavors and aromas of a Moroccan souk, these chicken quarters may be grilled over an open fire or roasted in the oven. The marinade also doubles as a tangy sauce, says Marlena Spieler.*

4 chicken quarters (leg-thigh, breast-wing, or both)

8 garlic cloves, chopped

1 small to medium red onion, finely chopped

3 to 4 tablespoons fresh lemon or lime juice

2 tablespoons paprika

2 teaspoons cumin seeds, or 1 teaspoon ground cumin

3 tablespoons chopped fresh cilantro

1 teaspoon salt

½ teaspoon coarsely ground black pepper

Large pinch red pepper flakes

¼ teaspoon ground ginger

2 pinches saffron threads

3 to 4 tablespoons olive oil

Chicken stock, as needed

∞ Combine the chicken, garlic, onion, lemon juice, paprika, cumin, cilantro, salt, pepper, pepper flakes, ginger, saffron and olive oil; let marinate at least 2 hours at room temperature, or up to 2 days in the refrigerator, turning from time to time.

Preheat the oven to 450 degrees.

Place the chicken and its marinade in a roasting pan and add enough chicken broth to come ½ inch up the sides of the pan. Roast for 20 to 40 minutes (depending on the cuts used), or until the chicken is brown on the outside, juicy and succulent within.

Skim off the fat from the roasting juices, then serve the chicken with the juices spooned over.

SERVES 4

# Sumatran Peanut Chicken

*Copeland Marks is an East Coast writer who is an expert at spicy cuisines. When we were doing a special issue on fiery foods, we turned to him. This was one of the dishes he recommended, and it has become one of our favorites.*

1 medium onion, sliced (½ cup)

2 garlic cloves, sliced

½-inch piece fresh ginger, sliced

4 or 5 fresh hot red chiles, seeded and sliced

⅛ teaspoon ground pepper

⅛ teaspoon ground turmeric

1 teaspoon salt, or to taste

2 cups coconut milk

1 salam leaf (kari, or curry, leaf)

1 slice galangal, fresh or dried (laos)

1 chicken (about 3 pounds), cut into 8 serving pieces, loose skin and fat discarded

⅓ cup dry-roasted peanuts

∞ Combine the onion, garlic, ginger, chiles, pepper, turmeric, salt and ¼ cup of the coconut milk in a blender or food processor; blend to a smooth paste. Transfer to a sauté pan and stir in the remaining coconut milk. Bring to a boil over medium heat. Add the salam, galangal, chicken and peanuts and cook, uncovered, over low heat for 30 to 40 minutes, turning the chicken frequently and basting with the pan juices, until almost all the liquid has evaporated.

Serve with a rice pilaf or plain steamed rice.

SERVES 6

**NOTE:** Salam and laos may be found in Middle Eastern, Indian and some Asian markets.

# Chicken Sautéed with Fresh Chiles, Garlic and Basil

*This is a good example of Thai cuisine, says Ayla Algar. It's colorful, fragrant and bursting with clean, intense flavors.*

2 garlic cloves, minced

2 teaspoons minced lemongrass

2 teaspoons minced young ginger or regular fresh ginger

1 tablespoon minced cilantro root

2 tablespoons Asian fish sauce (nam pla), or as needed

1 tablespoon rice vinegar

1 teaspoon sugar

1 tablespoon tapioca powder or cornstarch

1 pound boneless chicken, cut into ¼-inch strips

¼ cup peanut oil

3 tablespoons minced garlic

½ teaspoon red pepper flakes

1 tablespoon minced red onion

2 or more green serrano chiles, seeded and cut into strips

2 or more red serrano chiles, seeded and cut into strips

2 or 3 pickling cucumbers, cut into 6 pieces lengthwise

1 cup slightly underripe cherry tomatoes

Handful Thai basil, regular basil or mint leaves

◉◉ Combine the garlic, lemongrass, ginger, cilantro root, fish sauce, vinegar, sugar and tapioca powder or cornstarch; toss with the chicken in a bowl, cover and refrigerate for a few hours.

Heat a wok until very hot. Add the oil and heat. Stir in the garlic, pepper flakes and onion; cook a few seconds, stirring constantly. Add the chicken and stir-fry 2 or 3 minutes, or until it turns opaque. Add the fresh chiles, cucumbers and tomatoes; stir-fry a few seconds. Taste and, if desired, add more fish sauce. Stir in the basil, remove from heat and serve immediately with rice.

SERVES 2 OR 3

**NOTE:** Fish sauce is available in Asian markets, and in the ethnic-food section of some supermarkets. Thai basil is harder to find, but is carried by some Asian markets and farmers' markets.

## Low-Fat Chicken

To lower the fat in chicken, skin the breast and replace with a coating of mustard, fresh herbs and unbuttered bread crumbs. Roast in a preheated 400-degree oven until browned and bubbly. The crust not only enhances the flavor but holds in the moisture.

# Grilled Chicken with Eggplant Cream

*In this Turkish dish by Middle Eastern food expert Ayla Algar, simple grilled chicken attains regal splendor. In fact, the dish was created for Sultan Murad IV, and its name, Hunkar Begendi, means "the monarch was pleased."*

1 small onion, sliced

Salt

½ cup olive oil

2 tablespoons fresh lemon juice

1 teaspoon chopped fresh thyme

1 teaspoon minced garlic

Freshly ground pepper to taste

2 pounds boneless chicken, cut into 1-inch pieces

2 medium eggplants (about 2½ pounds total)

Juice of ½ lemon

2 cups water

7 tablespoons unsalted butter

4 tablespoons flour

1½ to 2 cups hot milk or light cream

½ cup grated kasseri or Gruyère cheese

2 cups small cherry tomatoes

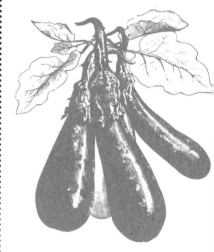

◎◎  Rub the onion slices with a little salt. Add the olive oil, lemon juice, thyme, garlic and pepper. Coat the chicken with this mixture; cover with plastic wrap and refrigerate several hours or overnight.

Place the eggplants over a wood fire or directly on a gas burner. Cook on all sides until thoroughly soft and the skins are black and charred. Let cool, then peel, removing all the pieces of burnt skin.

Put the eggplant in a bowl and add the lemon juice and the water; let stand 15 minutes. Drain the eggplant and squeeze dry.

Melt the butter in a saucepan; blend in the flour and cook 3 or 4 minutes, stirring all the time. Take small pieces of the eggplant, which should be soft and pulplike, and stir into the butter-flour paste. Add all the eggplant, mixing well with a wooden spoon until the mixture is smooth. Gradually stir in enough milk or cream to make a thick paste. While adding the liquid, stir briskly. When the mixture is smooth, add the cheese and stir a few seconds. Remove from heat, cover and keep warm.

Thread the chicken pieces and tomatoes on skewers and grill until done to your liking, taking care not to overcook.

Place the hot eggplant cream on a serving dish or on individual dinner plates. Then arrange chicken and tomatoes over the eggplant.

SERVES 4

# Chicken Thighs with Fennel, Lemon and Garlic

*Michael Bauer devised this one-pot dish, inspired by Richard Olney. Because of their meatiness and density, chicken thighs work much better than white meat for this recipe. Slices of lemon are cooked in a fennel- and garlic-laced broth. The lemon melts down, adding a lovely tart flavor. If it's too puckery, add a teaspoon or so of sugar. This dish is wonderful with a sprightly Pinot Grigio.*

8 to 12 chicken thighs, boned and skinned

Flour

Salt and pepper to taste

2 tablespoons olive oil

1½ cups dry white wine

12 garlic cloves, quartered

1 lemon, peeled, seeded and sliced

3 fennel bulbs, sliced

Sugar to taste (optional)

Zest of 1 lemon, finely chopped

2 tablespoons chopped fennel tops

∞ Lightly coat the chicken with flour that has been well seasoned with salt and pepper.

Heat the oil in a skillet over medium-high heat. Add the chicken and sauté until browned on all sides. Remove the chicken from the pan; set aside.

Add the wine to the pan and simmer, scraping up all the browned bits on the bottom. Add the garlic and lemon slices; let boil about 5 minutes. Add the fennel, cover and cook about 10 minutes. Stir well, then return the chicken to the pan, placing it on the fennel. Cover and simmer 30 minutes.

Just before serving, taste the sauce. If it's too tart, add a little sugar. If necessary, boil the sauce rapidly to reduce excess juices. Remove the chicken from the pan.

Combine the zest and fennel tops and stir most of the mixture into the fennel, reserving a little for garnish. Spoon the fennel onto serving plates and top with the chicken. Garnish with the remaining lemon zest–fennel top mixture.

SERVES 4 TO 6

# Orange-Mustard Chicken Wings

*Thoroughly glazed and wonderfully sticky, these are just the way chicken wings should be, says Georgeanne Brennan. Serve with plain white rice, a green salad and lots of napkins.*

2 tablespoons vegetable oil

2 garlic cloves, chopped

½ onion, chopped

1 cup orange marmalade

½ cup Dijon mustard

2 tablespoons Worcestershire sauce

1 tablespoon dry mustard

1 tablespoon packed brown sugar

2 tablespoons cider vinegar

½ teaspoon salt

24 chicken wings (about 2½ pounds)

@@ Heat the oil in a saucepan over medium heat. Add the garlic and onion and sauté until translucent. Stir in the marmalade, Dijon mustard, Worcestershire, dry mustard, brown sugar, vinegar and salt. Reduce heat and simmer for 10 minutes, stirring often. Remove from heat and let cool.

Put the chicken wings into a large glass or ceramic bowl. Pour the sauce over the wings, turning to make sure they are well coated. Let stand for 1 hour or more, turning the wings from time to time.

Preheat the oven to 350 degrees. Line a baking sheet with foil.

Place the chicken wings on the baking sheet and bake for 20 to 30 minutes, basting occasionally with the sauce left in the bowl.

SERVES 4

**Fat-Free Sauté**

Onions and garlic don't have to be sautéed in oil; they also can be "sautéed" in a little broth or water. A dash of vinegar near the end helps to add a high note to the flavor.

# Sticky Chicken Wings

*Another version of sticky chicken wings, this one by Bruce Cost. These Asian-accented wings make great appetizers or hors d'oeuvres.*

18 chicken wings
2 small dried red peppers, stemmed, seeded and coarsely chopped
¼ cup dry white wine
1½ cups boiling water
1 cinnamon stick
4 whole star anise
3 tablespoons dark soy sauce
1½ tablespoons sugar
¾ teaspoon salt
½ cup chopped scallions, green part included

@@ Heat a wok to nearly smoking; add the chicken wings, red peppers and wine. Cook, stirring, until the wine has almost evaporated.

Add the boiling water, cinnamon and anise; cover and simmer for 5 minutes. Uncover and add the remaining ingredients, except the scallions. Cover and simmer for 15 minutes.

Increase the heat to high and cook, stirring, until the liquid is gone and the wings have a sticky brown glaze. Stir in the scallions.

Serve hot, warm or at room temperature.

SERVES 3 OR 4

# Chicken-Fennel Sausage

*Merle Ellis, "the Butcher," created these chicken-fennel sausages long before the low-fat wave. The combination is superb.*

    3 pounds chicken thigh meat

    3 pounds boneless pork butt

    5 garlic cloves, chopped

    4 tablespoons fennel seeds

    2 tablespoons paprika

    2 teaspoons white pepper

    1 tablespoon black pepper

    2 teaspoons cayenne pepper

    ½ bunch Italian parsley, chopped

    1 bunch fresh sage, chopped

    ⅓ cup Pernod

    Hog casings (optional)

Cut the chicken and pork into strips. Combine all ingredients—except the hog casings—in a glass bowl. Refrigerate overnight.

Grind the mixture twice through the medium plate of a meat grinder.

If desired, stuff into hog casings and twist into links. Or, form into patties.

YIELDS ABOUT 6 POUNDS (ABOUT 4½ POUNDS COOKED)

# Sumatran Butterflied Cornish Game Hens

*Copeland Marks has devised this exotic way to prepare Cornish game hens. Use 3 chiles for a spicy dish; 7 chiles for an incendiary one. Serve with mountains of steamed rice to help tame the heat.*

2 Cornish game hens, about 1½ pounds each

4 shallots, sliced

2 garlic cloves, sliced

1 tablespoon ground coriander

3 to 7 fresh hot red chiles, seeded and sliced

½-inch piece fresh ginger, sliced

¼ teaspoon ground turmeric

Salt to taste

2 tablespoons fresh lime juice

2 cups coconut milk

2 stalks lemongrass, or 1 lemon slice

◎ Preheat the broiler.

Split open the hens from the breast side and flatten them out into a butterfly shape. Discard loose skin and fat. Broil the hens for 3 minutes on each side.

Using a blender or food processor, process the shallots, garlic, coriander, chiles, ginger, turmeric, salt, lime juice and ½ cup of the coconut milk to a smooth sauce. Marinate the hens in the mixture for 15 minutes.

Transfer the hens and their marinade to a large skillet and cook over medium heat for 10 minutes. Add the remaining coconut milk and the lemongrass. Bring to a boil, reduce heat and simmer for 30 minutes, basting occasionally, until the hens are tender and almost all the liquid has evaporated.

SERVES 2 TO 4

# Roasted Cornish Game Hens with Vinegar

*A bumper crop of homemade vinegar was the inspiration for this recipe by Fran Irwin. Marinating in a simple combination of vinegar and green onions gives bland Cornish hens a real boost in flavor. Serve with wild rice pilaf and a green vegetable.*

    4 Cornish game hens, rinsed and patted dry
    2 to 3 cups white wine vinegar or tarragon or champagne vinegar (see Note)
    ½ cup water (optional)
    4 green onions, trimmed and cut in 2-inch lengths
    Red seedless grapes, stemmed (optional)
    Thyme sprigs (optional)

∞ Place the hens in a large heavy-duty self-sealing plastic bag (you may have to use 2 bags). Add the vinegar, water and green onions. Seal the bag and refrigerate for 24 hours, turning occasionally.

Preheat the oven to 400 degrees.

Remove hens from the marinade; discard marinade. If desired, fill the cavities with grapes and thyme sprigs. Tie together the legs of each hen with kitchen string. Place the hens on a rack in a roasting pan and roast for 1 hour, or until juices run clear.

Remove the strings before serving. Pan drippings may be degreased and spooned over the hens.

SERVES 4

**NOTE:** Use enough vinegar to come at least halfway up sides of hens. If the vinegar is very acidic, add the water (the hens tend to "pickle" in a high-acid vinegar).

Duck

Cooking
| Weight | Temp. | Time |
| --- | --- | --- |
| 3–4¼ lbs | 325° | 1¾–2 hrs |
| 4¼–5 lbs | 325° | 2–2¼ hrs |

Goose

Cooking
| Weight | Temp. | Time |
| --- | --- | --- |
| 7–8 lbs | 325° | 2–2¼ hrs |
| 11 lbs | 325° | 2½–2¾ hrs |

# Jasmine Tea-Smoked Duck Breasts

*Tea-smoking is an important technique in Chinese cuisine, and the food most commonly smoked is duck. Joyce Jue came up with this method for preparing tea-smoked duck breasts, which are easier and a little quicker than smoking a whole bird. The breast is first marinated in a basic ginger–green onion mixture, then steamed, and finally smoked in a wok with tea leaves, aromatic herbs and spices. The duck comes out butter-tender with a delicate, haunting flavor. It can be used as a main course, or may be sliced for an appetizer or to top a mixed salad dressed with balsamic vinegar.*

4 duck breast halves, with or without bones

**Marinade**

2 tablespoons Sichuan peppercorns

2 tablespoons coarse salt

2 tablespoons sugar

2 green onions, cut in 1½-inch lengths and crushed

4 quarter-sized slices fresh ginger, shredded

¼ cup rice wine or dry sherry

**Smoking Mixture**

¼ cup Sichuan peppercorns

¼ cup white long-grain rice

¼ cup jasmine tea leaves

2 cinnamon sticks, broken into pieces

4 whole star anise, broken into pieces

⊚⊚ Pat the duck dry with paper towels. Prick the skin with a fork in several places. Put on a heat-resistant shallow plate that will fit comfortably into a wok. Set aside.

To make the marinade: Toast the peppercorns and salt in ungreased pan over medium-high heat, shaking the pan occasionally, until the mixture is aromatic, about 3 minutes. Grind to a fine consistency in a mortar or spice mill. Mix with the sugar, green onions, ginger and wine; pour over the duck and massage it in. Let marinate 4 hours or overnight in the refrigerator.

To steam: Fit a steaming rack into a wok. Pour boiling water into the wok to come within 1 inch of the rack. Return the water to a boil. Pour off the excess marinade around the duck. Put the duck, in its dish, on the rack. Cover and steam over medium-high heat for 30 minutes. Drain. Let cool for 2 hours or, better, refrigerate for several hours or overnight.

To smoke: Line the inside of the wok with enough heavy-duty foil to extend generously over the rim. Mix together the smoking ingredients and distribute over the bottom of the wok. Place a wire cake rack in the wok, cover the wok and set over medium-high heat. When the mixture begins to smoke, put the duck on the rack. Cover. Bring the excess foil up over rim of the lid; press to seal. Smoke for 15 to 20 minutes. The duck should be light golden brown.

To crisp the skin: Preheat the oven to 425 degrees. Place the duck breasts on a baking sheet and roast for 5 to 8 minutes. Pat off grease with paper towels.

SERVES 4

# Wild Ragout of Duck

*Duck is often on the menu at the Bay Wolf restaurant in Oakland. Here, chef/owner Michael Wild has brought together duck breasts, Pinot Noir, bacon and a few simple vegetables in a rich, robust stew.*

½ bottle Pinot Noir

1 pint duck stock (or chicken, turkey or veal stock)

4 duck breasts

1 leek (white and light green part only), well washed and julienned

¼ pound mushrooms, sliced

2 shallots, minced

¼ pound bacon, cubed

Salt and pepper to taste

1 tablespoon to ½ cup heavy cream (optional)

1 cup shelled peas, blanched

◎ Combine the wine and stock and place in a pot large enough to hold a steaming rack for the duck. Bring to a simmer and place the duck breasts on

## Skimming the Fat

An easy and effective way to degrease stocks, soups and stews is to let the food cool, then refrigerate overnight, or until the fat rises to the top and solidifies. Simply lift off the layer of chilled fat and discard.

a steaming rack in the pot. Cover and steam until the duck is three quarters cooked, about 10 minutes. (The legs also may be used, but they need to steam about 25 minutes, or until a skewer passes easily through the flesh.)

Slowly sauté the leek, mushrooms, shallots and bacon for 10 minutes, until cooked through. Pour off the bacon fat.

Let the duck cool slightly, then pull off the skin. Cut each breast into 6 to 8 pieces. Reduce the wine mixture to one third of its original volume. Add the cooked vegetables and bacon. Season with salt and pepper. Whisk in a bit of cream if the sauce tastes sharp. Add the duck to the sauce and simmer until cooked through.

Serve the stew in soup plates, sprinkling on the peas to garnish.

SERVES 4 TO 6

# Salt-Seared Duck Legs with Fresh Apricots

*Fresh apricots, with their natural sweetness, pair beautifully with the sturdy flavor of duck. If fresh fruit isn't available, dried apricots work just fine. Georgeanne Brennan usually slices the meat off the legs, then serves it atop a mound of bitter greens, with the juices poured over the top. It also goes well with creamy mashed potatoes and braised spinach.*

½ teaspoon salt

2 duck legs

½ cup Riesling or other fruity white wine

2 tablespoons fresh lemon juice

1 tablespoon minced onion

1 tablespoon finely grated fresh ginger

2 tablespoons packed brown sugar

8 apricots, halved and pitted (see Note)

Sprinkle the salt in a nonstick skillet just large enough to hold the duck legs. Heat the salt over high heat, then add the duck legs and sear 2 to 3 minutes on each side, or until the skin is crisp and browned. Remove the duck. Reduce the heat to low; add the wine and lemon juice, scraping the pan with a wooden spoon to dislodge any bits stuck to the bottom of the pan. Add the onion and return the duck to the skillet. Cover tightly and cook over low heat for 12 to 15 minutes for rare meat, another 4 to 5 minutes for medium, longer if desired. Check occasionally to see if more liquid is needed. (If so, add a little more wine or water.)

While the duck is cooking, combine the ginger and sugar; set aside.

Three to 4 minutes before the duck is ready, tuck the halved apricots around the legs. Sprinkle with the ginger-sugar mixture and replace the cover. After 2 minutes, turn the legs, cover, and cook another minute or two, until the apricots are soft and the sugar has dissolved into the juices to form a sauce.

SERVES 2

**NOTE:** Dried apricot halves may be substituted for fresh. Add them when you return the legs to the skillet, and let simmer with the duck.

# John Carroll's Wine-Braised Turkey Breast

*A turkey breast, braised in wine, herbs and vegetables, cooks on top of the stove, leaving the oven free for other things. It is much faster to prepare than a whole roasted turkey and also is easier to carve, says author John Carroll. The sauce, prepared from the braising liquid, practically makes itself—and there is plenty for mashed potatoes and stuffing.*

1 whole turkey breast, skin on (about 6 pounds)

Salt and freshly ground pepper to taste

2 tablespoons vegetable oil

2 carrots, peeled and thinly sliced

2 celery stalks, thinly sliced

1 onion, thinly sliced

2 garlic cloves, mashed

2 cups turkey or chicken broth

1½ cups dry red wine

3 tablespoons softened butter

3 tablespoons flour

¼ cup heavy cream

## Basic Turkey-Roasting Times

| Weight | Cooking Temp. | Time |
| --- | --- | --- |
| 6–8 lbs | 325° | 2–2½ hrs |
| 8–12 lbs | 325° | 2½–3 hrs |
| 12–16 lbs | 325° | 3–3¾ hrs |
| 16–20 lbs | 325° | 3¾–4½ hrs |
| 20–24 lbs | 325° | 4½–5½ hrs |
| + 24 lbs | 300° | 14 min/lb |

Differences in the shape and tenderness of individual birds, as well as the temperature of the bird when put into the oven, may affect the cooking time slightly. For best results, use a roasting thermometer, which will read 175 to 180 degrees when the bird is properly cooked.

@@ Season the turkey breast all over with salt and pepper.

Heat the oil over medium heat in a Dutch oven or roasting pan. Add the turkey skin side down and brown in the hot oil. Remove the turkey, leaving the fat in the pan. Add the carrots, celery, onion and garlic and cook about 10 minutes, stirring occasionally, until wilted. Add the broth and wine and bring to a boil. Return the turkey to the pan, cover, and simmer over low heat for 1½ to 2 hours, or until a meat thermometer registers 170 degrees when inserted in the thickest part of the breast. Turn the turkey 2 or 3 times during cooking, and make sure the liquid is just gently bubbling. Remove the pan from the heat, and set aside for 20 minutes, with the cover askew (the turkey should be skin side down in the cooking liquid).

Transfer the turkey to a platter and keep it warm.

Strain the cooking liquid; you will have about 3½ cups. Rapidly boil it down to about 2½ cups to concentrate the flavor.

Meanwhile, blend together the butter and flour until smooth. Add to the reduced liquid, whisking constantly until blended. Add the cream and simmer for 3 minutes. Season with salt and pepper. Serve with the turkey.

SERVES 8 TO 10

# Tandoori Turkey with Pomegranate Juice

*This spicy masterpiece by Laxmi Hiremath offers an unusual twist on the traditional holiday bird. A whole turkey marinates in pomegranate juice, yogurt and Indian spices for up to 3 days. Just before roasting the turkey, you can pack carrots, celery and leeks into the cavity.*

A 12- to 14-pound turkey

3 lumps fresh ginger (each about 2 inches long)

24 garlic cloves

3 cups coarsely chopped onions

1½ cups plain yogurt

2 tablespoons ground coriander

1 tablespoon ground cumin

¾ teaspoon cayenne pepper

2 teaspoons whole cloves, ground

1 tablespoon cardamom seeds, ground

3 teaspoons kosher salt

2 cups fresh pomegranate juice (see Note)

2 large red bell peppers, seeded, deribbed and sliced

2 large green bell peppers, seeded, deribbed and sliced

2 tomatoes, sliced

2 large lemons, cut into wedges

◉◉ Wash the turkey; pat dry and place in a large casserole.

Combine the ginger, garlic, onions, yogurt, spices and salt in a blender; process until finely pureed. Rub the marinade into turkey cavity, turning several times, pushing marinade into slits and coating evenly. Pour the pomegranate juice over the turkey and rub gently. Cover and refrigerate for at least 10 hours or up to 3 days, rubbing the marinade into the turkey from time to time.

Preheat the oven to 450 degrees.

Truss the turkey with string. Place on a rack set in a large, heavy roasting pan. Roast 30 minutes. Reduce oven temperature to 325 degrees. Brush the turkey with the marinade and roast until a meat thermometer inserted in thickest part of a thigh registers 175 degrees, about 3 to 3¾ hours total roasting time. Baste occasionally with pan juices. Transfer the turkey to a serving platter and let rest for 10 minutes before carving.

Garnish the platter with the peppers, tomatoes and lemon wedges.

SERVES 12 TO 14

**NOTE:** Pomegranate juice is available in Near Eastern groceries and some specialty markets.

# Chapter 7

# Fish and Shellfish

*Fish is one of the best ideas for a quick dinner, but for whatever reason, many people are intimidated by the thought of cooking it.*

*Not only can it be grilled or sautéed and be on the table in minutes, but it's easy to enhance the flavor with a variety of dipping sauces and salsas. We've included many options designed to be mixed and matched.*

*On nights when time is at a premium, there are few dishes simpler than oven-fried fish fillets, where the fish is coated with mustard and mayonnaise and topped with a frothy egg white meringue. In addition, our recipe for butter-steamed salmon with mint vinaigrette can be on the table in 10 minutes and is truly company-fare caliber.*

*Although quick is not a word that comes to mind for cioppino, a classic San Francisco fish stew, it's ideal for a casual dinner party. Or, for a singular sensation, we have two recipes for mussels: one steamed in a spicy coconut broth and the other cooked with white wine and herbs.*

*One of the most distinctive dishes, a real showstopper, is a soufflélike spoon bread with peppered oysters.*

# Cracked Crab

*According to purists, the best way to eat Dungeness crab is to steam it, crack it and dip it into drawn (unsalted, clarifed) butter. Mary Etta Moose, of the ever-popular Moose's in North Beach, agrees with that philosophy.*

1 tablespoon whole black peppercorns

1 bay leaf, crumbled

1 cup dry white wine

2 cups water, or enough to almost cover the crabs

1 celery stalk, chopped

A few parsley stems (without leaves)

1 lemon, cut into wedges, plus extra lemon wedges for garnish

2 live Dungeness crabs

Clarified unsalted butter (see page 28) or melted butter, for dipping

∞ Select a pan just large enough to hold the crabs side by side. Heat the empty pan over low heat. Add the peppercorns and bay leaf and heat very briefly to release their flavoring oils. Immediately add the remaining ingredients (except the crabs), squeezing the lemon in before adding it. Bring to a boil and add the crabs. Cover, lower the heat and simmer 10 to 12 minutes. Remove the crabs and let cool until you can handle them comfortably.

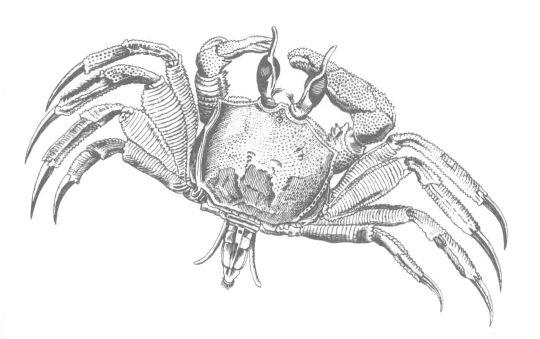

## Tips on Cooking and Cracking Crab

If cooking and cracking your own crab seems daunting, don't worry: It won't after you've done the first one. Here are some simple guidelines:

**Boiling.** Bring a large pot of water to a rolling boil, add the live crab, cover, and let the water return to a boil. Cook 15 minutes for a small crab (1½ pounds or less), 20 to 25 minutes for a 2½-pounder. Remove the crab and run a little cold water over it to cool the shell, then clean and crack to serve warm. To serve cold, surround the crab with ice before cleaning and cracking.

**Steaming.** Fill a wok or other large steaming pot with water and bring to a boil; plunge the live crab into the boiling water for about a minute. Retrieve the crab (turn off the heat under the pot) and clean, cut up and crack.

Toss the pieces in a large bowl with soy sauce, a dash of rice wine or sherry and a generous amount of shredded ginger and scallions. Let marinate for a few minutes.

Drain off enough water from the pot to keep the

level an inch or so below the steaming rack, then bring it back to a boil. Transfer the crab pieces with their marinade to a shallow bowl or plate that will fit on the rack; cover the wok and steam until all visible meat is opaque, 12 to 18 minutes, depending on size.

**Cleaning.** This step is the same whether the crab is cooked or raw. With the crab on its back, carefully lift the pointed apron on the underside, watching out for the spines underneath. Grasp the apron and twist it away. Do the same with the jaws at the front of the crab.

Holding the crab by the legs, pull off the top shell, which can be used for presentation. Pull off and discard the gills on each side of the body and all the spongy matter in the center. Only the shell and meat should remain.

**Cracking.** For serving Western style, the body is usually left whole or split in half and the legs and claws twisted off. Cracking each of the shell segments with a mallet makes the meat easier to extract. Provide individual nutcrackers for each person.

Disjoint the crabs and serve while still slightly warm, with lemon wedges and drawn butter. Provide bibs, napkins, nutcrackers, cocktail forks, hot finger towels and finger bowls with lemon squeezed into them.

SERVES 4

# Baltimore Crab Cakes

*Marion Cunningham went on a year-long search for the best crab cakes. She discovered them in Baltimore and fell in love with the sweet crab flavor and creamy texture. The secret ingredient—mayonnaise, which helps add moisture and brings out the best in the seafood.*

1 cup mayonnaise

1 tablespoon plus 1 teaspoon Dijon mustard

2 cups saltine cracker crumbs

2 cups fresh crabmeat

2 tablespoons oil

Lemon wedges

Tabasco sauce

Combine the mayonnaise and mustard in a mixing bowl and stir until well blended. Add 1 cup of the cracker crumbs and the crabmeat and mix well.

Put a large piece of waxed paper on the counter and spread the remaining cup of cracker crumbs on it.

Divide the crab mixture into 8 equal portions and pat each into a ball. Gently flatten each ball into a round about 3 inches in diameter. Lightly coat top and bottom of each cake in the crumbs.

Heat a large skillet over medium heat and film the bottom with the oil. Place the cakes in the skillet and fry over medium heat until golden on each side.

Serve hot with lemon wedges and Tabasco.

SERVES 4

# Grilled Shrimp with Papaya-Rocotillo Salsa

*Shrimp is one of the best seafoods for grilling. The smoked overtones of the fish are set off by Jacqueline McMahan's sweet-fiery papaya salsa.*

3 tablespoons fruity olive oil

3 tablespoons fresh lime juice

2 garlic cloves, minced

½ teaspoon freshly ground pepper

½ teaspoon salt

12 large raw shrimp, shelled

Papaya-Rocotillo Salsa (recipe follows)

∞  Soak 4 wooden skewers in water.

Combine the olive oil, lime juice, garlic, pepper and salt; mix well. Add the shrimp and let marinate 1 hour.

Remove the shrimp from the marinade and thread 3 shrimp onto each skewer. Grill over medium coals or a gas grill for about 2 minutes per side.

Serve with Papaya-Rocotillo Salsa.

SERVES 4 AS AN APPETIZER

## Papaya Rocotillo Salsa

*The rocotillo chile is a kissing cousin to the habanero, but not nearly as hot.*

2 rocotillo chiles, seeded and minced (see Note)

½ red bell pepper, seeded, deribbed and diced

1 ripe papaya, peeled, cut into small dice

¼ cup diced red onion

¼ cup minced fresh cilantro

¼ cup orange juice

¼ cup pineapple juice

Juice of 1 lemon

1 tablespoon honey

¼ teaspoon salt

Charles Solomon,
chef/owner of the Heights,
makes a basil oil that
maintains its bright green
color through the addition
of vitamin C. To 1½
pounds basil leaves and 2
cups olive oil, he pulverizes
and adds one and a half
500-milligram caplets of
vitamin C. He then purees
the mixture in a blender.
The unstrained puree can
then be used to thicken and
flavor sauces, or may be
drizzled over fish or grilled
chicken.

◎◎  Combine the chiles, bell pepper, papaya, onion and cilantro with the
juices and honey. Add just a bit of salt to bring out the flavors.

YIELDS ABOUT 3 CUPS

**NOTE:** If you cannot find rocotillos, substitute serrano chiles (about 4).
The flavor will be quite different but it will still be good.

# Martin Yan's Prawns with Fragrant Tea

*Oolong tea leaves make a marvelous sauce for prawns, steamed the Chinese
way in a bamboo steamer. Creator Martin Yan suggests orange spice tea as a
substitute, creating a sweeter perfumed flavor.*

### Shrimp

1 egg white, lightly beaten

2 teaspoons cornstarch

2 teaspoons Shaoxing wine or dry sherry

¼ teaspoon salt

Pinch white pepper

¾ pound medium shrimp, peeled (leave tail intact) and deveined

### Sauce

¼ cup chicken broth

1 tablespoon Shaoxing wine or dry sherry

1½ teaspoons good-quality ground Chinese oolong tea

¼ teaspoon sugar

Pinch white pepper

Fresh mint leaves for garnish

◎◎  To cook the shrimp: Combine the egg white, cornstarch, wine, salt
and white pepper in a bowl. Add the shrimp and stir to coat. Set aside for
30 minutes.

Place a steaming rack in a wok. Pour in water to just below the level of
the rack and bring to a boil. Place the shrimp in a heatproof dish and set the

dish on the rack. Cover and steam for 7 minutes, or until shrimp feel firm and turn pink.

To make the sauce: While shrimp are steaming, combine the broth, wine, tea, sugar and pepper in a small saucepan and bring to a boil; reduce heat and keep warm.

To serve: Strain the sauce and pour in the center of a round platter. Arrange the shrimp over the sauce. Garnish with mint leaves.

SERVES 4

# Mussels Cooked in an Aromatic Tomato Sauce

*In this Mediterranean-influenced dish by Janet Fletcher, plump mussels steam in a hearty tomato sauce that has been seasoned with garlic, red pepper flakes and wine. Serve with good country-style bread for mopping up all the juices.*

3 tablespoons olive oil

1 cup minced onion

½ cup minced celery

3 garlic cloves, minced

⅛ teaspoon red pepper flakes

1 cup chopped canned tomatoes

¾ cup dry white wine

3 tablespoons minced fresh parsley

Salt to taste

3 pounds mussels, scrubbed and debearded

◉ Heat the olive oil in a large pot over medium-low heat. Add the onion and celery and sauté until the celery is soft, about 15 minutes. Add the garlic and pepper flakes; sauté 1 minute. Add the tomato, wine and 2 tablespoons of the parsley. Simmer until the mixture loses its raw wine taste, about 10 minutes. Season with salt.

Increase the heat to high. Add the mussels, cover and cook, shaking the pot occasionally, until the mussels open, about 5 minutes.

Divide mussels and sauce among warm bowls. Top each portion with some of the remaining parsley.

SERVES 4

# Mussels in Spicy Coconut Milk

*Lemongrass is one of the most versatile flavorings and is used heavily in Thai cuisine. It has a pure lemon flavor with a hint of orange-blossom perfume. Niloufer Ichaporia pairs it with sweet coconut milk and mussels to create a fantastic broth that can be eaten like a soup when the shellfish has disappeared.*

3 pounds fresh mussels

¼ cup peanut oil

8-inch piece lemongrass, finely julienned

1 bunch scallions, coarsely chopped, including some of the green tops

2-inch piece fresh ginger, peeled and julienned

3 small fresh green or red chiles, thinly sliced (or slit and
    leave whole if you prefer less heat)

3 or 4 garlic cloves, chopped

2 cans (13.5 ounces each) unsweetened coconut milk

Salt to taste

Handful regular or Thai basil leaves

6 lime wedges

Scrub and debeard the mussels; set aside.

Heat the oil in a large wok or skillet over high heat. When hot, add the lemongrass, scallions, ginger, chiles and garlic. Stir-fry for a couple of minutes, until the seasonings begin to color. Add the coconut milk and bring to a simmer. Season with salt. Add the mussels, cover and cook until they open, about 3 minutes. Uncover and stir in the basil leaves.

Serve the mussels in wide soup bowls over steamed Indian basmati or Thai jasmine rice. Pass lime wedges at the table.

SERVES 6

**NOTE:** A 2-inch piece of fresh turmeric, peeled and julienned, is a delicious addition to the other seasonings, or add ½ teaspoon ground turmeric.

# Mussels Steamed in White Wine and Herbs

*Like the Atlantic Coast in Normandy and Brittany, the rocky shores of Northern California are home to huge populations of shiny blue-black mussels. California mussels, says Georgeanne Brennan, make a delectable version of the classic French moules marinière. As the mussels open, their juices release to mingle with the wine, herbs and garlic, creating a savory broth that begs to be sopped up with bread.*

1 cup dry white wine

6 branches fresh thyme, or 2 tablespoons chopped fresh thyme

1 bay leaf

8 pounds fresh mussels in the shell, scrubbed and debearded

2 garlic cloves

1 tablespoon butter

⚭ Combine the wine, thyme and bay leaf in a pot large enough to hold all the mussels. Add the cleaned mussels and grate the garlic cloves directly over them. Add the butter. Cover, turn heat to medium and cook just until the mussels open, about 10 minutes.

Serve the mussels in soup bowls with a ladle or two of broth over them.

SERVES 8

## All About Steaming

The microwave is the most convenient steaming tool in the kitchen. When you add liquid to the pan and cover it with plastic, you're steaming.

Chinese steamers are among the best for stove-top steaming. Boiling water (sometimes flavored) is in the bottom and the steamer, filled with vegetables, fish or meat is placed on top. When the pan is covered, the steam evenly cooks the food.

# Spoon Bread with Peppered Oysters

*Plump oysters are hidden beneath this airy, soufflelike spoon bread.*
*Georgeanne Brennan likes to serve it as a main course accompanied with*
*an arugula salad with thinly sliced radishes, dressed with only salt, pepper*
*and an excellent olive oil.*

2½ tablespoons butter

8 to 10 medium live oysters in the shell, or 1 (10-ounce) jar oysters,
    drained and juices reserved

2 to 2¼ cups milk

1 teaspoon salt

¼ cup minced fresh parsley

⅔ cup cornmeal

3 eggs, separated

2 tablespoons black peppercorns, finely ground

◉ Preheat the oven to 375 degrees.

Thoroughly grease the bottom and sides of a 10 x 10 x 2–inch deep
baking dish with ½ tablespoon of the butter.

Shuck the live oysters, if using, reserving their juices. Combine the
reserved oyster juices and 2 cups milk; add more milk if necessary to make
2¼ cups liquid.

Place the remaining butter in a medium saucepan; add the milk mixture,
the salt and parsley. Cook over medium-high heat just until bubbles form
along the edge of the pan. Slowly pour in the cornmeal, stirring constantly to
prevent lumps. Cook 1 to 2 minutes, stirring constantly. Remove from heat
and let cool 3 or 4 minutes.

Beat the egg whites until stiff.

Beat the egg yolks into the cornmeal mixture, then gently fold in the
beaten whites.

Sprinkle the oysters on both sides with the pepper and place them in a
single layer in the bottom of the baking dish. Spoon in the cornmeal mixture
and spread it evenly across the oysters.

Bake for 25 to 30 minutes, or until a knife inserted near the center comes
out clean, but the very center is still creamy.

SERVES 4 TO 6

# Crispy Fried Squid with Three Hot Sauces

*One of the most popular dishes on any San Francisco menu is fried squid. Marlena Spieler's at-home version bests them all. She accompanies the crisp calamari with three relishes: a lemony jalapeno and onion mix, a garlicky tomato salsa and a quick tomato chutney, which calls for mustard oil (available at specialty, Indian and Middle Eastern groceries; or see Note for how to make your own). Make them all or choose just one; they also add a dash of flavor to just about any broiled or grilled fish.*

> 4 to 5 pounds squid, cleaned
>
> 2 cups flour, or as needed
>
> Vegetable oil for frying
>
> Salt and cayenne pepper to taste
>
> Hot sauces of choice (recipes follow)

∾ Cut the squid into ½-inch strips. Toss with flour.

Heat about 2 inches of oil in a heavy skillet. When hot enough to instantly fry a tiny crouton of bread, the oil is ready. Fry the squid in batches until lightly browned, removing and draining finished squid on paper towels.

Season the squid with salt and cayenne. Serve immediately, accompanied with sauces of choice.

SERVES 4

## Lemony Jalapenos en Escabeche Salsa

> 5 or 6 jalapenos en escabeche (pickled jalapenos), plus a tablespoon of the marinade
>
> 1 onion, chopped finely
>
> 3 garlic cloves, chopped
>
> 1 to 2 tablespoons chopped parsley
>
> ¼ teaspoon ground cumin (optional)
>
> Juice of 3 or 4 lemons

∾ Combine all ingredients. Serve with fried squid.

YIELDS ABOUT 1½ CUPS

## To Clean Whole Squid

Cut off the tentacles just above the eyes, then remove and discard the small hard beak in the center. Rinse the squid under cold water, pulling off the skin with your fingers (it comes off easily). Insert your finger into the body of the squid and pull out the intestines and quill. Rinse the body cavity with cold water. Leave the body whole for stuffing, or cut into rings, squares, etc.

## Garlicky Salsa

6 to 10 garlic cloves

3 jalapeno chiles, stemmed but not seeded

5 ripe tomatoes, diced

½ cup fresh cilantro leaves

Juice of 1 lemon

1½ teaspoons ground cumin

Salt to taste

⚭ Puree the garlic in a food processor or blender, then add the remaining ingredients. The salsa should be somewhat smooth, only a little chunky.

YIELDS ABOUT 2 CUPS

## Tamatar Chatni (Tomato Chutney)

½ medium onion, chopped

2 teaspoons chopped fresh ginger

½ to 1 jalapeno or other fresh hot chile, seeded and minced

2 teaspoons mustard oil (see Note)

½ teaspoon ground turmeric

½ teaspoon ground coriander

4 medium tomatoes, coarsely chopped

½ teaspoon sugar

Salt to taste

⚭ Gently sauté the onion, ginger and chile in the mustard oil until the onion has softened. Sprinkle in the turmeric and coriander, cook a minute or so, then add the tomatoes, sugar and salt. Cook over medium heat until the mixture thickens, about 10 minutes. Let cool to room temperature.

YIELDS ABOUT 1½ CUPS

**NOTE:** Mustard oil may be found in Indian markets and some Near Eastern groceries. If you cannot find it, heat about ¼ cup canola oil in a small saucepan; add a teaspoon or so of yellow mustard seeds. When the seeds begin to pop and splutter (have a lid handy to cover the pan), remove the pan from the heat. Let the oil cool, then strain. This is not as pungent as true mustard oil, but it will do when only small quantities are called for.

# Hog Island Oysters with Bolinas Crabmeat

*Jeremiah Tower, owner of Stars restaurant, is one of the most innovative chefs in America. In this recipe, he tops fresh oysters in the shell with a mixture of crabmeat, diced potatoes and cream, delicately accented with tarragon. Serve as an elegant first course, or as a brunch or special lunch dish.*

24 live oysters in the shell

Rock salt

1 large potato, peeled, cut into ⅛-inch dice

1 cup half-and-half

¼ teaspoon salt

½ pound fresh crabmeat

1 sprig fresh tarragon, stemmed and chopped

Freshly ground pepper to taste

Lemon wedges for garnish

Preheat the oven to 425 degrees.

Open the oysters. Cut the muscles to free oysters from their shells and pour the juices into a small saucepan, keeping each oyster in its shell. Arrange the shells in a shallow baking pan filled with rock salt.

Add the potato, half-and-half and salt to the saucepan with the oyster juices. Simmer for 15 minutes, or until the potatoes are tender. Stir often. Mix in the crabmeat, tarragon and pepper. Mound on top of the oysters. Bake for 15 minutes.

Serve with lemon wedges.

SERVES 6

# Malaysian Squid Satay with Dipping Sauce

*Few people realize that squid is great on the grill. Bruce Cost marinates it first in a Malaysian-style sauce, and serves the calamari with a lively peanut-lime-chile dipping sauce.*

3 pounds squid, cleaned and cut in rings

1 tablespoon cumin seeds

2 tablespoons coriander seeds

3 small dried red peppers

2 tablespoons Thai fish sauce

2 tablespoons fresh lime juice

1 tablespoon packed brown sugar

**Dipping Sauce**

2 tablespoons peanut oil

2 tablespoons chopped garlic

2 tablespoons chopped fresh ginger

2 tablespoons chopped dried red peppers, seeds and all

3 tablespoons fresh lime juice

¼ cup Thai fish sauce

2 teaspoons sugar

1 tablespoon chile oil

¼ cup roasted peanuts, ground to a coarse paste

¼ cup finely minced cilantro leaves

◉◉ Thread the squid rings and tentacles (through the fleshy part) on bamboo skewers, leaving about 3 inches of skewer for a handle. Wrap handle and tip in aluminum foil (or soak skewers 1 hour in water before using).

Combine the cumin, coriander and red peppers; toast in a dry skillet until fragrant. Grind to a powder. Mix well with the fish sauce, lime juice and brown sugar. Add the squid and let marinate on a tray for 30 minutes, turning from time to time.

Meanwhile, get a hot fire going on a grill; combine all the ingredients for the dipping sauce.

Grill the squid about 90 seconds on each side. Serve with the dipping sauce on the side.

SERVES 4 TO 6

# Butter-Steamed Salmon with Mint Vinaigrette

*Mint, minced onion and balsamic vinegar are refreshing against the buttery-textured fish. "This dish couldn't be easier," says Maria Cianci, "and takes only about 10 minutes to make."*

4 center-cut pieces salmon fillet (6 to 8 ounces each), skinned and pin bones removed
8 teaspoons butter
Salt and freshly ground pepper to taste
¼ cup water

**Mint Vinaigrette**

6 tablespoons finely chopped fresh mint
3¾ tablespoons balsamic vinegar
4 teaspoons minced onion
⅛ teaspoon salt
⅛ teaspoon pepper
6 tablespoons corn or other neutrally flavored oil

∞ Cut 2 slits in each salmon fillet, each about 1 inch long and three fourths the depth of the fillet. Fill each slit with 1 teaspoon butter. Season the fish with salt and pepper. Place the fillets in a skillet large enough to hold them without touching each other. Add the water. Cover the skillet and place over medium-high heat. Simmer until the salmon is just cooked through, 6 to 8 minutes.

While the salmon cooks, make the vinaigrette: Combine the mint, vinegar, onion, salt, and pepper. Let stand 5 minutes. Whisk in the oil.

Carefully plate each cooked fillet with as much melted butter as possible; drizzle each fillet with 2 tablespoons of the vinaigrette.

SERVES 4

## Substituting Fish

Here's an easy guide to determine which fish can substitute for others in various recipes.

Lean (less than 1½ percent fat): The cod family, including cod, haddock, pollock; various species of hake; rockfish or "Pacific snapper," including Pacific and Atlantic ocean perch; lingcod; all the flatfish, including sole, flounder, sand dabs and halibut (but not Greenland halibut or so-called turbot); true red snapper from the Southeast; Hawaiian opakapaka, onaga and ta'ape; mahi-mahi; orange roughy; most shellfish, including crustaceans (crab, lobster, shrimp), scallops, most clams.

Moderate (1½ to 4½ percent fat): Sea bass, including groupers, the black sea bass of the Atlantic Coast and sea bass from Chile and New Zealand; California white sea bass, sea trout, weakfish, black drum and Louisiana redfish; sharks, skates and rays; monkfish; swordfish; oysters, mussels and squid.

Rich (5 to 12 percent fat): Salmon, mackerel and tuna; bluefish and the herring family, including shad and sardines.

15 percent fat: Sablefish (also called butterfish or black cod).

15 to 20 percent fat: Eel.

# Pan-Grilled Salmon on a Bed of Asian Greens

*As salmon fillets sear in the frying pan, their natural juices mingle with cayenne, lemon juice and white wine to make a tart sauce, sufficiently spicy to dress the greens. Spinach may be substituted for the Asian greens in this Georgeanne Brennan recipe.*

1 teaspoon butter
2 skinless salmon fillets
¼ teaspoon salt
½ teaspoon cayenne pepper
¼ cup fresh lemon juice
¼ cup dry white wine
1½ cups mixed young greens (mizuna, red mustard, tat-soi, spinach)

◉◉ Melt the butter in a small, preferably nonstick frying pan over medium-high heat. Add the salmon and sear 1 to 2 minutes on each side. Sprinkle with salt and cayenne. Turn the fillets, then add the lemon juice and wine. Reduce heat to low, cover, and cook 2 to 3 minutes, or until the salmon is just tender and flakes easily.

Divide the greens between 2 serving plates. Pour half of the pan juices over each, and top with a salmon fillet.

SERVES 2

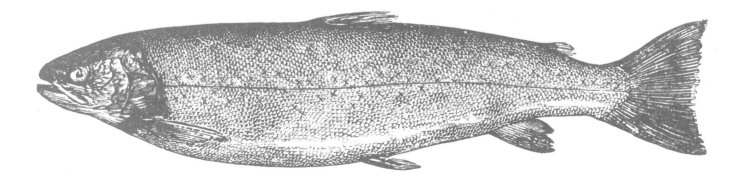

# Narsai's Gravlax (Salmon Marinated in Dill and Aquavit)

*A longtime columnist for* The Chronicle, *Narsai David has become known for many of his recipes, but his easy-to-make gravlax is one of our favorites. It's served with a light mustard and dill sauce that has the consistency of mayonnaise.*

1 teaspoon each dried dill weed and dill seed, or 1 tablespoon chopped fresh dill

2 pounds salmon fillet with skin

2 tablespoons coarse salt

4 tablespoons sugar

¼ teaspoon freshly ground black pepper

¼ teaspoon ground allspice

¼ cup aquavit

Mustard Dill Sauce (recipe follows)

◎◎ Mix together the dill weed and dill seed, if using; sprinkle half of the mixture over the bottom of a flat pan or dish that is big enough to hold the salmon.

Slash the skin side of the salmon 3 or 4 times with a sharp knife. Set the salmon skin side down in the pan. Sprinkle with the remaining dill.

Blend together the salt, sugar, pepper and allspice; distribute evenly over the salmon, patting lightly into the flesh. Pour the aquavit over the fish.

Cover the pan with clear plastic wrap and place a weight on top—a couple of large cans of juice or soup (or anything else) work well. Refrigerate for at least 2 days, spooning the juices over the fish from time to time. After the first day, remove the weights.

The salmon will keep in the refrigerator for up to 5 days. After that it becomes too salty.

To serve: Thinly slice the fish across the grain on a diagonal, cutting the flesh away from the skin. May be served with thinly sliced whole-grain bread and Mustard Dill Sauce.

SERVES 8 TO 12 AS A FIRST COURSE

## Baking in Foil

One of the easiest and cleanest ways to cook fish is to combine fillets and vegetables or herbs in foil packets. These ideas are from Jackie Mallorca:

*For halibut:* Preheat the oven to 400 degrees. Lightly butter the center of a 12 x 16–inch sheet of foil. Place a 6-ounce fillet of fish in the middle, add salt and pepper, about a tablespoon of dry white wine and a tablespoon of chopped fresh herbs such as tarragon or chives. Fold the foil over the fish, like closing a book. Crimp the edges tightly together for a D-shaped package. Place on a baking sheet and bake for about 8 minutes.

*For salmon:* Preheat the oven to 400 degrees. Spread a teaspoon of Asian sesame oil over a 12 x 16–inch sheet of foil. Arrange about a cup of cleaned spinach leaves on the foil. Place an 8-ounce fillet of salmon on the spinach. Season with salt and pepper and drizzle with another teaspoon of sesame oil. Add another cup of leaves and fold as directed above. Place on a baking sheet and cook for 10 minutes.

### Mustard Dill Sauce

¼ cup Dijon mustard

1 teaspoon dry mustard

3 tablespoons sugar

2 tablespoons white wine vinegar

⅓ cup olive oil

¼ cup chopped fresh dill, or 2 tablespoons dried dill

◎◎ Mix together the mustards, sugar and vinegar. Slowly drizzle in the oil, whisking constantly to create a light mayonnaiselike consistency. Stir in the dill.

YIELDS 1 CUP

# Steamed Sea Bass with a Compote of Oranges and Lemons

*This simple presentation, from Marlena Spieler, brings out the best in sea bass. The warmed citrus complements the sweetness of the fish and takes the place of a heavier sauce.*

1½ pounds sea bass fillets

Handful bay leaves or seaweed

2 tablespoons butter (optional)

Coarse salt and black pepper to taste

4 oranges, peeled and segmented

2 lemons, peeled and segmented

¼ cup olive oil, or to taste

1 red bell pepper, roasted, seeded and cut into strips

Handful fresh green herbs or other greens (mint leaves, arugula, fennel)

◎◎ Place the fish fillets in a single layer in a steamer on top of a bed of either bay leaves or seaweed. Top with butter and season with salt and pepper. Steam until the fish is just cooked through; it should be opaque and slightly firm to the touch.

Warm the orange and lemon segments in the olive oil. Do not fry. Season with salt and pepper.

Place the fish on warm plates and surround with little mounds of the citrus, strands of red pepper and herb leaves.

SERVES 4 TO 6

# Baked Shark on a Bed of Potatoes and Artichokes, Catalan Style

*Fish with artichokes and potatoes is typical Balearic Island fare, according to Marlena Spieler, who enjoys the robust flavors of Mediterranean food. Use any firm, white-fleshed fish—halibut, swordfish, tuna, sea bass—for this meal-in-a-casserole.*

⅔ to ¾ pound baking potatoes

Olive oil

3 artichoke hearts, blanched and sliced (frozen OK, but not as good as fresh)

Salt and pepper to taste

1½ to 2 pounds shark steaks (or halibut, swordfish, tuna, sea bass)

2 or 3 tomatoes, halved

6 garlic cloves, chopped

2 teaspoons chopped fresh parsley

2 green onions, chopped

½ to 1 teaspoon chopped fresh rosemary

½ to 1 teaspoon chopped fresh thyme

Fresh lemon juice

◎ Preheat the oven to 375 or 400 degrees. Boil the potatoes in water to cover for 10 minutes. Drain. Let cool until you can handle them, then peel and slice.

Coat the bottom of a ceramic casserole or other baking dish with olive oil, then layer in overlapping slices of potato and artichoke, sprinkling with salt and pepper as you go. Top with the fish, then tuck the tomato halves into any empty spaces. Drizzle olive oil over the top. Sprinkle with garlic, parsley,

Other than seared sashimi-style tuna, fish should be cooked until the center is just turning opaque but is still moist.

To test for doneness, try using the skewer test: When a thin wooden skewer slips in and out of the middle of the fish with just a bit of raw-meat resistance, whisk it off the heat. Try the test first on a piece of raw fish so you can feel the contrast.

Remember that fish continues to cook for a minute or two after coming off the heat, more with thicker cuts.

Another method: Place the fish on a work surface and measure at its thickest point. For each inch of thickness, allow 10 minutes of cooking time, no matter what the method.

green onions and herbs. Drizzle on a generous amount of lemon juice, then season with more salt and pepper.

Bake for 25 to 30 minutes, or until the fish and vegetables are cooked through.

SERVES 4

# Grilled Tuna Steaks with Sephardic Chile Relish

*This easy grilled tuna from Marlena Spieler is served with a sprightly relish made from tomatoes, chiles, garlic, cumin, lemon juice and lots of cilantro.*

½ to 1 medium jalapeno chile, seeded and chopped

4 garlic cloves, chopped

1 cup coarsely chopped fresh cilantro

¼ teaspoon ground cumin

¼ cup fresh lemon juice

2 tablespoons olive oil

4 tuna or salmon steaks (4 to 6 ounces each)

Salt and pepper to taste

2 medium tomatoes, coarsely chopped or diced

Combine the jalapeno, garlic, cilantro, cumin and lemon juice. Mix 1 tablespoon of this mixture with the oil, then brush onto the fish. Season with salt and pepper.

Grill 3 to 4 minutes on each side, or until the fish feels firm.

Combine the tomato with the remaining jalapeno-cilantro mixture.

Serve each steak hot from the grill, accompanied with a spoonful of the chile relish.

SERVES 4

# Sesame-Crusted Tuna with Miso Consomme

*Ken Oringer, who was the chef of Silks in the Mandarin Oriental hotel before moving to Boston, created this recipe. It's a spectacular dish for a dinner party because of its intriguing presentation and its East-West flavors. The sautéed tuna is served in a miso broth with vegetables and slices of Asian pear, which gives a subtle sweetness to the blend.*

½ pound thin asparagus

1 turnip, thinly sliced

4 cups chicken broth

4 tablespoons red miso paste

4 blocks (5 ounces each) sashimi-quality tuna

½ cup white and black sesame seeds

1 teaspoon Japanese togarashi (pepper) seasoning

Salt to taste

Lemon olive oil (see Note)

¼ cup sliced mushrooms (black trumpet, shiitake or other wild mushroom)

2 heads baby bok choy, leaves separated

Pepper to taste

1 Asian pear, stemmed, thinly sliced

2 scallions, julienned

20 watercress leaves

◎◎ Trim all but the top 3 inches from each asparagus spear.

Blanch or steam the turnip slices until tender. Set aside.

Put the chicken broth in a saucepan and cook over high heat, whisking in the miso, until reduced to 2 cups. Remove from heat, cover, and let steep 15 minutes.

Coat the tuna with the sesame seeds, then season with togarashi and salt. Sauté over medium-high heat, turning occasionally, until warm on the outside but still rare in the center. Set aside.

Heat a little lemon olive oil in a sauté pan. Add the mushrooms, asparagus and bok choy; cook, stirring, for a minute or so, then add ¼ cup of the reserved miso broth. Season with salt and pepper. Cook until the vegetables are glazed and tender.

## A Crisper Crust

To get a crisper crust on fish, Kirk Webber of Cafe Kati suggests replacing some of the flour used in breading with cornstarch.

Place the turnips in the remaining miso broth to keep them warm.

To serve: Cut each tuna block into 5 horizontal slices. Place equal amounts of the sautéed vegetables and a few turnip slices in the center of 4 large soup bowls. Arrange a few pear slices on top to form a level "bed." Alternate pear slices, turnip slices and tuna on top of the vegetables to create a "napoleon" effect, ending with a sesame seed-coated slice of tuna. Drizzle with a little lemon olive oil and scatter scallions on top. Pour warm miso broth around the sides and garnish with watercress leaves.

SERVES 4

**NOTE:** Lemon olive oil is sold in stores, or you can make your own by adding a little lemon zest or peel to olive oil and letting it sit overnight.

# Tonno al Salmoriglio

*This specialty of the Italian island of Lipari, as interpreted by Marlena Spieler, consists of fresh tuna marinated in a spicy Salmoriglio sauce. This sauce is based on olive oil and lemon juice. Traditionally, a little sea water was also added.*

6 garlic cloves

½ to ¾ cup olive oil

Juice of 2 lemons

3 tablespoons balsamic vinegar

Salt to taste

Cayenne pepper or chopped fresh chiles to taste

Crushed dried oregano to taste

¼ cup chopped fresh Italian parsley

2 to 3 pounds fresh tuna steaks

Roasted red pepper strips for garnish

Combine the garlic, olive oil, lemon juice and vinegar. Season with salt, cayenne pepper or chiles and oregano. Stir in the parsley. Pour half of the marinade over the tuna. Let marinate about 30 minutes.

Grill the tuna over hot coals until it just starts to flake. Serve hot from the grill, sauced with the remaining marinade and garnished with roasted red peppers.

SERVES 8

## White-Wine Fish Stock

Melt 2 tablespoons butter in a large stockpot over low heat. Add 1 cup diced onion and 1 cup diced carrot, cover and cook until the vegetables are soft but not browned. Add 5 pounds well-rinsed heads, bones and trimmings from lean fish; 10 parsley sprigs; 1 bay leaf; 1 teaspoon white peppercorns; 1½ cups dry white wine and 8 cups water. Bring to a boil, reduce heat to low and simmer uncovered for no longer than 35 minutes, skimming occasionally. Strain. Refrigerate for up to 2 days, or freeze for longer storage. Yields about 2 quarts.

## Basic Court Bouillon for Fish

Combine 1 quart water and 1 cup dry white wine in a nonaluminum saucepan. Add ½ onion, sliced; ½ cup sliced carrots; 2 or 3 parsley sprigs; 1 bay leaf; 6 peppercorns, cracked; ¼ teaspoon anise or fennel seed; and ½ teaspoon salt. Bring to a boil, reduce heat and simmer 15 to 20 minutes. Strain before using. Don't simmer longer or the broth will have a strong calcium flavor.

## Basic Fish Velouté

Melt 5 tablespoons unsalted butter in a heavy skillet over medium-low heat. When the foam subsides, blend in 6 tablespoons flour. Cook, stirring constantly, until the mixture no longer has a raw flour aroma, about 15 minutes. The mixture should not brown.

Remove from heat.

Bring 4 cups fish stock to a boil in a saucepan; remove from heat. Little by little, whisk in the flour mixture. Return to the heat and simmer gently for 20 minutes, skimming as needed. Season with salt and white pepper. Strain and refrigerate. When chilled, remove fat that has solidified on top. Reheat, then strain into storage containers and refrigerate or freeze until ready to use. Yields 4 cups.

## Quick Fish Stock

Use bottled clam juice as a quick substitute for fish broth; it works especially well if you add a squirt of lemon or lime and fresh herbs.

# Cioppino

*Cioppino is a classic San Francisco fish stew. Unfortunately, it's rarely found at restaurants outside Fisherman's Wharf, where it's only a shadow of what it should be. Here's a recipe created by the late Jane Benet,* The Chronicle's *food editor for more than 30 years. As with the bouillabaisse of southern France, cioppino relies on whatever fresh fish and shellfish are available. We like plenty of crab, but you can substitute firm-fleshed fish for part of the crab.*

1 cup fine olive oil

2 large onions

1 large bunch Italian parsley, trimmed

2 large garlic cloves

2 large cans solid-pack tomatoes, with juice

2 cans tomato sauce, 6 ounces each

2 bay leaves

1 teaspoon dried Greek oregano

Salt and coarsely ground black pepper to taste

2 cups dry white wine

1 pound medium shrimp, cooked, shelled and deveined

2 pounds uncooked sea trout, bass, rock cod, halibut or other firm fish, skinned, boned and cut into bite-sized pieces

3 or 4 cooked crabs

Heat the oil slowly in a large, deep, heavy kettle.

Chop the onions, parsley and garlic together until fine, then sauté in the oil until golden. Add the tomatoes, tomato sauce, bay leaves, oregano and salt and pepper. Simmer, covered, for 1 hour.

Add the wine, shrimp and the fish. Cook 10 minutes, stirring occasionally. Add the crabs, leaving the claw meat in the shells and cracking them. Correct the seasoning and cook another 8 to 10 minutes to heat through. Serve in soup plates.

SERVES 6 TO 10, DEPENDING ON APPETITES

# Malabar Fish Curry with Coconut Milk

*This simple classic from the coastal region of Southern India, as adapted by Laxmi Hiremath, makes a quick and satisfying entree for a dinner party.*

4 half-inch-thick fish fillets (red snapper, sole, bass or whitefish), 5½ ounces each

2 tablespoons fresh lemon juice

½ teaspoon salt, or to taste

½ teaspoon freshly ground pepper

2½ tablespoons mild vegetable oil

8 fresh or dried curry leaves, or ¼ cup minced fresh cilantro

1 cup chopped onion

2 teaspoons grated fresh ginger

1 or 2 serrano chiles, seeded and minced

¼ teaspoon ground turmeric

½ teaspoon ground cumin

2 tablespoons unsweetened flaked coconut

1½ cups coconut milk

Place the fish in a shallow dish and rub well with lemon juice. Sprinkle with salt and pepper. Set aside to marinate for at least 30 minutes.

Heat 1½ tablespoons of the oil in a heavy frying pan over medium-high heat. Add the fish and cook until just opaque, about 2 minutes per side. Remove with a slotted spoon and set aside.

Heat the remaining 1 tablespoon oil in the same pan. Add the curry leaves, onion, ginger, chiles and turmeric. Cook until the onion is soft, about 3 minutes. Add the cumin, coconut and coconut milk. Cook, uncovered, until the sauce is slightly thick, 8 to 10 minutes. Gently slip in the fish fillets; cook 1 or 2 minutes and remove from heat. Transfer the fish to a heated platter. Spoon the sauce over the fish.

SERVES 2

**NOTE:** Dried (and sometimes fresh) curry leaves are available at Indian grocery stores.

## Fish Tip

To remove the odor of raw fish from hands, utensils and cutting boards, rub with the cut side of a lemon.

# Poached Fish with Papaya, Tomatillo and Chile Salsa

*This salsa is so good, Georgeanne Brennan claims she could eat a bowl of it by herself. The combination of perfumed papaya, citrusy tomatillo and fiery chile is the perfect panacea for lagging summer appetites.*

3 papayas, peeled, seeded and cut into ¼-inch cubes

6 tomatillos, husked and finely chopped

6 serrano chiles, seeded and minced

⅛ teaspoon salt

¼ cup fresh lime juice

1 tablespoon butter

1 tablespoon vegetable oil

¼ teaspoon ground cumin

½ teaspoon cayenne pepper or ground chile

4 firm fish steaks (sea bass, salmon, halibut), about ½ inch thick

¼ cup fresh lemon juice

¼ cup water

∞ Combine the papayas, tomatillos and chiles in a bowl; season with the salt and lime juice. Set aside while you prepare the fish.

Combine the butter and oil in a nonstick skillet; heat until the butter foams. Toss in the cumin and cayenne or ground chile and stir for a second or two until the spices are fragrant. Add the fish and cook over medium heat for 2 or 3 minutes on each side. Add lemon juice and water, cover, and cook over low heat for 3 to 4 minutes, or until the fish flakes easily.

Transfer the fish to serving plates and pour some of the pan juices over each serving. Serve with the salsa on the side.

SERVES 4

## How to Poach

One of the best techniques for low-calorie cooking, poaching can also add flavor to dishes. When poached, chicken becomes plump and tender, fish moist and delicate.

Choose a pan that just fits the item to be poached. Season the liquid (water, stock or vegetable juice) and put enough liquid in the pan to cover the food when it is added. Bring the liquid to a boil, then reduce the heat to simmer. Add the food and adjust the heat so the liquid barely bubbles. If the liquid covers the food, no lid is needed.

When the food is cooked through, remove with a slotted spoon. The liquid may be reduced and strained to produce a sauce or used in a soup.

# Basic Asian Steamed Fish with Garlic and Lime

*In this country-style Thai recipe by Joyce Jue, a whole fish is steamed in a simple garlic-chile-lime marinade. The quality of the dish depends on the fish—purchase the freshest you can find and cook it the same day you buy it. Serve with wedges of lime. The fish would also be especially good with any of the relishes used with the Crispy Fried Squid recipe on page 250.*

A 1- to 1½-pound whole trout, sea bass, perch or red snapper

4 fresh green hot chiles (such as jalapenos, serranos or Thai chiles), cut in half and crushed

6 garlic cloves, chopped

2 tablespoons Thai fish sauce (nam pla)

4 tablespoons fresh lime juice

½ cup chicken stock

2 green onions, cut in half lengthwise, then into 2-inch lengths

2 stalks lemongrass, tender heart section only, cut into 2-inch lengths and crushed

Cilantro sprigs

◉◉ Scale and clean the fish, then rinse under cold water. Pat dry with paper towels. Make diagonal slashes (almost to the bone) 2 inches apart on both sides of the fish. Set the fish on a heat-proof plate that is at least 1 inch smaller than the diameter of your wok.

Mix together the chiles, garlic, fish sauce, lime juice and chicken stock. Adjust for a predominantly sour taste. Pour over the fish. Scatter the green onions and lemongrass over the fish.

Fill a wok with 2 inches of boiling water. Place a steaming rack or trivet in the wok. Bring the water to a full boil, then set the plate with the fish on the rack. Cover tightly. Reduce heat to medium-high and steam for 12 minutes, or until the fish is done (the flesh by the bone should be opaque white).

Garnish with cilantro. Accompany with steamed rice.

SERVES 4 WITH OTHER ENTREES

## Keeping Fish Moist

One of the best ways to intensify the flavor of lean white fish, such as rock cod, sole, cod, flounder and trout, is to leave the skin intact. This works especially well when grilling because the fat in the skin helps to baste the fish and keep it moist. Bones left in the fish also retard drying out during cooking.

# Fish Fillets with Mustard Meringue

*Marion Cunningham adapted this recipe from the* Classic West Coast Cookbook *by Helen Evans Brown. Don't be intimidated by the steps of baking the fish, beating egg whites and blanching and sautéing spinach with lemon zest. All these tasks can be completed in about 10 minutes while the fish is baking. The almost souffléed meringue on top adds an unusual twist and makes this easy dish ideal dinner-party fare.*

2 pounds red snapper or sole fillets

Salt to taste

2 bunches spinach, stemmed

2 tablespoons butter

2 teaspoons grated lemon zest

2 tablespoons fresh lemon juice

2 egg whites

2 teaspoons Dijon mustard

⅔ cup mayonnaise

⅓ cup grated Parmesan or romano cheese

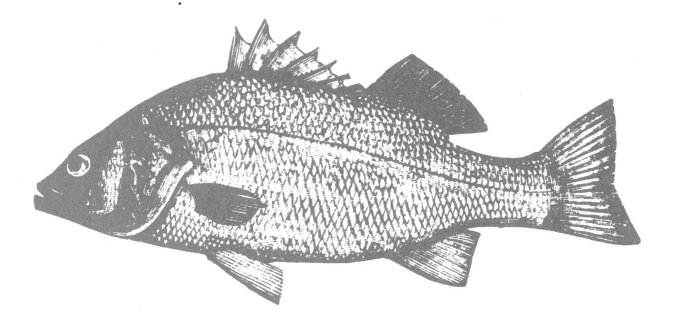

◎◎ Preheat the oven to 425 degrees.

Butter a shallow baking dish just large enough for the fish fillets, then place the fish in the dish. Bake for 8 to 10 minutes, or until the fish feels firm and the flesh turns opaque. Don't overbake. Remove from the oven and set aside.

Put a large pot of lightly salted water over high heat. When the water boils, add the spinach and cook 5 seconds; drain.

Put the pot over medium heat; add the butter, swirling the pot until the butter melts. Add the lemon zest and 1 tablespoon of the lemon juice. Gently mix with the spinach. Taste and add the remaining lemon juice and more salt, if needed. Set aside.

Beat the egg whites until stiff peaks form. Stir the mustard into the mayonnaise, then gently fold the mixture into the egg whites. Sprinkle the cheese over the mixture and gently fold it in.

Spread the egg-white mixture over the fish. Broil about 6 inches from the heat element until the topping puffs a little and turns golden, about 3 to 5 minutes. Watch carefully.

Quickly portion the spinach onto serving plates. Top with the fish and serve.

SERVES 4

# Chapter 8

# Breads, Waffles and Muffins

The Chronicle *is lucky to have two of the best home bakers in the country—
Flo Braker and Marion Cunningham—and they are the backbone of this
chapter. From popovers, biscuits and waffles to chocolate chip bread, bread
sticks and cake buns, they have the ultimate recipes.*

*In addition, one of our contributors, Jackie Mallorca, is allergic to wheat so
you'll find a delicious recipe for rice flour and yogurt pancakes. And you'll
also find recipes for corn fritters, jalapeno corn bread, banana chocolate chip
bread and even pizza dough.*

*For those who like to do things ahead, Sharon Cadwallader created four
baking mixes—including a buttermilk whole-wheat version and a
multigrain—along with suggestions for how to use them.*

# Basic Crepes

*Crepes are a quick way to give leftovers a new life; just about anything can be wrapped up. In making the batter remember that the amount of flour and liquid in each batch will depend on a host of variables: the density of the flour, the atmospheric humidity and so forth. Adjust the flour/liquid ratio accordingly: You want a batter the consistency of thick cream, says Marlena Spieler.*

3 eggs

1 cup low-fat milk

¼ cup water

⅔ cup all-purpose flour, plus more as needed

Pinch salt

3 tablespoons oil (bland vegetable oil, olive oil or melted butter)

Butter or oil for the pan

⊚⊚ Whisk the eggs until lightly beaten. Add the milk, water, flour, salt and oil. Whisk until the lumps disappear.

Place a crepe pan over medium-low heat. When hot, brush the pan with butter or oil. Spoon 3 or 4 tablespoons of the batter into the pan, swirling it around so the batter covers the bottom of the pan in a thin layer. Cook until the crepe is no longer runny on top and the edges pull up slightly. Turn the crepe and quickly cook the top side. Flip the crepe onto a plate and repeat with the remaining batter. (Note: The first crepe of each batch almost never turns out—making a convenient snack for the cook.)

SERVES 4 (ABOUT 3 CREPES PER PERSON)

# Easy Waffles

*This all-purpose batter by Flo Braker lends itself to numerous flavor variations.*

2¼ cups sifted cake flour

1 tablespoon sugar

2 teaspoons baking powder

## Egg Tips

To test raw eggs in the shell for freshness, place in a bowl and cover with water. If the eggs stay on the bottom of the bowl, they're fine; if they float, throw them out.

To bring chilled eggs to room temperature quickly, place them in a bowl and cover with very hot tap water. They'll reach room temperature in a few minutes.

½ teaspoon salt

3 tablespoons unsalted butter, melted

1¼ cups milk

2 eggs, separated

◎◎ Preheat a waffle iron at least 10 minutes before using.

Sift the flour, sugar, baking powder and salt into a large bowl.

Stir the butter into the milk, then blend in the egg yolks. Add the milk mixture to the flour mixture and whisk to combine.

Beat the egg whites until soft peaks form, then fold them into the batter just until blended.

Pour about ½ cup batter onto each hot waffle grid. Bake until the waffles are golden and almost all the steam stops, about 3 to 4 minutes.

YIELDS EIGHT 4½-INCH SQUARE WAFFLES

# Raised Waffles

*These yeast-raised waffles are crispy on the outside and light and tender on the inside. "They're the very best waffles you have ever eaten," promises Marion Cunningham. The batter will keep for several days in the refrigerator.*

½ cup warm water

1 package active dry yeast

2 cups warm milk

½ cup (1 stick) butter, melted

1 teaspoon salt

1 teaspoon sugar

2 cups all-purpose flour

2 eggs

¼ teaspoon baking soda

◎◎ Use a rather large mixing bowl—the batter will rise to double its original volume. Put the water in the mixing bowl and sprinkle in the yeast. Let stand for 5 minutes. Add the milk, butter, salt, sugar and flour to the yeast mixture and beat until smooth and blended (Cunningham uses a hand rotary beater to smooth out the lumps).

Quick Hazelnut
Waffles

Toast and chop hazelnuts, then dust them with flour. Fold into a whole-wheat waffle batter. Pour into a hot waffle iron and cook according to recipe directions. Serve with maple syrup or with tiny bits of orange zest and powdered sugar.

Cover the bowl with plastic wrap and let stand overnight at room temperature.

Just before cooking the waffles, beat in the eggs, then add the baking soda and stir until well mixed. The batter will be very thin.

Cook on a very hot waffle iron (use about ½ to ⅓ cup batter per waffle grid). Bake until the waffles are golden and crisp to the touch.

YIELDS 8 AVERAGE-SIZED WAFFLES

# French Toast with Orange and Triple Sec

*Danny Wilser, chef/owner of one of the city's most popular breakfast places, Ella's, created this recipe. The batter gets a double dose of orange—from freshly squeezed juice and from orange-flavored liqueur.*

3 eggs

½ cup heavy cream

Grated zest and juice of 1 orange

1 tablespoon Triple Sec or other orange liqueur

¼ teaspoon vanilla extract

¼ teaspoon ground nutmeg

8 thick slices of day-old white bread

4 tablespoons unsalted butter

Fruit preserves or maple syrup (optional)

◉◉ Beat the eggs in a large bowl with the cream, orange zest and juice, liqueur, vanilla and nutmeg. Soak the bread slices in the batter for 15 minutes.

Melt the butter in 1 or 2 large sauté pans, or on a griddle. Regulate the heat so the butter doesn't burn. Cook the bread slowly in the butter. The heat should not be too high, or the bread won't cook through. Cook on both sides until golden brown.

Serve with fruit preserves or maple syrup, if desired.

SERVES 4

## Low-Fat French Toast

Here's a quick fuss-free method of making French toast. Coat the bread in the traditional egg batter. Instead of frying, bake on a lightly oiled baking sheet in a preheated 500-degree oven for 6 minutes; turn and bake about 4 minutes longer.

# Rice Flour and Yogurt Pancakes

*Jackie Mallorca, a great cook who happens to be allergic to wheat, created these light and delicious pancakes. If refrigerated, the flour mixture will keep for weeks, the liquid mixture for 3 days.*

⅔ cup brown rice flour

⅓ cup cornstarch

1 tablespoon sugar

1 teaspoon baking powder

Pinch salt

1 large egg

2 tablespoons vegetable oil

½ cup plain low-fat yogurt

½ cup low-fat milk

Sift the rice flour, cornstarch, sugar, baking powder and salt into a large bowl. In a second bowl, mix the egg with oil and yogurt; stir in the milk. Pour the liquid ingredients over the dry ingredients and mix until just blended.

Heat a nonstick skillet over medium heat.

Pour the batter by tablespoonfuls into the skillet. Cook the pancakes until golden brown on both sides, 2 minutes or less. Stack on warm plates.

Serve with butter and preserves, honey or syrup.

YIELDS 26 PANCAKES, 2¾ INCHES IN DIAMETER

# Cornmeal Buttermilk Pancakes

*The crunch of cornmeal and the tang of buttermilk pair wonderfully in Marlena Spieler's wake-up call. Blackberries or blueberries may be added. This recipe will accommodate about 2 cups of fruit (toss lightly in flour before adding to the batter).*

2½ cups finely ground cornmeal

1 cup all-purpose flour

1 tablespoon plus 1 teaspoon baking powder

Pinch salt

3 tablespoons sugar

5 eggs, lightly beaten

2 cups buttermilk

2 cups milk

¼ cup melted butter or vegetable oil, plus extra for the pan

◎ Combine the cornmeal, flour, baking powder and salt; stir to blend.

Combine the sugar, eggs, buttermilk, milk and butter or oil. Stir into the dry ingredients, mixing only until it forms a batter. (A few lumps won't hurt.)

Make silver dollar-sized pancakes on a very hot lightly greased griddle, taking care to stir the batter before each batch (the cornmeal settles).

SERVES 8

## Substitute for Buttermilk

If you've run out of buttermilk, an easy substitute is to stir 1 tablespoon fresh lemon juice or distilled white vinegar into 1 cup milk. Stir, and let stand 5 minutes, or until the milk clabbers (curds form).

# Popovers

*Marion Cunningham's popovers are easy and impressive. Omit the cheese and serve them with unsalted butter and homemade strawberry jam for a bountiful breakfast or brunch. Add the cheese and they make fine companions to earthy soups, stews and chili.*

3 large eggs
1 cup milk
1 cup all-purpose flour
½ teaspoon salt
¼ cup grated cheese, such as sharp cheddar or Parmesan (optional)

◉◉  Preheat the oven to 400 degrees. Use either individual ¾-cup glass baking dishes or black nonstick popover pans (¾-cup capacity) that are hung separately on thin bars. If using baking dishes, put the filled dishes directly onto the oven rack rather than on a baking sheet so the heat will surround each dish. Butter each dish.

Break the eggs into a large mixing bowl and beat until well mixed. Add the milk and stir to blend. Add the flour and salt and beat briskly until smooth.

To make 8 small popovers, fill the containers half full; to make 4 large popovers, fill the containers two thirds full. If using cheese, pour half of the batter into the dishes, sprinkle in the cheese, then top with the remaining batter.

Bake for 25 to 35 minutes, or until golden. As soon as the popovers come out of the oven, make 2 or 3 slits in each with the point of a sharp knife (this releases steam and keeps the popovers from collapsing).

YIELDS 4 LARGE OR 8 SMALL POPOVERS

# Giant Apple Popover

*Use Granny Smith, Fuji or Golden Delicious apples (or a combination); these varieties won't turn mushy when baked, says Flo Braker, who adapted this from a Richard Sax recipe.*

### Apples

2 apples (8 ounces each), preferably Granny Smith, Fuji and/or Golden Delicious, peeled, cored and cut into ¼-inch slices

4 tablespoons unsalted butter

¼ cup sugar

⅛ teaspoon ground cinnamon

1 tablespoon fresh lemon juice

### Batter

2 eggs

1 cup milk at room temperature

1 tablespoon melted butter or vegetable oil

2 tablespoons packed brown sugar

1 teaspoon vanilla extract

1 cup all-purpose flour

½ teaspoon salt

2 tablespoons powdered sugar for garnish

Sauté the apple slices in butter in a large skillet. Add the sugar and cinnamon. Cook just until the slices are tender but not soft, about 8 to 10 minutes. Stir in the lemon juice. Arrange the apple mixture in a pie pan. Let cool 20 to 30 minutes before preparing the batter.

Adjust the rack to the middle of the oven; preheat the oven to 425 degrees.

To make the batter: Combine the batter ingredients in a blender or food processor; process about 40 seconds, scraping down the sides of the bowl a couple of times and blending until the mixture is completely smooth.

To make by hand: Whisk together the eggs, milk, butter, sugar and vanilla in a large bowl. Add the flour and salt and beat until very smooth (about the consistency of heavy cream).

Pour the batter over the apples in the pie pan. Bake for 20 minutes; reduce the oven temperature to 350 degrees and bake until the popover is golden brown and firm, about 20 minutes longer. Do not open the oven door until the end of the baking time or the popover will collapse.

Sprinkle powdered sugar over the top. Cut into wedges and serve hot.

SERVES 6 TO 8

# Cafe Beaujolais Coffee Cake

*Margaret Fox, chef/owner of Cafe Beaujolais in Mendocino, says customers frequently comment: "This is like the coffee cake I grew up with." Their mothers and/or fathers must have been great cooks.*

2¼ cups all-purpose flour

½ teaspoon salt

2 teaspoons ground cinnamon

¼ teaspoon ground ginger

1 cup packed brown sugar

¾ cup granulated sugar

¾ cup corn oil

1 cup chopped walnuts or pecans

1 teaspoon baking soda

1 teaspoon baking powder

1 egg, beaten

1 cup buttermilk

◉◉ Preheat the oven to 350 degrees. Liberally grease a 9 x 13 x 2–inch baking pan.

Combine the flour, salt, 1 teaspoon of the cinnamon, the ginger, both sugars and the corn oil in a large bowl and mix well. Remove ¾ cup of this mixture to a smaller bowl and add to it the nuts and remaining cinnamon; mix well.

To the mixture in the large bowl, add the baking soda, baking powder, egg and buttermilk; stir to combine (small lumps in the batter are OK). Pour the batter into the prepared pan. Sprinkle the flour-nut mixture over the top.

Bake for 40 to 45 minutes, or until the cake tests done (a cake tester inserted in the middle will come out free of raw batter). Serve warm. Great for breakfast.

SERVES 12

# Narsai's Cafe Scones

*These crumbly scones were served at Narsai's Cafe in the posh, now-departed I. Magnin department store on Union Square. They are lightly flavored with nutmeg, orange and currants. The recipe may be varied by substituting chopped dried fruit, such as apples, peaches or apricots, for the currants.*

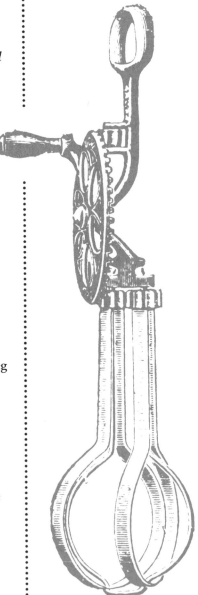

2½ cups all-purpose flour

1 tablespoon double-acting baking powder

4 to 5 tablespoons sugar

½ teaspoon ground nutmeg

Grated zest of 1 orange

½ cup (1 stick) butter

1 egg

¾ cup half-and-half or milk

⅔ cup dried currants or finely chopped dried peaches, apricots or apples

3 tablespoons heavy cream or milk

◎ Preheat the oven to 400 degrees. Lightly grease a baking sheet.

Combine the flour, baking powder, 3 tablespoons of the sugar, the nutmeg and orange zest in a large bowl; mix well. Cut in the butter as if making pie dough. Mix until crumbly.

Beat the egg with the half-and-half or milk. Add to the flour mixture along with the dried fruit. Mix only enough to incorporate the flour.

Gently press the dough into a ball. Divide into 12 equal parts and form each part into a ball. (Or, gently press the dough into a 9-inch circle and cut into 8 or 10 pie-shaped wedges for a more traditional scone shape.) Place the scones on the baking sheet; brush lightly with cream or milk and sprinkle with the remaining 1 to 2 tablespoons sugar.

Bake for 20 to 25 minutes, or until the scones are lightly browned.

YIELDS 12 SCONES

# Hotel St. Francis Currant Scones

*The St. Francis has a long history in San Francisco. At the turn of the century, it was the place for women to gather for lunch or tea. These scones, served with strawberry jam and clotted cream, were one of the most popular items on the menu.*

4½ cups unbleached all-purpose flour

⅓ cup granulated sugar

1 tablespoon baking powder

1 teaspoon salt

1 cup (2 sticks) unsalted butter

¾ to 1 cup dried currants

2 eggs

1¼ cups heavy cream

**Topping**

1 egg beaten with 2 tablespoons milk

⅓ cup packed brown sugar

Preheat the oven to 400 degrees. Lightly grease a baking sheet.

Combine the flour, sugar, baking powder and salt in a large bowl. Cut the butter into small pieces and scatter over the dry ingredients. Using your fingertips, work the butter into the flour until the mixture resembles cornmeal. Stir in the currants.

Beat together the eggs and cream. Slowly drizzle ½ cup at a time over the dry ingredients, tossing the mixture with a fork. Drizzle in the egg-cream mixture wherever it appears to be dry. Loosely press the dough into a ball. Place on a floured board and knead 4 or 5 times to blend well. Discard any dry crumbs.

Roll out the dough on a floured surface until it is 1 inch thick. Cut into scones using a 2-inch round cutter. Place the scones on the baking sheet. Brush the egg-milk mixture over each scone. Sieve brown sugar over the tops.

Bake for 14 to 15 minutes, or until the scones are golden and the sugar has caramelized.

Serve warm, with strawberry jam and clotted cream.

YIELDS 18 TO 20

# Baking Powder Biscuits

*Few breads are as homey or comforting as baking powder biscuits, but finding the right recipe is quite a chore. Look no further. Marion Cunningham has produced this simple no-fail biscuit.*

2 cups all-purpose flour
1 tablespoon baking powder
1 teaspoon salt
⅓ cup vegetable shortening
1 cup milk

Preheat the oven to 425 degrees. Grease a baking pan.

Combine the flour, baking powder and salt in a large mixing bowl. Using a fork, stir the dry ingredients until well mixed.

Add the shortening to the flour mixture. Flour your hands and break the chunk of shortening into 5 or 6 pieces. Lightly rub the flour and shortening together, reaching down to the bottom of the bowl to include all the flour. When there are no longer big pieces of shortening left, add the milk all at once.

Stir the mixture with a fork until it becomes a sticky mass of dough. Transfer the dough to a floured board. Dust your hands with flour, then knead the dough about 10 times.

Pat the dough into a circle about 9 inches in diameter and ¾ inch thick. Cut out biscuits using a 2-inch-diameter cookie cutter. Place the biscuits in the baking pan—touching each other for biscuits with softer sides; not touching for crisper biscuits.

Bake for 12 or 15 minutes, or until the biscuits are golden brown.

YIELDS ABOUT FOURTEEN 2-INCH BISCUITS

## Checking Baking Powder

One of the most persistent baking problems is cakes and breads that don't rise properly. The culprit generally is old baking powder that has lost its power. Double-acting powder works in two stages: first, to start the bubbles that make the batter rise, and again when it heats up. Replace an open tin about every 6 months.

# Buttermilk Biscuits

*Buttermilk gives a tart taste and moist texture to these delightful old-fashioned biscuits, devised by Marion Cunningham.*

½ cup vegetable shortening

2¼ cups all-purpose flour

2½ teaspoons baking powder

½ teaspoon baking soda

1 tablespoon sugar

½ teaspoon salt

1¼ cups buttermilk

Preheat the oven to 425 degrees. Grease a baking sheet. Put the shortening into a small plastic bag, flatten to a thin sheet and place it in the freezer. Tear off 2 pieces of waxed paper, each about 15 inches long.

Combine the flour, baking powder, baking soda, sugar and salt in a flour sifter and sift onto one sheet of waxed paper. Put the empty sifter on the other sheet of waxed paper. Lift the waxed paper containing the sifted ingredients and pour them into the sifter; sift onto the paper. Sift back and forth 4 more times, the last time sifting the ingredients into a large mixing bowl.

Remove the shortening from the freezer. Cut it into small bits, about ¼ inch square, and scatter over the dry ingredients. Using your fingertips, lightly rub the shortening into the flour, occasionally tossing the mixture so all the particles of shortening are coated with flour. When the mixture has bits of flour-covered shortening throughout, add the buttermilk, a little at a time, stirring lightly with a fork.

Transfer the sticky mass of dough to a floured work surface. Dust your hands with flour and gently knead the dough, adding only enough flour to make the dough manageable. (The less flour used, the lighter the biscuits will be.) Pat out the dough to a ½-inch-thick circle. Cut out biscuits, using a 2-inch-diameter cutter. Invert the biscuits and place them touching each other in 3 rows in the center of the baking sheet.

Bake for 12 minutes, or until lightly golden. Serve hot or warm.

YIELDS 19 BISCUITS

# Sage-Polenta Biscuits

*Jeannette Ferrary, author of half a dozen cookbooks, including* Season to Taste, *created these biscuits, which get their coarse texture from cornmeal.*

1½ cups all-purpose flour

½ cup cornmeal

2 teaspoons baking powder

2 tablespoons sugar

2 teaspoons chopped fresh sage

½ teaspoon salt

¼ cup cold butter or corn-oil margarine, cut into pieces

½ cup milk or heavy cream, plus 1 tablespoon for glaze

2 egg whites, lightly beaten

Cumin seeds

Preheat the oven to 450 degrees.

Combine the flour, cornmeal, baking powder, sugar, sage and salt in a large bowl. Cut in the butter or margarine until the mixture is crumbly. Stir in ½ cup milk or cream and the egg whites until the mixture holds together.

Transfer the dough to a lightly floured surface and knead gently about 10 times. Roll out the dough to ½-inch thickness and cut biscuits, using a 3-inch round cutter. Place the biscuits on an ungreased baking sheet. Brush each biscuit with the remaining milk or cream, then sprinkle with a few cumin seeds.

Bake about 12 minutes, or until the tops are golden.

YIELDS 1 DOZEN

## Beating Whites

When beating egg whites, make sure both bowl and beaters are completely clean and free of grease. If a speck of yolk (a greasy substance) gets into the whites, remove it using a piece of the egg shell (the sharp edges easily cut through the viscous whites).

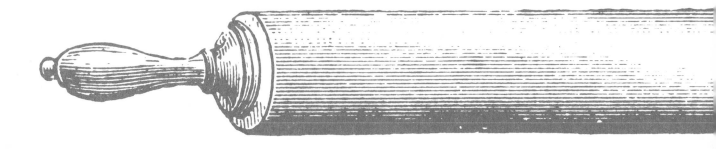

# Jalapeno Corn Bread

*Why would anyone want to eat plain old corn bread when they could have this version, which is liberally peppered with chiles? If you prefer corn bread with a crisp, golden crust, bake this in a cast-iron pan, says chile aficionado Jacqueline McMahan.*

2 eggs

1 cup milk

1 can (16½ ounces) cream-style corn

1 cup yellow cornmeal

¼ cup all-purpose flour

¼ cup sugar

1 teaspoon salt

½ teaspoon baking soda

½ teaspoon baking powder

3 jalapeno chiles or marinated nacho chiles, minced

1 cup grated cheddar cheese

4 tablespoons butter, melted

1 canned jalapeno chile, halved and seeded

Place a 9- or 10-inch cast-iron skillet or a 9-inch square baking pan in the oven. Preheat the oven to 375 degrees.

Beat together the eggs, milk and corn. Stir in the cornmeal, flour, sugar, salt, baking soda, baking powder, minced chiles, the cheese and 3 tablespoons of the melted butter. Blend well.

Use the remaining tablespoon of butter to coat the skillet or baking pan—be careful, the pan will be hot. Pour the batter in the pan. Place the jalapeno halves in the center.

Bake for 45 minutes, or until the top is golden brown.

SERVES 8

# Herbed Corn Fritters

*This is a basic corn-fritter batter to which Georgeanne Brennan adds finely chopped fresh thyme and winter savory. Although you could pour traditional pancake syrup over these fritters, they are meant to be savory rather than sweet. Try them on their own, without adornment, or halved and topped with stew, sautéed vegetables, greens or a creamy cheese sauce.*

4 or 5 ears fresh corn

1½ cups all-purpose flour

2¼ teaspoons baking powder

1 teaspoon salt

1 teaspoon pepper

½ teaspoon cayenne pepper

1 tablespoon minced fresh winter savory or chives

1 tablespoon minced fresh thyme

1 egg, separated

¾ cup milk

1½ teaspoons vegetable oil, plus oil for deep-frying

Cook the corn in boiling water for 3 to 4 minutes. Cut the kernels off the cobs; set aside in a colander to drain.

Sift together the flour, baking powder, salt, pepper and cayenne. Mix in the herbs.

Combine the egg yolk, milk and 1½ teaspoons oil; beat well.

Beat the egg white until stiff peaks form.

Stir the flour mixture into the egg-yolk mixture, then gently fold in the egg white. Finally, fold in the corn.

Heat oil to 375 degrees in a deep fryer or skillet. Drop batter by heaping tablespoonfuls into the hot oil. Fry until the fritters are golden brown, about 4 or 5 minutes. Remove with a slotted spoon and drain on paper towels. Serve hot.

YIELDS 18 TO 24

## Cleaning Copper Bowls

To clean a copper egg-white bowl before using, wash it well in hot soapy water, then rinse. Shake out excess water, then pour in ½ cup or so distilled vinegar. Add a tablespoon or more table salt and, using your hand, "scour" the inside of the bowl with the mixture. Rinse well with hot water and dry with a clean dish towel.

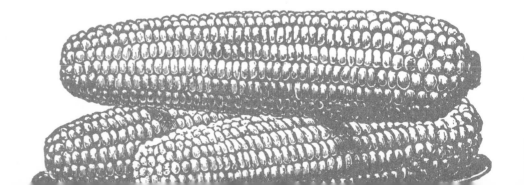

# Simply Perfect Dinner Rolls

*Unlike most bread doughs, this tender egg-rich dough, created by Flo Braker, needs only a few minutes of kneading in an electric mixer. After being shaped and baked, the rolls may be served immediately, or packed into containers and frozen until needed.*

1 cup milk

¾ cup (1½ sticks) unsalted butter

¼ cup sugar

½ teaspoon salt

1 package active dry yeast

¼ cup warm water (105 to 110 degrees)

3¾ cups unbleached all-purpose flour

2 large eggs at room temperature

◎ Heat the milk, butter, sugar and salt in a saucepan just until the butter melts; remove from heat and cool slightly.

Dissolve the yeast in the warm water in a large bowl.

When the milk mixture is lukewarm (85 degrees), beat into the yeast. Using an electric mixer (preferably with a paddle attachment) on low speed, gradually add 2 cups of the flour, then beat on medium speed for 2 minutes. Add the eggs and beat, scraping the sides of the bowl, until well blended. Gradually add 1 cup flour at low speed, beating an additional 2 minutes.

Remove the beaters. Using a wooden spoon, stir in the remaining ¾ cup flour until the dough is smooth and elastic. (The dough will not be as stiff as for some breads.)

Place the dough in a large oiled bowl; turn the dough so the oiled surface is on top, cover the bowl with plastic wrap and set in a warm place until the dough has doubled in volume, about 1½ hours.

Gently punch down the dough and shape as desired (instructions follow).

Adjust the rack in the lower third of the oven; preheat the oven to 375 degrees.

To make old-fashioned pan rolls: Divide the dough in half, forming each half into a thick rope, about 20 inches long. Cut each into 18 equal portions. Using your fingertips, shape each piece into a 1¾-inch ball (tuck edges under to form smooth tops). Place the rolls, sides not quite touching, into 2 greased

## Yeast-Dough Tip

When working with yeast dough, wet your hands to keep the dough from sticking to them. Coating your hands with vegetable oil works well, too, although it's messier.

8-inch square baking pans. Cover loosely with a cloth towel and let rise until doubled, 45 minutes to 1 hour. Bake about 20 minutes, or until pale gold. Yields 36 rolls.

To make knots: Divide the dough into 4 equal parts. Roll each part on a lightly floured surface into a 9-inch-long rope. Cut each rope into 8 equal pieces. Roll each piece into an 8-inch-long rope. Tie each rope loosely into a knot. Place the knots on a parchment-lined baking sheet, 1½ inches apart. Cover loosely with a cloth towel and let rise until doubled, 45 minutes to 1 hour. Bake for 12 to 15 minutes, or until pale gold. Yields 32 rolls.

To make snails: Divide the dough into 3 equal parts. Roll each part on a lightly floured surface into a 12-inch-long rope. Cut each rope into 12 pieces. Roll each piece into a 7-inch-long rope. Anchor one end of one rope with a fingertip, and wind the free end around and around; tuck the free end underneath the coil. Gently lift the roll with your fingertips and place on a parchment-lined baking sheet. Continue forming the snails, placing them 1½ inches apart on the baking sheet. Cover loosely with a cloth towel; let rise until almost doubled, 45 minutes to 1 hour. Bake for 12 minutes, or until pale gold. Yields 36 rolls.

To freeze: Remove the rolls from the oven to cooling racks. When completely cool, place in airtight plastic containers and freeze. To serve, place the frozen rolls on a parchment-lined baking sheet and heat in a preheated 325-degree oven just until hot, about 10 minutes.

# Walnut Bread

*Flo Braker usually makes the dough for this bread early in the evening, lets it rise overnight at room temperature, then forms and bakes it early the next day. Serve it with salads, or with cheese and fresh fruit. It's also excellent toasted for breakfast.*

> 1 package active dry yeast
>
> Pinch sugar
>
> ½ cup hot water (110 degrees)
>
> 1½ cups lukewarm water (85 degrees)
>
> 2 tablespoons sugar
>
> ½ cup walnut oil

## The Secret of Sourdough

San Francisco sourdough really is different. Typically, sourdough is made up of about a dozen different identifiable bacteria, but about 25 years ago researchers at the University of California at Davis found an unknown bacteria in five of San Francisco's most famous breads. It was named *Lactobacillus sanfrancisco*. It's the only place this bacteria exists; it works with the yeast to produce that marvelous sour flavor.

3 cups unbleached all-purpose flour

1 tablespoon salt

2 cups whole-wheat flour

1 cup walnut pieces, toasted

Cornmeal

Kosher salt

Sprinkle the yeast and a pinch of sugar over the hot water in a large bowl. Set aside for 15 minutes to proof.

Add the lukewarm water, sugar, oil, unbleached flour and salt to the yeast mixture; mix until well blended. Add the whole-wheat flour and stir, then knead it in. Turn out the dough onto a floured board and knead until smooth and elastic, 10 to 15 minutes. Place the dough in an oiled bowl, turning it to grease the top. Cover and let rise in a warm place for 2 to 4 hours, or until doubled in bulk.

Punch down the dough. Work briefly and gently with your hands to press out bubbles and deflate it. Working on a lightly floured surface, knead in the walnuts until they are evenly distributed.

Grease a large baking sheet and sprinkle with cornmeal. Divide the dough in half. Shape each half into a round loaf, pressing in any loose walnuts. Place the loaves on the baking sheet. Sprinkle the tops with kosher salt. Cover loosely with plastic wrap. Let rise in a warm place until doubled in bulk, about 1 hour.

Adjust the rack in the lower third of the oven; preheat the oven to 400 degrees.

Bake the loaves for 45 minutes, or until they are deep brown and sound hollow when tapped on the bottom.

YIELDS 2 LOAVES

# Italian Bread Sticks

*These crunchy sticks make delicious accompaniments to informal foods: Dip them in olive oil; spread them with caponata, unsalted butter or mustard; serve them with soups, sliced meats or cheese; or munch them alone. Being handmade, these bread sticks aren't uniform in shape or size. Flo Braker's recipe was inspired by bread master Bernard Clayton, Jr.*

1 package active dry yeast

2 teaspoons sugar

⅔ cup warm water (105 to 115 degrees)

¼ cup olive oil

2 cups unsifted all-purpose flour

1 teaspoon salt

Sprinkle the yeast and a pinch of the sugar over the water in a large bowl; set aside until the mixture bubbles slightly, about 6 minutes. Stir in the oil and remaining sugar.

Add 1 cup of the flour and beat until smooth. Add the salt and the remaining flour, and beat, then knead until smooth.

Turn out the dough onto a lightly floured surface and knead until it is smooth and elastic, about 10 minutes. Place the dough in a bowl, cover tightly with plastic wrap, and set aside in a warm place until the dough has doubled in bulk, about 1 hour.

Punch down the dough. Divide the dough in half, and divide each half into 18 equal pieces. Roll each piece between the palms of your hands into 7- to 8-inch pencil-shaped ropes. Place the bread sticks about ½ inch apart on greased baking sheets. Cover loosely with plastic wrap and let rise in a warm place until almost doubled in size, about 30 minutes.

Adjust the rack to the lower third of the oven. Preheat the oven to 325 degrees.

Using your fingertips, gently pick up each bread stick and pull to make it 2 to 3 inches longer before setting it back on the baking sheet.

Bake for 25 minutes, or until the bread sticks are light golden brown. Remove the bread sticks to wire racks to cool. Store in an airtight tin or wrap in aluminum foil.

YIELDS 3 DOZEN

## Storing Whole-Wheat Flour

Whole-wheat flour can quickly become rancid when stored at room temperature. Buy only as much as you will use within a couple of months, and keep it in an airtight container in the refrigerator or freezer.

**VARIATIONS:** For whole-wheat bread sticks, substitute 1 cup whole-wheat flour for 1 cup of the all-purpose flour. The whole wheat gives these sticks an appealing flavor with extra crunch, almost nutty in texture.

For seeded bread sticks, after punching down the dough in the bowl, knead in 5 teaspoons of fennel, caraway, poppy or sesame seeds. Cover loosely with plastic wrap and let rest 10 minutes before forming into bread sticks.

# Flat Bread with Caramelized Onions and Rosemary

*We used to call this pizza, but that's too common. Today, chic restaurants list it under the appetizer menu as "flat bread." Lance Dean Velasquez was the chef at Moose's, a popular North Beach restaurant, when he created his delectable version, which is made with yogurt.*

> 2 cups bread flour
>
> 1 package active dry yeast
>
> 1½ teaspoons sugar
>
> 1½ teaspoons salt
>
> ½ cup warm (120 degrees) water
>
> ½ cup plain yogurt
>
> ½ cup whole-wheat flour
>
> Melted butter
>
> Caramelized Rosemary Onions (recipe follows)

Combine 1 cup of the bread flour, the yeast, sugar and salt in a processor; process 10 seconds. Add the water; process 1 minute; scrape down the sides of the processor. Add the yogurt; process 5 seconds. Add the remaining bread flour; process 1 minute. Add the whole-wheat flour; process 30 seconds (the dough will be soft and sticky).

Remove the dough to a floured board; sprinkle lightly with flour. Knead until the dough is smooth and elastic, about 2 minutes. Place the dough in a greased bowl. Cover and let rise in a warm place for about 45 minutes. Punch down the dough; form into 8 balls. Cover loosely with a kitchen towel and let rise in a warm place until doubled, about 15 minutes.

Preheat the oven to 500 degrees (if you have a pizza brick, place it in the oven). Butter 2 baking sheets.

Place each ball of dough on a buttered surface and flatten to a 6-inch oval. Place the ovals on the baking sheets and brush with melted butter.

Bake 5 minutes, or until light brown. Spread the caramelized rosemary onions on top.

YIELDS 8 FLAT BREADS

## Caramelized Rosemary Onions

2 onions, thinly sliced
½ cup (1 stick) unsalted butter
Leaves from 1 rosemary sprig, finely chopped
Salt and pepper to taste

◉◉ Cook onions in butter over medium heat, stirring frequently, until golden brown, adding rosemary leaves toward the end of the cooking time. Cool. Season to taste with salt and pepper.

# Basic Pizza Crust Dough

2 envelopes active dry yeast

1 cup warm water (105 degrees)

1 teaspoon sugar

1 teaspoon salt

2 tablespoons olive oil

3 cups all-purpose flour, plus more if needed

◍ Dissolve the yeast in the water in a small bowl. Add the sugar and let stand until foamy, about 5 minutes.

Processor method: In a food processor fitted with a dough blade, combine the yeast mixture, salt, 1 tablespoon of the olive oil and 3 cups flour. Process until the ingredients come together into a ball. If the dough is too wet, add more flour, a little at a time, until the dough has a smooth, firm texture. Continue to process for 3 to 4 minutes after the ball is formed, or until the dough is smooth and silky, but firm. Turn out the dough onto a well-floured board and knead until elastic, 6 or 7 minutes.

Hand method: Follow the same steps as the processor method, but use only 2 cups flour to start and work the ingredients together with a fork or your fingertips. Gradually add more flour until the dough forms a stiff ball. Knead the dough on a well-floured board until it is smooth and elastic, 6 or 7 minutes.

Oil a large bowl with the remaining 1 tablespoon olive oil. Place the dough in the bowl and turn to coat the surface with oil. Cover the bowl with a clean cloth and let stand in a warm place until the dough has doubled in size, 1 to 1½ hours. Punch down the dough in the bowl, cover and let it rest for 30 minutes before forming.

YIELDS ENOUGH DOUGH FOR TWO 13-INCH PIZZAS

# Banana Chocolate Chip Bread

*We can't think of a better combination than banana, chocolate and walnuts for an easy-to-put-together tea bread. This loaf bakes up dense, moist and delicious. One key to its marvelous flavor, says Flo Braker, is to toast the nuts before chopping them and adding them to the batter.*

1¾ cups plus 2 tablespoons all-purpose flour

1½ cups sugar

½ teaspoon baking powder

1 teaspoon baking soda

¾ teaspoon salt

1 cup finely chopped toasted walnuts

1 cup mashed banana (about 2 medium bananas)

2 large eggs, lightly beaten

¼ cup plus 1 tablespoon buttermilk

½ cup vegetable oil

1 teaspoon vanilla extract

½ cup chocolate chips

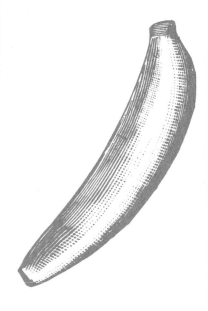

◎◎  Adjust the rack in the lower third of the oven; preheat the oven to 350 degrees. Grease and flour a 9 x 5 x 3–inch loaf pan.

Sift the flour, sugar, baking powder, baking soda and salt into a large bowl. Stir in the walnuts.

Combine the banana, eggs, buttermilk, oil and vanilla; add to the flour mixture. Stir until just combined. Fold in the chocolate chips. Spoon the batter into the prepared pan.

Bake for 1 hour and 15 to 20 minutes, or until a cake tester inserted in the loaf comes out clean. Cool 10 minutes in the pan, then turn the loaf out onto a rack to cool completely.

Slice thinly to serve.

SERVES 16

# Spicy Cake Buns

*These buns are a cross between scones and muffins but quicker to make than either one, says Flo Braker.*

2½ cups unsifted all-purpose flour
½ teaspoon baking powder
½ teaspoon baking soda
½ teaspoon salt
½ teaspoon ground cinnamon
¼ teaspoon ground cloves
¼ teaspoon ground ginger
¼ cup granulated sugar
½ cup packed light brown sugar
½ cup vegetable shortening
1 large egg
1 cup buttermilk
½ cup raisins
3 tablespoons granulated sugar for the tops

◉ Adjust the oven rack to the lower third of the oven. Preheat the oven to 375 degrees. Grease and flour a large baking sheet.

Sift the dry ingredients (except the brown sugar) into a large bowl. Add the brown sugar, shortening, egg and buttermilk and beat with an electric mixer until the batter is blended and smooth, about 1 to 2 minutes. Stir in the raisins.

Drop the batter by the heaping tablespoonful onto the prepared baking sheet. Sprinkle each mound with ½ teaspoon sugar.

Bake about 15 minutes, or until the buns are golden brown.

Serve warm or at room temperature.

YIELDS 18

# The Very Best Blueberry Muffins

*After trying dozens of recipes, Flo Braker moved these muffins to the top of her list.*

2 cups unsifted all-purpose flour

½ cup sugar

1 tablespoon baking powder

1 teaspoon baking soda

½ teaspoon salt

2 large eggs

¾ cup buttermilk

6 tablespoons unsalted butter, melted

2 teaspoons finely grated lemon zest

1 teaspoon vanilla extract

1 cup blueberries

2 tablespoons sugar mixed with ½ teaspoon ground cinnamon

Adjust the oven rack to the middle of the oven; preheat the oven to 400 degrees. Grease 12 muffin cups, then flour them.

Sift together the flour, sugar, baking powder, baking soda and salt.

Combine the eggs, buttermilk, butter, lemon zest and vanilla. Stir into the dry ingredients just until moistened. Do not beat until smooth or the muffins will be grainy. Fold in the berries, mixing until just combined.

Fill the muffin cups three-quarters full. Top each muffin with a sprinkling of cinnamon sugar.

Bake for 20 to 25 minutes, or until the muffins are golden and pull away from the sides of the cups. Let the muffins cool 15 to 20 minutes before removing from cups.

YIELDS 12 MUFFINS

## Lumpy Muffins

Remember that the batter for muffins should be lumpy. Be careful not to overmix, which will create a dense heavy product.

# Multigrain Baking Mix

*Why pay big bucks for those packaged baking mixes? Sharon Cadwallader created this dry mix for pancakes, waffles and muffins. Once you have the mix on hand, breakfast is only minutes away.*

2 cups quick-cooking oats

4 cups whole-wheat flour

1 cup brown rice flour

½ cup natural wheat germ

½ cup oat bran

1 cup dry milk powder

3 tablespoons baking powder

2 teaspoons salt

½ teaspoon cream of tartar

Combine all ingredients and mix well.
Store in a covered container in the refrigerator. Will keep up to 3 months.
YIELDS APPROXIMATELY 9¼ CUPS MIX

## Before You Bake

Use ice cream scoops for measuring food consistently, quickly and easily. They're great for scooping solid vegetable shortening, peanut butter, cookie dough, cupcakes and muffin batter.

# Multigrain Muffins

2 eggs

5 tablespoons canola oil

2 tablespoons warmed honey

⅔ cup warm water

2 cups Multigrain Baking Mix

Preheat the oven to 400 degrees. Grease a 12-cup muffin tin.
Beat the eggs with the oil, honey and water. Add to the baking mix, stirring just enough to moisten all the ingredients. Spoon into the muffin cups and bake for 18 to 20 minutes, or until the muffins are lightly browned.
YIELDS 12 MUFFINS

# Multigrain Pancakes

2 eggs, separated
5 tablespoons canola oil
2 tablespoons warmed honey
1½ cups warm water
2 cups Multigrain Baking Mix (see page 295)

Beat the egg yolks with the oil, honey and water. Add to the baking mix, stirring just enough to moisten all ingredients.

Beat the egg whites until stiff peaks form, then fold them into the batter. Spoon onto a hot greased griddle and cook over medium heat until surface bubbles appear. Turn once and cook until lightly browned.

YIELDS 16 TO 18 PANCAKES

**VARIATION:** For multigrain waffles, follow directions for making pancakes, but increase the oil to 6 tablespoons. Spoon into a hot greased waffle iron. Yields 6 to 8 waffles.

# Whole-Wheat Baking Mix

*Here's Sharon Cadwallader's whole-wheat baking mix for pancakes, waffles and muffins.*

6 cups whole-wheat flour

1¼ cups flaked bran (not bran cereal)

1¼ cups toasted wheat germ

¾ cup powdered milk

4 tablespoons baking powder

2 teaspoons salt

½ teaspoon cream of tartar

◎ Mix together all ingredients, stirring to blend well. Store in a covered container in the refrigerator. Will keep up to 3 months.

YIELDS ABOUT 9 CUPS

# Whole-Wheat Pancakes

1 cup Whole-Wheat Baking Mix

1 tablespoon packed brown sugar

2 eggs

2 tablespoons vegetable oil

¾ cup milk, or more as needed

◎ Combine the baking mix and sugar in a large bowl.

Beat the eggs with the oil and milk, then add to the baking mix, stirring just long enough to moisten all ingredients. Thin the batter with more milk, if desired.

Spoon onto a hot greased griddle. Turn the pancakes when bubbles appear on the surface.

YIELDS 10 TO 12 PANCAKES, 3 TO 3½ INCHES IN DIAMETER

**VARIATION:** For whole-wheat waffles, follow the directions for making pancakes, but increase the amount of oil to 3 tablespoons. Separate the eggs and fold the stiffly beaten whites into the batter before baking. Yields four 9-inch waffles.

# Whole-Wheat Muffins

1 cup Whole-Wheat Baking Mix (see page 297)

1 tablespoon packed brown sugar

1 egg

2 tablespoons canola oil

¾ cup milk

◎◎ Preheat the oven to 400 degrees. Grease 6 muffin cups.

Combine the baking mix and sugar in a bowl. Beat the egg with the oil and milk, then add to the baking mix, stirring just enough to moisten all ingredients.

Spoon the batter into the muffin cups. Bake for 18 to 20 minutes, or until a cake tester comes out clean when inserted into the center of a muffin.

YIELDS 6 MUFFINS

# Buttermilk Whole-Wheat Baking Mix

*Buttermilk powder gives this whole-wheat mix, by Sharon Cadwallader, a nice tang and texture.*

4 cups whole-wheat flour

2 cups gluten flour

1 cup natural wheat germ

1 cup bran flakes

1 cup buttermilk powder

3 tablespoons baking powder

2 teaspoons salt

½ teaspoon cream of tartar

1½ cups (3 sticks) butter or margarine at room temperature

◎◎ Combine the flours, wheat germ, bran flakes, buttermilk powder, baking powder, salt and cream of tartar in a large mixing bowl; stir well. Cut in the butter or margarine with a pastry blender until the mixture resembles coarse meal.

Store in a covered container in the refrigerator. Will keep well for up to 2 months.

YIELDS ABOUT 10 CUPS

**NOTE:** Buttermilk powder is sold in cans and packets in the baking goods section of supermarkets. Gluten flour and bran flakes (not bran flake cereal) are available at health food stores.

# Buttermilk Pancakes

2 eggs, separated

1 cup warm water

1½ cups Buttermilk Whole-Wheat Baking Mix

∞ Beat the egg yolks with the water, then add to the baking mix, stirring just long enough to moisten all ingredients. Beat the egg whites until stiff peaks form and fold into the batter. Spoon onto a hot well-greased griddle or frying pan and fry until browned on both sides.

YIELDS 12 TO 14 PANCAKES

**VARIATION:** For buttermilk waffles, follow the directions for pancakes but add 2 tablespoons oil to the yolk-and-water mixture before combining with the baking mix. Yields 4 average-sized waffles.

# Buttermilk Muffins

2 eggs

1 cup warm water

3 tablespoons packed brown sugar (optional)

2 cups Buttermilk Whole-Wheat Baking Mix (see page 298)

½ cup raisins (optional)

Preheat the oven to 425 degrees. Grease 12 muffin cups.

Beat the eggs with the water and optional sugar, then add to the baking mix, stirring just enough to moisten all ingredients. Stir in the optional raisins.

Spoon into the muffin cups and bake for 18 to 20 minutes, or until the muffins are lightly browned.

YIELDS 12 MUFFINS

# Drop Biscuits

2 cups Buttermilk Whole-Wheat Baking Mix (see page 298)

⅔ cup warm water

Preheat the oven to 375 degrees. Liberally grease a baking sheet.

Combine the baking mix and water and stir until just moistened.

Drop by the spoonful onto the baking sheet and bake for 10 minutes, or until the biscuits are brown.

YIELDS 16 BISCUITS

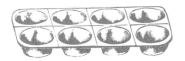

How to Blend Flour

Use a fine-meshed sieve instead of a flour sifter for simultaneously sifting and blending flour mixtures.

# Two-Flour Baking Mix

*For this mix, Sharon Cadwallader combines unbleached white and whole-wheat flours, producing a versatile combination for pancakes, waffles, muffins and biscuits. The mix will keep in the refrigerator for up to 2 months.*

    5 cups unbleached all-purpose flour
    4 cups whole-wheat flour
    ¼ cup plus 1 tablespoon baking powder
    3 teaspoons salt
    1 teaspoon cream of tartar
    2 cups (4 sticks) butter or margarine

∽ Combine the dry ingredients in a large bowl and mix well. Cut in the butter or margarine with a pastry blender or 2 knives until it resembles coarse meal. Store in a covered container in the refrigerator. Keeps well for up to 2 months.

YIELDS ABOUT 11 CUPS

# Two-Flour Biscuits

    2 cups Two-Flour Baking Mix
    ½ cup water

∽ Preheat the oven to 425 degrees. Lightly grease a baking sheet.
Combine the baking mix and water; stir with a fork until well blended. Roll out the dough on a lightly floured surface until it is ½ inch thick. Cut into biscuits with a 2-inch-diameter biscuit cutter and place on the baking sheet. Bake for 8 to 10 minutes, or until golden brown.

YIELDS 18 TO 20 BISCUITS

# Two-Flour Muffins

2 cups Two-Flour Baking Mix (see page 301)

2 tablespoons packed brown sugar

1 egg

1 cup milk

∞ Preheat the oven to 400 degrees. Grease 12 muffin cups.

Mix together the baking mix and sugar.

Beat the egg with the milk, then add to the baking mix, stirring just enough to moisten all ingredients. Spoon into the muffin cups and bake for 18 to 20 minutes, or until a cake tester comes out clean when inserted into the center of the muffins.

YIELDS 12 MUFFINS

**NOTE:** ½ cup chopped nuts or raisins may be added to the batter.

# Two-Flour Pancakes

1 egg

2 tablespoons honey

1½ cups milk

2 cups Two-Flour Baking Mix (see page 301)

∞ Beat together the egg, honey and milk; add to the baking mix, stirring just enough to moisten all ingredients. Spoon onto a hot greased griddle and fry the pancakes until golden, turning once.

YIELDS 12 TO 14 PANCAKES

**VARIATION:** For two-flour waffles, follow the directions for making pancakes, adding 2 tablespoons oil to the liquid ingredients. Yields 4 or 5 average-sized waffles.

# Chapter 9

# Salsas, Sauces and Chutneys

*Short of a live-in chef, there's nothing better for the harried cook than an arsenal of relishes, chutneys and quick sauces stashed in the refrigerator or pantry.*

*With little effort these bright flavors can be marshalled to transform the most mundane foods. Pickled onion rings reinvigorate a tired turkey sandwich; ginger-pickled vegetables add a tart counterpoint to roasted pork tenderloin; salsa cruda not only makes a great topper for grilled meats, but can be tossed with pasta as a quick week-night dinner. And with our recipe for yellow tomato ketchup, even frozen French fries will be a treat.*

*Those who like sweet-and-fiery blends will warm to the various chutneys, which add an exciting element to a Western-style meal.*

*In addition, this chapter includes several fun appetizers that can add a spark to cocktail hour: old-fashioned party mix (don't laugh, you may well become addicted); an olive-cheese ball; an easy Middle Eastern eggplant dip; and hot jalapenos that are perfect to accompany ice-cold beer.*

# Piquant Pickled Peppers

*Choose one kind of pepper or a combination for these refrigerator pickles. Dan Bowe likes to use the sweeter varieties of pale greenish-yellow, red and golden bell peppers, with a few poblanos and cherry peppers thrown in to give the pickles a hot-sweet note. Select a fragrant olive oil for the final touch; it cuts the acidity of the peppers.*

3 pounds peppers

½ small red or yellow onion, cut into ¼-inch slivers

8 garlic cloves, lightly crushed

3 cups distilled vinegar or combination of vinegars

3 cups water

3 teaspoons salt

¼ cup sugar

4 sprigs fresh thyme

Needles from 1 small sprig fresh rosemary

½ small dried chipotle chile, broken into several pieces

¼ cup fruity olive oil

Wash the peppers. Seed and derib the large ones and cut into 1-inch strips. Keep small peppers whole, but cut 2 slits on opposite sides of each pepper, just below the cap. This will allow the pickling solution to penetrate, soften and flavor the peppers.

Choose a 3- to 4-quart glass jar with a tight-fitting lid. Pack the peppers, onions and garlic into the jar, pressing down without squashing the vegetables.

Bring the vinegar, water, salt and sugar to a boil in a large nonaluminum pan. Reduce heat to a simmer. Add the herbs and chipotle and simmer 3 to 5 minutes. Pour over the peppers. Place in a well-ventilated place to cool. Once cooled, top with the olive oil. Place the lid on the jar and close tightly.

Refrigerate for at least 48 hours, or up to 1 month. The longer the peppers sit in the brine, the better they get.

YIELDS 2 QUARTS

## New Flavor Twists on Mayonnaise

Commercial mayonnaise is a great boon to the busy cook; it may be flavored in many ways to create a quick sauce for fish, poultry or vegetables (excellent as a dipping sauce for artichokes and asparagus).

**Tarragon Mayonnaise.** Finely mince ¼ cup fresh tarragon leaves. Blend in ½ cup mayonnaise, 1 teaspoon fresh lemon juice and ½ teaspoon salt. Yields a scant ¾ cup.

**Garlic Mayonnaise.** Finely mince 4 garlic cloves. Blend into ½ cup mayonnaise; season with ½ teaspoon salt and ½ teaspoon freshly ground black pepper. Yields ½ cup.

**Red Pepper Mayonnaise.** Put 1 red bell pepper that has been roasted, peeled, seeded and chopped into a food processor. Add a peeled garlic clove and process until pureed. Add 1 cup mayonnaise, ½ teaspoon salt and ½ teaspoon freshly ground black pepper. Process until well blended. Yields about 1½ cups.

# Pickled Shallots

*These tangy shallots come from Catherine Brandel, formerly of Chez Panisse and now an instructor at the Culinary Institute of America in St. Helena. Add them to salads or meat dishes, or simply nibble them whenever you feel like it. The shallots turn a pretty rosy pink from the red wine vinegar. They retain a crunch because they're not cooked; they simply steep in a sweet-sour solution. The solution should not be hideously pickley. Taste it because the amount of water and sugar depends on the strength of the vinegar you use.*

¾ cup red wine vinegar (more or less depending upon strength)

¼ cup sugar

½ cup water

1 bay leaf, bruised

3 or 4 sprigs fresh thyme, bruised

¾ pound shallots, thinly sliced (do not use shallots that are withered or sprouting)

Combine all ingredients except the shallots in a nonaluminum saucepan and bring to a boil.

Put the shallots in a clean, dry jar and cover with the hot sweet-sour solution. Let cool, cover and store in the refrigerator. These will keep at least 2 weeks.

YIELDS ABOUT 1 PINT

# Pickled Onion Rings

*At the Straits Cafe in San Francisco, these quick onions are served as a side dish with the house specialty, tandoori beef, but they are also delicious with other highly seasoned dishes, or use them in salads or sandwiches. They are easy to prepare and store well for several days in a covered container in the refrigerator.*

1 large Bermuda onion

½ teaspoon salt

¼ cup sugar

½ cup distilled white vinegar

ꙮ Cut the onion from top to bottom into very thin slices (about ¹⁄₁₆ inch). Toss the slices in a bowl with the salt; let sit 5 minutes. Remove the slices and gently squeeze out the juices.

Combine the sugar and vinegar in a medium bowl; mix until the sugar dissolves. Add the onion slices; toss well. Let marinate at room temperature for at least 2 hours. Drain before serving.

SERVES 8

# Ginger Pickled Vegetables

*The balance of sweet, sour and hot in these pickles by Dan Bowe is very refreshing. While he favors using very small baby carrots, you can use a combination of vegetables.*

1 pound vegetables (choose 1 or a combination): whole baby carrots, or larger carrots, peeled and cut into ¼-inch rounds; small Icicle radishes or larger radishes, cut into ¼-inch rounds; small pickling cucumbers or English cucumbers, cut into ¼-inch rounds or 3- to 4-inch-long spears

½ small yellow onion, cut into slivers

2 garlic cloves, minced

2 teaspoons salt

2 teaspoons grated fresh ginger

½ cup rice vinegar

## Quick Marinated Carrot Coins

*Here's a recipe Michael Bauer has used for years. The flavor gently infuses the carrot coins, bringing out a pleasant sweetness.*

8 carrots

3 tablespoons white wine vinegar

1 tablespoon olive oil

1 garlic clove, minced

2 tablespoons grated onion, or 1 teaspoon onion powder

Salt to taste

White pepper to taste

Chopped fresh parsley for garnish

ꙮ Cut the carrots into coins. Make the dressing with the vinegar, oil, garlic, onion or onion powder and salt. Pour over the carrots and refrigerate overnight, or until ready to serve. Drain before serving. Sprinkle with pepper and parsley.

¼ cup sugar

¼ cup cilantro leaves

2 to 4 slices (¹⁄₁₆ inch thick) jalapeno chile

☙ Combine the vegetable(s) of choice, the onion, garlic and salt in a large bowl; toss well to distribute the salt. Let sit at room temperature for at least 2 hours, but not longer than 6 hours. Rinse thoroughly, then drain and dry.

Combine the ginger, vinegar, sugar, cilantro and jalapeno slices (use just 2 slices for a mild mix). Add to the vegetables and toss to mix. Place in a nonaluminum bowl or a heavy-duty self-sealing plastic bag. Let marinate for 8 hours at room temperature, tossing once or twice.

Store in the refrigerator. These pickles will keep (and continue to improve in flavor) for up to 3 weeks.

YIELDS 1 POUND PICKLED VEGETABLES

# Pickled Jerusalem Artichokes

*These simple no-cook pickles by Narsai David marinate in the refrigerator for 2 weeks until they pick up all the flavor from the marinade.*

2½ pounds Jerusalem artichokes, trimmed and sliced (should yield about 1 quart)

3 garlic cloves

1½ teaspoons pickling spice

¼ cup sugar

1 cup white wine vinegar or other vinegar at 5 percent acidity

¾ to 1 cup hot water

☙ Pack the Jerusalem artichokes into a 1-quart plastic tub or canning jar. Add the garlic, pickling spice, sugar and vinegar. Add water to barely fill the container. Cover with the lid and shake to help dissolve the sugar.

Refrigerate for 1 to 2 weeks (or until marinated to your liking) before using. These keep well in the refrigerator for up to 6 months.

YIELDS 1 QUART

# Absolutely Fabulous Okra and Fennel

*One of our staff editors who hates the slimy qualities of okra challenged chef Dan Bowe to come up with something "absolutely fabulous." Surpassing our expectations, he created these refrigerator pickles that require no hot-water processing. The okra is crunchy and piquant, and the fennel and fennel seeds add a mild licorice note to the blend.*

1 pound fennel

¾ pound okra

1 cup distilled white vinegar

2 tablespoons balsamic vinegar

2 cups rice vinegar

3 cups water

½ cup sugar

2 teaspoons grated fresh turmeric, or a pinch of ground turmeric

1½ teaspoons fennel seeds, toasted and lightly crushed

1 tablespoon salt

1 teaspoon freshly ground black pepper

Trim the fennel, then cut into 1-inch strips; rinse and dry. Prepare the okra by trimming just the stem portion, making sure not to cut into the caps.

Combine the fennel and okra in a 3- to 4-quart glass jar.

Bring the vinegars, water and sugar to a boil in a nonreactive saucepan. Remove from heat and add the turmeric, fennel seeds, salt and pepper. Immediately pour over the okra and fennel; place the lid on the jar and close tightly. Refrigerate at least 3 days or up to 1 month, turning the jar over once or twice a day for the first 4 or 5 days.

YIELDS ABOUT 2 QUARTS

# Almost Raw Chow Chow

*Marion Cunningham's relish is a great addition to any meat or poultry dish. It's also the ideal relish for the Thanksgiving table.*

1 small cauliflower, broken into small flowerets

2 carrots, peeled and chopped

1 small green bell pepper, seeded, deribbed and chopped

1 small sweet red bell pepper, seeded, deribbed and chopped

1 large cucumber, peeled, seeded and chopped

2 yellow onions, chopped

2 cups chopped cabbage

¾ cup sugar

3 tablespoons flour

2½ tablespoons dry mustard (Colman's)

1½ teaspoons ground turmeric

1½ teaspoons celery seed

1 teaspoon salt

2½ to 3 cups cider vinegar

Bring a large pot of salted water to a boil; add the cauliflower and carrots. Simmer about 2 minutes. Add the peppers. Simmer about 30 seconds, then drain the vegetables.

Put the blanched vegetables into a large bowl and add the cucumber, onions and cabbage. Set aside.

Mix together the sugar, flour, mustard, turmeric, celery seed and salt in a small bowl.

Bring 2½ cups vinegar to a boil, stir a little into the dry ingredients and blend until smooth. Stir this paste into the vinegar and return to the stove. Cook over medium heat, stirring constantly, until smooth and thickened. Stir into the vegetable mixture.

Pack the vegetables into 4 pint jars; cover with lids. Refrigerate until needed. If the mixture seems a little dry, add a few tablespoons vinegar to each jar.

YIELDS 4 PINTS

# Sichuan Cucumber Pickle

*These cucumbers by Bruce Cost are great with any meal, but they're particularly good with roast chicken.*

3 pounds cucumbers

2 tablespoons coarse salt

4 to 6 tree ear mushrooms

⅓ cup sugar

⅓ cup rice vinegar

1 tablespoon light soy sauce

3 tablespoons peanut oil

1 tablespoon Sichuan peppercorns

8 small dried red peppers

2 tablespoons julienned fresh ginger

4 to 6 fresh red chiles, seeded and cut into julienne strips

1 tablespoon Asian sesame oil

◉ Cut off the ends of the cucumbers. Cut each cucumber in half lengthwise, scrape out the seeds, then cut into thin half-moon slices. Toss with the salt and let sit for 1 hour.

Meanwhile, place the tree ears in a bowl and pour in hot water to cover; let soak for 30 minutes. Drain, rinse well and drain again.

Combine the sugar, vinegar and soy sauce.

Put the peanut oil in an enamel or stainless steel saucepan with the peppercorns and dried peppers. Heat until the peppers begin to smoke. Turn off the heat and cover for 10 minutes. Reheat the oil and add the ginger, fresh chiles and the tree ears; stir briefly. Pour in the vinegar-sugar mixture and continue to heat and stir just until the sugar dissolves. Remove from heat and stir in the sesame oil.

Wrap the cucumber slices in a damp cloth and wring to extract the moisture. Place the cucumbers in a bowl; pour in the pickling sauce, including the fresh and dried ingredients. Let marinate for 1 hour before serving.

SERVES 6 TO 8

## Using Juice as Sauce

Those with a juicer have a head start on a quick sauce for dinner.

**Asparagus.** Warmed and swirled with butter, the juice makes a great sauce for chicken or fish. Use it in a vinaigrette with lemon juice and olive oil; especially nice for seafood salads or on grilled halibut or sole. A pound of blanched asparagus makes about a cup of juice.

**Arugula.** It's best when whisked into oil and drizzled on the plate as a flavor accent. Ideal for grilled chicken or vegetables. It's also good in a vinaigrette for a tomato and mozzarella salad. A pound of arugula (blanched lightly before juicing) produces just over a cup of juice.

**Celery.** It's great as a poaching liquid for steamed fish. Reduced, it works well for seafood, especially when paired with fennel juice. It can also make a good flavor base for a bean soup. A pound of celery produces a generous cup of juice.

**Carrots.** Seasoned with rosemary or basil, the juice may be used as a poaching liquid for chicken. It also may be used in risotto. A pound of carrots produces about ¾ cup juice.

**Beets.** The syrupy sweet juice is best cut with lemon or lime. Reduced to a glaze, it makes a colorful flavor enhancer for sea bass, salmon or pork. A pound of beets produces about 1 cup juice.

# Fire-and-Ice Relish

*Marion Cunningham suggests using this quick relish with peppers and onions as a salad, combined with fresh tomatoes and cucumbers. It's also a good accompaniment to grilled or broiled steak or lamb chops.*

¼ cup cider vinegar

½ teaspoon salt

1½ teaspoons celery seed

1½ teaspoons mustard seed

4 teaspoons sugar

⅛ teaspoon cayenne pepper

⅛ teaspoon black pepper

¼ cup water

3 cups cherry tomatoes, cut in half (or quartered, if large)

1 large green bell pepper, seeded, deribbed and coarsely chopped

1 large red onion, finely chopped

◉◉  Combine the vinegar, salt, seeds, sugar, cayenne, black pepper and water in a small saucepan; bring to a boil and boil for 1 minute. Remove from heat and immediately pour over the tomatoes, pepper and onion. Let cool to room temperature, then refrigerate for at least 3 hours before using, stirring once or twice.

YIELDS 3 CUPS

**TIP:** For a zesty salad, arrange Bibb or butter lettuce leaves, 3 sliced tomatoes, and thin slices of cucumber on individual plates. Drain the relish (save the marinade for more vegetables) and spoon evenly over the salad.

# Hot Tomato Relish (Gujarati Kasundi)

*This popular relish comes from Gujarat in western India. It makes a wonderful dipping sauce for any kind of finger food, says Laxmi Hiremath.*

>    1 tablespoon mild vegetable oil
>    ½ teaspoon mustard seeds
>    1½ tablespoons slivered garlic
>    ½ teaspoon ground turmeric
>    1 teaspoon cayenne pepper
>    ½ teaspoon salt
>    5 vine-ripened tomatoes, peeled, seeded and chopped
>    ¼ cup distilled white vinegar

◎◎  Heat the oil in a medium skillet over medium-high heat. Add the mustard seeds and garlic. Cook, stirring, until the mixture starts to brown, about 4 minutes. Add the turmeric, cayenne, salt and tomatoes. Stir and cook for 2 minutes. Add the vinegar and bring to a boil. Reduce heat, cover and simmer until thick, about 10 minutes.

Spoon into a hot, clean jar, cover and let cool to room temperature. Store in the refrigerator. Keeps well for several weeks.

YIELDS ¾ CUP

# Tunisian Pepper-Tomato Relish

*Garlic and cayenne or fiery harissa influence this exotic relish from Joanne Weir. Spread it on slices of baguette, or use it as a condiment with grilled fish, chicken, lamb and beef.*

>    3 vine-ripened tomatoes, peeled, seeded and chopped
>    3 large red bell peppers, roasted, peeled and seeded
>    2 garlic cloves, minced
>    1 teaspoon ground cumin
>    ¼ teaspoon cayenne pepper or harissa
>    1 tablespoon olive oil

2 tablespoons fresh lemon juice

¼ cup chopped fresh parsley

Salt and freshly ground pepper to taste

Put the tomatoes in a skillet and sauté over high heat until thickened, 6 to 8 minutes. Transfer to a bowl.

Mince the peppers and add to the tomatoes. Add the garlic, cumin, cayenne or harissa, olive oil, lemon juice and parsley. Mix well. Season with salt and pepper.

May be made 1 day in advance, but do not add the garlic until serving time. Store in the refrigerator. Bring to room temperature before serving.

SERVES 6

# Salsa Cruda

*When you get the hang of it, you'll be able to chop up the ingredients for Jacqueline McMahan's fresh salsa in minutes. Use it on tacos, as a dip with tortilla chips, or as a garnish for roast chicken or grilled meats.*

8 plum tomatoes

½ cup diced red onion

2 to 3 jalapeno chiles, seeded and minced

1 to 2 garlic cloves, minced

½ to 1 teaspoon salt

2 to 3 tablespoons minced fresh cilantro

1 tablespoon fresh lime juice or flavorful vinegar

Core, seed and dice the tomatoes. Place them in a bowl and add the remaining ingredients; stir to mix.

YIELDS ABOUT 2 CUPS

**NOTE:** Salsa cruda keeps well for a day or two in the refrigerator. If you want to keep it longer, put it in a saucepan and simmer for 5 minutes (or microwave). This brief cooking actually sets the flavors and helps preserve the salsa.

## Juicing Ginger

Ginger juice can give a subtle edge to many dishes. Simply put a few slices in the garlic press and capture the juices in a bowl. It's particularly good with chicken, shellfish and seafood.

# Chiles

## How Hot Is Hot?

The heat in all chiles, whether hot or mild, is due to the flavorless, odorless, colorless chemical known as capsaicin.

In 1912, William Scoville, a Detroit pharmacologist, measured capsaicin by having a panel of hardy souls sip a sweetened solution of dried chiles dissolved in alcohol. Each concoction had decreasing amounts of capsaicin, and the panel tasted through the various solutions until they no longer burned.

The results were converted into Scoville units—with no mention made as to what happened to all those tasters.

In recent years, this subjective test was converted to a chemical process, but with the results still expressed as Scoville units.

Scoville units can range from zero (the good old bell pepper) to more than half a million (the Red Savina habanero chile).

Disagreement is common, and even chiles of the same variety may vary in heat, but the ratings give a general idea of relative chile heat.

## Ranking the Heat in Chiles

### Dried Chiles

*Ancho*
Also labeled: Pasilla
Description: Almost triangular, about 3 x 5 inches; thick-fleshed, reddish brown and wrinkled
Heat and flavor: 1,000–1,500 Scoville units; complex, rich and sweet (Mexican cooks consider it indispensable)
Substitute: Mulato

*California*
Also labeled: New Mexico
Description: Slender, tapering, about 1 x 5 inches, smooth and reddish
Heat and flavor: 1,000–1,500 Scoville units; mild heat, delicate flavor
Substitute: Guajillo

*Cascabel*
Description: Smooth, round, 1½ inches in diameter; mahogany color
Heat and flavor: 1,500–2,500 Scoville units; richly flavored, with nutlike, medium heat
Substitute: Guajillo

*Cayenne, Red*
Description: Clear, bright red. Resembles a chile de árbol but is shorter, about 2 to 4 inches long.
Heat and flavor: 30,000–50,000 Scoville units; smoky, dusty tones with a pungent, acidic flavor
Substitute: Chile de árbol

*Chile de Árbol*
Description: Brick red, 2 to 4 inches long, pointed
Heat and flavor: 30,000–50,000 Scoville units; flavor takes a back seat to fast, searing heat
Substitute: Cayenne pepper

*Chipotle*
Description: Oblong, 2 to 3 inches long; hard, brown or dark red, wrinkled
Heat and flavor: 2,500–5,000 Scoville units; smoky, complex heat
Substitute: Canned chipotles in adobo sauce

*Guajillo*
Description: Smooth, orange red, tapering; about 1 x 5 inches
Heat and flavor: 2,500–5,000 Scoville units; sweet, berrylike flavor with medium heat
Substitute: California

*Habanero*
Description: Orange-tan, about 1 inch in diameter; slightly wrinkled, with pointed end
Heat and flavor: 150,000–300,000 Scoville units, "hottest in the world"; lacks some of the fruitiness of the fresh
Substitute: Chile de árbol or cayenne pepper

*Mulato*
Also labeled: Ancho or pasilla
Description: Often mistaken for the ancho, but it is darker brown when held up to the light
Heat and flavor: 1,500 Scoville units; slight acidic bite to heat
Substitute: Ancho

*New Mexico*
Also labeled: Colorado, California
Description: Several varieties; most about an inch wide and 5 to 6 inches long; bright red, shiny and slightly wrinkled
Heat and flavor: 1,500–10,000 Scoville units; medium, clear heat; incomparable flavor, fruity and sun dried
Substitute: California

### Fresh Chiles

*Anaheim*
Description: Slender, about 7 inches long; bright green
Heat and flavor: 500–1,500 Scoville units; gentle as a lamb
Substitute: Poblano or fresh New Mexico green

*Cayenne, Green*
Description: Skinny, 5 to 6 inches long; bright green
Heat and flavor: 30,000–40,000 Scoville units;

milder than red cayenne; sweet
Substitute: Jalapeno, serrano, güero

*Cayenne, Red*
Description: Skinny, 5 to 6 inches long; deep red
Heat and flavor: 30,000–50,000 Scoville units; hot and sweet
Substitute: Jalapeno or serrano

*Red Fresno*
Also labeled: Jalapeno (mistakenly); caribe or cera
Description: Plump, 2 to 4 inches long, pointed tip; mellow red
Heat and flavor: 5,000 Scoville units; sweet and hot
Substitute: Jalapeno

*Guero (blondie)*
Also labeled: Yellow wax
Description: 3 inches long; pale yellow
Heat and flavor: 2,000–5,000 Scoville units; sweet but sharp
Substitute: Jalapeno, fresno, serrano

*Habanero*
Also labeled: Manzana
Description: Round or heart-shaped; 2 inches in diameter; orange or lime green
Heat and flavor: 100,000–300,000 Scoville units; floral, fruity, incendiary
Substitute: Serrano

*Jalapeno*
Description: Plump, 2 to 3 inches long; dark green
Heat and flavor: 2,500–5,000 Scoville units; rich and medium hot
Substitute: Fresno, guero, serrano

*Poblano*
Also labeled: Pasilla
Description: Heart-shaped, about 5 inches long; dark green
Heat and flavor: 1,000–1,500 Scoville units; rich and velvety
Substitute: Anaheim

*Serrano*
Description: Skinny; 2 inches long; bright green
Heat and flavor: 10,000–23,000 Scoville units; delayed, biting heat
Substitute: Jalapeno, Fresno

## Chile Tips

**How to Select.** The most important thing about a fresh chile is its freshness. Fresh means shiny and firm; if the flesh has started to wrinkle, if the stem looks dried or if it has begun to blacken around the base, the chile is old.

**How to Handle.** If your hands tend to be sensitive or you're not used to working with the hotter chiles, wear surgical gloves when cutting them. Chopping a few jalapenos with your bare hands may not hurt, but if you're handling massive quantities, you'll certainly feel it.

Wash your hands extremely well after working with chiles—and even then don't assume you've removed all the oil. Even if you can't feel the heat on your tongue when you lick your finger, there may still be a residue and it will burn when it comes into contact with more sensitive parts of your skin. Be extremely careful about touching your face, especially your nose and eyes.

If you do rub chile oil into your eyes, flush them immediately with cold running water.

**How to Roast.** Blacken peppers or chiles by turning them over a gas burner or by putting them on a stainless steel cooling rack placed over an electric burner. The gas-burner method works best because the flame just chars the surface without actually cooking the flesh. Place the blackened peppers or chiles in a plastic bag and let steam for 5 minutes or so. The blackened skin will easily slip off. Use a paring knife to remove any tough spots. Do not worry about removing every last bit of blackened skin; a few bits add character.

**Quenching the Flames.** When chiles bite back, don't guzzle water, beer or wine. Instead, try quenching the flames by eating rice, bread or a tortilla. These soft, starchy foods help mop up the spicy oils.

Milk—which contains casein, a protein that literally grabs capsaicin—will also help douse the fire. Raita, the yogurt-cucumber dish in Indian cuisines, serves the same function.

Some chile eaters find piping-hot liquids such as tea soothing. Others find sucking an orange or lemon helpful.

The capsaicin is concentrated in the chile's white tissue, which holds the seeds. If you want to cut the heat, discard this tissue, as well as the seeds, which are often hot because they're in such close contact with the white stuff.

**Storing Chiles.** Because dried chiles attract bugs, store them in sealable plastic bags in the freezer.

# Velvet Chipotle Salsa for Enchiladas

*This heavenly sauce by Jacqueline McMahan demonstrates that Mexican food can be complex and delicate. If you have any sauce left after making enchiladas, try using it on pasta or slathered on chicken.*

3 dried chipotle chiles

1 guajillo or dried California chile

½ onion

1 head garlic, top sliced off to expose the cloves

2 teaspoons fruity olive oil

2 tomatoes (about ½ pound)

3 cups water (may use part chicken broth)

1 sprig fresh thyme

½ teaspoon salt

¼ to ½ cup half-and-half

2 tablespoons heavy cream or Mexican crema (optional)

◎◎ Preheat the oven to 375 degrees.

Place the chiles in a bowl, cover with boiling water and let soak for 15 to 30 minutes.

Place the onion and garlic on a square of foil, drizzle with olive oil and wrap up tightly. Bake for 45 minutes.

Cut the tomatoes in half and place in a 3-quart saucepan along with the water, thyme, salt, the soaked and drained chiles, and the roasted onion and garlic. Simmer for 45 minutes.

Transfer the tomatoes, chiles, half of the onion and 3 of the garlic cloves to a food processor; process to a smooth puree. Add a little of the cooking liquid to facilitate blending. Discard the remaining onion and garlic. Pour the remaining cooking liquid into a bowl and reserve.

Push the puree through a sieve placed over the saucepan. Add half of the reserved cooking liquid, the half-and-half and cream. (Discard the remaining cooking liquid.) Simmer for 5 minutes to thicken.

YIELDS 3 TO 3½ CUPS

## How to Make Low-Fat Tortilla Chips

Spray cooking oil on both sides of soft corn tortillas. Cut the tortillas into wedges and spread on oiled baking sheet(s). Bake in a preheated 375-degree oven for 10 to 15 minutes, or until crisp. Sprinkle with salt and/or chile powder.

# Chipotle-Corn Salsa

*This salsa is perfect for a late-summer barbecue when corn and tomatoes are at their peak. Jacqueline McMahan suggests serving it with any grilled meats. Adapted from a recipe by Michele Anna Jordan of the Jaded Palate Catering Company in Sonoma.*

2 ears very fresh corn

2 vine-ripened tomatoes

1 small red onion, diced

¾ cup diced red bell pepper

2 jalapeno chiles, minced (save some of the seeds)

2 teaspoons pureed canned chipotle chiles

Juice of 2 limes

1 tablespoon olive oil

¼ cup chopped fresh cilantro

Salt to taste

◉◉ Remove the husks and silk from the corn and rinse the ears. Simmer the corn in rapidly boiling water for 2 minutes; drain and immediately plunge the ears into a bowl of cold water to stop the cooking. Cut the kernels off the cobs.

Cut the tomatoes into the same size dice as the onions and bell peppers. Combine the corn with the diced and minced vegetables; sprinkle in the reserved jalapeno seeds. Stir in the chipotle puree, lime juice, olive oil, cilantro and salt.

YIELDS ABOUT 3 CUPS

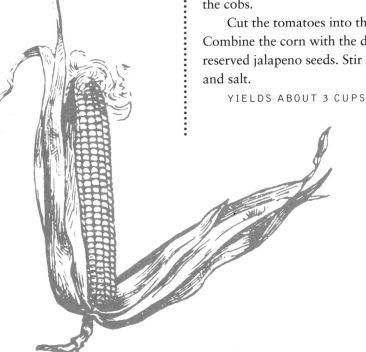

# Tomato-Chipotle Salsa

*Jacqueline McMahan, always on the lookout for a new salsa, discovered this one in Oaxaca, Mexico. It was just one of an array offered with the hotel's breakfast lineup: scrambled eggs, black beans and crispy little rolls. Four chipotles will make a very hot salsa, so cut the amount in half for a milder effect.*

2 large tomatoes

6 or 7 fresh tomatillos, husked

¼ cup diced red or white onion

4 chipotle chiles, cut in strips and seeded

2 garlic cloves

Salt to taste

◉◉ Broil or grill the tomatoes until the skins sear and begin to split. Peel the tomatoes, cut in half and remove the seeds.

Grill or broil the tomatillos just until they have softened, about 2 minutes.

Put the tomatoes, tomatillos, onion, chiles and garlic in a food processor and chop, using on and off pulses. Season with salt.

YIELDS 2 CUPS

# Three-Chile Salsa

*One of Jacqueline McMahan's favorite salsas is made with dried chiles, tomatoes, water, salt and garlic. The different varieties of chiles give a complexity of flavor that belies its simplicity.*

2 tomatoes

6 chiles de árbol

4 cascabel chiles

2 guajillo chiles

¼ cup water

1 garlic clove

½ to 1 teaspoon salt

◎◎  Preheat the oven to 400 degrees.

Place the tomatoes on a baking sheet and roast until the skins blacken, turning as necessary; set aside.

Toast the chiles in a dry skillet until they soften. The arbol chiles should change to a toasty red but should not blacken. Use scissors to snip the chiles into slivers. Shake out the seeds.

Combine the tomatoes and any juices, the chile slivers, water, garlic and salt in a blender. Whir until smooth.

YIELDS ABOUT 1½ CUPS

# Grape Salsa

*This easy salsa, from Jacqueline McMahan, offers the contrast of sweet grapes, tart lemon and fiery jalapenos. It makes an exotic but quick way to perk up a simple sautéed chicken breast or roasted pork tenderloin.*

    2 cups Red Flame or Muscat seedless grapes (or a combination)

    1 tablespoon fresh lemon juice

    1 tablespoon rice vinegar

    1 teaspoon olive oil

    1 garlic clove, pressed

    1 jalapeno chile, seeded and minced

    2 tablespoons chopped fresh chives

    ¼ cup chopped fresh cilantro

    4 tablespoons toasted slivered almonds, crushed

    Pinch salt

    ⅛ teaspoon cayenne pepper

◎◎  Cut the grapes in half. Combine with the remaining ingredients and stir to mix. Set aside for at least 1 hour before using.

SERVES 6

# Cilantro Tomatillo Salsa

*Serve Jacqueline McMahan's sauce as a dip, over eggs or spooned on fish or chicken.*

14 small tomatillos

1 cup cilantro leaves (loosely packed)

2 garlic cloves

2 jalapeno chiles, some of the seeds removed

¼ cup chopped red onion

½ teaspoon salt

∞ Soak the tomatillos in hot water for a few minutes, then remove the husks. Place the tomatillos in a dry skillet over medium heat. Keep turning the tomatillos until they soften; this takes about 5 minutes. Watch them carefully; you don't want them to split.

Transfer the tomatillos to a food processor, add the remaining ingredients and roughly blend, leaving some texture.

YIELDS ABOUT 2½ CUPS

# Tomato Coulis

*Generally speaking, a coulis is a thick puree or sauce, most often made with tomato. This one, by Georgeanne Brennan, may be made ahead because it keeps in the refrigerator for up to 4 days. You can use it on almost everything, but it's particularly fine on pasta. It freezes well, too, so you can stash a batch to dress up last-minute meals.*

2 tablespoons olive oil

1 garlic clove, crushed and minced

5 pounds very ripe tomatoes, peeled and roughly chopped

½ teaspoon salt

½ teaspoon pepper

½ to 1 tablespoon sugar (optional)

1 tablespoon minced fresh thyme

## Making Flavored Vinegars

These are from cooking teacher Heidi Haughy Cusick:

**Raspberry vinegar.** Half-fill a 1-pint mason jar with fresh raspberries, cover with a good-quality white-wine vinegar. Cover and store on a windowsill or other sunny place for 3 to 4 weeks, until the vinegar has a rich pink color. When the berries have sunk to the bottom, strain the vinegar into a sterilized bottle. Stored in a cool, dark place, it will keep for 1 year.

**Tarragon vinegar.** Blanch sprigs of fresh tarragon. Place ¾ cup tarragon leaves in a 1-pint mason jar; cover with white-wine vinegar. Let steep for a couple of weeks. Strain the vinegar into a sterilized bottle. (Use the leaves to flavor mayonnaise.) Will keep for a year. Great for potato salad or to deglaze a pan of sautéed chicken.

⊚⊚   Heat the oil in a saucepan large enough to hold all of the tomatoes. Add the garlic and sauté for 2 or 3 minutes; do not let it brown. Add the tomatoes and cook over low heat for 30 minutes. Add the salt, pepper and sugar, if needed. Simmer until the sauce thickens, 30 minutes to 1 hour, depending upon the type of tomato. Skim any clear liquid off the top. Stir in the thyme and simmer 10 minutes. Let cool, then ladle into jars.

    Store in the refrigerator.

YIELDS ABOUT 3 CUPS

# Yellow Tomato Ketchup

*You may never go back to store-bought ketchup when you try Georgeanne Brennan's tangy-sweet version. Use as an accompaniment to vegetables, such as crispy potato pancakes, or with omelets, frittatas, soufflés, pork chops, sausages, fish or chicken.*

    5 pounds very ripe yellow tomatoes, peeled, seeded and roughly chopped

    2 large yellow bell peppers, seeded, deribbed and coarsely chopped

    2 onions

    10 garlic cloves

    1 cup white wine vinegar

    Juice and zest of ¼ lemon

    ¾ cup sugar

    1½ teaspoons salt

    2 teaspoons mustard seeds

    1 tablespoon black peppercorns

    1 tablespoon coriander seeds

    1 teaspoon whole cloves

    1-inch-long cinnamon stick

    1-inch knob fresh ginger, cut into 3 or 4 pieces

⊚⊚   Place the tomatoes in a large saucepan. Add the peppers, onions, garlic, ½ cup of the vinegar, the lemon zest and juice. Cook over medium heat, stirring frequently, until the vegetables are soft and cooked through, 15 to 20 minutes. Transfer the mixture to a food processor and process until coarsely pureed but not liquefied. Return the mixture to the pan; add the sugar, salt and remaining ½ cup vinegar.

Place the mustard seeds, peppercorns, coriander, cloves, cinnamon stick and ginger on an 8-inch square of cheesecloth. Gather up the corners and tie with kitchen string. Add to the tomato mixture. Simmer over low heat, stirring occasionally, until the mixture thickens, about 1 hour. Watch carefully so it does not burn. The ketchup will be slightly thinner than most commercial ketchups.

Ladle the ketchup into clean, dry, hot jars with sealable lids, filling the jars to within ½ inch of the rims. Wipe the rims clean. Cover with lids and process for 30 minutes in a hot-water bath.

Remove the jars and let cool at least 12 hours. Check the lids for a complete seal. Store in a cool, dark place. Will keep for up to 1 year. Once opened, keep refrigerated. Store any jar lacking a good seal in the refrigerator for up to 10 days.

YIELDS ABOUT 2 QUARTS

# The Best Red Chile Sauce

*Use Jacqueline McMahan's sauce for making enchiladas or chile colorado. Or spoon it over eggs.*

12 dried New Mexico chiles

1 onion, halved and rubbed with olive oil

2 garlic cloves

2 teaspoons dried oregano

About 1 cup water

Salt to taste

Preheat the oven to 350 degrees. Place the chiles on a baking sheet and toast in the oven for 5 minutes; remove from the oven. Wrap the onion halves in foil, put directly on the oven rack and roast for 45 minutes.

While the onion is roasting, transfer the chiles to a deep bowl and pour boiling water over them. Add the garlic and let steep about 45 minutes, until the chiles are soft (keep pushing them down into the hot liquid). Remove the garlic and chiles from the soaking water. Remove stems and seeds from chiles.

## Infused Basil Oil

John Ash, the chef of Fetzer Vineyards, shared this recipe for basil oil: Blanch a bunch of basil (this helps it retain the bright color). Dry well and put in a blender or food processor. Cover generously with oil, then blend. Pour into a jar, let it settle, then strain. Will keep 10 to 12 days in the refrigerator. Great to drizzle on pizza, pasta or over grilled chicken, pork or fish.

Working in batches, place the chiles in a blender along with the garlic, oregano and water (do not use the chile-soaking water—it is too bitter). Puree for 2 to 3 minutes. Season with salt. Transfer the puree to a saucepan, add the roasted onion (cut into chunks) and simmer for 20 minutes. Add more water if the sauce seems too thick.

YIELDS 2 CUPS

# Cranberry-Raisin Sauce

*This light honey-scented relish by Sharon Cadwallader is delicious with poultry, or any vegetarian, nut or grain dish.*

    1 package (12 ounces) fresh cranberries
    1½ cups water
    ¾ cup mild honey
    3 tablespoons fresh lemon juice
    ½ teaspoon ground cinnamon
    ½ teaspoon ground ginger
    ½ teaspoon ground cloves
    1 cup yellow raisins
    ⅔ cup coarsely chopped pecans

Combine the cranberries, water, honey, lemon juice, cinnamon, ginger and cloves in a large pot. Bring to a boil, reduce heat and simmer, uncovered, for 5 minutes. Add the raisins and continue to simmer for 4 to 5 minutes. Remove from heat and stir in the pecans. Pour into sterilized jars and cover tightly. Refrigerate. Bring to room temperature before serving.

YIELDS 2 PINTS

# Smoky Cranberries

*Jacqueline McMahan believes that chipotles (smoked jalapeno chiles) are good with everything. She proves it here with this intriguing cranberry relish. The chipotle adds a smoky heat that complements the tart cranberries. The relish also makes an amazing bread spread after Thanksgiving when you don't think you can face another turkey sandwich.*

1 bag (12 ounces) cranberries

Grated zest of 1 orange

1 red apple, cored, cut into pieces

½ jalapeno chile, seeded

1 cup orange juice

1 tablespoon honey

½ cup sugar

1 dried chipotle chile

Combine the cranberries, zest, apple and jalapeno in a food processor. Chop roughly. Transfer the mixture to a large saucepan. Add the orange juice, honey, sugar and chipotle chile. Simmer for 8 to 10 minutes.

Serve as a relish with the turkey or on next-day turkey sandwiches, using sturdy Italian bread.

YIELDS 2¼ CUPS

## Getting the Zest

If you don't have a citrus zester, use a vegetable peeler and peel the zest off in long strips, as you would a potato. Don't press too hard and you'll get only the colored zest. Turn the strip over; if there's any white pith (which is bitter) left, gently scrape it off with the blade of the peeler. To cut: Stack the peels on top of each other and slice thinly; then mince.

# Peach Chutney with Pistachios

*Laxmi Hiremath's chutney has a delightful thick and chunky texture. Use only tree-ripened peaches for the best flavor. Let the chutney ripen for at least 1 day before using.*

2⅔ cups sugar

½ cup distilled white vinegar

1 teaspoon mustard seeds, lightly crushed

1 teaspoon fennel seeds, lightly crushed

1 teaspoon whole cloves

½ teaspoon ground cumin

1 teaspoon ground coriander

1 teaspoon red pepper flakes

¾ cup dried currants

½ teaspoon salt

4 pounds peaches, peeled, pitted and sliced into ¼-inch-thick wedges

¼ cup fresh lemon juice

1 cup slivered pistachios

Put the sugar into a large, heavy nonaluminum saucepan. Add the vinegar, mustard seeds, fennel, cloves, cumin, coriander, pepper flakes, currants and salt. Bring to a boil, stirring constantly. Reduce the heat, cover, and simmer until the mixture is thick, about 12 minutes.

Meanwhile, toss the peaches with the lemon juice. When spice mixture is thick, add the peaches, stir gently and cook, uncovered, for 10 minutes. The peaches should retain their shape. Remove from heat. Stir in the pistachios.

Spoon the chutney into hot sterilized jars. Seal, cool and refrigerate. The chutney keeps well in the refrigerator for up to 6 months.

YIELDS 8 CUPS

# Coconut Chutney

*In Southern India, this chutney is paired with savory lentil crepes and rice cakes, but it also goes well with shrimp, shellfish and salmon. Traditionally, freshly grated coconut is used, but Laxmi Hiremath has found that packaged sweetened coconut produces amazingly good results. Those who like a fiery chutney are free to add more chiles.*

    1½ fresh hot green chiles, seeded (if desired) and chopped
    ½ teaspoon cumin seeds
    2 large garlic cloves
    ⅓ teaspoon salt
    ¼ cup chopped fresh cilantro with tender stems
    1 cup packaged sweetened flaked coconut
    1 cup plain yogurt
    1 tablespoon mild vegetable oil
    ½ teaspoon mustard seeds
    1 small dried red pepper, crumbled
    10 kari (curry) leaves, preferably fresh

☙ Combine the chiles, cumin, garlic, salt, cilantro, coconut and yogurt in a blender and process until finely pureed. Transfer to a bowl. Set aside.

Heat the oil in a small skillet over medium-high heat. Add the mustard seeds, red pepper and kari leaves. When the seeds sputter and the pepper turns dark red, remove from heat. Pour over the coconut chutney, scraping the skillet with a rubber spatula. Mix gently.

Serve immediately, or cover and refrigerate for up to 4 days.

YIELDS ABOUT 1½ CUPS

# Fresh Mint Chutney with Garlic

*Serve Laxmi Hiremath's fragrant chutney with an assortment of crackers, or as a condiment for lamb curry or simple barbecued or roast lamb. It's also delightful for breakfast, spooned on Indian-style sausages and scrambled eggs.*

    2 cups fresh mint leaves with tender stems
    1 fresh hot green chile, seeded and chopped

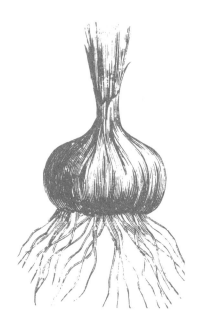

2 large garlic cloves

¼ cup water

½ teaspoon salt

¼ cup plain yogurt, stirred to blend

❧ Combine the mint, chile, garlic, water and salt in a blender and finely puree. Transfer to a serving bowl. Whisk in the yogurt. Serve immediately, or cover and refrigerate for up to 5 days.

YIELDS 1 CUP

# Tamarind Chutney with California Dates

*This hot, sweet-and-sour chutney from Laxmi Hiremath is a great dipping sauce for onion rings, fried zucchini and other vegetables or chips.*

4 ounces tamarind pulp, cut into pieces

2 cups hot water

½-inch piece fresh ginger

⅓ teaspoon red pepper flakes

½ teaspoon ground coriander

¼ cup packed light brown sugar

¼ teaspoon salt

2 tablespoons chopped California dates or other dates

1 ripe banana, peeled and thinly sliced

❧ Combine the tamarind and water in a glass bowl. Cover and let soak for 1 hour. Break up the tamarind pulp with a spoon or your fingers. Strain it through a sieve into a nonaluminum saucepan, pressing on the solids with the back of a spoon to extract as much tamarind as possible. Add the ginger, pepper flakes, coriander, sugar and salt. Cook, uncovered, over medium heat until the mixture is thick, about 10 minutes, stirring occasionally. Discard the ginger.

At this point you may cool, cover and refrigerate the chutney for up to 2 weeks. Bring to room temperature before continuing. If the chutney is too thick, add water to the desired consistency.

Just before serving, stir in the dates and banana.

YIELDS ABOUT 1½ CUPS

# Hot and Sweet Cranberry-Tangerine Chutney

*This Indian relish from Laxmi Hiremath is a refreshing change from the standard cranberry sauce. It goes well with lamb, pork, chicken or turkey (and it's particularly good on turkey sandwiches). Stored in a glass jar with a tight-fitting lid, it will keep well for up to 6 months in the refrigerator. Just give it a good stir before using.*

1 bag (12 ounces) cranberries, stemmed and washed

2 small tangerines (unpeeled), halved, seeded and cut into ½-inch wedges

¼ cup chopped onion

1 cup sugar

1 tablespoon grated fresh ginger

½ teaspoon cayenne pepper

¼ teaspoon ground cinnamon

4 green cardamom pods, husked and seeds ground

⅓ teaspoon salt

¼ cup chopped walnuts

Combine all the ingredients except the walnuts in a large, heavy nonaluminum pan. Cook over medium heat, stirring, until the sugar dissolves. Increase the heat and boil until the cranberries pop, 3 to 4 minutes. Remove from heat and stir in the nuts.

When completely cool, spoon the chutney into sterilized jars. Heat seal or cover and refrigerate. Let chutney ripen for at least 2 days before serving. Serve at room temperature.

YIELDS 3 CUPS

Carol Field, an authority
on California cuisine, uses
balsamic vinegar on salad
greens along with olive oil.
She then adds a scattering
of toasted walnuts and
freshly grated Parmesan
cheese.

Carlo Middione, owner
of the Vivande restaurants,
dusts sea bass with flour,
sautés it, then deglazes the
pan with balsamic vinegar
and capers. He also sprinkles the vinegar on sautéed
zucchini, cantaloupe and
honeydew melon.

Michael Chiarello,
chef/owner of Tra Vigne in
the Napa Valley, likes it
drizzled on roasted sea
bass and scallops.

Chuck Williams, owner
of Williams-Sonoma,
sprinkles it on strawberries,
sliced peaches, pears,
oranges and avocados. He
also likes to make a simple
sauce for sautéed chicken
breasts by adding a splash
of balsamic to the pan
juices.

Loni Kuhn, a San
Francisco cooking teacher,
uses it in vegetable soup or
at the end of making
risotto. She also likes it
with kale, sautéed in olive
oil, garlic and red pepper
flakes, because it smooths
the flavors.

# Baba Ghanoush

*Marlena Spieler loves eggplant, and this fire-roasted puree is her favorite way
to use it. Baba ghanoush may be varied and garnished as whim dictates. Serve
it as a salad, as an appetizer with triangles of pita bread, or as a sauce for
grilled vegetables or meats. Topping the puree with lots of cilantro is a fresh
and spunky touch. When pomegranates are in season, omit the olive garnish
and scatter a handful of pomegranate seeds over the top. This classic dish calls
for tahini, which is a sesame paste, available in Middle Eastern markets.*

2 globe eggplants, unpeeled

3 to 5 garlic cloves, finely chopped

½ to ⅔ cup tahini, more if needed

Juice of 1 to 2 lemons

Dash Tabasco or cayenne pepper

½ teaspoon ground cumin, or to taste

Salt to taste

2 tablespoons olive oil

2 tablespoons chopped fresh cilantro

Paprika or cayenne pepper to taste

Salty Mediterranean-type olives

◎ Place the eggplants over an open fire, either on a barbecue or over a gas
burner. Cook slowly until charred, turning until the eggplants are deflated,
evenly blackened and tender. Place in a pan and let cool.

When the eggplants are cool enough to handle, peel and coarsely chop the
flesh. Use a little of the smoky juices that leach out of the charred vegetable as
flavoring. Stir in the garlic, tahini, lemon juice, Tabasco or cayenne, cumin
and salt. Adjust seasoning as needed. Chill until ready to serve.

When ready to serve, garnish with a drizzle of olive oil, a sprinkling of
cilantro and paprika or cayenne, and a scattering of olives.

SERVES 8

# Michael Bauer's Party Mix

*When we were doing a story on retro comfort food, everyone laughed when party mix was mentioned. However, a gallon bag disappeared within an hour, and it's constantly requested. Most versions these days omit the bacon grease and add all kinds of other embellishments—but this version still is the best. Margarine is used instead of butter because it keeps better.*

7 cups (7 ounces) Rice Chex

7 cups (11 ounces) Wheat Chex

7 cups (7 ounces) Corn Chex

1 box (15 ounces) Cheerios

1 package (9 ounces) thin pretzels

1 can (12.5 ounces) Spanish peanuts

⅓ cup bacon grease

½ cup margarine

2 tablespoons Tabasco

1 heaping teaspoon chile powder (with salt)

Preheat the oven to 200 degrees.

Mix together the cereals, pretzels and peanuts in a large roasting pan and set aside.

Melt together the bacon grease, margarine and Tabasco, then stir into the dry ingredients. Sprinkle on the chile powder and stir again.

Bake for 2 hours, stirring every 20 minutes.

YIELDS ABOUT 50 CUPS

## Flavoring Vodka

Flavored vodkas are all the rage, great for sipping or using for cooking. The recipe is simple:

Almost any fruit (fresh or dried) may be used: apricots, berries, grapes, pears, peaches, pineapple. Or use chiles, herbs and spices for a spirited twist.

Wash the produce well, then peel, slice or cube it, if necessary. Loosely fill a container with the fruit, then add vodka to cover. Cover the container and let stand at room temperature until the vodka has taken on the flavor of the fruit. John Hurley, owner of Garibaldi's Cafe, recommends the following times for letting the mixture steep:

a week for pineapple and grapes;

5 days for berries;

a week to 10 days for pears, peaches and apricots;

2 weeks for dried fruit.

# Little Jalapenos for Munching

*On those hot summer evenings, when you pull your chair out-of-doors to enjoy a quiet glass of wine or a cold beer, you need something to munch— such as these fiery little peppers with a tangy goat cheese filling by Jacqueline McMahan. Accompany them with slices of chewy baguette or warm tortillas.*

1 tablespoon olive oil

½ cup cider vinegar

1 garlic clove, minced

½ teaspoon salt

1 small can roasted jalapeno chiles (not pickled), marinade reserved

**Filling**

½ cup crumbled mild goat cheese, such as a queso ranchero

2 teaspoons mayonnaise

1 tablespoon unflavored yogurt

1 tablespoon minced fresh cilantro

2 teaspoons reserved chile marinade, or more as needed

Cilantro leaves for garnish

⊚⊚  Mix together the olive oil, vinegar, garlic and salt. Carefully cut each chile in half, then place in the marinade. Let marinate for a couple of hours to overnight.

Blend together the goat cheese, mayonnaise, yogurt, cilantro and 2 teaspoons of the chile marinade, or enough to make the mixture moist. Using a small spoon, fill each pepper half with goat cheese mixture. Press a cilantro leaf into the top of each.

May be made several hours ahead; cover and refrigerate. Serve with crackers, baguette slices or warm tortillas—and lots of icy beer.

YIELDS ABOUT 14 STUFFED JALAPENO HALVES

# Olive Cheese Balls

*This recipe came to Flo Braker's attention many years ago after it won a national contest.*

36 small pimiento-stuffed green olives, drained

¾ cup all-purpose flour

½ teaspoon paprika

⅛ teaspoon salt

4 tablespoons unsalted butter, softened

1 cup (4 ounces) coarsely shredded cheddar or Asiago cheese at room temperature

◎ Drain the olives well on paper towels. Adjust the rack to the lower third of the oven; preheat the oven to 400 degrees. Line a baking sheet with bakers' parchment.

Combine the flour, paprika and salt; stir briefly to mix. Blend together the butter and cheese. Add the flour mixture, blending to form a smooth dough.

Using a teaspoon of dough at a time, shape into a ball, then flatten the dough in the palm of your hand. Center a drained olive on the dough and wrap the dough around the olive to encase it completely. Roll in the palms of your hands to form a smooth ball. Place on the baking sheet.

Bake 12 to 15 minutes, or until the dough is set. Serve hot or lukewarm (we even like them at room temperature).

YIELDS 3 DOZEN

# Chapter 10

# Desserts

*Californians are probably no different from people in the rest of the country: We love sweets. If there is any difference at all, it's that many of the offerings are fruit based.*

*We've included several desserts that seem more popular on the West Coast than in the rest of the country: an at-home version of crème brûlée, a rich buttery custard; lemon-scented biscotti, the Italian crisp cookie designed for serving with fresh fruit or dunking in coffee or dessert wine; and a rosemary-polenta pound cake, which follows the emerging trend of putting savory herbs in sweet courses.*

*Of course, we also have our share of rich peanut butter cookies, homey slumps, grunts and cobblers, ice cream, and one of the best angel food cakes we've ever tasted.*

# Strawberry Angel Pie

*There's no better showcase for the first strawberries of the season than Marion Cunningham's angel pie. The crust is a golden meringue; it holds lemon custard topped with sweetened berries folded into whipped cream. Remember, meringues are temperamental, so don't be alarmed when the crust collapses a bit and cracks as it cools. The cracks won't show when the shell is filled.*

4 eggs at room temperature, separated
¼ teaspoon salt
¼ teaspoon cream of tartar
1½ cups sugar
¼ cup fresh lemon juice
1 tablespoon grated lemon zest
1½ cups heavy cream
⅓ cup powdered sugar
2 cups strawberries, hulled and sliced

Preheat the oven to 275 degrees. Butter a 9-inch pie pan.

Combine the egg whites, salt and cream of tartar in a large mixing bowl. Beat with an electric mixer until soft peaks form. Slowly add 1 cup of the sugar and beat until shiny stiff peaks form. Spread the mixture in the pie pan, building a rim about 1 inch higher than the edge of the pan.

Bake for about 1 hour, or until the meringue is lightly golden and firm to the touch. Let cool in the turned-off oven with the door open.

While the crust is cooling, beat the egg yolks until they are thick and pale yellow. Slowly beat in the remaining ½ cup sugar. Add the lemon juice and zest. Cook over low heat, stirring constantly, until the mixture thickens. Be patient; this takes about 5 minutes, but you don't want the yolks to burn. Remove from the heat and let cool to room temperature.

Beat the cream until it is stiff enough to hold peaks (you should have about 3 cups). Refrigerate until time to assemble the pie.

Sprinkle the powdered sugar over the strawberries; gently toss so they are evenly sweetened.

To assemble: Gently fold 1 cup of the whipped cream into the lemon custard, mixing only until well blended. Spread the mixture over the bottom of the meringue shell.

Fold the strawberries into the remaining 2 cups whipped cream and pile on top of the lemon filling. If desired, decorate the pie with whole berries, or a little strawberry juice drizzled on top.

SERVES 8 TO 10

# Apple-Quince Pie

*Flo Braker's streusel-topped pie is one of the best uses for quince, which are available in the fall from just before Thanksgiving to Christmas. One of our editors likes to add 2 to 3 teaspoons of grated fresh ginger to the apple-quince mixture.*

One 9-inch unbaked pie crust (see page 337)

**Streusel**

½ cup packed light brown sugar

½ cup granulated sugar

1 cup all-purpose flour

½ cup (1 stick) unsalted butter at room temperature

**Filling**

¼ cup packed dark brown sugar

¼ cup granulated sugar

3½ tablespoons flour

½ teaspoon ground cinnamon

¼ teaspoon ground nutmeg

2½ pounds firm tart apples, peeled, cored and cut into ⅛-inch slices (about 8 cups)

1 ripe quince, peeled, cored and cut into ⅛-inch slices (about ¾ cup)

1 tablespoon fresh lemon juice

3 tablespoons unsalted butter, melted

◎◎  To make the streusel: Combine the ingredients in a large bowl and mix with your fingertips until the mixture resembles coarse crumbs.

Adjust the rack in the lower third of the oven; preheat the oven to 450 degrees.

To make the filling: Mix the sugars, flour and spices in a small bowl. Combine the apple and quince slices in a large bowl, sprinkle with the spice-sugar mixture and toss gently and briefly with a rubber spatula. Sprinkle with the lemon juice and melted butter, tossing again just to combine.

Spoon the filling into the pastry-lined pan, mounding it slightly higher in the center. Top with half of the streusel, patting to form a thin topping on the fruit. (Store the remaining streusel in the refrigerator or freezer.)

Bake for 10 minutes, then reduce the oven temperature to 350 degrees and bake for 30 to 40 minutes longer, or until the bottom crust is golden. Remove from the oven to a cooling rack.

Serve lukewarm or at room temperature with vanilla ice cream or frozen yogurt.

SERVES 6 TO 8

# The Perfect Pie Crust

*The recipe may be doubled for an 8- or 9-inch double-crust pie.*

1 cup unsifted all-purpose flour
¼ teaspoon salt
3 tablespoons unsalted butter, chilled
¼ cup vegetable shortening, chilled
3 to 4 tablespoons ice water

◉◉ Combine the flour and salt in a large bowl; stir to mix. Divide butter into 6 to 8 pieces; scatter over the flour. Using a pastry blender, cut in the butter until the largest pieces are pea-sized. Divide the shortening into 6 to 8 pieces and scatter over the butter-flour mixture. Cut in with a pastry blender until the fragments range in size from bread crumbs to small lima beans. Sprinkle the ice water, 1 tablespoon at a time, evenly over the flour mixture, tossing with a fork. Add more ice water until the mixture is moist enough to stick together.

Gather the dough together. Place on a sheet of plastic wrap and form into a disc about 4½ inches in diameter. Wrap and refrigerate for at least 2 hours.

Lightly flour a work surface. Place the dough on the floured surface and roll it into a 12½-inch circle (pastry will be about ⅛ inch thick). Drape the dough over the rolling pin and ease it into a 9-inch pie pan. Fit the dough into the pan using your fingertips. Using kitchen scissors, trim the dough overhang 1 inch from the rim of the pan. Fold excess pastry under, forming a rim, then flute.

To prebake: Prick the bottom of the crust with the tines of a fork. Line shell with foil, carefully fitting it against the dough; fill with dried beans or pie weights. Bake in a 450-degree oven for 10 minutes. Remove the foil and weights, and return the crust to the oven until it is lightly browned, 3 or 4 minutes longer. Do not let it get too brown.

YIELDS ONE 9-INCH PIE SHELL

## Substituting Honey for Sugar

When substituting honey for sugar, use ⅔ to ¾ cup honey for each cup of sugar called for in the recipe. Decrease the liquid in the recipe by 25 percent and reduce the baking temperature by 25 degrees.

# Lattice-Top Fresh Berry Pie

*Flo Braker prefers using a Pyrex pan for pie crusts because you can see when the bottom crust is done. Use a combination of your favorite berries: blueberries, raspberries, boysenberries, olallieberries and blackberries.*

2 cups all-purpose flour

¼ teaspoon salt

6 tablespoons unsalted butter, chilled and cut into ¼-inch pieces

⅔ cup vegetable shortening, chilled

⅓ cup ice water

**Berry Filling**

6 cups fresh berries, any combination

⅔ cup sugar

⅛ teaspoon salt

3 tablespoons tapioca

2 tablespoons unsalted butter, melted

**Glaze**

2 tablespoons milk

2 tablespoons sugar

☙☙ Combine the flour and salt in a large bowl and stir to disperse the salt. Scatter the butter over the flour. Using a pastry blender, cut in the butter until the size of peas. Scatter the shortening over the butter-flour mixture, and cut it in until the fragments range in size from bread crumbs to lima beans. Sprinkle ice water, a tablespoon at a time, evenly over the flour mixture, using a fork to distribute the moisture.

Gather up the dough, using the side of the bowl to help shape it. Divide the dough in half, shape each half into a 4½-inch disc, wrap in plastic and refrigerate for at least 2 hours.

Roll out 1 portion of dough to a 13-inch circle. Fit it into a 9-inch pie pan with a lightly greased bottom. Trim the overhang to 1 inch beyond the rim of the pan. Refrigerate while preparing the lattice.

Roll out the second portion of dough to a 13-inch circle. Roll up onto the rolling pin and transfer to a baking sheet; cover with plastic wrap and refrigerate until time to apply the lattice.

Adjust the rack in the lower third of the oven and preheat the oven to 450 degrees.

Place the berries in a 3-quart mixing bowl. Combine the sugar, salt and tapioca; sprinkle over the fruit. Toss gently until mixed. Wait for 15 minutes, gently tossing occasionally, to allow the tapioca to soften in the berry juices.

To form the lattice, remove the pastry-lined pan and circle of pastry from the refrigerator.

Add the melted butter to the berry filling and pour into the pastry-lined pan, spreading it evenly.

Using a ruler and pastry wheel (or sharp-edged chef's knife), cut the entire pastry circle into strips. Brush the strips with a light coating of milk. Place the strips in parallel rows, about ½ inch apart, across the filling. Arrange another row of strips at right angles to the first to form a lattice. (Not all the strips may be needed.) Cut overhanging strips even with the bottom crust. Lift the bottom crust and fold it up and over the ends of the strips, pressing with your fingertips to seal and build a ridge. Crimp the ridge with your fingertips. Sprinkle the lattice with the 2 tablespoons sugar.

Bake for 10 minutes. Reduce the oven temperature to 350 degrees and bake for 35 to 45 minutes, or until the bottom crust is golden brown, the filling is bubbling and the lattice is light golden brown. Remove from oven to a cooling rack. Serve lukewarm or at room temperature.

SERVES 8

# Blum's Coffee Toffee Pie

*Blum's was a tremendously popular local chain of cafe/sweet shop/ice cream parlors. Some of us still remember going to the Blum's on Union Square for a cup of coffee and a bite—or two—of something sweet. Unfortunately, Blum's closed its doors in the 1960s. A few of the recipes survive, however, kept alive by people like cookbook author John Carroll, who gave us this one.*

**Chocolate Dough**

1 cup all-purpose flour

½ cup (1 stick) butter, softened

¼ cup packed brown sugar

1 square unsweetened chocolate, grated

1 teaspoon vanilla extract

2 tablespoons (or more) milk

¾ cup chopped walnuts

**Filling**

½ cup (1 stick) butter, softened

¾ cup sugar

2 teaspoons powdered instant coffee

1 square unsweetened chocolate, melted

2 eggs

**Topping**

1½ cups heavy cream, chilled

6 tablespoons powdered sugar

1½ tablespoons nonfat dry milk

1½ tablespoons powdered instant coffee

1 tablespoon grated unsweetened chocolate

## Whipping Cream

To whip cream easily in warm weather, first place the bowl, cream and whisk (or beaters) in the freezer for 7 to 10 minutes.

◉ Preheat the oven to 375 degrees. Set out a 9-inch pie plate.

To make the dough: Combine the flour, butter, brown sugar and chocolate in a bowl and mix until well blended, using your fingertips, a pastry blender or a food processor. Add the vanilla, 2 tablespoons milk and the walnuts and mix well. The mixture should form a cohesive but not sticky mass. If it is too dry, add a few drops milk. This is a cookielike dough, not harmed by handling. The easiest way to get it into the pan is to take walnut-sized pieces and press them onto the bottom and sides of the pan, making sure you distribute them evenly, with no gaps or thin spots. Press the dough well up the sides too, then crimp the edges. Prick all over with a fork and press a piece of heavy-duty foil snugly into the pie shell.

Bake for 8 minutes, then remove the foil and bake for about 10 minutes more, or until the shell is dry and crisp. Remove to a rack and let cool completely before filling.

To make the filling: Put the butter in the large bowl of an electric mixer and beat until fluffy. Beating on high speed, gradually add the sugar. Beat in the instant coffee and melted chocolate. Add 1 egg and beat on the highest speed for 5 minutes. Add the second egg and beat for 5 minutes more. Spread the filling evenly in the cooled pie shell, then cover and refrigerate for at least 6 hours, or overnight.

To make the topping: Combine the cream, powdered sugar, dry milk and instant coffee in a large bowl and beat with an electric mixer until stiff. Spread in peaks and swirls over the chilled pie. Sprinkle with the grated chocolate. Refrigerate for at least 2 hours before serving.

SERVES 8

# Frangipane Tart

*Frangipane is a gooey almond paste that's used to fill many classic desserts. Here, Flo Braker features it in a rich and delicious tart. Once the filling has cooled, you can add a fresh-fruit topping: kiwi slices, pineapple or berries. The dough for this tart is easy to make and press into the pan. Sugar added to the dough reduces the risk of shrinkage or toughness.*

2 cups unsifted all-purpose flour

½ cup sugar

⅛ teaspoon salt

¾ cup (1½ sticks) unsalted butter, softened

1 large egg, lightly beaten

**Frangipane Filling**

1½ cups blanched almonds, finely ground

1 cup sugar

1 cup unsalted butter

4 large eggs

1 tablespoon rum

½ teaspoon vanilla extract

½ teaspoon almond extract

½ cup jam or preserves (any flavor)

◎ Adjust the rack to the lower third of the oven; preheat the oven to 350 degrees.

Place the flour, sugar and salt in a food processor and process briefly to mix. Add the butter and process just until the mixture resembles cornmeal. Add the egg and process until the dough just comes together into a ball. Press into an ungreased 10 x 15–inch jelly-roll pan. Bake 5 to 10 minutes, or until the pastry is set but not yet colored.

To make the filling: Combine all the filling ingredients in a food processor and process until just combined.

Spread the jam thinly over the dough, then spread the filling evenly over the jam. Return to the oven and bake for 25 to 30 minutes, or until light golden on top.

Cut into 2½-inch squares.

YIELDS 24 SQUARES

**NOTE:** Filling may be used for two 9-inch round tart pans. Bake each for 25 minutes.

# Ohio Lemon Pie

*This recipe, from Marion Cunningham, is a traditional Shaker dessert. Lemons are sliced thinly—rind and all—then mixed with sugar and allowed to stand for 3 to 5 hours before they're baked in a pastry crust. The resulting pie has an intense taste of candied lemon.*

2 lemons
2 cups sugar
Pastry for a 2-crust 8-inch pie (see page 337)
4 eggs

Using a vegetable brush or nylon scouring pad, scrub the lemons under hot water to rid them of dirt and chemical sprays. Dry the lemons and trim off stem ends. Slice the lemons as thin as paper, rind and all. Remove and discard the seeds. Place the lemons in a bowl and sprinkle 1½ cups of the sugar over them. Mix well and let stand for 3 to 5 hours.

Preheat the oven to 450 degrees.

Roll out half of the pastry and fit into an 8-inch pie pan.

Beat the eggs until they are well mixed. Arrange the lemon slices in layers in the pie shell, sprinkling the remaining sugar between each layer. Pour the beaten eggs over the lemons.

Roll out the remaining pastry and fit it over the top of the pie. Trim, then crimp the edges. Cut steam vents in the top.

Bake for 15 minutes. Reduce the oven temperature to 400 degrees and bake about 20 minutes (check after 15 minutes), or until the tip of a knife comes out clean when inserted into the center of the pie.

Remove the pie from oven to a wire cooling rack. Let cool to room temperature before serving. Refrigerate any leftover pie.

SERVES 6

# Fresh Peach Pie

*We've tried lots of peach pies in our time, but former food editor Jane Benet's is the best. The quick-cooking tapioca gives it a great texture, without robbing the fruit of any flavor.*

Pastry for 2-crust 9-inch pie (see page 337)

8 to 10 peaches, peeled, pitted and sliced

Juice of 1 lemon

¾ cup sugar, or to taste

Pinch ground nutmeg

3 tablespoons quick-cooking tapioca

2 tablespoons unsalted butter

Preheat the oven to 425 degrees.

Roll out half of the pastry and line a 9-inch pie pan with it, trimming the edges.

Combine the peaches with the lemon juice, sugar, nutmeg and tapioca; toss together thoroughly, then spoon into the prepared pie shell. Cut the butter into pieces and distribute over the fruit. Roll the remaining pastry to a circle 2 inches larger than the pan; cut decorative slits in it for escape of steam. Moisten the edges of the bottom crust with water, then place the top crust over the peaches. Trim the edges but leave about ½ inch overhang. Fold the overhanging pastry under the bottom crust and crimp with your fingers or a fork, either of which should be floured to avoid sticking. Cut steam vents in top crust.

Bake for 15 minutes, then reduce oven temperature to 375 degrees and continue baking about 20 to 25 minutes, or until the peaches are tender when pierced and the crust is golden.

Serve at room temperature.

SERVES 6 TO 8

# Pumpkin Chiffon Pie

*If the pumpkin growers had a contest, we're convinced this pie, by Flo Braker, would win. Both egg whites and lightly whipped cream give the filling a light,*

*creamy texture. A bit of orange juice and zest bring out admirable qualities in
the pumpkin.*

2 tablespoons fresh orange juice

2 tablespoons cold water

1 envelope (1 tablespoon) unflavored gelatin

1 cup packed brown sugar

2 cups pumpkin puree, fresh or canned

1 teaspoon ground cinnamon

¼ teaspoon ground ginger

¼ teaspoon ground cloves

3 egg yolks

¼ teaspoon salt

2 teaspoons finely grated orange zest

3 egg whites

2 tablespoons granulated sugar

1 cup heavy cream

9-inch baked pie shell (see page 337) or cookie crumb crust (see page 347)

◉◉  At least 4 hours before serving the dessert, combine the orange juice and
water in a small dish. Sprinkle the surface with the gelatin and set aside for
5 minutes to soften.

Combine the brown sugar, pumpkin puree, spices, egg yolks and salt in a
saucepan. Cook over medium heat until thickened, stirring constantly.
Remove from heat and add the softened gelatin, stirring until it is dissolved.
Stir in the orange zest and pour the mixture into a large bowl. Refrigerate
until mixture becomes cool and syrupy, about 30 minutes.

Beat the egg whites until soft peaks form, then add the sugar and beat
until slightly stiffer peaks form. Whip the cream just until soft peaks form.
Fold the egg whites into the pumpkin mixture, then fold in half of the
whipped cream. Pour the filling into the pie crust. Spoon dabs of the remaining whipped cream on top. Run the blade of a kitchen knife around the filling
to swirl the two mixtures together.

Refrigerate for about 3 hours, or until set.

SERVES 6 TO 8

# Deliteful Raspberry Cheese Pie

*This satin smooth, raspberry-studded cheesecake, by Flo Braker, is utterly seductive. The combination of ricotta and cream cheese lightens the filling a bit. The cookie-crumb crust may be used with other fillings, too.*

One 9-inch Cookie Crumb Crust, preferably made with store-bought chocolate wafers or chocolate sandwich cookies (recipe follows)

**Filling**

⅓ cup plus 2 tablespoons part-skim ricotta cheese

12 ounces cream cheese at room temperature

1 cup sugar

2 large eggs at room temperature

1 teaspoon vanilla extract

¼ cup fresh lemon juice

1 teaspoon finely grated lemon zest

1 cup fresh raspberries at room temperature

**Decoration**

2 ounces semisweet chocolate, melted

30 fresh raspberries

∞  Adjust the rack to the lower third of the oven; preheat the oven to 350 degrees.

Using an electric mixer on low speed, cream the ricotta until it is smooth. Add the cream cheese and continue to beat until the mixture is creamy. Add the sugar and mix until smooth. Add the eggs, 1 at a time, and continue mixing on low until the mixture is slightly runny. Stir in the vanilla, lemon juice and zest. Gently fold in the raspberries. Pour into the crust.

Bake for 40 minutes. Slide a baking sheet with no sides under the pie and remove it to a wire rack to cool completely.

For the decoration: Pour the melted chocolate into a small handmade paper cone and pipe thin lines of chocolate back and forth over the surface of the pie. Imagine the pie cut into 10 wedges and arrange a cluster of 3 raspberries on each wedge. Refrigerate until serving time.

SERVES 10

## Cookie Crumb Crust

1¼ cups crumbs (chocolate wafers, chocolate sandwich cookies, gingersnaps, graham
    crackers, zwieback, vanilla cookies, biscotti, etc.)
1 tablespoon sugar, or to taste (optional)
5 tablespoons unsalted butter, melted

Combine the crumbs, sugar and butter in a medium bowl and mix until thoroughly coated. Transfer to a lightly buttered 9-inch pie pan; press evenly over the bottom and up the sides of the pan.

If the recipe directs, bake in the lower third of a preheated 350-degree oven for 8 to 10 minutes. Otherwise, chill until ready to fill. If the filling bakes in the crust, fill and bake after pressing evenly into pan.

YIELDS ONE 9-INCH PIE SHELL

**NOTE:** To spice up the crust, add ⅛ to ¼ teaspoon ground cinnamon or a combination of finely grated lemon zest and ground ginger. A couple of tablespoons of finely ground nuts, such as pecans or hazelnuts, add another flavor dimension.

# Lattice-Topped Rhubarb Strawberry Pie

*The sweetness of berries and tangy flavor of rhubarb are perfect companions in this pie from Flo Braker. She uses tapioca as a thickener because it doesn't mask the flavors or colors. Be sure to make a high fluted edge on the shell to hold in the fruit and its juices.*

Pastry for a double-crust 9-inch pie (see page 337)

1 cup sugar

¼ cup instant tapioca

⅛ teaspoon salt

4 cups (about 1½ pounds) fresh rhubarb, leaves trimmed, cut into 1-inch lengths

2 cups strawberries, hulled and sliced in half

2 tablespoons butter

Adjust the rack to the lower third of the oven; preheat the oven to 425 degrees.

Roll out two thirds of the pastry and use it to line a 9-inch pie pan. Refrigerate the remaining pastry.

Combine the sugar, tapioca and salt in a large bowl. Add the rhubarb and berries and toss to mix. Let stand for 15 to 20 minutes.

Spoon the fruit and juices into the pie shell; dot with butter.

Roll out the remaining pastry into a rectangle, ⅛ inch thick. Cut into strips ¾ to 1 inch wide and weave them over the top of the pie into a lattice.

Bake for 15 minutes, then reduce the oven temperature to 375 degrees and continue to bake until the filling is bubbling and the crust is golden brown, 35 to 45 minutes longer. Place on a wire rack to cool.

SERVES 6

# Lemon Polenta Pound Cake

*This cake was created by Shanna Masters to serve at a dinner honoring some of San Francisco's top chefs. For that meal, she paired it with lemon curd, softly whipped cream and fresh blueberries. The pound cake packs a lemony wallop, and the cornmeal adds a rustic texture and a slight crunch.*

½ cup yellow cornmeal

1 cup all-purpose flour

½ teaspoon baking soda

½ teaspoon salt

3 eggs, separated

½ cup (1 stick) butter

1 tablespoon grated lemon zest

1¼ cups sugar

6 tablespoons fresh lemon juice

2 tablespoons evaporated milk

Preheat the oven to 350 degrees. Line a medium loaf pan with parchment or waxed paper.

Combine the cornmeal, flour, baking soda and salt; set aside. Beat the egg whites until stiff; set aside.

Cream the butter, lemon zest and sugar until fluffy, then add the egg yolks and mix well. Add the lemon juice and milk alternately with the dry ingredients. Blend just until the dry ingredients are moistened. Carefully fold in the beaten egg whites. Spoon the batter into the prepared pan.

Bake for 1 to 1¼ hours, or until a cake tester inserted in the center of the cake comes out clean. Let the cake cool 15 minutes in the pan before turning out onto a rack to cool. Remove the lining paper.

YIELDS 1 LOAF

# Heavenly Angel Cake

*When Marion Cunningham wants to know something, she goes to the kitchen and experiments. She tested dozens of recipes before settling on this one, which is higher and not as sweet as most angel food cakes. It has a tender crumb that is moist but not gummy.*

1 cup sifted cake flour

1½ cups sugar

1½ cups unbeaten egg whites (approximately 12)

2 tablespoons cold water

1½ teaspoons cream of tartar

½ teaspoon salt

1½ teaspoons vanilla extract

½ teaspoon lemon extract (optional)

½ teaspoon lemon zest (optional)

Few drops almond extract (optional)

∞ Preheat the oven to 325 degrees.

Sift and measure the flour, then add ½ cup of the sugar. Sift together 3 times (use 2 pieces of waxed paper to sift back and forth on).

Put the egg whites into a mixing bowl, add the water, cream of tartar, salt and flavorings—yes, all at once! Beat until barely stiff enough to hold a peak when the beater is lifted. Don't beat until the egg white mixture is dry (this is most important, because if the whites are too stiff the air will be knocked out by folding in the remaining dry ingredients).

Gradually add the remaining cup of sugar, 2 tablespoons at a time, beating gently after each of the first few additions, then fold in rather than beating the last amount. Add the sifted flour and sugar, 3 or 4 tablespoons at a time, and fold gently until blended. Spoon the batter into an ungreased 10-inch tube pan. Tap the pan sharply on the table a couple of times to break the large air bubbles.

Bake for 50 to 60 minutes, or until a cake tester comes out clean when inserted in the center of the cake. Cool upside down (this is important, because the cake will collapse if left to cool right-side up).

SERVES 10 TO 12

## The Magic of Water

Plain water can make a difference in some recipes, according to cookbook author Marion Cunningham.

To make angel food cake lighter and higher, add 2 tablespoons cold water to the egg whites before beating them.

Add 2 tablespoons water to ½ cup vinaigrette dressing to give it balance and make it seem less oily.

Use water in place of milk in scrambled eggs, or add a tablespoon or so of water to beaten eggs when making an omelet; the results will be lighter and creamier.

# Chocolate Ancho Chile and Orange Cake

*The smoky nuances of dried ancho chiles add a warm background to the chocolate in Jacqueline McMahan's cake, while the orange keeps the flavor from being ponderous. It's an unlikely combination, but it works!*

1 cup (2 sticks) unsalted butter at room temperature

1½ cups sugar

5 eggs at room temperature

1¾ cups sifted all-purpose flour

½ teaspoon salt

Grated zest of 2 oranges

2 tablespoons orange juice

1 teaspoon baking soda

½ cup Chocolate Syrup (recipe follows)

4 tablespoons Ancho Chile Puree (recipe follows)

2 teaspoons vanilla extract

Orange Glaze (recipe follows)

Preheat the oven to 350 degrees. Butter a 10-inch bundt pan.

Beat the butter with an electric mixer, then gradually beat in the sugar. Add eggs, 1 at a time, beating well after each. Slowly beat in the flour and salt. Divide the batter in half. To half of the batter, add the orange zest, orange juice and ½ teaspoon of the baking soda. Spoon the batter into the prepared pan.

To the remaining batter, add the chocolate syrup, ancho puree, vanilla and the remaining ½ teaspoon baking soda. Spread over the orange batter.

Bake for 45 to 50 minutes, or until a cake tester inserted into the middle of the cake comes out clean. Cool the cake in its pan on a rack for 10 minutes, then unmold onto a plate. Brush with the orange glaze. (The warm cake will rapidly absorb all the glaze.)

You may drizzle an additional ¼ cup chocolate syrup over the cake just before serving, if desired.

SERVES 10

## Chocolate Syrup

½ cup water
¼ cup butter
2 tablespoons honey
8 ounces semisweet chocolate
1 ounce unsweetened chocolate

Combine water, butter, honey, and both kinds of chocolate in a saucepan. Heat gently, stirring, until the syrup is silky and smooth.
YIELDS ABOUT 1½ CUPS

## Ancho Chile Puree

4 ancho chiles
Boiling water to cover

Rinse chiles. Place in a bowl and cover with boiling water; let soak for at least 2 hours. Remove seeds and stems from the chiles. Place the chiles and ½ cup of their soaking water in a blender. (If the soaking liquid tastes bitter, use fresh water instead.) Puree on high speed until smooth. May be refrigerated for up to 1 week, or frozen for longer storage.
YIELDS ¾ CUP PUREE

## Orange Glaze

Juice of 1 orange
½ cup powdered sugar
1 tablespoon Grand Marnier

Combine orange juice, sugar, and liqueur.
YIELDS ABOUT ¾ CUP

# Chocolate Buttermilk Cake

*It's the buttermilk that makes Flo Braker's chocolate cake so light and tender.*

2 cups sifted cake flour

1 teaspoon baking soda

¼ teaspoon salt

½ cup (1 stick) unsalted butter, softened

1 cup sugar

2 eggs

1 teaspoon vanilla extract

2 ounces unsweetened chocolate, melted and cooled

1 cup buttermilk

Chocolate Buttermilk Frosting (recipe follows)

## Melting Chocolate

When melting milk chocolate or white chocolate, place the chocolate in a bowl and place the bowl over water no hotter than 95 degrees.

◎ Have all ingredients at room temperature. Adjust the rack to the lower third of the oven; preheat the oven to 350 degrees. Grease and flour two 9-inch cake pans.

Sift together the flour, baking soda and salt; set aside.

Using an electric mixer, preferably with a paddle attachment, cream the butter until smooth. Add the sugar and continue to cream until light and fluffy. Add the eggs, 1 at a time, beating well after each addition. Beat in the vanilla, then the cooled melted chocolate.

Add the dry ingredients alternately with the buttermilk, beginning and ending with dry ingredients. Spoon equal amounts of batter into each pan, spreading it to level the top.

Bake for 22 to 25 minutes, or until a wooden toothpick inserted into the center of the cakes comes out clean. Cool in the pans on a wire rack for 10 minutes. Invert and remove pans; cool completely on racks before frosting.

SERVES 10

## Chocolate Buttermilk Frosting

2 cups powdered sugar

⅛ teaspoon salt

2 tablespoons unsalted butter, softened

3 tablespoons buttermilk

4 ounces unsweetened chocolate, melted

1 teaspoon vanilla extract

◉◉ Cream together the sugar, salt and butter. Slowly add the buttermilk, mixing until well blended and smooth. Blend in the cooled melted chocolate and vanilla. If the frosting is too runny, add additional powdered sugar, 1 tablespoon at a time; if too thick, add additional buttermilk, 1 teaspoon at a time, to achieve a spreading consistency.

Spread the frosting between layers and around the sides and on top of the cake.

YIELDS ABOUT 2 CUPS, ENOUGH TO FILL AND FROST TWO 8- OR 9-INCH CAKE LAYERS

# German Chocolate Cake

*This classic recipe, which is published on the back of the Baker's Chocolate package, is one of Marion Cunningham's favorites. The cake has a mild chocolate flavor, delicate enough to let the rich coconut-pecan filling and topping star.*

4 ounces Baker's German's Sweet Chocolate

½ cup boiling water

1 cup butter or margarine at room temperature

2 cups sugar

4 eggs, separated

1 teaspoon vanilla extract

2¼ cups all-purpose or cake flour

1 teaspoon baking soda

½ teaspoon salt

1 cup buttermilk

Coconut-Pecan Frosting (recipe follows)

## Making More Layers

When cutting a cake in two to make thinner layers, Flo Braker recommends using waxed dental floss. Stand in front of the cake, hold a length of dental floss tautly between your hands and, starting at the side of the cake farthest away from you, gradually pull the floss through the cake toward you. The cut will be smooth and even.

∞ Preheat the oven to 350 degrees. Butter and flour three 9-inch round cake pans. Line the bottom of the pans with buttered parchment, waxed paper or foil (shiny side up). Melt the chocolate in the boiling water. Cool.

Cream the butter and sugar until fluffy. Add the egg yolks, 1 at a time, beating well after each addition. Blend in the vanilla and chocolate.

Mix the flour with the soda and salt, then add alternately with the buttermilk to the chocolate mixture, beating after each addition until smooth. Fold in the beaten egg whites. Divide the batter among the prepared pans.

Bake for 30 to 35 minutes, or until a cake tester comes out clean when inserted into the center of the cakes. Cool in the pans for 5 minutes before turning out onto a rack to cool completely.

Fill and frost (top only) with Coconut-Pecan Frosting.

SERVES 10 TO 12

## Coconut-Pecan Frosting

*This is the traditional frosting for German Chocolate Cake.*

1 cup evaporated milk

1 cup sugar

2 egg yolks, slightly beaten

½ cup (1 stick) butter

1 teaspoon vanilla extract

1⅓ cups Baker's Angel Flake coconut

1 cup chopped pecans

∞ Mix together the milk, sugar, egg yolks, butter and vanilla in a saucepan. Cook and stir over medium heat until thickened, about 12 minutes. Stir in the coconut and pecans. Cool until thick enough to spread, beating occasionally.

YIELDS 2¼ CUPS, ENOUGH TO FILL AND FROST THREE 9-INCH CAKE LAYERS

# Lemon Pudding Cake

*This moist mousselike cake by Marion Cunnigham has an intense lemony tang. Serve with lightly whipped cream.*

1½ cups milk

4 tablespoons butter

3 eggs, separated

1 cup sugar

½ cup all-purpose flour

⅓ cup (5 tablespoons) fresh lemon juice

Grated zest of 1 lemon

⅛ teaspoon salt

Preheat the oven to 350 degrees. Butter a 1½-quart baking dish. Get out a slightly larger pan at least 2 inches deep, which will hold the cake pan comfortably.

Put the milk and butter into a small saucepan and heat until hot and the butter has melted. Remove from the heat and set aside.

Put the egg yolks into a mixing bowl and whisk until blended. Add the sugar, flour, lemon juice, lemon zest, salt and the hot milk mixture. Stir until thoroughly blended.

Beat the egg whites until stiff but still moist, then fold them into the batter. Spoon the batter into the baking dish. Set the dish in the larger pan and pour in enough hot water to come halfway up the sides of the baking dish.

Bake for 35 to 45 minutes, or until the cake springs back when touched lightly in the center. Remove from the oven and let cool. Don't refrigerate.

Serve with softly whipped cream.

SERVES 6

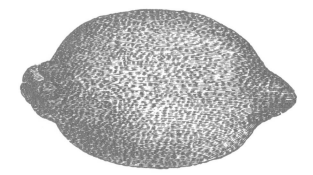

# Peanut Butter Pound Cake

*If you're not already addicted to peanut butter, one bite of Flo Braker's cake will do it. Before you begin, be sure all ingredients are at room temperature.*

1 cup (2 sticks) unsalted butter

1½ cups sugar

½ cup creamy peanut butter

5 large eggs

2 cups unsifted all-purpose flour

∞ Adjust the rack in the lower third of the oven; preheat the oven to 350 degrees. Grease and flour a 9 x 5–inch loaf pan.

Using an electric mixer, cream the butter until light; add the sugar and beat until fluffy. Add the peanut butter and beat until fluffy. Add the eggs, 1 at a time, beating well after each addition. Blend in the flour in 2 additions, mixing until thoroughly combined. Pour the batter into the prepared baking pan and spread evenly.

Bake for 65 minutes, or until golden brown and a toothpick inserted in the center comes out clean.

SERVES 12

## Greasing the Pan

Use a paper towel rather than your fingers to grease baking pans. Then lightly flour the pan to ensure easy removal.

# Poppy Seed Bundt Cake

*The whiteness of this cake, from Flo Braker, contrasts beautifully with blue-black poppy seeds to create a simple yet sophisticated dessert.*

⅓ cup poppy seeds

¾ cup milk

1 teaspoon vanilla extract

2 cups sifted cake flour

2 teaspoons baking powder

⅛ teaspoon salt

¾ cup (1½ sticks) unsalted butter at room temperature

1 cup sugar

3 egg whites at room temperature

◉◉ Place the poppy seeds in a small bowl. Add the milk and vanilla; stir to blend. Set aside for an hour.

Sift together the flour, baking powder and salt.

Position the rack in the lower third of the oven; preheat the oven to 350 degrees. Grease and flour a 9-inch bundt or tube pan.

Beat the butter until creamy, add ¾ cup of the sugar and beat until light and fluffy, about 3 minutes. Add the flour mixture alternately with the milk mixture, in 3 or 4 additions, beating until well blended and smooth after each.

Beat the egg whites until soft peaks form. Gradually add the remaining ¼ cup sugar, beating until the whites form stiff, glossy peaks. Fold the whites into the batter. Spoon the batter into the prepared baking pan.

Bake for 45 minutes, or until the cake springs back when lightly touched in the center and a toothpick inserted in the center comes out clean. Let cool in the pan on a wire rack for 10 minutes before turning the cake out of the pan to cool completely.

SERVES 12

# Rosemary Polenta Pound Cake

*There's been a trend at restaurants in the last few years to flavor desserts with savory herbs. In the wrong hands this technique can be overpowering, but when done by Mark Elkin, former pastry chef at Oliveto, it can add an intriguing background flavor. The buttermilk smooths the mixture and the polenta adds a coarser texture.*

1½ cups buttermilk

1 cup polenta

3¼ cups all-purpose flour

1 tablespoon baking powder

1½ teaspoons baking soda

¾ teaspoon salt

3 tablespoons finely chopped fresh rosemary

1½ cups (3 sticks) unsalted butter at room temperature

1½ cups sugar

3 eggs

Mix together the buttermilk and polenta; let soak for 45 minutes.

Preheat the oven to 350 degrees. Butter and flour two 8-inch tube cake pans.

Sift together the flour, baking powder, baking soda and salt. Stir in the rosemary. Cream the butter and sugar until light and fluffy. Add the eggs 1 at a time, beating well after each addition. Fold the soaked polenta alternately with the dry ingredients into the creamed mixture. Divide the batter between the prepared pans.

Bake for 40 minutes, or until a toothpick inserted into the middle of a cake comes out clean. Let cakes cool 5 minutes before turning out on racks to cool.

YIELDS 2 CAKES; EACH CAKE SERVES 8

# Jane Benet's Fruitcake (Best Recipe)

*A lot of people hate fruitcake, but this one is different: It's dark, rich, moist and not as sweet as commercial cakes. In fact, this version, which has been handed down in the Benet family for many, many years, is the only one that some editors in the Food Department will eat.*

1 pound (3 cups) blanched almonds

½ pound (2 cups) pecans

¼ pound (1 cup) walnuts

1 pound (2 cups) shredded citron

½ pound (1 cup) lemon peel

½ pound (1 cup) orange peel

½ pound (1 cup) candied pineapple

1 pound (2 cups) candied cherries

2 pounds (6 to 7 cups) seedless raisins

1 pound (2 cups) dried figs

1 pound (2 cups) pitted dates

1 pound (3 to 3½ cups) dried currants

1 glass (about ½ cup) brandy

1 glass (8 to 10 ounces) jam (blackberry preferred)

4 teaspoons ground cinnamon

½ teaspoon ground allspice

2 teaspoons ground nutmeg

½ teaspoon ground cloves

2 cups (4 sticks) butter at room temperature

1 pound brown sugar

1 cup molasses

12 eggs, beaten until foamy

1 pound (3½ to 4 cups) all-purpose flour

2 teaspoons salt

Whole blanched almonds and candied cherries for garnish

◎◎ Preheat the oven to 275 or 300 degrees.

## Measuring Dried Fruit

When shopping for ingredients, it's handy to have a list of bulk equivalents.

A pound of raisins, dried apricots, prunes, dried peaches, dried pears or dried figs will measure 3 to 3½ cups.

A pound of fresh dates or cut-up candied fruits and peels will measure 2 cups.

A pound of dried apples will yield 5 cups.

A pound of shelled almonds or Brazil nuts will yield 3 cups; a pound of shelled walnuts or pecans will yield 4 cups.

Chop the nuts and fruits (grind the dates and figs—they're very sticky) and combine them in a bowl. Add the brandy, jam and spices; mix well. Cream the butter, add the sugar, molasses and beaten eggs; mix thoroughly. Add the flour and salt and mix to a batter consistency. Pour over the fruit mixture and stir to combine. A little more flour may be needed, or a little more brandy. What dough there is should be fairly stiff, not runny.

Grease pans well (see Notes), then line with heavy waxed or parchment paper. Fill the pans three fourths full and bake until a straw comes out clean (probably from 2 to 3 hours, depending on sizes). Have a pan of hot water in the bottom of the oven for moisture during baking. You can decorate the tops of the cakes with almonds and cherries pressed into them before baking.

When done, turn out the cakes onto racks to cool. Pour a little brandy slowly over the top of each one. In 15 minutes, invert onto waxed paper, remove the baking paper and pour more brandy slowly over each cake. This must be done gradually, but a warm cake absorbs the liquid much better than a cold one. When completely cool, wrap the cakes well and store in airtight containers for at least 1 month before slicing.

YIELDS ABOUT 17 POUNDS OF FRUITCAKE

**NOTES:** We now often substitute 4 pounds of mixed candied fruits for the citron, peels and candied pineapple and cherries in the recipe.

Fruitcakes may be baked in all sizes and shapes. To estimate baking time, check this list of pan sizes and amounts:

An 8½ x 4½ x 2¾–inch foil loaf pan holds about 4 cups of batter and takes about 2 hours to bake.

A 5½ x 3 x 2½–inch loaf pan holds about 1¾ cups batter and takes about 1½ hours to bake.

A 4½ x 1½–inch round foil pan holds from 1 to 1¼ cups of batter and takes about 1¼ to 1½ hours to bake.

A 3-quart tube pan or mold takes about 2½ quarts of batter and from 2½ to 3 hours or more to bake, depending on tube size.

A 7½-inch ring mold holds 3 cups batter and takes about 1 hour and 45 minutes to bake.

A 6-ounce juice can will hold ½ cup batter and bakes in about 50 minutes.

Cupcake pans measuring 1¾ x ¾ inches each will hold a heaping tablespoon of batter and take about 20 minutes to bake.

# Caribbean Christmas Cake

*Here is a thoroughly modern fruitcake from Shanna Masters. This one, too, holds top honors in the flavor department, with tropical notes from banana, pineapple, coconut, ginger, cardamom and rum.*

### Light Fruit Mixture

Zest of 1 lemon, minced

½ cup dried banana slices

½ cup diced dried pineapple

¾ cup sugar

¼ teaspoon ground nutmeg

2 whole cardamom pods

### Dark Fruit Mixture

1 cup raisins

1 cup dry red wine (preferably Cabernet Sauvignon)

1 cup packed brown sugar

1 vanilla bean, halved lengthwise

⅔ cup shredded coconut

3 tablespoons chopped candied ginger

¾ cup shelled pumpkin seeds (pepitas)

½ cup plus ⅔ cup all-purpose flour

2 cups pecan halves

### Light Batter

⅓ cup butter, softened

⅓ cup sugar

3 egg whites

1 cup all-purpose flour

3 tablespoons rum

2 tablespoons light corn syrup

### Dark Batter

½ cup (1 stick) butter, softened

½ cup sugar

3 egg yolks

1 whole egg

1⅓ cups all-purpose flour

## Cutting the Fat in Baking

One of the easiest ways to cut down on fat in baked goods is to substitute buttermilk and low-fat yogurt for whole milk and sour cream. If you use buttermilk, add at least ¼ teaspoon baking soda to the recipe to balance the acid of the buttermilk.

¼ cup dry red wine

2 tablespoons light corn syrup

◉◉ One week before baking: To make the light fruit mixture, combine the lemon zest, bananas, pineapple, sugar and spices in a saucepan; add water to barely cover. Simmer for 15 minutes, adding more water, if necessary, to keep fruit mixture barely covered. Let cool, then transfer to a container, cover and let macerate for 1 week, stirring once or twice a day.

To make the dark fruit mixture, combine the raisins, wine, brown sugar and vanilla bean in a saucepan. Simmer for 15 minutes, adding a bit more wine, if necessary, to keep the raisins from becoming too dry and caramelizing. Cool, then transfer to a container, cover and let macerate 1 week, stirring once or twice a day.

On baking day: Line two 11 x 4 x 2–inch loaf pans with parchment. Preheat the oven to 275 degrees.

Stir the light fruit mixture; discard the cardamom pods and add the coconut, candied ginger, pumpkin seeds and ½ cup flour; stir to mix well.

Stir the dark fruit mixture, discard the vanilla bean and add the pecans and ⅔ cup flour; stir to mix well.

To make the light batter: Cream the butter and sugar. Stir in the egg whites, 1 at a time, mixing well after each. Mix in ½ cup of the flour, then the rum and corn syrup. Add the remaining ½ cup flour and mix well. Fold in the light fruit mixture; set aside.

To make the dark batter: Cream the butter and sugar. Stir in the egg yolks and whole egg, 1 at a time, mixing well after each addition. Mix in half of the flour, then the wine and corn syrup. Add the remaining portion of flour and mix well. Fold in the dark fruit mixture.

To assemble and bake: Spread a shallow layer of dark batter in each prepared loaf pan. Spoon equal amounts of light batter lengthwise down the center of the dark batter in each pan. Top with the remaining dark batter. Bake for approximately 1¾ hours, or until a cake tester inserted into the center of the cakes comes out clean.

Cool the cakes in their pans until just warm to the touch, then remove; peel away the parchment. Wrap the fruitcakes tightly in wine-soaked cheesecloth, if desired, then in plastic wrap, then in foil. Store in a cool place for at least 2 weeks before slicing.

YIELDS 2 FRUITCAKES

# Raised Cheesecake

*Encased in a buttery pastry crust, this cheesecake, by Marion Cunningham, is*
*light as a mousse, with a rich cream flavor.*

**Pastry**

1 cup all-purpose flour

½ cup (1 stick) butter, softened

1 egg yolk

2 tablespoons sugar

**Filling**

1 pound cream cheese, softened

1 tablespoon all-purpose flour

½ cup sugar

4 eggs, separated

¼ cup heavy cream

¼ cup sour cream

2 teaspoons vanilla extract

¼ teaspoon salt

⊚⊚  Preheat the oven to 400 degrees.

To make the pastry: Mix together the flour and butter until well blended.
Add the egg yolk and sugar and blend well.

Remove the rim of a 9-inch springform pan. Press about half of the pastry
onto the bottom of the springform. Bake about 8 minutes; cool.

Reassemble the springform. Press the remaining pastry halfway up the
inside of the rim. Don't worry if it isn't even. Set aside.

Reduce the oven temperature to 350 degrees.

To make the filling: Put the cream cheese into a mixing bowl and beat
until soft. Add the flour and sugar and mix well. Add the egg yolks, heavy
cream, sour cream and vanilla; beat well.

Beat the egg whites with the salt until they hold stiff peaks, but are not
dry. Fold the whites into the cheese mixture, then pour into the pan. Bake for
about 45 minutes.

Let cool. Serve at room temperature.

SERVES 8 TO 10

**NOTE:** This freezes well.

## Quick Caramel Sauce

*This rich, delicious sauce is from Marion Cunningham.*

1 cup light brown sugar
¼ pound (1 stick) butter
½ cup whipping cream

◎◎ Combine all ingredients in a sauce pan. Cook over medium heat for about 3 minutes, until the sugar dissolves and the sauce is smooth. Whisk briefly before using.

YIELDS 1½ CUPS

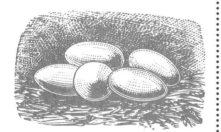

# Peach-Almond Custard and Brioche Napoleon

*Elizabeth Falkner, the pastry chef at the hot restaurant, Rubicon, created this dessert which can be made ahead and assembled right before serving. The brioche acts as a sandwich, surrounding a scoop of custard and fresh fruit.*

### Custard

1 cup milk

3 cups heavy cream

1 vanilla bean, split and scraped, or 2 teaspoons pure vanilla extract

10 egg yolks

¾ cup sugar

2 tablespoons Cointreau

1 teaspoon almond extract

6 ripe peaches

3 tablespoons sugar

2 tablespoons Amaretto

Pinch ground nutmeg

2 tablespoons fresh lemon juice

1 loaf brioche or challah

Unsalted butter, melted

1 pint berries, or caramel sauce (purchased or homemade) and toasted sliced almonds

◎◎ To make the custard: Preheat the oven to 300 degrees.

Scald the milk and cream with the vanilla bean, if using. Remove from the heat and let steep for 15 minutes; strain.

Combine the egg yolks and sugar in a mixing bowl; stir to blend. Add a ladleful of the hot milk mixture and blend well, then stir the mixture into the remaining hot milk; mix well. Skim the surface, then stir in the Cointreau, almond extract and vanilla extract, if using. Pour into a 2-quart ovenproof dish and set in a larger pan filled halfway with hot water.

Bake for 1 to 1½ hours, or until the custard is set. Cool, then refrigerate overnight.

To assemble: Peel, pit and slice the peaches; toss with the sugar, Amaretto, nutmeg and lemon juice. Cut the brioche or challah into twelve ½-inch-thick slices; toast or grill on both sides. Brush with butter. Place a slice on each serving plate. Top each slice with a large spoonful of custard, then 4 or 5 peach slices. Place another slice of brioche on top. Garnish with fresh berries, or drizzle caramel sauce over the top and sprinkle with toasted sliced almonds.

SERVES 6

# The Ultimate Autumn Brown Betty

*Flo Braker's dessert is one of the best and easiest baked fresh fruit treats. Bread is layered in a pan with fruit, then it's moistened with water and baked to a crispy brown.*

2 quinces

1 firm Bartlett pear

1 large Golden Delicious or Fuji apple

⅓ cup granulated sugar

⅓ cup packed brown sugar

1 tablespoon fresh orange juice

6 cups soft bread cubes

½ cup (1 stick) unsalted butter, melted

1 tablespoon finely grated orange zest

½ cup water

½ cup pomegranate seeds (optional)

Adjust the rack to the lower third of the oven and preheat the oven to 350 degrees. Lightly butter the bottom only of a 2½-quart, 2-inch-high baking dish.

Peel and core the quinces, then coarsely chop. Place in a large bowl. Core and coarsely chop the pear and apple; add to the quinces. Add the sugars and toss with your fingertips to mix. Add the orange juice and toss just to mix.

Place the bread cubes in a large bowl, drizzle the melted butter over the bread and toss. Add the orange zest and toss again.

Place 2 cups of the bread cubes in an even layer in the baking dish. Cover with half of the fruit mixture, top with 2 cups bread cubes, then a final layer of fruit mixture. Top with the remaining bread cubes. Pour the water over top. Cover the baking dish with aluminum foil.

Bake for 1 hour. Remove the foil and bake 10 minutes longer, or until most of the bread cubes on top are slightly crisp and golden, the fruit is tender and the liquid absorbed.

Serve warm with heavy cream or crème fraîche, if desired.

Sprinkle pomegranate seeds on top for a refreshing touch.

SERVES 8

# Fresh Apricot Cobbler

*Apricots have such a short season, and this cobbler, by Georgeanne Brennan, is the ultimate way to show them off.*

4 cups halved and pitted fresh apricots

1 teaspoon fresh lemon juice

½ cup sugar

2 tablespoons flour

**Topping**

1 cup all-purpose flour

1¼ teaspoons baking powder

½ teaspoon salt

¼ cup butter, cut in bits

⅓ to ½ cup milk

◉◉ Preheat the oven to 425 degrees. Grease a deep-dish baking dish.

Place the apricots in a bowl and drizzle with the lemon juice. Mix together the sugar and flour and add it to the apricots, turning to coat the fruit. Transfer the apricots to the baking dish.

To make the topping: Sift together the flour, baking powder and salt. Using a pastry blender or your fingertips, quickly work in the butter until pea-sized particles form. Do not overwork. Gradually pour in the milk, stirring until the mixture sticks together. Pat or roll out to a ¼-inch-thick sheet, large enough to cover the apricot mixture. Place the pastry on top of the apricots, rolling and tucking as necessary, leaving a gap or two on the sides or making gashes in the pastry for steam to escape.

Bake for 15 to 20 minutes; reduce oven temperature to 325 degrees and bake 10 minutes longer, or until the apricots are tender.

Serve hot, warm or at room temperature.

SERVES 4 TO 6

# Mixed Plum Cobbler with Tender Dumplings

*Flo Braker's cobbler, which is topped with dumpling batter, has a homespun flavor. Serve warm, topped with a scoop of ice cream (vanilla, cinnamon, ginger or almond).*

### Fruit

½ cup granulated sugar

1 tablespoon packed brown sugar

2 tablespoons cornstarch

1 cup water

2¾ pounds assorted plums, pitted and cut into ½-inch-thick slices (6 cups)

1 teaspoon finely grated orange zest

⅛ teaspoon almond extract

### Tender Dumplings

1 cup all-purpose flour

3 tablespoons sugar

2 teaspoons baking powder

½ teaspoon salt

⅓ cup oats (old-fashioned or quick)

5 tablespoons unsalted butter

½ cup milk

### Topping

⅛ teaspoon ground cinnamon

2 teaspoons sugar

⊚⊚ Adjust the rack to the lower third of oven; preheat the oven to 400 degrees.

Mix together the sugars and cornstarch in a 2½-quart saucepan. Stir in the water. Add the plum slices. Cook over medium heat until the mixture thickens, about 5 to 6 minutes. Remove from heat and stir in the orange zest and almond extract. Pour the mixture into an 8-inch square baking pan.

To make the dumpling dough: Sift the flour, sugar, baking powder and salt into a large bowl. Stir in the oats. Cut in the butter until the mixture resembles coarse meal. Add the milk and stir to blend. Spoon the dough over the fruit. Combine the cinnamon and sugar and sprinkle over the top.

Bake for 25 minutes, or until the dumplings are golden and the filling is bubbling. Serve warm.

SERVES 6 TO 8

**VARIATION:** For cobbler pies, prepare the plum filling and divide among six 8-ounce ramekins. Prepare the dumpling dough and spoon over the filling. Sprinkle with cinnamon sugar. Bake in a preheated 400-degree oven for 25 minutes, or until dumplings are golden and the filling is bubbling. Serve warm. Serves 6.

# Fruit Clafouti

*Clafouti is a classic French dessert, but there are many different versions: Some are cakelike, others are almost like custard. In this example by Phil Ogiela, pastry chef at 231 Ellsworth in San Mateo, a milk and egg batter is poured over fruit, producing an easy, creamy dessert.*

    1 cup crème fraîche or ½ cup buttermilk plus 1 cup heavy cream

    3 tablespoons all-purpose flour

    2 tablespoons sugar

    ⅛ teaspoon salt

    2 medium eggs

    1 teaspoon vanilla extract

    1½ cups raspberries, blackberries or sour cherries

Preheat the oven to 300 to 325 degrees. This clafouti may be baked in a low ceramic ornamental dish or an 8- or 9-inch tart shell. Traditionally, it is baked and served in a ceramic mold.

Place the crème fraîche or buttermilk mixture in a mixing bowl. Add the flour, sugar and salt. Stir to combine. Stir in the eggs, then the vanilla. Arrange the fruit in the dish or mold and pour the filling over it.

Bake for 40 minutes, or until the filling is set and starts pulling away from the sides of the pan.

SERVES 8 TO 10

## Quick Crème Fraîche

If you can't find this French delicacy at your supermarket, here's an easy way to reproduce it at home: Combine 1 cup heavy cream and 1 tablespoon buttermilk. Let stand at warm room temperature for 8 to 12 hours, then cover and refrigerate.

# Fresh Apricot Clafouti

*This clafouti, by Georgeanne Brennan, has a buttery cakelike texture.*
*If apricots aren't available, use any stone fruit.*

1 cup milk
¼ cup heavy cream
¼ cup packed brown sugar
3 eggs
1 tablespoon almond extract
⅛ teaspoon salt
⅔ cup all-purpose flour, sifted
18 apricots, halved and pitted

◎ Preheat the oven to 350 degrees. Butter a 1½-inch deep 12-inch-diameter baking dish (or use a 12 x 18–inch rectangular baking dish).

Combine the milk, cream, brown sugar, eggs, almond extract, salt and flour in a mixing bowl and beat with an electric mixer until frothy, about 5 minutes. Pour enough of the batter into the prepared baking dish to cover the bottom with a layer about ¼ inch deep. Put the dish in the oven for 2 minutes.

Remove from the oven and arrange the apricot halves face down evenly over the batter, which is now slightly set. Pour the remaining batter over the apricots. Bake until puffed and brown and a knife inserted in the center comes out clean, about 30 to 35 minutes.

Serve warm from the oven, plain or sprinkled with powdered sugar.

SERVES 6 TO 8

# Gingered Persimmon and Asian Pear Crisp

*Dan Bowe's dessert takes advantage of two Asian varieties of fruit,*
*persimmons and pears. The crisp ginger-oat topping also works well with*
*other fruit, including apples, peaches or nectarines.*

4 to 6 Fuyu persimmons, peeled and cut into ½-inch slices

1 large Asian pear, cored and cut into ½-inch slices

½ cup tangerine juice

2 tablespoons granulated sugar

½ teaspoon salt

1 tablespoon grated fresh ginger

¼ teaspoon ground cardamom

**Oat Crumble Topping**

4 tablespoons cold unsalted butter

2 tablespoons light brown sugar

½ teaspoon finely chopped tangerine zest

⅛ teaspoon salt

2 tablespoons flour

¼ teaspoon ground cardamom

½ cup whole oats, toasted (see Note)

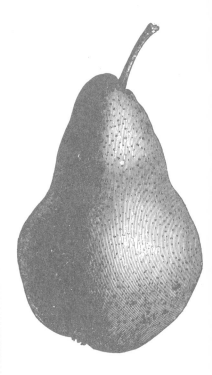

◉ Preheat the oven to 375 degrees.

Combine the persimmons, pear, juice, sugar, salt, ginger and cardamom in an 8-inch square baking pan.

Combine the butter, brown sugar, tangerine zest, salt, flour and cardamom in a food processor; pulse a dozen times or so to combine. Add the oats, pulsing just to combine. Sprinkle the topping over the fruit.

Bake for 40 minutes, or until the fruit is bubbling and the top is deep brown. Let cool 15 minutes before serving.

Top with big scoops of French vanilla ice cream, if desired.

SERVES 8

**NOTE:** Spread the oats on a baking sheet and toast in a preheated 350-degree oven for 5 to 7 minutes, or until lightly browned.

# Cranberry, Apple and Orange Grunt

*A grunt, which is similar to a cobbler and is sometimes called a slump, is a perfect vehicle for the mix of winter fruit chosen by Dan Bowe.*

4 navel oranges

1 package (12 ounces) cranberries

1 large apple, peeled, cored and cut into ½-inch slices

½ cup water

½ cup sugar

⅛ teaspoon ground cloves

¼ teaspoon ground nutmeg

**Topping**

1½ cups all-purpose flour

1 tablespoon baking powder

½ teaspoon salt

4 teaspoons sugar

4 tablespoons cold unsalted butter, cut into ½-inch cubes

¾ cup milk

3 tablespoons preserves (apricot, peach or berry)

◉◉ Preheat the oven to 350 degrees.

Peel 3 oranges, removing skin and pith. Cut the oranges in half, then cut each half into ½-inch-wide slices. Juice the remaining orange. Combine the cranberries, apples, water, sugar, spices, orange juice and slices; toss to combine. Transfer to a 10-inch ovenproof skillet. Boil until the cranberries begin to pop. Reduce the heat to a brisk simmer and cook for 20 minutes.

To make the topping: Combine the flour, baking powder, salt, sugar and butter in a processor. Pulse several times. Add the milk and pulse a few times, until the mixture is combined and moist. Remove the dough to a floured work surface. Roll into a 9 x 12–inch rectangle. Spread the preserves evenly over the dough, stopping ½ inch short of the edge. Starting with a long side, roll the dough into a tight log. Slice into 12 rounds and arrange on top of the fruit, allowing about ½ inch between rounds.

Bake for 20 minutes, or until the topping is golden brown.

SERVES 8 TO 10

# Rhubarb Grunt

*Marion Cunningham created this rhubarb dessert in which butter in the batter is replaced by cream, producing a rich shortcakelike topping.*

1½ pounds rhubarb, cut into ½-inch pieces

1¼ cups sugar (approximately, depending on how sour the rhubarb is)

3 tablespoons butter, cut into small pieces

**Topping**

1 cup self-rising flour

3 tablespoons sugar

½ teaspoon salt

1 cup heavy cream, whipped

◎ Preheat the oven to 375 degrees.

Spread the rhubarb over bottom of an ungreased shallow 9 x 5–inch baking dish. Sprinkle with sugar and toss to coat the rhubarb evenly. Dot with butter.

To make the topping: Put the flour, sugar and salt in a mixing bowl and stir to blend. Gently stir in the whipped cream and mix until well blended. Spread over fruit (it's sticky, so dampen your fingers with cold water to spread easily), or drop over the fruit by spoonfuls.

Bake for 45 minutes, or until the fruit is bubbling and the top golden brown.

SERVES 6

## Hold That Peak

To stabilize whipped cream, Marion Cunningham suggests adding 2 tablespoons nonfat dry milk per cup of cream before you begin beating.

# Perfect Spanish Flan

*A cool wedge of Jacqueline McMahan's rich flan is just what the palate needs after a spicy meal. A classic California rancho dessert, flan is also good for breakfast with a cup of coffee.*

1¾ cups sugar

6 egg yolks

2 whole eggs

2 cans (12 ounces each) evaporated milk

2 teaspoons vanilla extract

◉◉ Preheat the oven to 350 degrees.

Place 1 cup of the sugar in a heavy saucepan and caramelize over medium heat. At first, swirl the pan over the heat, but do not stir (this will cause the sugar to clump). After about 8 minutes, when the sugar has begun to liquefy, stir with a wooden spoon. When the caramel turns light brown, quickly (and carefully—burns are painful) pour into a 2-quart high-sided metal mold, such as an aluminum flan mold or charlotte mold. Tip the pan so the caramel coats the bottom and sides of the mold. Work fast; caramel hardens quickly.

Whisk together the egg yolks, whole eggs, evaporated milk, the remaining ¾ cup sugar and the vanilla. The mixture should be well blended but not frothy. Pour into the caramelized mold. Cover tightly with foil (this prevents the top from overcooking). Place the mold in a larger pan (such as a roasting pan) and pour in about 1½ inches of hot water.

Place on the bottom rack of the preheated oven and bake for approximately 65 minutes. After 55 minutes, open the oven door and test the flan by inserting the thinnest knife you own into the middle—do not go all the way to the bottom. If large curds cling to the knife, the flan is not yet done. Give it about 10 minutes longer. If just a film of custard clings to the knife, the flan is done. When you jiggle the mold, the custard should shimmer in the middle but look cooked around the edge.

Remove from the oven to a wire rack. Let cool. The flan will continue to cook for about an hour after being removed from the oven. During this time it will set up.

Refrigerate at least 2 hours before serving.

To unmold: Run a thin, sharp knife around the edge of the flan. Move the pan from side to side to see if the flan is slipping and free from the edges of the pan. Place a flat serving platter with a raised rim on top of the mold. Holding the platter and mold together tightly, flip them over. The flan should slip easily onto the platter, along with most of the caramel sauce. Use a spoon to remove more caramel and spoon it around the custard. The bottom of the pan will have a hard layer of caramel still on it. Don't worry, it always does. That's why Latin cooks make extra caramel.

To serve: Cut the flan into wedges, spooning caramel sauce over each heavenly piece.

SERVES 12 TO 14

# Zabaglione of Muscat de Baumes de Venise

*Zabaglione is a frothy, cooked egg mixture, traditionally made with Marsala, that's often served in stemmed glasses with strawberries or other fruit at the bottom. Marlena Spieler makes hers with a sweet French dessert wine. Serve with fresh fruit or crisp, delicate cookies.*

4 eggs

¼ cup sugar

1 cup Muscat de Baumes de Venise wine

Juice of 1 lemon, or to taste

∞  Beat the eggs with the sugar until light and frothy. Gradually add the wine, beating well, then place the whole bowl (a metal such as stainless steel works best for this) into a saucepan of very hot water and stir constantly over low heat until the mixture thickens. When just about to boil—whatever you do, don't let it boil or sweet scrambled eggs will be on your menu—remove from the heat and whisk in the lemon juice. Taste for seasoning and pour into cups. Serve immediately.

SERVES 4

# Crème Brûlée

*The most popular dessert in San Francisco these days is this rich and silky custard topped with a thin layer of caramelized sugar. Restaurants have an advantage over the home cook because they can caramelize the topping under a salamander or use a blowtorch. Flo Braker came up with this at-home version that's every bit as good as the best restaurant crème brûlée.*

1 cup packed brown sugar

3 cups heavy cream

½ cup granulated sugar

6 egg yolks

2 teaspoons vanilla extract

Grand Marnier (optional)

◉◉ Spread the brown sugar in a thin layer over a baking sheet. Let dry at room temperature for 48 hours, raking with your fingers occasionally to help remove the moisture.

Adjust the rack in the lower third of the oven; preheat the oven to 300 degrees. Place a sieve over a large bowl.

Combine the cream and granulated sugar in a saucepan and heat just to dissolve the sugar. Do not boil.

Blend the egg yolks and vanilla in a mixing bowl; add the warm cream, stirring with a whisk to combine. Pour the mixture through the sieve. (The sieve will catch any cooked egg yolk particles and deflate bubbles that may occur from the stirring.) Pour the custard into 8 ungreased round 3-ounce porcelain ramekins. Place the ramekins in a baking pan. Pour hot water into the pan to come halfway up the ramekins.

Bake for 25 minutes, or until the custards are just set. Do not overbake. Remove the ramekins and set aside to cool a bit, then refrigerate (the custards will firm as they cool).

Adjust the rack 5 to 6 inches from the broiler unit; preheat the broiler about 10 minutes before glazing the sugar.

At serving time, gingerly blot the surface of each chilled custard with a paper towel, then sprinkle dried brown sugar in a thin layer over each custard. Gently pat with your fingertips. Set the ramekins in a baking pan

Core large apples and stuff with a mixture of blue cheese, ricotta and toasted walnuts. Bake in a preheated 375-degree oven for about 40 minutes, or until the apples are tender. Pears also work well for this dessert. Great with a dessert wine such as Quady Essencia (an orange Muscat).

filled with ice water to come halfway up ramekins. Place under the preheated broiler and broil just until the sugar is golden and melted.

Serve immediately, or refrigerate until chilled and serve cold.

If desired, crack each sugar crust before serving and pour a teaspoon or so of Grand Marnier on top.

SERVES 8

# Creamy Saffron Yogurt with Almonds (Shrikhand)

*This rich-tasting dessert, from Laxmi Hiremath, gets its exotic, almost lemony flavor from green cardamom—the most delicate of the cardamoms. If you cannot find green cardamom pods, use regular brown cardamom, available in most supermarkets. If you don't have saffron, don't fret—the dessert is very good without it.*

4 cups plain yogurt

½ teaspoon saffron threads

¼ cup sour cream

⅓ cup sugar

Seeds from 4 green cardamom pods, ground

Fresh fruit: sliced strawberries, peaches or mangoes, or orange segments

2 tablespoons toasted sliced almonds

◉◉  Line a colander with a double thickness of cheesecloth.

Spoon the yogurt into the cheesecloth, gather up the corners and tie with string just above the yogurt. Hang the bag above the sink, where it can drain, for at least 15 hours. Or, place the cheesecloth bundle in a colander or large sieve, set in a large bowl and refrigerate for 15 to 48 hours, or until the yogurt firms up and about 2 cups whey has drained into the bowl. You should have about 1¾ cups of yogurt cheese.

Place the saffron threads in a small pan and toast over low heat until brittle. Cool and crush with a rolling pin.

Transfer the yogurt cheese to a bowl. Add the saffron, sour cream, sugar and cardamom. Mix thoroughly. Refrigerate until well chilled.

Nothing is better than
tangy cheese to finish off
the red wine after a multi-
course meal. Georgeanne
Brennan stuffs figs with
Gorgonzola for an easy,
impressive before- or after-
dinner treat.

Simply take 15 ripe figs
and about 5 ounces of
cheese cut into 15 pieces.
Slice each fig halfway
from the stem to the base.
Gently open and put in
the cheese. Arrange on
a platter and serve.

(May be made up to 4 days ahead. Store in a covered container in the
refrigerator.)

To serve, scoop into sundae dishes or goblets. Top with fruit of choice
and garnish with almonds.

SERVES 2 OR 3

# Mexican Rice Pudding

*Mexican rice pudding is exquisitely rustic and comforting. The play of vanilla
and cinnamon in Jacqueline McMahan's recipe is totally captivating.*

4 cups milk (low-fat or whole milk)

4 eggs, separated

4 tablespoons flour

¾ cup sugar

Pinch salt

1 cup hot steamed rice (white or brown)

1½ teaspoons vanilla extract

½ teaspoon ground cinnamon

Heat the milk. Beat the egg whites to stiff but not dry peaks; set aside.

Blend together the egg yolks, flour, sugar, salt and ½ cup of the hot milk.
Using a whisk, beat the yolk mixture into the remaining milk. Cook, stirring,
over medium heat for 5 minutes. Add the hot rice and continue cooking and
stirring for 10 minutes, or until the custard has thickened. Remove from heat
and stir in the vanilla.

Pour the hot custard over the top of the beaten egg whites and gently fold
until blended (the custard will poach the egg whites). Sprinkle cinnamon over
the top.

SERVES 8

# Mangoes with Sticky Rice

*This Thai dessert has found many fans in the Food Department. It's sweet and chewy and showcases the sweet perfumed flavor of mango. In Thailand, when mangoes are out of season, you won't find this dessert. However, Joyce Jue has substituted papaya and nectarines with great success.*

2 cups sweet glutinous rice

2¼ cups cold water

1½ cups unsweetened coconut cream

¾ cup sugar

½ teaspoon salt

2 mangoes, peeled, pitted and sliced

Toasted unsweetened coconut flakes for garnish

∞ Wash the rice under cold water until the water runs clear. Drain. Put the rice into a saucepan, add the water and let soak for 1 hour or, better yet, overnight.

Bring the rice to a boil and stir to separate the grains. Boil for 5 minutes. Cover the pan, reduce the heat to low and simmer for 20 minutes. Turn off the heat and let the rice rest, covered, for 10 minutes.

Combine the coconut cream, sugar and salt in a saucepan. Bring to a boil and cook, stirring constantly, until reduced by one third. Pour three quarters of the coconut cream into a large mixing bowl and add the rice; gently mix until thoroughly blended.

To serve: Mound about ¾ cup sweet rice on each dessert plate. Arrange mango slices around the rice. Top with a tablespoon of the remaining sweetened coconut cream and sprinkle with toasted coconut flakes. Serve at room temperature.

SERVES 6

# Banana-Macadamia Cookies

*Banana and macadamia nuts give these tropical-inspired cookies, by Shanna Masters, a rich crunch and a moist chewiness.*

1½ cups sugar

1 cup (2 sticks) butter, softened

2 eggs

2 bananas, mashed

3¼ cups all-purpose flour

1 teaspoon baking soda

¼ teaspoon salt

2 teaspoons cream of tartar

1 cup chopped macadamia nuts

½ cup sugar mixed with ½ teaspoon ground nutmeg

Semisweet chocolate chips (optional)

Cream together the sugar and butter. Add the eggs and mix well. Stir in the bananas.

Combine the flour, soda, salt and cream of tartar; stir to blend. Add to the creamed mixture, stirring until the dry ingredients are moistened. Mix in the nuts. Refrigerate until chilled.

Preheat the oven to 350 degrees. Line a baking sheet with parchment.

Drop the dough by the tablespoonful (or scoop) into the sugar-nutmeg mixture, turning carefully to coat. Place the cookies about 3 inches apart on the baking sheet and flatten slightly.

Bake about 8 minutes, or until the edges start to brown. Cool on the baking sheet before removing to a rack.

If desired, melt chocolate chips and drizzle over the tops of the cooled cookies.

YIELDS ABOUT 3½ DOZEN COOKIES

# Lemon-Scented Cornmeal Biscotti

*Biscotti are crisp cookies that are baked as an oblong loaf, then cut into slices and baked again. These lemon-flavored cookies, from Marlena Spieler, are excellent with coffee or as an accompaniment to fresh fruit.*

½ cup (1 stick) unsalted butter at room temperature

⅔ cup sugar

2 egg yolks

¼ cup brandy

¼ teaspoon finely grated lemon zest

¼ teaspoon lemon extract

1½ cups all-purpose flour

1½ cups cornmeal

¼ teaspoon salt

¼ teaspoon baking powder

4 to 6 dried pears, diced (optional)

◎ Mix the butter with the sugar, egg yolks, brandy, lemon zest and lemon extract. Stir in the flour, cornmeal, salt, baking powder and optional pears. Refrigerate the dough for 30 minutes.

Preheat the oven to 350 degrees. Grease a baking sheet and dust with cornmeal.

Shape the dough into an oblong loaf or loaves on the baking sheet. Bake for 25 minutes, or until firm (tops may crack a bit; don't worry). Remove from the oven. Reduce the oven temperature to 300 to 325 degrees.

When the loaves are cool enough to handle, slice them on the diagonal into ½- to ¾-inch slices. Place on the baking sheet and bake for about 20 minutes, turning once. Each side should appear toasty, but the cookies should not burn. Cornmeal biscotti take longer to bake than other biscotti because of the density of the dough.

YIELDS APPROXIMATELY 18 COOKIES

**VARIATION:** For the Swedish version, substitute rye flour for the cornmeal, eliminate the brandy and substitute orange juice for the water.

# Hazelnut Coconut Cookies

*The combination of hazelnut and coconut is magical in these wickedly rich and chewy cookies developed by Shanna Masters.*

½ cup granulated sugar

½ cup powdered sugar

½ cup (1 stick) butter, softened

1 egg

1 teaspoon vanilla extract

1½ cups all-purpose flour

½ teaspoon ground nutmeg

½ teaspoon baking soda

½ teaspoon salt

¾ cup hazelnuts, toasted, peeled, and chopped (see Note)

1 cup sweetened flaked coconut

Preheat the oven to 350 degrees. Line a baking sheet with parchment.

Cream together the sugars and butter. Add the egg and vanilla and mix well.

Combine the flour, nutmeg, soda and salt. Add to the creamed mixture and blend well. Stir in the nuts and coconut. Drop by the tablespoonful onto the baking sheet. Allow about 3 inches between each cookie. Flatten slightly with the bottom of a glass that has been dipped in sugar.

Bake for 10 minutes, or until light brown. Let cool a few minutes on the baking sheet before removing to racks to cool completely.

YIELDS ALMOST 2 DOZEN COOKIES

**NOTE:** To toast and peel hazelnuts, spread the nuts on a baking sheet and toast in a preheated 350-degree oven just until you can smell them. Transfer the nuts to a kitchen towel and rub to remove the skins (don't worry if a bit of skin remains on the nuts).

## How to Avoid Black Bottoms

When you are baking cookies that have lots of butter in the dough, the bottoms often get dark or burned before the cookies are baked through. Stack 2 baking sheets together—pros call it "double-panning"—to retard the heat a little.

# Marbled Brownies

*The marble effect of these rich brownies, by Flo Braker, comes from drawing a knife through layers of chocolate and cream cheese batters.*

### Filling

6 ounces cream cheese, softened

¼ cup (½ stick) butter, softened

½ cup sugar

2 eggs

2 tablespoons flour

1 teaspoon vanilla extract

### Brownies

1 cup all-purpose flour

1 teaspoon baking powder

½ cup (1 stick) unsalted butter

4 ounces unsweetened chocolate

4 eggs

1½ cups sugar

⅔ cup chopped walnuts

1½ teaspoons vanilla extract

## Sprinkling Flour

A small shaker filled with flour is handy for applying a couple of tablespoons of flour to a well-greased pan. Tap out excess flour.

☙ Adjust the rack in the lower third of the oven; preheat the oven to 350 degrees. Grease and flour a 13 x 9–inch pan.

To make the filling: Cream the cream cheese with the butter. Add the sugar and continue to cream until the mixture is light and fluffy. Stir in the eggs, 1 at a time. Add the flour and vanilla. Set aside.

To make the brownies: Combine the flour and baking powder; whisk briefly to combine. Place the butter and chocolate in a small saucepan; place over low heat until melted and smooth. Set aside to cool.

Put the eggs in a medium bowl and whisk until frothy, then gradually add the sugar, whisking until thick and light in color. Add the flour mixture, then stir in the chocolate mixture. Add the nuts and vanilla.

Spread half of the brownie batter in the pan; spread the cream cheese filling on top. Spoon dollops of the remaining brownie mixture over the cheese filling. Using a table knife, cut through batter a few times to create a marbled effect.

Bake for 40 to 45 minutes. Cool before cutting.

YIELDS 36 BARS

# Chocolate Cookies "to Die For"

*When Jacqueline McMahan bakes these cookies she claims she has to mediate fights over who gets the last one. The flavor of the chocolate is enhanced by a bit of black pepper and a pinch of cayenne. Sounds strange, but once you try them you'll know why the spices are there. She adapted her recipe from the Totally Chile Pepper Cookbook (Celestial Arts).*

½ cup dried currants

2 tablespoons Kahlua or other coffee-flavored liqueur

2 ounces unsweetened chocolate

4 ounces bittersweet chocolate

3 tablespoons butter

7 tablespoons flour

¼ teaspoon baking powder

¼ teaspoon salt

⅛ teaspoon ground cinnamon

½ teaspoon freshly ground pepper

Pinch cayenne pepper

2 eggs at room temperature

¾ cup sugar

2 teaspoons vanilla extract

1 cup chocolate chips

◎ Preheat the oven to 350 degrees. Line baking sheets with parchment paper.

Combine the currants and Kahlua in a saucepan; warm over low heat. Combine the unsweetened and bittersweet chocolates and the butter in another saucepan and melt over low heat, stirring frequently. Set aside to cool.

Combine the flour, baking powder, salt, cinnamon, pepper and cayenne in a small bowl; stir to blend.

Beat the eggs and sugar in a large bowl until pale and thick, about 5 minutes. Add the vanilla and melted chocolate; stir to combine. Fold in the flour mixture. Gently stir in the currants, any remaining Kahlua and the chocolate chips. (The dough will be loose.) Drop by spoonfuls onto the lined cookie sheets.

Bake 8 to 10 minutes, until the tops are shiny and the cookies slightly puffy. Let cool 5 minutes before transferring to racks to cool completely.

YIELDS ABOUT 18 COOKIES

# Orange Chocolate Chip Cookies

*Orange and chocolate are a classic combination, but you rarely find it in cookies. Here, Shanna Masters has achieved just the right balance, the citrus provides a subtle background to the chocolate.*

1 cup granulated sugar

1 cup packed brown sugar

½ cup (1 stick) softened butter

2 tablespoons oil

Grated zest of 1 orange

2 eggs

2 cups all-purpose flour

½ cup whole-wheat flour

1 teaspoon baking soda

1 teaspoon salt

½ cup chopped walnuts

1 cup semisweet chocolate chips

◎◎ Preheat the oven to 350 degrees. Line a baking sheet with bakers' parchment.

Cream together the sugars, butter, oil and orange zest. Add the eggs and mix well.

Combine the flours, soda and salt and stir to mix. Add to the creamed mixture and blend well. Stir in the nuts and chocolate chips. Drop by the tablespoonful or scoop onto the baking sheet; flatten slightly to make thick, round disc shapes. Allow about 3 inches between each cookie.

Bake for 10 minutes, or until the cookies are light brown. Let cool on the sheet a few minutes before transferring the cookies to a rack to cool completely.

YIELDS ABOUT 2½ DOZEN COOKIES

# Super-Duper Peanut Butter Chocolate Chip Cookies

*Not since Reese's has there been a better pairing of chocolate and peanut butter than in these cookies by Flo Braker. A cup of Rice Krispies in the batter adds a pleasant crunch.*

2⅓ cups all-purpose flour

½ teaspoon baking powder

1 teaspoon baking soda

⅛ teaspoon salt

1 cup (2 sticks) unsalted butter, softened

⅓ cup creamy peanut butter

1 cup packed brown sugar

⅔ cup granulated sugar

2 eggs

2 teaspoons vanilla extract

1 cup toasted, chopped walnuts

1 cup semisweet chocolate chips

1 cup Rice Krispies

◉ Adjust the rack to the lower third of the oven; preheat the oven to 350 degrees. Line baking sheets with parchment paper.

Sift the flour, baking powder, baking soda and salt onto a sheet of waxed paper.

Using an electric mixer on low speed, cream the butter, peanut butter and both sugars just until thoroughly blended. Mix in the eggs and vanilla until well combined. Blend in the dry ingredients, then the walnuts and chocolate chips. Lightly stir in the Rice Krispies by hand (be careful not to crush the cereal).

Drop rounded tablespoons of batter about 2 inches apart onto the baking sheets. Bake 9 to 11 minutes, or until cookies are golden.

YIELDS ABOUT 4 DOZEN COOKIES

# Ginger Jack Cookies

*These chewy cookies, by Marion Cunningham, leave a trail of heat in the back of the throat from the generous use of candied ginger. Cunningham loves these cookies with vanilla ice cream.*

1¼ cups vegetable shortening

1 cup granulated sugar

1 cup packed brown sugar

2 eggs

1 teaspoon vanilla extract

2 cups all-purpose flour

1 teaspoon baking soda

½ teaspoon baking powder

½ teaspoon salt

2 cups cornflakes

1 cup uncooked oatmeal

1¼ cups finely chopped candied (crystallized) ginger

◉ Preheat the oven to 350 degrees. Grease baking sheets.

Put the shortening into a mixing bowl and, using the back of a large spoon, cream it around the sides of the bowl. Slowly add both sugars and continue to cream and blend until the mixture is smooth. Add the eggs and vanilla and mix well.

Combine the flour, baking soda, baking powder and salt; stir with a fork until mixed. Add to the creamed mixture and beat until thoroughly mixed. Add the cornflakes, oatmeal and ginger. Mix well.

Drop by teaspoonfuls 1½ inches apart on the prepared baking sheets. Bake about 8 minutes, or until the edges of the cookies are lightly golden. Transfer the cookies to racks to cool.

Store or freeze in airtight plastic bags.

YIELDS ABOUT 7 DOZEN 2-INCH-DIAMETER COOKIES

# Zesty Lemon Bars

*It seems everyone is making lemon bars these days, but Flo Braker's version has a pure lemon flavor and a great crust.*

 **Crust**

*1.5* — 1 cup all-purpose flour

 ¼ cup powdered sugar

 ½ cup (1 stick) unsalted butter

**Filling**

*3* — 2 tablespoons flour

*1.5* — 1 cup sugar

*3/4* — ½ teaspoon baking powder

*3* — 2 eggs

*3* — 2 tablespoons fresh lemon juice

*3* — 2 teaspoons finely grated lemon zest

*4.5* — 3 tablespoons powdered sugar

Adjust the rack in the lower third of the oven; preheat the oven to 350 degrees. Grease a 9-inch square baking pan.

To make the crust: Briefly blend the flour and sugar in a medium bowl to combine. Cut in the butter until the mixture resembles oatmeal. Using your fingertips, press the mixture into the bottom of the pan. Bake for 15 minutes, or until pale gold.

To make the filling: Briefly blend the flour, sugar and baking powder to combine.

Blend the eggs, lemon juice and lemon zest in a medium bowl. Add the dry ingredients and blend until thoroughly combined.

Pour the filling over partially baked crust and bake 25 minutes. Cool, sprinkle powdered sugar over top and cut into bars.

YIELDS 18 BARS

# Joyce's Lemon Cookies

*Sometimes the best recipes just happen. Trying to create an intensely lemon cookie, Joyce McGillis, who was working with Marion Cunningham on the* Fannie Farmer Cookbook *revision, thought she had a lemon because the cookie failed to rise. After tasting them, however, the women knew they had a winner. These cookies are thin, crisp and almost puckery. They're great by themselves or served with ice cream or fresh fruit.*

¾ cup (1½ sticks) unsalted butter, softened

1¼ cups sugar

1 teaspoon vanilla extract

2 tablespoons grated lemon zest

¼ cup fresh lemon juice

1½ cups all-purpose flour

1½ teaspoons baking powder

½ teaspoon baking soda

½ teaspoon salt

Raw sugar (optional)

Cream together the butter and sugar with an electric mixer. Add the vanilla, lemon zest and lemon juice and beat until smooth.

Mix together the flour, baking powder, baking soda and salt. Add to the butter and blend well.

Turn the dough out onto a piece of waxed paper and form it into 2 logs about 1 to 1½ inches in diameter and about 1 foot long. Refrigerate for at least 2 hours, or wrap tightly and freeze.

Preheat the oven to 350 degrees.

Using a sharp knife, cut the logs into about ⅛-inch-thick slices and place about 3 inches apart on ungreased baking sheets. Sprinkle with raw sugar if desired. Cut only enough cookies to fill the baking sheets. Return the remaining dough to the refrigerator so it will stay cold.

Bake for 7 to 8 minutes, or until the cookies are light gold in color. Watch carefully during the last minute or two of baking. Remove from the oven and let the cookies cool slightly on the baking sheet before removing them to racks to cool completely.

YIELDS ABOUT 50 COOKIES

# Lime and Pepita Sugar Cookies

*The citric tang of lime and the crunch of pumpkin seeds may seem an esoteric combination for a cookie, but these are truly wonderful. Shanna Masters created these when she and her husband took off for a year-long boat outing. Cruising along the coast of Mexico inspired these chewy sugar-sparkled cookies.*

> 2 cups plus 5 tablespoons sugar
>
> ½ cup (1 stick) softened butter
>
> 2 tablespoons oil
>
> Grated zest of 2 limes
>
> 2 eggs
>
> ¼ cup fresh lime juice
>
> 3½ cups all-purpose flour
>
> ½ cup pepitas (hulled pumpkin seeds), chopped and toasted (see Note)
>
> 1 teaspoon baking soda
>
> 1 teaspoon salt

◎ Preheat the oven to 350 degrees. Line a baking sheet with bakers' parchment.

Cream together 2 cups sugar, the butter, oil and zest of 1 lime. Add the eggs and mix well. Stir in the lime juice.

Combine the flour, pepitas, soda and salt; stir to mix. Add to the creamed mixture; blend well.

Combine the remaining 5 tablespoons sugar and the lime zest in a small bowl; stir well to distribute the zest evenly in the sugar.

Using heaping tablespoonfuls or an ice-cream scoop, drop balls of dough into the sugar-zest mixture and turn to coat. Place on the baking sheet. Flatten each ball with 2 fingers, first in one direction, then at a 90-degree angle to the first to form round disc-shaped cookies about ¼ inch thick.

Bake for 9 to 10 minutes, or until the edges start to brown. Remove the cookies with a spatula to a rack to cool.

YIELDS ABOUT 3 DOZEN COOKIES

**NOTE:** To toast pepitas, heat them in a dry heavy skillet over medium heat. Toss or stir so they won't burn. When they begin to smell toasty, they're ready. Cool before adding to the dough.

# Killer Peanut Butter Fudge Cookies

*The name says it all. This creation, by Shanna Masters, is for those of us who love peanut butter cookies, but are constantly disappointed by the insipid peanut flavor.*

1 cup peanut butter

6 tablespoons vegetable oil

1 cup granulated sugar

1 cup packed brown sugar

2 eggs

1 tablespoon vanilla extract

⅔ cup cocoa powder

1 cup all-purpose flour

1 teaspoon baking soda

½ teaspoon salt

Preheat the oven to 350 degrees. Line a baking sheet with parchment.
Cream the peanut butter, oil and sugars. Add the eggs and vanilla. Mix well.

Combine the cocoa, flour, soda and salt; stir to mix. Add to the creamed mixture, kneading with the back of a wooden spoon to moisten the dry ingredients. The dough will be stiff and somewhat crumbly. Form the dough into balls by hand and place on the cookie sheet. Allow about 3 inches between each cookie. Flatten each ball to make a thick disc.

Bake for 8 to 9 minutes, or until set. Let the cookies cool a few minutes on the baking sheet before transferring them to racks to cool completely.

YIELDS ABOUT 2 DOZEN COOKIES

# A Better Oatmeal Cookie

*Richer, crispier and not at all like the spicy cakey variety, these oatmeal cookies by Shanna Masters really are the best.*

⅔ cup packed brown sugar

⅔ cup granulated sugar

½ cup (1 stick) softened butter

1 egg

2 teaspoons vanilla extract

1¾ cups old-fashioned oats

½ cup chopped pine nuts

½ cup chopped dried plums, prunes, or dried apricots

1½ cups all-purpose flour

¾ teaspoon baking soda

¾ teaspoon salt

Additional sugar

Preheat the oven to 350 degrees. Line a baking sheet with parchment.

Cream together the sugars and butter. Add the egg and vanilla. Mix well. Stir in the oats, pine nuts and dried plums, prunes, or apricots.

Combine the flour, soda and salt; stir to mix. Add to the creamed mixture, kneading with the back of a wooden spoon to moisten all the dry ingredients. The dough will be stiff. Form tablespoon-sized balls of dough and place on the baking sheet. Allow about 4 inches between each cookie. Flatten each ball slightly with the bottom of a glass that has been dipped in sugar.

Bake for 8 to 10 minutes, or until light brown. Let the cookies cool a few minutes on the baking sheet, then transfer to racks to cool completely.

YIELDS 2½ DOZEN COOKIES

# Polvorones (Powdered Sugar Cookies)

*These fragile melt-in-your-mouth cookies by Jackie Mallorca taste even better after they've been stored for 24 hours in an airtight container. Put them in miniature cupcake paper cases; it makes them easier to handle and looks festive.*

1 cup (5 ounces) hazelnuts

2 tablespoons sugar (preferably superfine)

1 cup cornstarch

½ teaspoon ground cinnamon

Pinch salt

½ cup (1 stick) cold unsalted butter, cut up

1 tablespoon Cognac

½ cup powdered sugar

◎◎ Preheat the oven to 325 degrees. Line a heavy baking sheet with parchment.

Combine the nuts and sugar in a food processor. Process until the mixture is very fine. Add the cornstarch, cinnamon, salt and butter. Process to mix, then add the Cognac.

Lightly dust a work surface with cornstarch. Turn the dough out of the processor onto the work surface (the dough will be very soft) and press it into a cohesive mass, dusting your hands with cornstarch if necessary, then roll into a 12-inch log. Quickly slice into ³⁄₁₆-inch-thick rounds; lightly roll each between your palms, forming a slightly flattened disc. Place the cookies on the baking sheet.

Bake for 25 to 30 minutes. The cookies should not color much. Let cool for 5 minutes on the baking sheet.

Sift the powdered sugar onto a sheet of waxed paper or foil. Place the warm cookies on the sugar, then sift more powdered sugar on top.

When completely cooled, place the cookies in miniature cupcake liners and store in an airtight tin.

YIELDS APPROXIMATELY 30 COOKIES

# Four-Star Rugelach

*These popular crescent-shaped cookies, by Flo Braker, are made from an easy-to-handle dough. Rugelach (ROOG-uh-luh) are flaky and rich, but not overly sweet. They store well in an airtight tin for up to one week.*

**Cream Cheese Dough**

2½ cups unsifted all-purpose flour

½ teaspoon salt

1 cup (2 sticks) unsalted butter, chilled

8 ounces cream cheese, chilled

¼ cup sour cream, chilled

**Filling**

½ cup sugar

1 teaspoon ground cinnamon

4 tablespoons strained apricot jam

1 cup finely chopped walnuts

½ cup dried currants

Process the flour and salt in a food processor just to combine. Cut the butter and cream cheese into cubes and scatter over the flour mixture, along with the sour cream. Process with on/off pulses just until the mixture comes together into a cohesive ball. Divide the dough into quarters; shape each quarter into a flat disc. Wrap each in plastic and refrigerate until firm, or freeze, well wrapped, up to 1 month.

When ready to assemble and bake, position the rack in the lower third of the oven. Preheat the oven to 350 degrees. Line a baking sheet with aluminum foil.

Combine the sugar and cinnamon in a small bowl.

Remove 1 dough package from the refrigerator 10 minutes before rolling it. Keep the remaining dough chilled.

Roll out the dough on a lightly floured work surface into a 10- to 11-inch diameter circle about ⅛ inch thick. Using a small metal spatula, spread 1 tablespoon of the jam very thinly over the dough. Sprinkle with 2 tablespoons of the cinnamon-sugar, then ¼ cup of the nuts and 2 tablespoons of the currants. Using a rolling pin, lightly roll to press the filling ingredients into the dough. Cut the circle into 16 pie-shaped wedges. Beginning at the wide end, roll up each wedge toward the point. Place the rolls 1 inch apart on the foil-lined baking sheet.

Bake for 15 to 20 minutes, or until golden brown. Cool 5 minutes, then transfer the cookies to a wire rack to cool completely.

Repeat shaping and baking with the remaining dough and filling.

YIELDS 64 RUGELACH

# Glasgow Shortie

*Rich with butter, these shortbread cookies have been a family favorite of* Chronicle *food writer Karola Saekel. The original recipe came from her mother-in-law, who immigrated to this country in 1922.*

2 cups all-purpose flour
2 tablespoons cornstarch
⅓ to ½ cup sugar
1 cup (2 sticks) butter at room temperature
1 teaspoon cool water

◉◉ Combine the flour, cornstarch and sugar in a bowl. Cut the butter into small pieces and rub into the dry ingredients until crumbly (the crumbs should be no larger than grains of rice). Blend in the water. Pat the dough into an ungreased 9-inch square baking pan, making the surface as even as possible. This is easily done by firmly pressing the bottom of another pan the same size against the crumbs. Refrigerate for 15 to 30 minutes to firm up the dough.

Preheat the oven to 325 degrees.

Prick the shortbread with a fork in about a dozen places. Put the pan on a baking sheet and place in the oven. Bake until golden, about 45 minutes. If the edges brown too fast, cover them loosely with strips of foil.

Place the pan on a rack and let cool to lukewarm. Cut the shortbread into 16 squares. Remove with a thin spatula and let cool completely.

Store in cookie tins, placing waxed paper between the layers. Store at room temperature for up to 10 days, or freeze.

YIELDS 16 COOKIES

# Coffee Ice Cream

*This easy recipe, from Marion Cunningham, owes its intense coffee flavor to instant coffee granules.*

    1 cup heavy cream
    1 cup milk
    ⅓ cup instant coffee granules
    1 cup sugar
    3 eggs
    1 teaspoon vanilla extract
    Pinch salt

◉◉ Combine the cream and milk in a heavy saucepan and heat to boiling. Add the coffee granules and blend.

Beat together the sugar and eggs until pale and thick. Add a little of the hot milk mixture to the egg mixture, stirring constantly. Pour back into the saucepan and cook over medium heat until slightly thickened. Be careful not to boil. Remove from the heat and add the vanilla and salt. Pour into an ice-cream maker and freeze according to manufacturer's directions.

YIELDS 3 CUPS

# Cranberry Sorbet

*Here's another way that Georgeanne Brennan has found to use tart cranberries; it's especially grand to serve as a between-course palate refresher for a more formal Thanksgiving or Christmas celebration. It's also an intriguing idea to serve it in small bowls along with the turkey.*

    2 cups cranberries
    ¼ cup fresh orange juice
    1 tablespoon grated orange zest
    3 cups water
    1 cup sugar
    1 tablespoon fresh lemon juice

Place the berries, juice, zest and ½ cup of the water in a saucepan; cook over medium heat until the berries pop, 5 to 7 minutes. Coarsely mash the berries. (You should have about 1½ cups.) Add the sugar, lemon juice and remaining water. Simmer, stirring often, until a syrup forms. Let cool, then refrigerate for 6 hours or overnight.

Freeze in an ice-cream maker according to manufacturer's instructions. Store in an airtight container in the freezer.

YIELDS ABOUT 1 QUART

# Ginger Ice Cream with Nectarine Caramel

*Dan Bowe created this extraordinary ice cream featuring the fresh tang of ginger, the juiciness of nectarines and the richness of caramel. For a more intense ginger flavor, squeeze the minced ginger through a garlic press directly into the cream mixture. This saves the time of steeping the ginger, then straining the mixture before continuing with the recipe.*

2-inch knob fresh ginger, peeled and minced

1 pint half-and-half

1 pint heavy cream

⅔ cup sugar

8 egg yolks

1 tablespoon vanilla extract

2 tablespoons minced crystallized ginger (about 2 small pieces)

**Caramel**

4 very ripe nectarines, peeled and pitted

¼ cup sugar

¼ cup water

¼ cup light corn syrup

Combine the ginger, half-and-half and cream in a 2-quart saucepan; bring to a simmer. Cover, remove from heat, and let steep at least 15 minutes, or up to 1 hour. Strain and return to the saucepan. Bring to a simmer.

Combine the sugar and egg yolks in a large bowl; mix well. Add about half of the simmering cream mixture, stirring constantly. Return this mixture to the saucepan with the remaining simmering cream and cook over medium heat, stirring constantly, until the custard thickens to the consistency of a thin milk shake. Pour into the now-empty mixing bowl. Stir in the vanilla and crystallized ginger. Let cool completely. Refrigerate for several hours.

Pour the custard into an ice-cream maker and freeze according to manufacturer's instructions.

The caramel may be added to the ice cream during the last few turns of the machine, or poured over the ice cream at serving time.

To make the caramel sauce: Place the nectarines in a juice extractor or a food processor and puree. Strain, if using a processor. (You should have about 1 cup juice.)

Combine the sugar and water in a small heavy saucepan and heat over medium-high heat, stirring to combine and dissolve the sugar. When the mixture begins to bubble, stop stirring and swirl the pan until the sugar turns a nice caramel color. Remove from heat and stir in the corn syrup. Let cool for 5 minutes, then stir in the nectarine juice. Let cool completely, then refrigerate until ready to use.

YIELDS 1 GENEROUS QUART

# Lemon Granita

*A granita, unlike a sorbet, doesn't need any fancy equipment. Simply pour the juice into a shallow pan, place in the freezer and stir and scrape every half hour or so. This produces a fine ice that melts as soon as it hits the tongue. For the best flavor in this refreshing dessert, by Flo Braker, use only freshly squeezed lemon juice, not the reconstituted variety.*

2 cups water
2 cups sugar
1½ cups fresh lemon juice (about 8 lemons)

◉◉ Combine 1 cup of the water and the sugar in a small saucepan; heat until the sugar dissolves. Refrigerate until cold.

Combine the sugar syrup with the lemon juice and the remaining 1 cup water; blend thoroughly. Pour into a freezer-safe container, such as a 9 x 13 x 2–inch metal pan. Freeze, stirring and scraping the mixture every 30 to 40 minutes—first with a rubber spatula, then with the tines of a fork—until the mixture has a grainy consistency and is completely frozen. This takes 3 to 4 hours.

Spoon into chilled stemmed glasses or bowls.

YIELDS 7 CUPS

# Fresh Rhubarb Sorbet

*Flo Braker cleverly uses tart rhubarb to make a tangy-sweet sorbet. A dessert wine is used to add flavor and a creamy, soft texture. One note: When cleaning the celerylike rhubarb stalks, remove all traces of leaves—they are toxic.*

1¾ pounds fresh rhubarb, cleaned and trimmed

¾ cup plus 2 tablespoons sugar

1½ cups dessert wine, chilled (see Note)

∞ Preheat the oven to 350 degrees.

Cut the rhubarb into 1½-inch pieces. Place in a large, shallow oblong ceramic or glass baking dish. Sprinkle the sugar over the top and bake for about 25 minutes, or until the rhubarb is soft. Set aside to cool.

Puree the rhubarb with its liquid in a food processor or blender. Refrigerate until well chilled.

Stir the wine into the rhubarb puree, then transfer to an ice-cream maker and freeze according to manufacturer's instructions.

YIELDS ABOUT 1 QUART

**NOTE:** Muscat Canelli, Muscat de Beaumes de Venise or a Late-Harvest Riesling are good choices for this sorbet.

# Glossary of Ingredients

**Achiote:** The seed of the annatto tree. Used as a coloring agent in foodstuffs such as cheese and butter, and as an ingredient in Latin American dishes. This brick red–orange seed with a somewhat musty flavor is available in whole, ground or paste form. It is carried in Latin American and some Asian markets.

**Arborio rice:** A short-grain Italian rice traditionally used for risotto.

**Arugula (rocket):** A bitterish salad green with a peppery mustard flavor. A great addition to mixed green salads, or use instead of lettuce on a sandwich; add it to soups and sautés, or use as a bed for roast meats and poultry.

**Balsamic vinegar:** A pungent sweet-sour Italian vinegar made from Trebbiano grapes. It is aged in different woods and in barrels of gradually diminishing sizes, until it is dark, thick, complex and richly flavored. The oldest vinegars will be the best; they will also be the most expensive.

**Basmati rice:** A long-grain rice with a perfumed nutlike flavor and a fine texture. Traditionally used in Indian and Middle Eastern cuisines.

**Borlotti bean:** Similar to a cranberry bean, this legume has maroon markings over an off-white background. Use any way you would a cranberry bean: soups, stews, vegetable side dishes. Available in specialty-food stores, farmers' markets and some produce markets and stands.

**Brown rice flour:** Milled from brown rice, this gluten-free flour is creamy white. It should be stored in the refrigerator or freezer. Available in natural-food stores.

**Cannellini beans (white kidney beans):** Used mainly in Italian cooking, these beans are similar to Great Northerns, but they retain their texture better when cooked. Available dried and canned.

**Cardamom:** Related to ginger, this aromatic Indian spice is an essential ingredient in curries. Three main varieties are available: white (tan), black and green. The pods range in size from ¼ to ½ inch long; the seeds inside are tiny and black, and have a pungent almost lemony flavor and aroma. Cardamom is available ground or in the pod.

**Chaat:** A northern Indian salad/snacklike dish often sold by street vendors. Chaats are boldly flavored; they can be sweet and spicy at the same time, and often combine fruit, vegetables, fresh chiles, mint and cilantro, tamarind or lime juice, nuts—even meat or seafood. Almost anything goes as long as the flavor is vibrant.

**Chaat masala:** A tangy and slightly smoky spice blend, based on dried mango, that is used for Indian chaats. It is available in Indian and some Middle Eastern markets.

**Chana dal:** A skinned split yellow lentil similar to yellow split peas. It is commonly used in Indian cooking as both a food and a spice.

**Chile caribe:** Dried red pepper flakes with seeds. Sold in jars or cellophane packages in most supermarkets.

**Chipotles en adobo:** Chipotle chiles in a spicy brick-red marinade. These are sold in cans in Latin American markets and some supermarkets. Once opened, transfer the chiles and their marinade to a clean glass jar with a tight-fitting lid and store in the refrigerator. They'll keep for several months.

**Clarified butter, desi ghee:** When butter is melted over low heat, the milk solids will settle to the bottom of the pan, leaving the clear (clarified) butter on top. See also *ghee.*

**Coconut milk, coconut cream:** Made from the grated and steeped meat of coconuts, this pearly white liquid is available in cans. When coconut milk stands, it separates, with the thick coconut cream coming to the top. Available in Asian markets and most supermarkets.

**Curry leaves:** See *kari leaves.*

**Daikon:** A giant white Japanese radish. Ranging from 6 inches to over 2 feet long, diakon has a peppery flavor and juicy, crisp texture. May be used like other radishes, or put into stir-fries or braises.

**Dashi:** Used in Japanese cooking, this soup stock is made with dried bonito (fish) shavings or flakes, dried kelp and water. The instant form, dashi-no-moto, is available in concentrate, granulated and powdered form. It is available in Japanese markets and the ethnic food section of some supermarkets.

**Desi ghee:** See *clarified butter.*

**Drawn butter:** Clarified unsalted butter.

**Escarole:** A bitter green with broad pale-green leaves. It is related to endive, but the flavor is milder. Used mainly in salads, but may also be used in a stir-fry or braise. Available year round.

**Fava beans (broad beans, horse beans):** Available fresh or dried, these legumes resemble large lima beans. The fresh beans must be shelled and peeled before using. Favas are commonly used in Mediterranean and Middle Eastern cuisines, and were used by the early California rancho cooks.

**Fenugreek:** An ocher yellow, square and somewhat flat seed with a bittersweet flavor. Available whole or ground, it is commonly used in Indian cooking: spice blends (notably curry powder), soups, stews and beverages.

**Galangal (Siamese or Thai ginger, laos):** Related to ginger, this thin-skinned rhizome is pale yellow with zebralike markings and pink shoots. It may be used fresh or dried. When dried, it is generally called laos. It is used extensively in the cooking of Thailand.

**Garam masala:** An Indian spice blend. May contain any number of spices, but commonly includes cinnamon, cloves, chile pepper, black pepper, coriander, cumin, cardamom, fennel, mace and nutmeg. Usually added to a dish just before it is finished, or sprinkled over the dish just before serving. Available in Indian, Middle Eastern and some specialty-food shops.

**Ghee:** Clarified butter that has been simmered until all the moisture has evaporated and the milk solids have "caramelized," giving the butter a nutty flavor, a higher smoking point (375 degrees) and a longer shelf life than regular clarified butter. It is used extensively in Indian cooking, and may be found in Indian, Middle Eastern and some gourmet stores.

**Harissa sauce:** A fiery hot sauce from Tunisia. It is a frequent accompaniment to couscous and tagines, and is used as a flavor enhancer—much like Tabasco—with stews and soups. It is available in Middle Eastern markets and some specialty stores.

**Jicama:** A Latin American root vegetable with a tan skin and white flesh. It has a crisp, somewhat juicy texture and sweet-starchy flavor. This bulbous root may be used raw in salads or as a garnish, or it may be cooked in soups, stews or stuffings. It is a good substitute for fresh water chestnuts in Asian stir-fries.

**Kari leaves (curry leaves):** Small, shiny, dark-green leaves of the curry bush (not related to curry powder). Used in Indian cooking. The flavor enhances lentil and rice

dishes, soups, stews and raitas. The fresh and dried leaves are carried in Indian markets, although supplies of fresh leaves are erratic.

**Lemongrass:** This lemon-flavored herb resembles a long, somewhat dried-out green onion with thin gray-green leaves and an off-white base. It is a common ingredient in Thai cooking. It is available in Asian markets, specialty-produce markets and some supermarkets.

**Lily buds (tiger lily buds, golden needles):** These are the dried buds of the day lily plant. Used in Chinese cooking, these 2- to 3-inch-long light golden buds have a delicate musky-sweet flavor. They must be rehydrated in warm water before using. Available in Asian markets.

**Lotus root:** This underwater rhizome of the water lily plant resembles a string of fat sausage links. However,

when cut, it reveals a beautifully porous, almost lacelike interior. Its delicate flavor has been likened to such different foods as artichokes and fresh coconut. Good in Asian stir-fries, braises, stews, soups and salads. Although lotus root is best fresh, it is also available canned.

**Mirin (sweetened rice wine):** This Japanese low-alcohol cooking wine, made from glutinous rice, is used in a multitude of dishes, including sauces, glazes, soups, dips. It is widely available in Asian markets and most supermarkets.

**Miso:** This Japanese fermented soybean paste comes in a variety of flavors and colors. Lighter misos are generally used for delicate soups and sauces; darker versions are used in heavier dishes. Available in Japanese markets and health-food stores. It should be stored in an

airtight container in the refrigerator.

**Mung beans (moong dal):** These small, oval, blue-green beans have a yellow flesh. They are sold either whole or split, hulled or unhulled. Native to India, and used extensively in China, they are among the most versatile dal. They have a tender texture and slightly sweet flavor.

**Mustard oil:** A pungent yellow oil made from mustard seeds. Used in Indian pickles and other dishes. Available in Indian markets and some Near Eastern and Asian grocery stores.

**Pancetta:** Italian unsmoked bacon that is cured with pepper, salt and spices. It is used, much like bacon, to flavor vegetable dishes, sauces, soups, stews, meats, pastas.

**Panko:** Japanese bread crumbs. Usually found in cellophane packages, these crumbs have the appearance of white flakes. Available in Asian markets and the ethnic section of some supermarkets. Regular bread crumbs may be substituted.

**Pecorino romano:** An Italian sheep's milk cheese with a sharp flavor and hard, granular texture. It is used much like Parmesan.

**Polenta:** A Northern Italian mushlike dish made from coarsely ground yellow cornmeal. Soft polenta often is used as a base for braised meats or stews; firm polenta often is cut into shapes and baked or fried in butter or olive oil.

**Portobello mushroom:** A common brown mushroom that has been allowed to grow. May reach 6 or 7 inches in diameter.

**Ricotta salata:** A hard ricotta cheese with a flaky texture. Typically used in salads.

**Sake:** A Japanese wine made from fermented rice. Traditionally, sake is served warm in small cups, but it also may be enjoyed chilled. It is mainly a beverage, but sometimes is used in marinades and sauces.

**Rocotillo chile:** Related to the habanero and Scotch bonnet chiles, this small chile is shaped something like a miniature pattypan squash. It has a fruity flavor and intense heat. Excellent in salsas.

**Shaoxing wine:** Chinese wine made of glutinous rice, rice millet and a special yeast. It is golden in color and similar to dry sherry in flavor and aroma. Sold in Asian markets and some supermarkets.

**Sichuan peppercorns:** These small reddish-brown berries have a woodsy-spicy fragrance and a strangely numbing quality, according to Asian food authority Bruce Cost. They are sold in cellophane

packets in Chinese markets.

**Soba:** A taupe-colored Japanese noodle made of wheat flour and buckwheat flour. Sold fresh or dried in Japanese markets and many supermarkets.

**Soy sauce:** This fermented soybean product comes in two forms: dark and light. Light soy sauce (also called thin soy sauce) has a more delicate flavor and is used mainly in seafood and vegetable dishes, soups and dipping sauces. Dark soy sauce (also called black soy sauce), is darker, thicker and has a stronger flavor. It generally is used for more robust dishes.

**Sweet glutinous rice (sweet rice, sticky rice):** A short-grain opaque white rice with a high starch content. When cooked, this staple of Asian cooking becomes quite sticky. Glutinous rice rarely is served by

itself as a side dish, but is used mainly as an ingredient. Available in Asian grocery stores and some supermarkets.

**Tahini:** Sesame seed paste. This Middle Eastern ingredient resembles peanut butter and is used to flavor dishes such as hummus and baba ghanoush. It is available in Middle Eastern markets and some supermarkets.

**Tamarind:** Also known as "Indian dates," tamarind seeds have a sweet-sour flavor and are used much like lemon juice. Unlike lemon juice, however, tamarind's sourness does not dissipate with prolonged cooking. Tamarind is available in Indian, Middle Eastern and some Asian and Latino markets in various forms: jars of liquid concentrate, cellophane-wrapped blocks of pulp with seeds, canned paste and whole dried pods.

**Tam chipotle chile:** A mildly hot, fresh-smoked jalapeno chile. The smokiness can vary depending on what kind of wood was used in the smoker. These chiles are available in farmers' markets and specialty produce shops.

**Tomatillos (Mexican green tomatoes):** Except for its papery husk, this fruit— a member of the nightshade family— resembles a small green tomato. It has a clean flavor with hints of lemon and herbs. Tomatillos can be used raw or cooked. They are available fresh in Latin American markets, farmers' markets and some specialty-produce markets; they're also available canned.

**Toovar dal:** A hulled ocher-colored split pea with a mild, earthy flavor. Used in Indian cooking for soups, stews, pilafs, sauces and sweets. Buy the washed variety as opposed to the oiled dal. If all you can find is the oiled variety, wash it well in several changes of warm water before use.

**Tree ear mushrooms (wood ear, cloud ear, black fungus):** A variety of dried mushroom used in Asian cuisines. Sold in cellophane packages, these mushrooms must be rehydrated in warm water before using. They have little flavor, but add a pleasant rubbery-crunchy texture to dishes. Available in Asian markets and some supermarkets.

**Udon:** A Japanese noodle made of white flour, salt and water. May be either flat or round. Available fresh or dried in Japanese markets and many supermarkets.

**Urad dal:** These small, oval ivory-white lentils come from black gram beans that have been washed, hulled and split. They are traditionally used in Southern Indian cooking, notably for savory cakes and pancakes.

**Zest:** The outermost skin of a citrus fruit. The easiest way to "zest" any citrus is with a potato peeler; it will take off only the colored outer skin, leaving the white pith behind.

# Mail-Order Sources

## Asian and Pacific Rim Ingredients

### Uwajimaya

519 Sixth Street, South
Seattle, WA 98104
(800) 889-1928
(206) 624-6248
Fax: (206) 624-6915
All major credit cards
accepted; no out-of-state
checks.

Products from all over
Asia, including Japan,
China, Thailand, Vietnam,
Cambodia, India and the
Philippines. Products
include a variety of
noodles, mushrooms,
sauces and condiments,
herbs and spices. Exotic
fruits and vegetables also
available for next-day
delivery. Carries Asian
cooking equipment, utensils
and dishes.

### Mo Hotta-Mo Betta

P.O. Box 4136
San Luis Obispo,
CA 93403
(800) 462-3220
(805) 544-4051
Fax: (805) 545-8389

### Maison Glass

111 East 58th Street
New York, NY 10022
(800) 822-5564
(212) 755-3316
Fax: (212) 755-4646
All major credit cards and
personal checks accepted.

Imported and domestic
gourmet specialties and
hard-to-get items. Over
4,000 different products,
including caviar, cheeses,
dried mushrooms and
truffles, mustard fruit,
herbs and spices from all
over the world. Also carries
a supply of rare game
meats and fowl.

## Cheeses and Charcuterie

### Vella Cheese Company of California

315 Second Street East
P.O. Box 191
Sonoma, CA 95476
(800) 848-0505
(707) 938-3232
Fax: (707) 938-4307
MasterCard, Visa accepted.

Variety of domestic
cheeses, plain and flavored.
All products are rennet-
free.

### Manganaro Foods

488 Ninth Avenue
New York, NY 10018
(800) 472-5264
(212) 563-5331
Fax: (212) 239-8355

### Maison Glass

See listing on this page.

### Dean and DeLuca

560 Broadway
New York, NY 10012
(800) 221-7714
(212) 226-7714
Fax: (800) 781-4054
American Express,
MasterCard, Visa accepted.
Catalog: $3, applied to first
order.

Wide selection of
gourmet and specialty
foods, with a large variety
of domestic and imported
cheeses, smoked items,
caviar, sausages and wursts.

## Dried Mushrooms

### Maison Glass

See listing on this page.

### Dean and DeLuca

See listing on this page.

## Imported and Domestic Specialty Foods

**Maison Glass**
See listing on page 407.

## Indian Ingredients

**Sri Emporium**
2190 Meridian Park Boulevard,
Suite J
Concord, CA 94520
(510) 686-2162
Fax: (510) 827-4862
MasterCard, Visa, Discover card
accepted; no out-of-state checks.

Large selection of Indian staples
such as rices, grains, lentils, flours,
pastes, oils, spices, condiments and
pickles.

**Taj Mahal Imports**
3095-C South Peoria Street
Aurora, CO 80014
(970) 751-8571
MasterCard, Visa, Discover card,
personal checks accepted.

Full line of Indian groceries,
staples, beans, breads, condiments,
sauces, pastes and canned goods.

**Dean and DeLuca**
See listing on page 407.

## Latin and Southwestern Products

**Chile Shop**
109 East Water Street
Santa Fe, NM 87501
(505) 983-6080
Fax: (505) 984-0737
MasterCard, Visa, Discover card
accepted.

A variety of dried chiles (both
whole and ground), chile blends,
salsas, condiments and other prepared
foods.

**Santa Fe School of Cooking**
116½ West San Francisco Street
Santa Fe, NM 87501
(505) 983-4511
Fax: (505) 983-7540
American Express, MasterCard, Visa
accepted.

Specializes in New Mexican and
other Southwestern ingredients, such
as sauces, condiments, beans and
Mexican herbs and spices. Carries a
large variety of chiles, as well as corn
and blue corn products.

**Mo Hotta-Mo Betta**
See listing on page 407.
MasterCard, Visa accepted.

Specializes in hot and spicy foods
from around the world. Over 700
products, including Southwestern and
Latin American ingredients, salsas
and sauces. Also carries a variety of

Asian, Pacific Rim, Caribbean and
regional American ingredients and
seasonings.

**Native Seeds/SEARCH**
2509 North Campbell, Suite 325
Tucson, AZ 85719
For information or catalog:
(520) 327-9123
Orders by mail or fax only:
(520) 327-5821
MasterCard, Visa, Discover card
accepted.

A nonprofit organization for the
preservation of traditional crops and
ingredients in the Southwest and
Northern Mexico. Selection of seeds,
beans, grains, herbs and spices, and
corn products. Also sells books and
materials on regional cooking and
indigenous agriculture.

## Italian Foods and Ingredients

**Manganaro Foods**
See listing on page 407.
All major credit cards and personal
checks accepted. Catalog without an
order: $1.50.

Imported Italian foods, oils and
vinegars, antipasti and holiday items.
Large selection of imported cheeses,
sausages and hams.

# Contributors' Notes

**Ayla Algar** teaches Turkish language at the University of California at Berkeley. She is the author of *Classical Turkish Cooking* (Harper Collins).

**Jane Benet,** who died in 1994, was the food editor of *The Chronicle* for more than 30 years before retiring in 1988.

**Dan Bowe,** *The Chronicle's* food stylist, is a San Francisco chef and food consultant.

**Flo Braker** of Palo Alto writes "The Baker," a column that appears every other week in the Food Section. A nationally recognized baker and teacher, she is the author of *The Simple Art of Perfect Baking* and *Sweet Miniatures* (both William Morrow).

**Georgeanne Brennan,** a cookbook author who lives in Yolo County, is the author of *Potager, The Glass Pantry, Fragrant Flowers* and *France: The Vegetarian Table* (all Chronicle Books). She is coauthor of *Beautiful Bulbs* and *Little Herb Gardens,* among other titles.

**Marion Cunningham,** the "Home Cooking" columnist for *The Chronicle,* lives in Walnut Creek and is known as the modern-day Fannie Farmer. She is the author of two revisions of *The Fannie Farmer Cookbook.* She has also written *The Fannie Farmer Baking Book, The Breakfast Book, The Supper Book* and *Cooking With Children* (all Alfred A. Knopf).

**Maria Cianci,** a *Chronicle* staff writer and restaurant critic, is a graduate of the Culinary Institute of America and has worked in restaurant kitchens and contributed to many food magazines.

**Sharon Cadwallader** is the author of the "Naturally" column syndicated by Chronicle Features. The Santa Cruz-based food writer is the author of *Savoring Mexico* (Chronicle Books).

**Bruce Cost,** a San Francisco resident and a former food columnist for *The Chronicle,* owns the Ginger Club in Palo Alto and is the author of *Ginger East to West* (Aris Books) and *Bruce Cost's Asian Ingredients* (William Morrow).

**Narsai David,** a former restaurant owner and "California Cuisine" columnist for *The Chronicle,* is the food editor of KCBS radio. He is the author of *Monday Night at Narsai's* (Simon & Schuster).

**Janet Fletcher,** a *Chronicle* food writer and former cook at Chez Panisse, lives in Oakland and is the author of many books, including *Pasta Harvest* (Chronicle Books).

**Joyce Goldstein,** a former "California Cuisine" columnist for *The Chronicle,* was the chef/owner of Square One restaurant in San Francisco. She is the author of *Feedback* (Richard Marek Publishers), *Back to Square One* and *Kitchen Conversations* (both by William Morrow), and of several books published by Williams-Sonoma, including *Festive Occasions.*

**Laxmi Hiremath,** an East Bay food writer and cooking teacher who grew up near Bombay, is the author of *Laxmi's Vegetarian Kitchen* (Harlow & Ratner).

**Joyce Jue,** who was born and raised in San Francisco's Chinatown, is *The Chronicle's* "East to West" columnist. She is the author of *Asian Appetizers* (Harlow & Ratner) and *Wok and Stir-Fry Cooking* (Cole Group) and is coauthor, with Chris Yeo, of *The Cooking of Singapore* (Harlow & Ratner).

**Jacqueline Higuera McMahan,** who grew up on a Bay Area rancho, writes the "North to South" column in *The Chronicle's* Food Section. She is the author of numerous books, including *California Rancho Cooking, The Salsa Book, The Chipotle Chile Cook Book, The Red and Green Chile Book, Healthy Fiesta* and *The Mexican Breakfast Cookbook* (all Olive Press).

**Marlena Spieler,** a Bay Area resident who also lives in London, is the author of numerous cookbooks, including *From Pantry to Table* (Addison Wesley), *The Flavor of California* (HarperCollins), *The Vegetarian Bistro* (Chronicle Books) and *Islands in the Sun* (Lowell House). She has also written, with Mary Berry, *Classic Home Cooking* (Dorling Kindersley).

# Permissions

The recipes on pages 50 and 312 are from *From Tapas to Mezes* by Joanne Weir. © 1994 by Joanne Weir. Reprinted by permission of Crown Publishers, Inc. ∞ The recipe on page 271 is from *The Fannie Farmer Cookbook* by Marion Cunningham. © 1990 by Marion Cunningham. Reprinted by permission of Alfred A. Knopf, Inc. ∞ The recipes on pages 43, 141, 180, 190, 214, and 390 are from *The Supper Book* by Marion Cunningham. © 1992 by Marion Cunningham. Reprinted by permission of Alfred A. Knopf, Inc. ∞ The recipe on page 356 is from *The Breakfast Book* by Marion Cunningham. © 1987 by Marion Cunningham. Reprinted by permission of Alfred A. Knopf, Inc. ∞ The recipes on pages 21 and 306 are reprinted from *The Cooking of Singapore* by Chris Yeo and Joyce Jue. © 1993 by Chris Yeo and Joyce Jue. Reprinted by permission of Harlow & Ratner. ∞ The recipes on pages 120, 10, 378, 312, and 326 are reprinted from *Laxmi's Vegetarian Kitchen* by Laxmi Hiremath. © 1995 by Laxmi Hiremath. Reprinted by permission of Harlow & Ratner. ∞ The recipe on page 66 is reprinted from *Bistro* by Gerald Hirigoyen. © 1995 by Gerald Hirigoyen. Reprinted by permission of Sunset Books. ∞ The recipes on pages 63 and 80 are reprinted from *Carlo Middione's Traditional Pasta*. © 1996 by Carlo Middione. Reprinted by permission of Ten Speed Press. ∞ The recipes on pages 62, 67, 71, 73, 79, 81, and 83 are reprinted from *Pasta Harvest* by Janet Fletcher. © 1995 by Janet Fletcher. Reprinted by permission of Chronicle Books. ∞ The recipes on pages 131 and 136 are reprinted from *Potager* by Georgeanne Brennan. © 1992 by Georgeanne Brennan. Reprinted by permission of Chronicle Books. ∞ The recipes on pages 36, 114, 153, and 175 are reprinted from *The Vegetarian Table: France* by Georgeanne Brennan. © 1995 by Georgeanne Brennan. Reprinted by permission of Chronicle Books. ∞ The recipe on page 230 is reprinted from *Citrus* by Ethel Brennan and Georgeanne Brennan. © 1995 by Ethel Brennan and Georgeanne Brennan. Reprinted by permission of Chronicle Books. ∞ The recipe on page 167 is reprinted from *Down to Earth* by Georgeanne Brennan. © 1996 by Georgeanne Brennan. Reprinted by permission of Chronicle Books. ∞ The recipe on page 202 is reprinted from *Back to Square One* by Joyce Goldstein. © 1992 by Joyce Goldstein. Reprinted by permission of William Morrow and Co., Inc. ∞ The recipes on pages 164 and 165 are reprinted from *Kitchen Conversations* by Joyce Goldstein. © 1996 by Joyce Goldstein. Reprinted by permission of William Morrow and Co., Inc. ∞ The recipe on page 19 is reprinted from *Italy in Small Bites* by Carol Field. © 1989 by Carol Field. Reprinted by permission of William Morrow and Co., Inc. ∞ The recipe on page 277 is reprinted from *Cafe Beaujolais* by Margaret Fox . © 1984 by Margaret Fox. Reprinted by permission of Ten Speed Press. ∞ The recipe on page 213 is reprinted from *The Islands in the Sun Cookbook* by Marlena Spieler. © 1996 by Marlena Spieler. Reprinted by permission of Lowell House.

# Index

# Chefs/Restaurants

# Table of Equivalents

The exact equivalents in the following tables have been rounded for convenience.

## US/UK

oz=ounce
lb=pound
in=inch
ft=foot
tbl=tablespoon
fl oz=fluid ounce
qt=quart

## Metric

g=gram
kg=kilogram
mm=millimeter
cm=centimeter
ml=milliliter
l=liter

## Weights

| US/UK | Metric |
|---|---|
| 1 oz | 30 g |
| 2 oz | 60 g |
| 3 oz | 90 g |
| 4 oz (¼ lb) | 125 g |
| 5 oz (⅓ lb) | 155 g |
| 6 oz | 185 g |
| 7 oz | 220 g |
| 8 oz (½ lb) | 250 g |
| 10 oz | 315 g |
| 12 oz (¾ lb) | 375 g |
| 14 oz | 440 g |
| 16 oz (1 lb) | 500 g |
| 1½ lb | 750 g |
| 2 lb | 1 kg |
| 3 lb | 1.5 kg |

## Oven Temperatures

| Fahrenheit | Celsius | Gas |
|---|---|---|
| 250 | 120 | ½ |
| 275 | 140 | 1 |
| 300 | 150 | 2 |
| 325 | 160 | 3 |
| 350 | 180 | 4 |
| 375 | 190 | 5 |
| 400 | 200 | 6 |
| 425 | 220 | 7 |
| 450 | 230 | 8 |
| 475 | 240 | 9 |
| 500 | 260 | 10 |

## Liquids

| US | Metric | UK |
|---|---|---|
| 2 tbl | 30 ml | 1 fl oz |
| ¼ cup | 60 ml | 2 fl oz |
| ⅓ cup | 80 ml | 3 fl oz |
| ½ cup | 125 ml | 4 fl oz |
| ⅔ cup | 160 ml | 5 fl oz |
| ¾ cup | 180 ml | 6 fl oz |
| 1 cup | 250 ml | 8 fl oz |
| 1½ cups | 375 ml | 12 fl oz |
| 2 cups | 500 ml | 16 fl oz |
| 4 cups/1 qt | 1 l | 32 fl oz |

## Length Measures

| | |
|---|---|
| ⅛ in | 3 mm |
| ¼ in | 6 mm |
| ½ in | 12 mm |
| 1 in | 2.5 cm |
| 2 in | 5 cm |
| 3 in | 7.5 cm |
| 4 in | 10 cm |
| 5 in | 13 cm |
| 6 in | 15 cm |
| 7 in | 18 cm |
| 8 in | 20 cm |
| 9 in | 23 cm |
| 10 in | 25 cm |
| 11 in | 28 cm |
| 12 in/1 ft | 30 cm |